The History
of Islam
(Volume Three)

First Edition: April 2001

Printed in Lebanon

ISBN 9789960892931

Supervised by

ABDUL MALIK MUJAHID

Headquarters:

P.O. Box: 22743, Riyadh 11416, KSA
Tel: 00966-1-4033962/4043432
Fax:00966-1- 4021659
E-mail: darussalam@naseej.com.sa
Website: http:// www.dar-us-salam.com
Bookshop: Tel & Fax: 00966-1-4614483

Branches & Agents:

K.S. A.
● Jeddah: Tel: 00966-2-6712299 Fax: 6173448
● Al-Khobar: Tel: 00966-3-8948106

U.A.E.
● Tel: 00971-6-5511293 Fax: 5511294

PAKISTAN
● 50 Lower Mall, Lahore
   Tel: 0092-42-724 0024 Fax: 7354072
● Rahman Market, Ghazni Street
   Urdu Bazar, Lahore
   Tel: 0092-42-7120054 Fax: 7320703

U. S. A.
● Houston: P.O. Box: 79194 Tx 77279
   Tel: 001-713-722 0419 Fax: 001-713-722 0431
   E-mail: Sales @ dar-us-salam.com
   Website: http:// www.dar-us-salam.com
● New York: 572 Atlantic Ave, Brooklyn
   New York-11217
   Tel: 001-718-625 5925

U.K.
● London: Darussalam International Publications Ltd.
   P.O. Box: 21555, London E10 6XQ
   Tel: 044-7947 306 706 Fax: 0044-208 925 6996
● Birmingham: Al-Hidaayah Publishing & Distribution
   436 Coventry Road, Birmingham B10 0UG
   Tel: 0044-121-753 1889 Fax: 121-753 2422

AUSTRALIA
● Lakemba NSW: ICIS: Ground Floor 165-171, Haldon St.
   Tel: (61-2) 9758 4040 Fax: 9758 4030

MALAYSIA
● E&D BOOKS SDN.BHD.-321 B 3rd Floor, Suria Klcc
   Kuala Lumpur City Center 50088
   Tel: 00603-21663433 Fax: 459 72032

SINGAPORE
● Muslim Converts Association of Singapore
   Singapore- 424484
   Tel: 0065-440 6924, 348 8344 Fax: 440 6724

SRI LANKA
● Darul Kitab 6, Nirmal Road, Colombo-4
   Tel: 0094-1-589 038 Fax: 0094-74 722433

KUWAIT
● Islam Presentation Committee
   Enlightment Book Shop
   P.O. Box : 1613, Safat 13017 KUWAIT
   Tel: 00965-244 7526, Fax: 240 0057

BANGLADESH
● 30 Malitola Road, Dhaka-1100
   Tel: 0088-02-9557214, Fax: 0088-02-9559738

The History of Islam

(Volume Three)

By
Akbar Shah Najeebabadi

Revised by
Safi-ur-Rahman Mubaralpuri

Edited by
Abdul Rahman Abdullah
Formerly
Raymond J. Manderola
Fordham University, USA
and
Muhammad Tahir Salafi

DARUSSALAM
GLOBAL LEADER IN ISLAMIC BOOKS
Riyadh • Jeddah • Sharjah • Lahore
London • Houston • New York

In the Name of Allâh the Most
Beneficent, the Most Merciful

Publishers Note

We are presenting before you the third volume of the book *History of Islam*. This book was originally written in the Urdu language in 1922 (1343 AH) by Akbar Shah Khan Najeebabadi. This was the time about 25 years before the partition of Indian Subcontinent into Pakistan and India. For the purpose of brevity, the compiler has presented the authentic events in concise form from the famous histories of Islam written in the Arabic and Persian languages by the great Muslim historians like Tabari, Ibn Athir, Mas'udi, Abul-Fida', Ibn Khaldûn and Suyuti, apart from getting benefited from the authentic books of *Ahadith* for the compilation of the part about the biography of the Prophet Muhammad ﷺ. So, this compilation is actually the extract of the works of the famous Muslim historians.

In the first volume, starting with the introduction of the history as a subject, the country, people and conditions of Arabia prior to the advent of Islam were discussed, and an account of the life of Prophet Muhammad ﷺ was presented including the hardships and opposition he faced while propagating the message of Islam, and the details of migration and the period after it until his death. After that the description of Rightly Guided Caliphate was also discussed in its full perspective.

In this second volume, starting with the Caliphate of Banu Umayyah, the martydom of Imam Husain ﷺ, and the Caliphate of the Abbasids, all areas have been covered as far as the expansion of Islam was.

This third volume begins with the description of the conditions of Spain before and after the rule of Muslims and the role played by Umayyad, Abbasid, Almoravid and Almohad Caliphs there and their encounters with the Christian Armies. Then some mention of the conquest of Morocco and North Africa has been given along with the details of Idrisia and Aghlabs rule there. After that detailed accounts of Ganghisid Mongols, Turks and Tartar Mangols have been produced. After that Islamic history of Persia is described giving the accounts of Saffariah, Samanid, Delmid, Gharnavid, Seljuk, Ghourid and Muluk Dynasties with the periods of Khwarizm Shah, Atabeks and Sistan Kings rule there. Then the Islamic history of Egypt and Syria is covered describing the Ubaidullah, Ayyubid and Mamluk Dynasties, and the rule of Atabek and Abbasid Caliphs. In the end, something about the Ottoman Dynasty and its Empire is dicussed including the description of the conquest of Constantinople.

We hope that the readers will find this volume also of great help in the study of Islamic history. The famous scholar Safi-ur-Rahman Mubarakpuri has revised the Urdu edition before its translation to check the authenticity aspect.

The translation was done by the Translation Department of Darussalam, and every care has been taken to reproduce the events and the names of the persons and places as accurately as possible. We thank all the persons who have cooperated with us to complete this task and produce it before you into a presentable form. May Allâh accept our humble efforts in this regard and send His peace and blessings on our Prophet Muhammad, his Companions and his followers.—*Amin!*

Abdul Malik Mujahid
General Manager
Darussalam

Table of Contents

Chapter - 3

Chapter - 4

Chapter - 5

Chapter-13

Chapter-14

Chapter-21

Chapter 1

Spain before the Muslims

Geographical Conditions

On the map of Europe is a peninsula in the southwest, which joins Europe with the African continent. The southern part of this peninsula, by joining the northern part of Morocco, intended to form an isthmus but the Mediterranean Sea prevailed in joining hands with the Atlantic Ocean, with the result that Europe and Africa remained about ten miles apart from one another. The Mediterranean Sea and the Bay of Biscay were making an attempt to form an island but the Pyrenees mountain range, by raising its high wall, separated this peninsula from France without allowing it to become an island. This southwestern peninsula of Europe came to be called Spain, Iberia, Hispaniah and Andalus (Andulus). It covers an area of about two hundred thousand square miles.

Produce and Climate

Its climate is temperate and better than all the other countries of Europe. It has a fertile land and may be compared to Syria and Egypt with respect to agricultural production. It is famous for silver mines and other precious minerals.

Two big rivers, Ebro River (Tagus) in the northeast and that of the
Guadalquivir (Wadi Al-Kabir) River in the southwest, flow to make this
peninsula a bed of flowers. This peninsula is enclosed in the north by
the Bay of Biscay and the Pyrenees, in the east by the Mediterranean
Sea, in the south by the Mediterranean, Gibraltar (Jabal Tariq) and the
Atlantic Ocean, and in the west by the Atlantic Ocean.

Details of Provinces and Territories

The details of the noted provinces and territories of this peninsula are as
follows: Portugal falls in the west, Galicia in the northwest, the
provinces of Asturia, Castile, Arbunia, Aragon in the north, the
provinces of Catalonia in the northeast, and Andalusia in the southeast.
Toledo lies at the center of Spain while the famous cities of Cordova and
Granada fall in the province of Andalusia, in the southern part of the
peninsula. Seville was also famous in the southwestern part. The most
fertile and valuable area of the peninsula falls in the southern part,
Andalusia and this part of the peninsula remained under the Muslim
control for a longer period than the other provinces.

Phoenician, Carthage, Roman, Gothic Rules in Spain

Phoenician Rule

Phoenicia or Canaan was a country that was the western part of Sham
and forms part of the eastern coast of the Mediterranean Sea (including
present day Syria, Lebanon and Israel). Several hundred years before
Musa (Moses) a very powerful trading people lived in this country and
historians call them Phoenicians. Phoenician ships would carry
merchandise throughout the Mediterranean Sea. Vast wealth let them
lay the foundation of a unique society and civilization and by capturing
Palestine and establishing a Red Sea port, they established relations with
India and China. Through the Mediterranean Sea and crossing Gibraltar,
they spread their trade routes to England. The northern and southern
ports of the Mediterranean Sea were under their control and they had
the mightiest Navy in the world. They set up colonies at various places.
Among those colonies was Carthage (Tunis) a city of northern Africa,
which was later made the capital of an independent state.

Cities, towns and ports were established by them on the coastal areas of Spain. Gradually, the Phoenicians began to rule there and Spain became a province of their state. At the decline of Phoenician rule, some of their members set up a mighty empire in Carthage (Tunis). They ruled for hundreds of years. They were worshippers of fire and stars. Their civilization had no parallel in their times. The Carthaginians rule of Spain left a deeper effect than the Phoenicians because they were nearer to Spain than Syria.

Roman Rule in Spain

When the Roman Empire was founded in Italy confrontations took place between the Romans and the Carthaginians. After victory over the Carthaginians, the Romans set up their rule in Spain. They ruled over Spain for five hundred years. Viceroys were sent to Spain from Rome who collected annual tribute from the country and sent it to the ruling parties of the Roman Empire.

Goth Rule

With the acceptance of Christianity the Roman Empire suffered a two-fold calamity. One, the Goths, resembling the Mongols, rose from middle and eastern Europe and started launching attacks on Rome. The pleasure loving Romans could not withstand the onslaught of the hard-working Goths. During the same time, the Roman Empire was divided into two parts. One had Rome as its capital and the eastern Roman Empire made Constantinople its capital. These Gothic plunderers later accepted Christianity in the same manner as the Seljuk Turks accepted Islam adopting the religion of those they conquered. Just as the Seljuks had, after accepting Islam, founded their rule so, after accepting Christianity the Goths crossed the Pyrenees captured Spain and established their rule.

Like the eastern and western Roman Empires, the Goths also founded two separate states named Eastern Goth and Western Goth. Since the western Goths became rulers and adopted religion simultanewusly, they kept themselves independent of the Roman Pope. Moreover, their acceptance of Christianity was more a matter of expediency than faith. But the power and influence of the spiritual leaders cast its effects on Spain too with the spread of Christianity in other countries of Europe. With the passage of time, the bishops gained so much power that they had their say in the election and enthronement of kings and it was not easy for a king to curtail their power. The Goth dynasty, which took its shape by 500 C.E., ruled over Spain for two hundred years.

During this period, the fighting qualities and ferocity of the Spanish Goths were changed into a life of luxury, pleasure and adornment. Even though the Goths had brought with them soldierly qualities and a fighting spirit they changed their outlook and way of life. Since the Goths had no character or high standard of living of their own, they crossed all limits by indulging in the pleasures of life under the influence of the Spaniards. In Short, Spain was the sum total of many civilizations. But it was not bereft of academic and other kinds of developments of the age. Christianity had also influenced it deeply by its growth and practices.

The Gothic dynasty ended after 700 C.E. and an eastern nation raised the standard of Islam in Spain by ending the rule of Persia, Rome, Syria, Egypt and Greece and by replacing Christianity and idolatry.

End of Gothic Rule

A religious sense grew within the Gothic state with the passage of time. It had a church of its own. The laws of the country were dictated by Christian narrow-mindedness, with the result that the Jews were put to disgrace and the Christian population treated them like their slaves. Their properties were confiscated and they had to serve the Christians in all manners. Concerning their rights, they had few and were reduced to the state of animals. The Spanish Christians were dominated by all kinds of superstitions. In respect to culture, the arts, science, trade and discipline the Jews were superior to the Christians who were generally pleasure loving and lazy while the Jews were hardworking. However, the Jews were a small minority and they could not fight for their salvation. The bishops went so deep into the State's affairs that the kings could not go against them. They had large estates and fertile lands. Their residences were made to look like wonderlands and their assemblies were resplendent with pleasures and luxuries and whatever they desired. No one had the courage to interfere with their evil acts. The verdicts and decrees issued by the bishops made the most respectable of people bow down. Each of the bishops possessed one or two hundred slaves and an injunction issued by a bishop had no appeal to any higher body whatsoever. Gothic rule had its capital in Toledo. The Archbishop of Spain lived in the capital. The Archbishop enjoyed so much power that he could order the deposition of a king. In other words, the Christian clerics were the total rulers of Spain.

Accession of Roderick (Larziq)

With regard to grandeur and magnificence the expanse of Gothic rule had reached its peak. They had under there sway most of the islands around the Mediterranean besides the Spanish peninsula. Some of the parts of the northern coast of Africa were also under their control. On the coast of the Mediterranean Sea, Byzantium/nes (Eastern Romans) ruled gloriously. When the Muslims had driven away the Romans from Syria and Palestine, the Goth king Witiza ruled in Toledo. When he noticed the bishops rising in power and their inhuman treatment to the Jews, he made an attempt to cut them down to size. Being informed of the plan, they accused the king of favoring the Jews and brought about his deposition. They replaced him with Roderick, a military commander, who belonged to the royal family. This was the end of Gothic rule and beginning of Roderick's rule. He was a seasoned commander of 70 or 80 years of age. On assuming the throne, he ruled with power and peace and did nothing to antagonize the Church.

Factors Leading to the Muslim Invasion of Spain

The Ceuta fort on the northern coast of Africa (Morocco) was still under Christian possession and a man named Count Julian was the garrison commander. He was a Roman commander and was deputed on behalf of the Caesar of Constantinople. Except for this fort, all other occupied territories of Africa had come under Muslim control. Julian had established friendly relations with the Christian rulers of Spain with the consent of Caesar of Constantinople. Since Spain was nearer to Ceuta, it was expedient from the standpoint of security. The last Gothic king, Witiza had married his daughter to Julian. The deposition of Witiza and the enthronement of Roderick displeased him but the support of the bishops kept Julian silent. Julian had a daughter named Florenda who was the maternal grand daughter of king Witiza. As per the practice of that time, young sons of kings, governors, commanders and men of high status were sent to live in the king's palace to learn etiquette and manners. The king treated them like a father and sent them to their parents after attaining puberty. Similarly, they would send their daughters to the queens with the same purpose in view. Florenda, the daughter of Julian, when she became a young lady, was raped by Roderick. Informed of this, Julian grew furious and whoever among the Goths heard of this felt annoyed. However, Count Julian kept his displeasure a secret and arrived in Toledo. He met king Roderick and pretended that his wife was seriously ill and wanted to see her daughter, Florenda before her death. Roderick could not oppose her departure. Thus, Julian took his daughter and came back to Ceuta. The Archbishop of Seville came to Julian to share his pain and both of them sat together to find out how to do away with Roderick's rule.

Musa bin Nusayr

Musa bin Nusayr was then the governor of the occupied western territories in Qairwan during the Caliphate of Waleed bin Abdul Malik. Tariq bin Zeyad, a slave of the Berber race was the Governor of Tanja city (Tangiers) and Commander of the Moroccan force on behalf of Musa bin Nusayr. Although Tariq was close to Julian the latter preferred to talk with Musa bin Nusayr. He took the Archbishop and a selected band of the Christians and reached Qairwan. Musa bin Nusayr showed him the utmost respect. They requested Musa bin Nusayr to invade Spain. But the Muslim Governor gave no clear reply. Thereupon the Archbishop said that Spain was under tyrannical rule and it was his (Musa's) duty to save the Spanish population from these excesses. Musa bin Nusayr then made inquiries about the military power and other conditions in Spain and then wrote to Caliph Waleed bin Abdul Malik in Damascus seeking his permission for the task ahead.

First Islamic Corps to Spain Under Turaif

Musa bin Nusayr then ordered five hundred soldiers under Turaif to accompany Julian in his ships and land on the coast of Spain to acquire first hand knowledge about the state of affairs there. Turaif landed on the Spanish coast and returned safely after making some small-scale raids for plunder. After a short time the Caliph permitted them to invade Spain but with the utmost caution.

Tariq bin Zeyad Ordered to Invade Spain

Acquainted with the state of affairs in Spain Musa bin Nusayr sent orders to Tariq bin Zeyad, the Governor of Tangiers to invade Spain. Tariq led a force of seven thousand in four boats. He was still on the way when he was overtaken by drowsiness and saw in dream that the Prophet (صلى الله عليه وسلم) gave him the good news of the conquest of Spain at his hands. Shortly after this, his eyes opened and he was sure of his victory.

Chapter 2

Islamic Rule In Spain

The Strange Order of Tariq

Tariq landed on the coast of Spain along with his men and his first order was to set the boats on fire and sink them. This was undoubtedly strange but in fact, it was an act of matchless bravery. As a seasoned military commander, he knew that compared with the huge enemy force he had with him a very small one. His soldiers might lose heart or a discouraging situation might lead them to retreat or wait for reinforcements before engaging the enemy. By sinking the warships, he let his forces know that retreat was out of the question. They were standing between their enemy and the sea. They were left with no choice but to go ahead and push their enemy back. They needed courage, determination and quick action because lack of courage and fighting spirit would lead them to annihilation.

The First Stage of the Islamic Force

The place Tariq landed on was called Lines Rock but from that day on it came to be called Jabal Tariq or Gibraltar.

The Attack of a Christian General and His Defeat

Tadmir, the military Commander of Roderick was very experienced and had led his force to victory in a number of encounters. He was encamped in the vicinity of Tariq's forces with a strong army. He launched a powerful attack before the Muslim forces had a chance to get settled. However, Tariq gave him a smashing defeat and he fled from the battlefield. He then wrote to Roderick the following day from a safe place:

> "O Emperor! Some strange people have invaded our territory. We fought with courage and bravery but tasted defeat and our troops could not withstand their onslaught. What is needed is your personal engagement. I am quite unaware of their identity and whereabouts".

Preparations of Roderick

Soon after receiving the horrible news Roderick set about building his army. He came from Toledo to Cordova where troops from all parts of the country began to concentrate. He then marched against the invaders at the head of one hundred thousand troops. Tadmir also joined him with his force, while all the seasoned commanders of Spain came forward to play important roles. But Tariq did not sit idle during this period. He continued his march occupying cities and towns and reached up to the Lorca valley.

The First Battle

The two forces clashed on the bank of a small river near Janda Lagoon adjoining Sidonia city on 28 Ramadan 92 A.H. (July 711 C.E.). Shortly after the departure of the Muslim forces under Tariq, Musa bin Nusayr dispatched five thousand soldiers as reinforcements, which joined Tariq before the confrontation. Now the twelve thousand men of Tariq bin Zeyad had to face a strong Christian force of one hundred thousand. The Muslim force knew little of the state of affairs of the country they had invaded. The Christian troops were the natives of the country and had come to the battlefield to save their motherland.

Tariq bin Zeyad, the Governor of Africa was the freed slave of Musa bin Nusayr who did not command extraordinary value. The Emperor of Spain was himself leading the army and all the resources of the country were at his command. The Muslim force had its greater part based on convert Berbers while the Christian force was inspired and encouraged by eminent bishops and religious guides. Had Tariq's force been defeated in this battle it would have been known as one of the insignificant events of history. But since twelve thousand Muslim troops defeated one hundred thousand well-equipped Christian troops, it came to be known as one of the most glorious battles ever fought by humans. While drawing his battle line Tariq made a fervid speech to the Muslim fighters, which fired them with new spirit, zeal and determination.

The greater part of Christian force consisted of cavalry clad in armor, while the Muslim side had only foot soldiers. The cavalry movement of the Christians was quite terrifying and it appeared very clear that they would crush the Muslim troops under their hooves without giving them an opportunity to take up their arms against the Christians. But the glittering Islamic swords dispelled the hovering clouds of the Christian force and left many lying dead and wounded. Their *takbir* (*Allah-o-Akbar* Allah is Great) rent the air and subdued all other shouts and noises on the battlefield.

Roderick's Escape from the Battlefield

Roderick fled the battlefield leaving behind not only a large number of soldiers dead and wounded but also his wide experience, courage and determination.

Causes of the Christians' Defeat

The Christians tasted defeat not because of their lack of courage but simply because of the daring deeds of Muslim fighters. Had they been cowards they would not have left behind great commanders, princes and bishops dead and wounded. The actual number of dead Christian soldiers is not known but history tells us that the horses left by the dead horsemen were sufficient for the entire Muslim army. The Christian soldiers could have escaped on horseback but they preferred to die fighting.

The Muslims were crowned with this victory on 5 Shawwal 92 A.H.
(711 C.E.). This was the beginning of Muslim rule in Spain. Tariq bin
Zeyad sent the good news of the Muslim victory to Musa bin Nusayr
the same day and he himself marched ahead to win the province of
Andalusia. Musa bin Nusayr grew happy and dispatched the glad
tidings to the Caliph. He then left Qairwan for Spain at the head of
eighteen thousand soldiers. Before his march, he sent orders to Tariq
not to go ahead but consolidate his position in the conquered
territories. However, Tariq had conquered Andalusia before the letter
reached him. But some big cities of the Peninsula and its capital,
Toledo still held military camps of the Christians and a joint attack
was possible at anytime. Thus, his march to the north and the conquest
of these cities was necessary to Zeyad who assembled his Commanders
and read out the order issued by Musa bin Nusayr. They were all
unanimous against the order pleading that if the campaign against the
Christians were stopped at the present stage the Christians would
with attacks on all sides, make the task of the conquest of the entire
Spain most difficult. Count Julian also supported this view.

Tariq's March to Cordova

The Governor of Cordova belonged to the royal family. The fugitives
of the battle of Lorca valley had taken refuge in the city. The fort of the
city was very strong and formidable. Tariq first asked them to yield in
a friendly manner but on their refusal, he besieged the fort. He then
appointed Mughith, the Roman, to continue the siege and he
proceeded to Toledo.

Conquest of Toledo

Tariq conquered Toledo rather easily in Rabia al-Thani 93 A.H. From
the royal treasury of Toledo he captured twenty-five crowns of former
Gothic kings. Every crown bore the name and tenure of the king.
Every king had a new crown to wear and it was preserved in the royal
treasury after his death. Tariq then marched to the remotest northern
province of Spain. Mughith, the Roman, in the meantime, conquered
Cordova and its surroundings. Thus, Tariq brought under his control
the Spanish peninsula from the south to the north. But the eastern and
western parts were yet to be conquered.

Musa bin Nusayr in Spain

Meanwhile, Musa bin Nusayr stepped into Spain along with his force. Count Julian, who was put by Zeyad there to look after the administration, gave a hearty welcome to Musa. Finding Musa angry with Tariq for overstepping his orders, Julian advised Musa to lead his campaign against the cities of the western provinces. Musa accepted the advice. Tariq joined him in Toledo. Musa not only reprimanded Tariq for disobeying his orders but also held him as a captive for a short time. After a few days, Musa sent Tariq in front at the head of a large army and proceeded at his back. While Tariq and Musa were engaged in conquering the northern and northwestern cities Abdul Aziz, the son of Musa started conquering the southern and southeastern territories. Tadmir, the commander of king Roderick, was then in the southeast. He came out to face Abdul Aziz. A number of battles took place. Tadmir retreated to the hills for safety and took to guerrilla attacks. At last, a peace accord was signed between the two on condition that Tadmir would give no shelter to the enemies of Islamic rule and religious freedom would be kept intact. On the finalization of the agreement, Abdul Aziz gave a small territory to Tadmir to rule over. Musa and Tariq also signed peace treaties with each city on easy terms including religious freedom for the Christians, disputes between the Jews and the Christians to be settled according to their religious scriptures, no interference on anyone accepting Islam, and safety for the Christians and their property. Musa and Tariq had also directed their troops not to kill old men, women and children except those who rose in arms to fight against the Muslims.

Conquering northern and western provinces Tariq and Musa marched up to the Pyrenees and then stepped into the southern territories of France and conquered them. But the Islamic force came back to the Pyrenees owing to the severity of the winter and shortage of supplies. He had a plan to conquer France, Austria, Italy, and the Balkans before arriving at Constantinople.

Full Islamic Control over Spain

Following his arrival in Spain and before his departure from Toledo, the capital towards the north Musa bin Nusayr sent Mughith, the Roman to

Damascus with valuable gifts and news of the conquest of Spain. Mughith came back from the headquarters of the Caliph after Musa had conquered Galicia province. However, the order of the Caliph issued to Musa bin Nusayr and brought back by Mughith was rather frustrating.

Musa Summoned

The Caliph ordered Musa to meet him in the court of the Caliph and in pursuance of the order Musa bin Nusayr deputed his son Abdul Aziz in Spain and left for the headquarters in the company of Mughith and Tariq. He took with him the treasure of Spain, golden utensils, ornaments and one-fifth of the total possessions captured along with a large number of slaves and slave-girls. He reached Damascus at a time when Caliph Waleed bin Abdul Malik was on his deathbed. His brother Sulaiman bin Abdul Malik was about to succeed him. When Sulaiman heard of Musa's arrival near Damascus he sent him (Musa) word not to make a hasty entrance into Damascus. But Musa paid no heed to the message of Sulaiman and appeared before Caliph Waleed bin Abdul Malik. On receiving such large and costly gifts from Musa bin Nusayr, Waleed became very happy. But the courtiers and ministers felt jealous.

Accession of Sulaiman bin Abdul Malik

Sulaiman bin Abdul Malik succeeded his brother Waleed bin Abdul Malik on Jamad al-Thani 96 A.H. Following the death of the latter immediately after coming to the throne Sulaiman bin Abdul Malik called Musa bin Nusayr to account in a severe manner and when Musa failed to clear the account received as tribute from the western countries he confiscated Musa's wealth and property. He put him in prison for failure to pay two hundred thousand gold coins he owed to the State.

End of Tariq

With the punishment given to Musa bin Nusayr, Tariq bin Zeyad also could not remain unaffected. He was neither shown any respect nor sent back to assume charge of Spain or Morocco. All the conquered territories in the west were under the control of Musa's sons. Spain was ruled over by Abdul Aziz bin Musa, Qairwan by Abdullah bin Musa and Morocco by Marwan bin Musa. Since Sulaiman bin Abdul Malik could not ignore their being at the helm, he held back Tariq who was considered as a member of Musa's family. He was allowed to be retired on pension and to settle in a city of Syria. On intercession, Musa bin Nusayr was released and sent to live in al-Qura valley after paying as much money as he could.

Death of Musa bin Nusayr

In a state of frustration Musa bin Nusayr passed away the next year 97 A.H. Historians have targeted Sulaiman bin Abdul Malik for his unkind treatment of Musa bin Nusayr. But he could not be blamed for what he did. Umar Farooq had already done the same in the case of Khalid bin Waleed and had him deposed from his command. Musa bin Nusayr remained in power for about sixteen or seventeen years and owed a lot of wealth to the public treasury. Had the case been overlooked it would have set a very bad example for other Governors, present and future.

Moreover, Sulaiman's ministers, advisers and courtiers never made him the target of their criticism for his treatment of Musa and Tariq nor have Muslim historians ever condemned him for his behavior.

European historians have very wrongly stated that Roderick suffered defeat owing to his weak power. Some others say rather baselessly that Roderick's subjects had revolted against him and went over to the Muslims side. Although the Spanish population had begun to look upon the Muslim character and style with respect, except for Count Julian and a bishop who had asked the Muslim ruler to invade Spain, no one lent any support to the Muslims. Moreover, the Muslims in the presence of their power of Faith and strength of heart were not in need of any intrigue or plots or outside help.

A False Episode

European historians have, in fact, fabricated many such stories to degrade the achievements of the Muslim forces. One of these says that when Tariq proceeded to the north from Toledo he met a group of fugitives who had a table or low wooden seat of Sulaiman (ﷺ) studded with gems and jewels and valued in the millions and Tariq wrested it from them. When Musa reached Spain he demanded the table, Tariq handed over the captured table after removing a leg of it and concealing it, he told Musa that he had received it in the same state. Musa bin Nusayr fitted a golden leg onto it but it looked different from the others. Presenting the table to the Caliph, Musa bin Nusayr submitted that he had found it in the spoils of war. Finding a leg different from others the Caliph inquired about it and Musa submitted that he had received the table from the Christians in the same state. Tariq then took out the fourth leg from under his clothes and said to the Caliph, "This is the fourth leg of the table". When the Caliph, came to know that Musa had taken the credit for the deed performed by Tariq he grew very angry and put Musa bin Nusayr in prison along with such a heavy fine that he would not be able to pay. European historians have invented many such stories with ulterior motives. One cannot, however, find a reason for Tariq to play such a heinous trick on his leader and immediate commanding officer, Musa bin Nusayr. Moreover, how could have Musa remained in the dark for so long although thousands of men were aware of such a plot. It means an ambitious and far-sighted conqueror like Musa bin Nusayr was so mean that he would snatch the credit from his freed slave, Tariq. Furthermore, nobody could in the packed court notice the hidden leg of the table. Among the historians of Spain and western countries, Ibn Khaldun is the most reliable and he has made no mention of such an event. According to Ibn Khaldun, the Caliph grew angry with Musa because the latter had resolved to conquer all of Europe by putting the Muslims into danger and it was for this reason he was called to headquarters.

As already mentioned, Musa bin Nusayr had entrusted Spain, Morocco and the other occupied territories to his sons. Thus, it was out of question that the Caliph would have taken Musa to task so severely over the leg of a table. It also seems strange that the Caliph made no attempt to depose his sons when he was so angry with their father. Even when, after sometime, he sent Muhammad bin Yazid as governor to look after the western countries, he left Abdul Aziz bin Musa to rule in Spain.

First Ruler of Spain

Although Musa and Tariq were the conquerors of Spain and they spent a long time conquering and making peace with the Christian powers, the person to be called the first ruler of Spain was Abdul Aziz, the son of Musa bin Nusayr.

Chapter 3

Rulers of Spain

Abdul Aziz bin Musa

With the departure of Musa bin Nusayr from Spain most of the cities rose in revolt. Abdul Aziz bin Musa had to put down the revolts with determination and a heavy hand. Since the commanding officers in the different cities were not sufficient in number, the Christian population felt encouraged to take up arms. But very soon, it dawned upon them that it was not an easy task to drive away the Muslims from Spain. Moreover, they had the feeling that Islamic rule was far better than the Gothic rule and a blessing from Allah Almighty.

Religious Freedom

The Muslims were the first to announce religious freedom. The Christian population also enjoyed it fully provided they would live in peace with the Muslims. The Christians of Spain had a large number of slaves who worked very hard. When Abdul Aziz announced that the slaves accepting Islam would enjoy full freedom from slavery, large number of slaves under the Christians embraced Islam and became free from slavery. This was not only a great service to humanity but also a device to increase the Muslim population.

Abdul Aziz had married Ajilona, the widow of Roderick and left her to follow her religion. The Muslim population also followed suit. They occupied the vacant Christian houses and began to live with them. Abdul Aziz appointed Christians as the administrators of cities and towns. Ajilona very soon began to influence her husband in state affairs. Although the Arabian Commanders disliked it, they could not do anything about it.

The new Caliph, Sulaiman bin Abdul Malik had accused Musa bin Nusayr of the case of non-payment of the spoils of war instead of holding him in honor for his conquests. Abdul Aziz had not uttered a word against the Caliph but Ajilona and other Christians began to take advantage of Abdul Aziz's agitated feelings. He also tried to win the support of Ajilona and the Christians to free Spain from the control of the Caliph. But in order to keep Caliph Sulaiman unaware Abdul Aziz sent a substantial amount along with gifts to Damascus. The correspondents of Caliph had already informed him of the dangerous designs of Abdul Aziz and those who carried spoils of war and gifts from Spain also supported the report.

Assassination of Abdul Aziz

The Caliph sent orders to five Muslim Commanders in Spain to kill Abdul Aziz if his evil intentions became dangerous. Abdul Aziz had his capital in Seville. When the Caliph's message came to Habib bin Ubaidah, he consulted the other four persons. Now all the five decided to kill Abdul Aziz. Thus, they arrested Abdul Aziz and assassinated him. Burying his body in Seville, they sent his head to the Caliph. Following this they replaced him by Musa bin Nusayr's sister's son Ayub bin Habib Lakhmi. Since the Caliph was not sure of the killing of Abdul Aziz, he had not sent anybody from Damascus to replace him and left the decision to them. Thus, the appointment of a close relative of Abdul Aziz as a ruler of Spain proves the good intentions of the group of five because they could have taken the leadership from his family. European historians have exaggerated on this subject in order to defame Caliph Sulaiman bin Abdul Malik's character.

Abdul Aziz bin Musa was assassinated in 98 A.H.

Ayyub bin Habib

After doing away with Abdul Aziz the "group of five" convened a meeting of the courtiers and commanders and obtained their consent for Ayyub bin Habib. However, he was elected on condition that his election was to be considered valid subject to the approval of either the governor or the Caliph otherwise it would be set aside forthwith.

Transfer of the Headquarters

With an eye on the large Christian and Jewish population and their growing influence Ayyub bin Habib shifted his capital to Cordova. It was a historic deed of the new ruler because Cordova, from then on, became the center of world attention. Ayyub also invited Berber and Arab tribes of Africa and Morocco to settle in Spain. Thus with the substantial increase in the Muslim population the possibilities of Christian insurgence was minimized to a certain extent. A number of forts were built on the frontiers and were manned by garrisons. Besides, Ayyub made an extensive tour of the country and managed to fulfill the needs of the different areas. Ayyub ruled for only for six months when a deposition order came. Muhammad bin Yazid of Qairwan feared his growing power and influence particularly because he belonged to the family of Musa and Abdul Aziz. He sent Harb bin Abdur Rahman bin Uthman to assume the post of governor. The Caliph latter sent his approval.

Harb bin Abdur Rahman Ghafqi

Shortly after coming to power Harb bin Abdur Rahman began to make the officials of Musa and Abdul Aziz's time the target of his excesses. He indulged in taking violent action against the Christians and the Jews. They had enjoyed kind treatment from the Muslim rulers in the past. At last, they sent a deputation to Qairwan to seek Harb's transfer from Spain. But Muhammad bin Yazid paid no heed. Following their failure they took the daring step of sending a deputation to Damascus. It took place when Caliph Umar bin Abdul Aziz had taken charge after Caliph Sulaiman bin Abdul Malik. When the deputation approached the new Caliph, he took the immediate step of deposing Harb bin Abdur Rahman and replaced him with Samh bin Malik Khulani. Harb ruled in Spain for two years and eight months.

Samh bin Malik

Even though Samh bin Malik was a military man and was also among the companions of Tariq bin Zeyad, he worked hard to promote justice and prosperity among the people. His rule was, in fact, the reflection of Umar bin Abdul Aziz's noble caliphate.

Census in Spain

Caliph Umar bin Abdul Aziz ordered a census in Spain to know the exact number of tribes and sections of people in the country. Samh then populated the Berbers in the deserted areas and induced them to take to agriculture and crafts, which they did with success. He then drew a geographical map of Spain delineating the population of every city and town, its physical position, distance between cities, rivers, mountains and other important details. The map was sent to the Caliph. Rules and regulations regarding trade and commerce, agriculture, *Jiz'yah* (poll tax) *ash'r* (one-tenth), *khum's* (one-fifth) and tribute were enacted . Besides, he built a number of mosques and bridges in various cities. Peace and justice prevailed over all of Spain. Samh achieved the same position among the Muslim Governors in Spain that Umar bin Abdul Aziz had among the Muslim umayyad Caliphs.

Expedition to Southern France

In view of Samh bin Malik's earlier style of governance nobody could expect that he would also be a great warrior. After finishing his task of consolidating and regulating his administration, he led his forces into southern France. This part of France had some strong states. The most belligerent to the Muslims was ruled by the fugitive Goths from Spain who had fled with as much possessions as they could carry with them. They were the worst enemy of the Muslims and their state was supposed to be strong and formidable. The Gauls ruled another State, their capital was in Toulousse. Crossing the Pyrenees Governor Samh invaded and captured Narbonne city and then the whole State. They also captured substantial spoils of war. His next target was Toulousse. After a fierce battle, the Muslim troops laid siege to the city. When Toulousse city was about to fall, the Duke of Acton, a Christian ruler appeared with a large force. Governor Samh had already much fewer troops, some of whom had been left in Narbonne. However, Samh drew the battle line dauntlessly and made an impassioned speech to his force. Thus, the scene of the battle between Tariq and Roderick was repeated.

Martyrdom of Samh

At a time when the Muslims were pushing the Christians back, an arrow hit the throat of Samh and he succumbed to it. Although the Muslim force felt discouraged, they did not give in. They elected Abdur Rahman bin Abdullah Ghafqi as their leader and commander who drew back with enough caution to deny the Christians any opportunity to chase them.

Abdur Rahman bin Abdullah Ghafqi

Historians have generally admired the courage and caution with which Abdur Rahman bin Abdullah Ghafqi pulled out his force safely from the battleground. While coming back from Toulousse to Narbonne, the Muslim forces could have been plundered on the way. But whenever and wherever the Christians made such attempts, they suffered a disaster. Having arrived in Narbonne Abdur Rahman Ghafqi set about bringing back courage, strength and normalcy to the Muslim force. He then marched against those who had shown signs of revolt owing to the Muslim setback in Toulousse.

Abdur Rahman's Deposition

While marching to France Governor Samh had deputed Anbasa bin Suhaim Kalbi to look after the administration. He had also dispatched reinforcements from Spain but Abdur Rahman had already finished his task. On his return from the battlefield, he (Abdur Rahman) was left to work as Governor. But in a short time, Abdur Rahman was deposed on charges of concentrating power in the hands of the army and the administration was once again handed over to Anbasa bin Suhaim Kalbi. Abdur Rahman paid allegiance to Anbasa without delay. Later, Anbasa appointed Abdur Rahman the Governor of eastern Spain where he had held the same post in the past.

Anbasa bin Sahim Kalbi

Upon taking charge of the Governorship Anbasa began many activities beneficial to everyone. During the early days of his rule, a Christian named Pelayo revolted in the mountainous areas and brought many Christians to his fold. Islamic force put down their insurgence with heavy hands and Pelayo, along with thirty men, escaped to the hills. The Muslims ignored their escape. They later took to robbery and plundering in the nearby areas. With scattered groups of Christians joining them, they gained strength and gradually laid the foundation for a parallel rule in Spain.

Conquest of Southern France

After managing the affairs of his country, Governor Anbasa invaded France. Since Narbonne was under Muslim rule, he experienced no difficulty in passing through the Pyrenees. He conquered Southern France and spread his troops towards the east and the west from the center. At one point, the Christian forces gave a good account of themselves but they could not withstand the heavy onslaught of the brave Muslims.

Martyrdom of Anbasa

The conquest was heading towards the final stage when Anbasa left his troops behind and stormed into the enemy ranks and was honored with martyrdom. Urwah bin Abdullah Fihri replaced him as the commander who was able to retreat safety and brought back his forces to Spain. This event took place in 107 A.H.

Urwah bin Abdullah Fihri

Urwah bin Abdullah was one of the renowned Commanders of Spain. People belonging to his family and tribe lived in Spain in large numbers. He was very honest, brave and sober. However, some people became angry with him and complained to the governer of Africa about him and he was replaced by Yahya bin Salma.

Yahya bin Salma

Yahya bin Salma Kalbi came to power at the end of 107 A.H. He was an extremist and unyielding by nature, with the result the people of Spain turned against him and he was deposed and replaced by Uthman bin Abi Ubaidah Lakhmi.

Uthman bin Abi Ubaidah Lakhmi

Uthman was appointed Governor by Ubaid bin Abdur Rahman, the ruler of Africa. Five months after his appointment he was replaced by Hudaifah bin al-Ahwas Qaisi.

Hudaifah bin al-Ahwas Qaisi

Hudaifah ruled Spain until the end of 110 A.H. But was deposed and replaced by Haitham bin Ubaid the next year.

Haitham bin Ubaid

Haitham bin Ubaid Kilabi belonged to the Syrian race and was inclined to harsh treatment and hard decisions, because of this the people of Spain turned against him. The Muslims and the Christians united in standing against him. Thus, a deputation left Spain to lodge a complaint to the Governor of Africa about Haitham as they had done in the past. The African ruler paid no heed to the complaint nor did he depose the ruler of Spain.

Meeting with failure the deputation approached the Caliph in Damascus. He sent Muhammad bin Abdullah Ashjai to investigate the matter in disguise. In the case Haitham was proved a wrong doer he was to be deposed instantly and the Governorship was to be assumed by Ashjai, otherwise Haitham was to be left in his place.

Deposition of Haitham

Haitham bin Ubaid waged Jihad on Manshah (La Mancha), conquered it and stayed there ten months. After a rule of two years, he was deposed.

Muhammad bin Abdullah Ashjai

Muhammad bin Abdullah Ashjai came to Spain, looked into the charges and found Haitham guilty. The investigator then assembled the people and placed before them the order of the Caliph. With the active support of the people, he deposed and arrested Haitham and sent him to the Caliph in chains. Muhammad bin Abdullah Ashjai then devoted all his time and energy to put the administration right. After being satisfied with the state of affairs in Spain, he made Abdur Rahman bin Abdullah Ghafqi governor in Spain and left for Damascus. This event took place in 113 A.H.

Abdur Rahman bin Abdullah Ghafqi Reinstated

assuming charge of the administration, he made an all-out effort to put it back to normal. As a part of his welfare works, he built madrasas (schools), mosques and bridges in most of the cities and towns. Finding time from working on the welfare projects, he set about making preparations to invade France.

Uthman Lakhmi rebels

As mentioned above, Uthman Lakhmi had also ruled Spain for a short period of five months. On being deposed, he was given a northern province to rule. The Pyrenees was in his province. Since he was reduced to the position of a ruler of a small piece of land, he felt indignant and agitated and was restless to form his own sovereign rule. Since Uthman belonged to the Berbers, he had little sympathy with Arabs and Syrians. He rather considered them his rivals. The Duke of Acton, the Gothic king, ruled over a large part of France. Following the battle of Toulousse, he wanted to strengthen his position against Charles Martel, the king of the northern part of France. In order to overpower his rival the Duke extended a hand of friendship towards Uthman. With a strong desire to win Uthman's friendship, he not only sent costly gifts but also gave him his daughter, famous for beauty, in marriage. In return for this marriage, the Duke of Acton made Uthman put in writing that he would not force his daughter to abandon Christianity and also refrain from using force against him (the Duke).

Uthman assassinated

When Abdur Rahman Ghafqi, the Governor of Spain decided to lead his campaign against France and pass through the Pyrenees he sent Uthman word to be ready to join his command with military forces and supplies. He showed his unwillingness to obey these orders. And when Abdur Rahman Ghafqi reached there, Uthman put up resistance to Ghafqi's forces in the pass of the Pyrenees. Abdur Rahman Ghafqi sent a commander ahead with some troops who fought Uthman and killed him. His Christian wife was captured and brought before Abdur Rahman.

Finishing his task in the Pyrenees Abdur Rahman Ghafqi entered France and set about conquering city after city. The Duke of Acton had already joined hands with Charles Martel under compulsion and came to the latter along with his forces and encouraged him to face the Muslims. Charles swung into action and began to make large scale preparations for all out war. The Bishops began to arouse Christian feelings against the Muslims. The Islamic forces landed across the river Jourdanne. The Christians were completely routed and the Muslim troops seized the city of Poitiers.

Fighting in the City of Tours

Muslim forces proceeded to the city of Tours, which lies in central France. Both forces remained encamped in front of one another for seven days. The Muslims were strange to the territory while the Christians were trying to save their country and were led by seasoned commanders like Charles Martel and the Duke of Acton. They had gone mad with anger and zeal. The Muslim force, one-tenth of the Christian troops, faced its enemy with exemplary courage. The two forces clashed on the eighth day and a fierce fight broke out which went on until evening. Taking advantage of the dark night the Duke of Acton made an ambush with his forces. The next day, at a time when the Christian forces were about to leave the battlefield the Duke attacked the Muslim force from behind. The front row of the Muslim forces was engaged with the invaders while the Christians who were retreating halted.

Martyrdom of Abdur Rahman

The sudden and unexpected two-pronged Christian attack tore apart the Muslim ranks. In such a state of confusion, Abdur Rahman Ghafqi, following the practice of his predecessors, drew his sword and plunged into the enemy ranks killing them in large numbers. At last, he was honored with martyrdom. The Muslim forces kept fighting the whole day despite the loss of their Commander. However, they retreated in the night. The next morning the Christians did not find the Muslims on the battlefield but they could not muster enough courage to chase them for fear of their having set an ambush. They left the battlefield in a hurry to avoid a sudden Muslim onslaught. The Christians left large numbers of troops dead and the biggest tragedy on the Muslim side was the loss of their Commander. The event took place in 114 A.H.

Abdul Malik bin Fihri

When the Governor of Africa, Ubaid bin Abdur Rahman came to know of the outcome of this battle and the martyrdom of Abdur Rahman Ghafqi he appointed Abdul Malik bin Qatn as Governor of Spain. He ordered him to avenge the martyrdom of Abdur Rahman Ghafqi on the French. Abdul Malik bin Qatn Fihri took charge of the Spanish administration in 115 A.H. and soon after streamlining the administration of the country, he set about making military preparations against France.

Abdul Malik bin Qatn being experienced and bright, encouraged high hopes of future successes. However, he made the blunder of leading his force against France during the rainy season, with the result that the swollen rivers and streams made his way very difficult. In view of the troubles faced by the Muslim force, Christian guerillas began to snipe at them. At last, Abdul Malik decided to withdraw but only after much loss of life and time.

Abdul Malik's Deposition

The African Governor was angry and replaced him by Utbah bin Hajjaj Saluli.

Utbah bin Hajjaj Saluli

Utbah bin Hajjaj took charge of the Spanish administration in 117 A.H. and appointed Abdul Malik bin Qatn Fihri as Governor of a small territory. It was a mistake committed by the new Governor. Instead of bringing him down in position, he should have sent him back to Africa.

Deeds of Utbah

He was very intelligent and just. He first brought about peace in Spain. He set up separate police departments to make the routes safe for travelers. He recruited horsemen to patrol all the streets and lanes. He also set up separate courts in every village to lighten the burden of the central courts. He opened at least one madrasa (school) in every village and settlement and set aside a portion of the total revenue to run these institutions. Wherever required he built mosques with a madrasa attached to each one. The Berber population in Spain had increased and their acts of barbarity had increased in the same proportion. Utbah engaged them in constructive jobs in a manner that they became disciplined and civilized. He brought down the rates on revenues and tax collection to a level that made all classes of society happy and satisfied.

He then turned to the French territories under Muslim control. He strengthened and fortified the occupied cities and territories, built forts and during this period, he defeated all French attacks.

The Berbers rose in revolt in Africa in 121 A.H. The African Governor called Utbah from Spain to tackle the situation and he punished the rebels adequately. But disorder and anarchy prevailed throughout Spain during his absence. It proved a heyday for conspirators and those with vested interests. Yusuf bin Abdur Rahman was then the Junior Commissioned officer of the territory north of the Pyrenees with the city of Narbonne as its capital. The Duke of Marseilles, the ruler of eastern France sought help from him against Charles Martel and offered his allegiance to Yusuf bin Abdur Rahman. Charles Martel attacked Marseilles, the capital of the Duke and reduced it to ashes. But he had to withdraw unsuccessfully from Narbonne.

Death of Utbah

When Utbah returned to Spain from Africa, he found clear signs of insurgence. Abdul Malik bin Qatn, the man once deposed by him, had already brought under his control a large section of the Spanish people and staked his claim to the Governorship of Spain. Utbah was planning to deal with the new developments when he was overtaken by death in Cordova in 123 A.H. Thus Abdul Malik bin Qatn captured Spain rather easily.

Abdul Malik bin Qatn

Abdul Malik bin Qatn Fihri was an old man of hundred years, but he was very active with a sound mind and youthful courage. He was originally an inhabitant of Madinah and had taken part in many battles fought in Madinah, Syria, Egypt, Iraq, Morocco and Spain. His body showed scars of hundreds of wounds. The Arabs looked down upon the Berbers of Africa and Morocco. The Berbers felt it deeply. When they found the Umayyads, the Arabs, showing signs of national superiority and arrogance they abhorred it. This is the reason why they joined every movement against the Arab rulers.

Kulthum bin Ayaz

A Syrian Commander, Kulthum bin Ayaz was sent by the Caliph to replace Ubaid bin Abdur Rahman, the Governor of Africa. The Berber Chief Maisarah was at that time plundering and creating trouble for the people. Kulthum took some rather reckless steps to put down the Berber uprisings. The Berbers had, on the other hand, made much progress and development with the blessings of Islam. They had become very experienced fighting side by side with the Arab soldiers, and they brought about setbacks for the Syrians.

Kulthum bin Ayaz at the Fort of Ceuta

Leaving a large number of soldiers dead on the battlefield Kulthum bin Ayaz took refuge in the Fort of Ceuta along with ten thousand Syrian soldiers. This fort was situated on the southern coast of the

Gibraltar Straits. Even though it was beyond the power of the Berbers to conquer the fort, food grain ran short and the besieged Syrians had to face starvation. Kulthum bin Ayaz sought the supply of food grains from Abdul Malik bin Qatn, the Governor of Spain but he gave no such help for his dislike for the Syrians. When a merchant of Spain, Zaid bin Amr came to know of the wretched plight of the besieged Syrian force in the Ceuta Fort, he dispatched several ships loaded with food grains. When it came to the knowledge of Abdul Malik, he killed Zaid bin Amr in disgrace.

Hanzala Appointed as Governor

When Hisham bin Abdul Malik the Caliph of Damascus came to know of the sad plight of Syrian force he sent Hanzala at the head of a large army. He defeated the Berbers and freed the Syrians. During the same period, Kulthum bin Ayaz passed away and Hanzala became the Governor of Africa.

Abdul Malik bin Qatn killed

With the news of Berbers' large-scale killings the Berbers of Spain rose as one man and attacked Abdul Malik bin Qatn and defeated him more than once. When he found putting down of Berber insurgence beyond his power, he wrote to Balj bin Bishr bin Ayaz Qushairi, the nephew of Kulthum bin Ayaz and Commander of a ten thousand man Syrian force to come to Spain and bring the situation under control. Balj bin Bishr put down the revolt in a short time. When the Syrian force narrated to the Spanish Arabs about their starvation and sufferings and the cruelties of Abdul Malik bin Qatn in the Ceuta Fort, Balj bin Bishr arrested Abdul Malik bin Qatn with the support of the people of Spain. Even though he wanted to keep Abdul Malik in captivity, his companions and the enemies of Abdul Malik forced him to kill the old man of 100. The event took place during the last days of 123 A.H.

Mutual Discord

Shortly after the control of Balj bin Bishr over Spain, Umayyah bin Abdul Malik and Qatn bin Abdul Malik, the two sons of Abdul Malik bin Qatn Fihri started making secret plans against Balj bin Bishr. Yusuf

bin Abdur Rahman the Governor of Narbonne also joined them, with
the result that even the Berbers, previously opposed to Abdul Malik,
joined the camp of Abdul Malik's sons. Together they marched on
Cordova. Balj bin Bishr also came out to face the attack. Thus two strong
Muslim forces came face to face in central Spain, Balj was seriously
injured and fell from his horse unconscious. However, the Syrians drove
away their enemies. Balj succumbed to his injuries. This event took place
in 124 A.H. He ruled Spain for eleven months. The Syrians and the
Spanish Arabs jointly made Thalba bin Salamah the ruler of Spain.

Thalba bin Salamah

Thalba bin Salamah, being a Yemenite, excessively favored the people
of Yemen. The sons of Abdul Malik Qatn, who had escaped following
their defeat, refrained from offering their allegiance to Thalba bin
Salamah and went about looting and plundering all over the country.
The Arab tribes, on the other hand, rose against Thalba because of his
excessive favor to the Yemenites and his hostility to the other Arabs.
At last, they lodged a complaint to African Governor Hanzala bin
Safwan about Ibn Salamah with the request of sending a new Governor.

Deposition of Ibn Salamah

Abul Khattab Hosam bin Darar Kalbi was sent to Spain and was
warmly welcomed by the people. He deposed Ibn Salamah and took
charge of the administration. The event took place in 125 A.H.

Abul Khattab Hosam bin Darar Kalbi

Abul Khattab deserved to be ruler by all accounts. The people of Spain
were fed up with the fighting and the discord that had become an
everyday experience. Almost all of them greeted the new ruler outside
of Cordova with great fanfare and displayed their total submission.
The sons of Abdul Malik also came and offered their allegiance.
Hosam started his rule with the utmost justice, tolerance, love and
generosity. He looked into the real causes of the disturbances and
managed to settle each tribe in a separate territory. In this way, he
very wisely spread the Syrians to distant places who had been
creating troubles of all kinds.

Political Mistake of Abul Khattab

The only political blunder Abul Khattab made was his excessive favor of the Yemenites. A strong undercurrent of dissatisfaction set in against him. Tribe after tribe began to express themselves against him. In the meantime, a dispute arose between his cousin and an Arab from the Canaan. The case came to the court of the ruler who gave his verdict in favor of his cousin despite his being in error. Displeased and dissatisfied with the court judgment the victim lodged a complaint with Bakr Damil bin Hatim bin Shimr Dhil Joshan, the chief of the Qais tribe about the ruler. Damil bin Hatim was very powerful and popular among the Arabs. He came to the ruler and protested against his improper attitude. After a hot exchange of words, the ruler asked his men to turn the chief out of the court. While pushing him out of the court, they struck a few blows at his neck so that his turban hung to one side of his head. When he came out of the court in a state of utter disgrace, someone asked him to put his turban right. He replied that, if willing, his people would set it right. On reaching home, he called the chieftains of his tribe and other influential Arabs and related to them what had happened. All of them promised to extend their help to him.

Damil bin Hatim then went on tour around the country and met influential people everywhere to give an account of the disgraceful treatment meted out to him. Since almost all of them were displeased with Abul Khattab, they lent their support to him. When he became satisfied that the people of Spain were against the ruler, he set up his center in the city of Sidonia and called his friends and men belonging to his tribe to come together. When they were concentrated at his headquarters he marched on Cordova. Thalba bin Salamah, a Yemenite and the former Governor of Spain also joined Damil bin Hatim. As a result of the clash between the two forces, Abul Khattab was defeated and arrested and sent to one of the strong forts of Cordova as a captive. Following this both Thalba and Damil occupied Spain. The event took place in 127 A.H. However, shortly after that he was released with the efforts of Abdur Rahman bin Hasan Kalbi. On being released, Abul Khattab left Cordova and met his people to win their support. Thus, a large number of Yemenites gathered round him. Damil and Thalba also rose to face him. It all happened at a time when the caliphate of Damascus was the target of the Abbasids' intrigue and the caliphate was passing through a state of chaos and disorder. The Umayyad Caliph Marwan was desperately seeking a decisive defeat of his enemies.

There was no one to look towards Spain as the seat of power itself was in danger. Abul Khattab remained as a captive in Spain between 127 A.H. and 129 A.H. and was then put to death. In 128 A.H., Thalba bin Salamah went to Abdul Rahman bin Habib, the ruler of Africa. With the news of Abul Khattab's assassination, the Governor of Africa sent Thalba bin Salamah as the Governor of Spain in 199 A.H.

Thalba bin Salamah

Thalba bin Salamah took the reins of power in Rajab, 129 A.H. and Damil bin Hatim, being his close friend, took over as the Chief Minister and Commander. Since Thalba too was a Yemenite, Damil bin Hatim brought peace between the Yemenite and other tribes. Thalba bin Salamah died a few days after. The people of Spain chose Yusuf bin Abdur Rahman Fihri as their ruler. As his abilities and services were known to everyone, there wasn't any objection raised.

Yusuf bin Abdur Rahman Fihri

Since Spain was no longer attached to the center of the caliphate and was inhabited by Muslims of many different tribes internal conflict began to build up and powerful men were aggrieved at the election of Yusuf. The Christians of the territory incited Abdur Rahman bin Alqama, the ruler of Arbonia to revolt but he was killed before he could take up arms. He was replaced by Ibn al-Waleed, who conquered Seville and proceeded to Cordova where Yusuf defeated and killed him.

Spain is divided into Provinces

Having put down the revolts Yusuf turned to streamlining the internal administration. The entire Spain was divided into four provinces and the French territory under Muslim control was made the fifth one. Names of the provinces are given below:

No.	Name of the province	Famous cities of the province
1.	Andalusia	Cordova, Carmona, Seville, Sidonia, Malaga, Ilbira, Jaen
2.	Toledo	Ubeda, Boeza, Marbella, Villena, Valencia
3.	Merida (Galicia)	Merida, Lisbon, Badajoz, Salamanca
4.	Saragossa	Saragossa, Tarragona, Barcelona, Lerida
5.	Arbonia (Catalonia)	Narbonne, Tolousse, Pampalona, Lugo

Impact of Change in Central Rule over Spain

Yusuf bin Abdur Rahman Fihri did not belong to any group. But when the news of the end of Umayyad caliphate and the establishment of Abbasid rule spread, Syrians everywhere began to face troubles because of the Abbasids. Damil bin Hatim was also surrounded but the people of the Qais tribe saved him. The entire country was torn by strife. Among the supporters of the Umayyad Abu Uthman Ubaidullah bin Uthman and Abdullah bin Khalid were two of the main supporters who were also related. Abu Uthman was the father-in-law of Abdullah bin Khalid. Together they ruled in Ilbira, the city of Andalusia. The city was dominated by Syrians. Yusuf bin Bakht and Husain bin Malik Kalbi were two famous chiefs. On refusal of help to Damil bin Hatim by Yusuf bin Abdur Rahman it was Abu Uthman and Abdullah bin Khalid who extended their help. Badr, the slave of Abdur Rahman al-Dakhil joined before they had left. They persuaded Damil bin Hatim to invite Abdur Rahman al-Dakhil to Spain. Damil favored the proposal, apparently because he did not want to embitter his relations with Yusuf. Abu Uthman and Abdullah bin Khalid then took leave from Damil and came to Ilbira and began to spread their point of view secretly among the people. Later they came to know that Damil bin Hatim was not sticking to his promise and liked the rule of Yusuf bin Abdur Rahman. Now losing hope of support from the Qais and Fihir tribes, Abu Uthman filled the Yemenites with the zeal of opposition, with the result that the Yemenite Commanders raised their standard in revolt. Thus both Yusuf bin Abdur Rahman and Damil bin Hatim became engaged in punishing them.

The Rule of Abdur Rahman al-Dakhil

When Abu Uthman found the Yemenite tribes in a state of fighting and killing he sent Badr along with eleven men by ship to bring Abdur Rahman bin al-Dakhil from Africa. Abdur Rahman bin al-Dakhil reached Spain in 138 A.H. and was received with great fanfare by Abu Uthman and the followers of the Umayyads. Abu Uthman collected for him a large number of supporters. Yusuf bin Abdur Rahman was then engaged in putting down revolts in the Saragossa province. With the news of Abdur Rahman al-Dakhil's arrival in Spain he finished his task quickly and came to Toledo and met Damil bin Hatim, he had made the blunder of killing all the captives he had already promised safety of life to. This act of his displeased many of his commanders who deserted him and joined Abdur Rahman al-Dakhil. With this news the Arab chiefs who were scattered in different places, particularly the Yemenites, joined Abdur Rahman al-Dakhil. Now Yusuf and Ibn Hatim were left alone with the Fihri and Qais tribes. The Syrian support for Abdur Rahman al-Dakhil was logical but the Yemenites who previously opposed the Syrians lent their support because of their hostile attitude towards Yusuf and because Abdur Rahman had come to take the leadership from Yusuf. Even the Fihri and the Qaisi liked the Umayyad prince but they were with Yusuf and Ibn Hatim because of their towering personalities. One reason of Abdur Rahman al-Dakhil's success was that he had, before his arrival, become a household name due to his high morals and character. His sympathetic attitude to the Hijazi and Yemenite Arabs also gained him a lot of popularity. Thus, even those hostile to the Umayyads looked upon him with love and sympathy.

Finally, Ibn Hatim and Yusuf marched to Cordova from Toledo and Abdur Rahman al-Dakhil proceeded from the other side. The two forces clashed on Dhul Hijjah 10, 138 A.H. (May 14,756 C.E.) and Abdur Rahman al-Dakhil won the battle after fierce fighting. Yusuf's son was captured along with some others while Yusuf and Ibn Hatim fled to safety. Ibn Hatim took refuge in Merida and Yusuf in Jaen, Abdur Rahman al-Dahkil then entered into Cordova and announced security of life to those who obeyed. Ibn Hatim and Yusuf collected forces once again. But finally, they were also forced to obey. Abdur Rahman al-Dakhil gave them peace and security on condition that they would live in Cordova and appear in the court once a day. In this way Abdur Rahman al-Dakhil and his descendants began to rule in Spain and the first phase of Islamic rule of Spain came to an end.

A Summary of the First Phase of Islamic Rule in Spain

Spain was far from Damascus, the seat of the Caliphate. The way to Spain passed through Copt and Berber territories. Messages took a long time to arrive from one another. Spain was conquered at a time when the provinces of Iraq, Syria and Iran had engaged the attention of the renowned commanders and statesmen of the Caliphate. Because of these circumstances, Spain never attracted the proper attention it needed. This was the reason why Spain generally remained under the control of the Governor of Africa. Since Spain had become famous for its fertility and opportunity, many people of the Hijaz, Syria and Iraq who had no important engagements in there own territories shifted to Spain. These Arabs were welcomed and treated with much respect and high posts were offered to them. The Berbers of Africa had come to Spain in the very beginning and continued to arrive. This is how Spain became a Muslim colony in such a short time. The country was mainly populated by Christians, who showed total submission to the Muslim rule. A large number of Jews also formed part of the population. Thus, the mixed population of Spain consisted of different elements. Scores of rulers came to Spain during the first fifty-years of Muslim rule. The Spanish Muslims retained their sense of freedom together with a democratic temperament. The Christian population never suffered any trouble and they had ample opportunity for economic development and academic progress. They received all of this simply in return for their allegiance.

At first, the Muslims had a great zeal for victory and reached the central areas of France. But very shortly in Spain, civil wars broke out and their military advances were halted and the Christian powers had time and opportunity to contemplate their plight. During these fifty years of Muslim rule, a different caliber of ruler came into power and the Spanish population saw an era of all-round development. Moreover, the victorious Muslim rulers began to marry Christian women who played a very effective role in softening their attitude to the Christians. They were no longer the objects of hate for them and the Muslims did a lot to educate and train the Christians. Gradually, they grew so strong that they would seek military help from their Muslim neighbors during their internal disputes.

When the Muslims came to Spain and the rule of Christian Goths came to end, the bishops and the commanders who had once fought the Muslims fled to the north. Muslim invaders had entered Spain from the southern side, which was fertile, pleasant and relatively warm and they populated this part of the country. The Arab people did not like the northern part, which was hilly and cold and less fertile. The Muslim invaders conquered the southern part but they entered the hilly areas of the Pyrenees only when they were chasing fugitives. Although this resulted in the Muslim conquest of Catalonia and Narbonne civil war broke out among the Muslims, and because of this they held back their advances.

Sovereign Christian Rule in the Northern Areas

Hilly Ranges of Spain

Pelayo

A minor act of negligence on the part of the early Muslim conquerors proved very costly in future. It has already been mentioned that Anbasa had left unpunished a privateer named Pelayo who had eluded the Muslims in the passes of the Pyrenees . When he set up his camp in the Pyrenees, he attracted the Christians who had been scattered and the bishops who brought the valuables of the Spanish churches. Thus, Pelayo's group in the hills grew strong in a very short time. Even though Pelayo's seat of power was, on all sides, surrounded by Muslim territories all of them ignored this group and never made a campaign against them thinking that they would never pose any real danger to the Muslims. It was logical to some extent for neither Pelayo nor the Christians ever mustered enough courage to descend from the high hills to take on the Muslims in the lowlands.

But the bishops who brought valuable gifts and relics to Pelayo made him a religious leader and a protector of the Christian relics. He remained confined to a small hilly area for about twelve or thirteen years. During this period he kept receiving supplies from the Christians. With the passage of time Pelayo rose in glory and the Christians would visit him from far off places, and pay him regards and see the relics. The negligence of Muslims encouraged the Christians to consider this an empire on its own and declared Pelayo their king and protector of their religion.

Alfonso

On Pelayo's death his son came to power but he too expired after two or three years. Then Alfonso, the son-in-law of Pelayo was elected king and commander. The Muslims, on the other hand, were so deeply engaged in civil wars that they did not turn their attention to the emerging hilly State. Alfonso invited the Christians of Galicia, Aragon, and Catalonia to settle in the hills. He went to the extent of raiding and capturing those Christians who were reluctant to leave their fertile lands and brought them to populate the areas around his capital.

The Capital of the Christian State

Asturias was made the capital of this sovereign rule of the Christians. Constant sermons of the bishops made the unwilling Christians come live there in peace. Gradually, the Christian population rose to such an extent that the area occupied by them became crowded. Although they could achieve no success in the open areas, they were able to capture hills along the Pyrenees. This became the foundation of a small Christian state. They had no connection with either the Christian rulers of France or of Italy the religious bigotry present there was stronger than that of France or Italy. Their rules of governance were enacted and supported by the bishops. In 138 A.H. Abdur Rahman al-Dakhil brought about the end of the caliphate era and Alfonso also died the same year.

Chapter 4

The Spainish Caliphs

Abdur Rahman bin Mu'awiyah, the Umayyad

Habits and Traits of Character

Abdur Rahman bin Mu'awiyah bin Hisham bin Abdul Malik bin Marwan bin Hakam was born in 113 A.H. His father, Mu'awiyah was cut short in the prime of his life when Abdur Rahman was only 5. His grandfather, Hisham bin Abdul Malik was then on the throne. He devoted his full attention to the education and training of his grandson. He had in mind to appoint Abdur Rahman his crown prince. But Hisham died when Abdur Rahman was only 12 years of age. Hisham's nephew Waleed replaced him. Abdur Rahman had in him kingly qualities from an early age. He kept away from evil and foul practices. He was well versed in courtly manners and the art of governance. He had also enjoyed the company of religious scholars and courtiers. As a young man, he learned swordsmanship and the art of warfare.

Emigration

When the Umayyad caliphate saw its end in 132 A.H. and the Abbasid caliphate came into power Abdur Rahman was 20 years old. Abdur Rahman had an estate on the bank of the Euphrates. While the Umayyads were being massacred by the Abbasids in Damascus, Abdur Rahman was away at his estate. When he came to know of the death of the Umayyad's, he shifted to a forest and encamped there for safety.

One day when Abdur Rahman was in his camp and his four-year old son, who was playing outside, rushed into the camp shocked and frightened. When Abdur Rahman went outside, he noticed the black Abbasid flag flying and moving towards him. He took his son and fled towards the river. He was on way to the river when the Abbasids appeared chasing and promising him peace and safety. He paid no heed to their promise. He plunged into the river with his son stuck to his chest and swam across the river. His enemies saw him helpless and held themselves back from jumping into the river.

Abdur Rahman in Africa

Abdur Rahman wandered from village to village in the guise of a traveler with his child on his lap. In such a wretched state, he reached Palestine where he came across his father's slave Badr who was heading for Egypt in the same state. Badr had with him some money and an ornament of Abdur Rahman's sister, which he gave to Abdur Rahman to improve his condition. He then started a journey as a merchant in the company of Badr and reached Egypt and contacted supporters of the Umayyads. After a short stay in Egypt, he left for the other territories of Africa.

Abdur Rahman's Plan to Found His Rule in Africa

The Governor of Africa showed Abdur Rahman his love and respect. However, when he came to know that Abdur Rahman wanted to found his rule in Africa and at the same time that the Abbasid caliphate was growing strong, he made a plan to arrest Abdur Rahman and send him to the Abbasid Caliph. But the plot was discovered and Abdur Rahman went into hiding along with his son and slave. Since the Governor of Africa had announced a substantial reward for the arrest of Abdur Rahman, the search was intensified and Abdur Rahman, the victim of circumstances, had to run for safety through forests and deserts facing starvation.

Once Abdur Rahman took refuge in the hut of an old woman. When a search party came to the hut, the old woman covered Abdur Rahman with cloth. Taking it to be a heap of clothes the party left the hut. Abdur Rahman was reduced to a plight that he neither had bread or shelter. After passing four or five years of a life fraught with dangers and beset with sorrows and suffering he came into contact with the Banu Nafusa, a branch of the Kinana tribe. When they discovered that Abdur Rahman's mother belonged to their tribe, they treated him like a relative and promised him all kinds of help and support. Abdur Rahman settled in Ceuta, an area where Banu Nafusa was in a majority. During all these years Abdur Rahman had learnt that it was not an easy matter to snatch power from the Governor of Africa. In Ceuta he had the opportunity of receiving intimate knowledge of the state of affairs in Spain as Ceuta was near to Spain. When he learned that Spain was continuously experiencing internal disturbances and discord and Yusuf, the ruler was preoccupied with the task of curbing violence and uprisings, Abdur Rahman a man of high ambition and exemplary courage and determination saw an opportunity for himself. He made no delay in sending his slave Badr to Spain with letters from him to the chiefs and other influential men sympathetic to the Umayyads.

Abdur Rahman in Spain

Badr contacted Abu Uthman and Abdullah bin Khalid and informed them of the task ahead. They called the Syrian and Arab chiefs and placed the matter before them. They all agreed on inviting prince Abdur Rahman to Spain. Fortunately, the supporters of the Umayyads inhabited the southeastern coast of Spain and Abdur Rahman experienced no trouble in landing there. When the party consisting of eleven men sent to invite Abdur Rahman landed in Ceuta, they approached him with Badr at their head while Abdur

Rahman was performing prayers. When the head of the party, Abu Ghalib al-Tammam saluted Abdur Rahman and told him that the people of Spain were awaiting his presence the latter asked his name. Abdur Rahman knew him to be Abu Ghalib al-Tammam who grew very happy at this recognition and announced that Spain was within his reach. Following this, Abdur Rahman boarded the ship without loss of time, upon landing he was greeted by men numbering in the thousands.

Cordova Occupied

The Umayyads and the Syrians in Spain rushed to offer their total submission and loyalty. Following this nearby cities and towns were seized. The rainy season stopped Yusuf's march to Cordova. Because of this, Abdur Rahman had a respite of seven months before he had to face Yusuf's attack, which finally resulted in Yusuf's defeat and Abdur Rahman, captured Cordova. After the victory was won a Yemenite chief, Abu Sabah said addressing his people that they had now revenged themselves against Yusuf and they should now kill Abdur Rahman to establish their own rule instead of the Umayyads. Since Abdur Rahman's forces had a large number of Syrians and Berbers, his opponents could not rise up against him. However, they kept waiting for an opportunity to cause Abdur Rahman some kind of setback. When he discovered their design against him, he simply formed a security squad for his safety and overlooked his opponents' activities. However, a few months later he had killed Abu Sabah for some fault he had committed.

The Appointments of Abdur Rahman

Since Abdur Rahman, the Umayyad was quite young and strange to the Governors, people, tribes and their tastes and traits he also appointed men to high posts who brought opposition from the Spanish people and some of them got posts far below their expectations. In short, a large section of the population felt disappointed and aggrieved. Friends, relatives and supporters of Yusuf Fihri and Damil bin Hatim were also hostile to Abdur Rahman's regime.

Rebellions

Despite showing no favor to any one section, he had to face a number of revolts in the initial stages of his reign. Yusuf Fihri was at that time kept in Cordova and was not allowed to leave. Two years after the conquest of Cordova, Abdur Rahman still had to devote most of his time and resources to curbing the opposition to his newfound rule. During these actions against his opponents, he felt the need to organize a force based on the Umayyads who survived the Abbasid onslaught. He felt that any such force could play a sincere role in safeguarding against opposing forces. Among the Umayyads surviving the Abbasid massacre in Egypt were Abdul Malik bin Umar bin Marwan bin Hakam and his son Umar bin Abdul Malik. Having heard of the conquest of Spain, they along with a dozen Umayyads came to Abdur Rahman. Welcoming their arrival Abdur Rahman appointed Abdul Malik bin Umar as the Governor of Seville and Umar bin Abdul Malik the governor of Moruba.

Since Abdur Rahman was alone in this strange country and he doubted the courage of the different groups and tribes to oppose the Abbasids, he kept himself confined to the rank of the Governor of Spain. He delivered addresses in the name of the Abbasid Caliph, although, he was their enemy at heart and considered the Abbasids his enemies. Due to this situation Abdur Rahman deemed it necessary to give his friends and close relatives high positions. Thus, when he appointed Abdul Malik and his son Umar as Governor he was opposed even more vehemently than before and the country was heading towards crisis and revolt.

Yusuf bin Abdur Rahman assassinated

On being incited by the people Yusuf bin Abdur Rahman, the former ruler of Spain escaped from Cordova but his sons Abu Zaid Abdur Rahman and Abul Aswad could not. And the minister of Yusuf bin Abdur Rahman Fihri Damil bin Hatim also failed to escape from Cordova. All three of them were put in prison. Yusuf Fihri reached Toledo and as per their resolution, his supporters from all sides gathered round him. In a very short time twenty thousand troops collected under his banner. Yusuf bin Abdur Rahman then invaded Seville and surrounded Abdul Malik bin Umar. But, in order to save time, he raised the siege and proceeded to Cordova. When Umar, the son of Abdul Malik heard of the siege on his father he proceeded to Seville. Both the father and son chased Yusuf bin Abdur Rahman's force. When Abdur Rahman found out about Yusuf's march at the head of twenty thousand men, he came out from Cordova to face Yusuf, Abdur Rahman attacked from the front and Abdul Malik and Umar came from behind. A large number of Yusuf's troops were killed and Yusuf fled to Toledo. Having reached near Toledo the Yemenites held consultations and considered that if they killed Yusuf and carried his head to Abdur Rahman he would forgive them for joining the revolt. They implemented their plan.

Yusuf Fihri was a brave and renowned Commander and had served Spain as Governor. He was known for his benevolence and politeness. But he was gullible too. He could believe his friends and supporters blindly and, at last, he lost his life because of this. In the wake of this bitter experience, Abdur Rahman was within his rights to kill the sons of Damil bin Hatim and Yusuf and he did so. However, Abul Aswad was put in a fort because of his young age. In order to create awe and terror in his enemies Abdur Rahman hung the dead bodies of the insurgents in public but such a brutal action created less fright and more sympathy for the Fihri family.

Abul Aswad bin Yusuf Fihri who was a captive in a fort declared himself blind after sometime. Every morning he went to the bank of the river outside the fort to answer the call of nature and then requested someone to take him back to the fort. Anyone of the soldiers moving about would return him back to the gate of the fort. When his blindness was fully established, his supervisors stopped keeping watch over him. In the meantime a slave of Abul Aswad began to pay regular visits to him. Abul Aswad set about sending messages to his friends and sympathizers through him and one day he escaped.

Managing Home Affairs

After doing away with Yusuf Fihri, Abdur Rahman paid his attention to affairs at home. Having displayed a good deal of royal power and grandeur he declared his sovereignty and expunged the name of the Abbasid Caliph from any official addresses in 146 A. H. The Abbasid caliphate was newly founded in the east and it was not yet free from dispute. With the news of Abdur Rahman's occupation of Spain, he felt aggrieved but could not dispatch an expedition against the newly proclaimed ruler. He was satisfied that addresses were still delivered in his name.

Abbasids' Action against Abdur Rahman

The Abbasid Caliph grew very upset when he knew that Abdur Rahman had removed his name from his addresses. He then wrote to Ala'a bin Mughith, the Commander in Africa to invade Spain. Ala'a bin Mughith marched to Spain. Hashim bin Abdu Rabbih, a relative of Yusuf bin Abdur Rahman Fihri, and the chief of Toledo was deeply frustrated at the damage done to the Fihris. He then lured away a large number of Berbers besides those who joined him out of their hate for the brutalities committed against the Fihris.

Hashim Fihri then sent word to Ala'a bin Mughith to invade Spain without delay and counted upon his support and sent a black flag representing the Abbasids. The message fired the courage of Ala'a bin Mughith. Abdur Rahman was quite unaware of the impending danger. Hashim raised his banner of revolt in 146 A.H. and captured northern Spain and fortified Toledo. Abdur Rahman proceeded from Cordova at the head of a force to curb the revolt and besieged Toledo. The insurgents from Toledo took on the attack bravely, with the result that the siege dragged on for several months without yielding a conclusion. Meanwhile, Ala'a bin Mughith landed at Beja with the black flag sent by Caliph Mansur, the Abbasid.

Taking Ala'a bin Mughith to be deputed by the Caliph of the Muslims the people of Spain gathered under the banner of the Caliph. They considered Abdur Rahman to be a rebel. He grew very anxious over this news. It was a crucial moment for him because the insurgents of northern Spain were still beyond his control. Abdur Rahman raised his siege of Toledo and turned to the fresh threat. He had reached Carmona near Seville when Ala'a bin Mughith appeared on the scene. A large number of Abdur Rahman's soldiers rushed to Ala'a bin Mughith. The people of Toledo, being free from the siege, sent a column to reinforce Ala'a's troops. Abdur Rahman had to take refuge in the fort of Carmona.

Courageous Act of Abdur Rahman

After surrounding Carmona Ala'a bin Mughith sent troops to nearby areas on a mission to plunder for supplies. The Berbers of Spain and other people also followed suit. The entire country of Spain was plunged into killings, plunder and disorder. Abdur Rahman remained besieged in the fort of Carmona for two months. In such a state of despair, Abdur Rahman told his companions that the time had come to go down fighting rather than to die of hunger. They started a large bonfire in the open and seven hundred fighters put the sheaths of their swords into it to declare that they would either become victorious or die fighting. Thus they threw open the gates of the fort and fell upon the enemy. The invaders had, after such a long siege, become careless about the besieged and were no longer on the alert. Seven hundred fighters like hungry lions launched an attack so heavy and unexpected that the besieging force fled leaving behind seven thousand corpses and Spain was restored to Abdur Rahman.

Macabre Joke

On this occasion Abdur Rahman played a macabre joke with Caliph Mansur Abbasi. He cut off the heads of Ala'a bin Mughith and all the Commanders of Abbasid force, he made holes in the ears of each one and fastened a paper in each one with his name and post. He then put all the heads in trunks and dispatched them very cautiously with the caravans of the pilgrims to Makkah. From there, it was sent to Caliph Mansur. When the trunk containing the head of Ala'a bin Mughith was opened there was a letter from Mansur directing Ala'a bin Mughith to invade Spain. It also contained the pieces of black flag sent by Mansur to Mughith. Mansur saw the heads and passed the simple remark: "Thank Allah there lies a sea between Abdur Rahman and me". Again, he said one day, "I am amazed at the courage, wisdom and prudence of Abdur Rahman that he founded his rule in a far off country in the absence of resources." The battle of Carmona took place during the last part of 146 A.H.

Rebels annihilated

Following the conquest of Carmona Abdur Rahman came to Toledo with the force headed by his slave Badr and Tammam bin Alqama who defeated the insurgents of the territory after a fierce battle. Prominent chiefs like Hisham bin Abdu Rabbih Fihri, Hayat bin Waleed Yahsabi and Uthman bin Hamza bin Ubaidullah bin Umar bin Khattab were arrested and killed by the order of Abdur Rahman.

A number of Yemenite tribes had joined Ala'a bin Mughith and most of them were killed by Abdur Rahman and his men in the battle of Carmona. The people of Yemen developed a deep desire to avenge their blood. In 147 A.H. Sayed Yahsabi, known as Matri rose in revolt and captured Seville. Abdur Rahman proceeded from Cordova to punish Matri. Matri then took refuge in a fort of Seville, which was besieged by Abdur Rahman. Attab bin Alqami was then in Sidonia city and had promised Matri to join him in the revolt. Thus, he marched at the head of an army.

Having heard this news Abdur Rahman sent his slave Badr at the head of an army to go and stand between Attab and Matri. Matri was killed and Khalifa bin Marwan was appointed as Commander. Nevertheless, they had to seek peace. Abdur Rahman granted the petition but demolished the fort. He then came back to Cordova. Following this, Abdullah bin Khrasha Asadi of Jaen rose in revolt. Abdur Rahman mobilized his army but Abdullah's companions deserted him with the result Abdullah Asadi sought forgiveness and was pardoned. Ghayath bin Mir Asadi revolted in 150 A.H. The Governor of Beja gave battle and Ghayath was killed in action and his force was defeated and dispersed. The same year, 150 A.H., Abdur Rahman laid the foundation stone of the fortification of the city of Cordova.

In 151 A.H., a person named Shaqna (Ibn Abdul Wahid) and a teacher by profession claimed that he was the descendant of Husain bin Ali and his name was Abdullah bin Muhammad. Very soon the credulous Berbers gathered around him while others also followed suit. When the number of his followers grew strong, he raised his standard of revolt in Pelencia, the northern province of Spain and captured Santarem. Abdur Rahman proceeded to punish him.

Having heard of the march of Abdur Rahman, Ibn Abdul Wahid fled to the hills. Abdur Rahman returned to Cordova. He then appointed Habib bin Abdul Malik as the Governor of Toledo and directed him to punish Ibn Abdul Wahid. Habib bin Abdul Malik deputed Sulaiman bin Uthman bin Marwan bin Uthman bin Affan to punish Ibn Abdul Wahid. But the latter captured Sulaiman and killed him. Following this he captured some nearby territories.

Having heard this Abdur Rahman himself proceeded from Cordova in 152 A.H. Ibn Abdul Wahid fled to the hills once again and Abdur Rahman had to return without engagement for the second time.

Abdur Rahman sent his slave Badr in 154 A.H. to attack him but Ibn Abdul Wahid took refuge in the hills. Later in 154 A.H., Abdur Rahman himself led an expedition but again could not get him.

In 155 A.H., Abdur Rahman sent Abu Uthman Ubaidullah bin Uthman at the head of a strong army but it proved an exercise in futility. Ibn Abdul Wahid killed a large part of Abu Uthman's force by playing a trick and plundered several cities as well. Compelled by the situation Abdur Rahman once again led his force in 155 A.H. and deputed his son Sulaiman in Cordova. When he arrived at the Santarem fort, he was informed that the Yemenite tribes and the people of Seville had revolted against him. He had to leave his task unfinished and he hurried back. He ordered Abdul Malik bin Umar to go ahead an attack Seville.

Abdul Malik reached Seville and sent his son Umayyah to snipe at the enemy. But, finding the people of Seville alert, he came back without doing his job. On inquiry, he gave the reason for his return. Abdul Malik accused his son of coming back for fear of death. He then charged him with cowardice and cut off his head. Following this he said addressing his men: "We all know how mercilessly we have been killed and had to leave our country. Now that we have this piece of land, Spain, to live on and we can't afford to lose it too. It is our obligation to keep it even at the cost of our lives." All of them supported the idea and vowed to lay down their lives for the purpose. The Yemenite tribes had a large and strong force in Seville and it was the last extension of their power. Because of this, the conquest of Seville was not an easy job. Abdul Malik bin Umar launched a powerful attack and his force gave him very active support. The people of Seville tasted defeat. Even though Abdul Malik received several injuries, he showed exemplary bravery and steadfastness in the battle. When at the end of the battle, Abdul Malik wanted to put down his sword his fingers refused to open out and the sword remained in his hand. Meanwhile Abdur Rahman appeared and said, seeing the blood stained sword in his hand and hearing the account of the battle: " Brother Abdul Malik", I wanted my son Hisham to marry your daughter." Following this remark Abdur Rahman appointed Abdul Malik bin Umar as his minister.

Two chiefs of Seville named Abdul Ghaffar bin Hamid and Hayat bin Flaqash and the rulers of Banila city and Seville respectively and Amr, the ruler of Beja fled the battlefield. They gathered the Arab tribes once again. Abdur Rahman attacked them in 157 A.H., and defeated and killed them and their supporters. These events created doubts and misgivings in the mind of Abdur Rahman concerning the Arab tribes. As a result of this, he began to recruit non-Arabs and slaves to curb the rising of Arab tribes against the throne. The same reasons had perhaps, compelled the Abbasids to prefer other forces to the Arabs even though they were themselves Arabs. They always feared their treason. Abdur Rahman sent an expedition in 160 A.H. against Ibn Abdul Wahid, which besieged Santarem Fort but returned unsuccessful after one month. At last, in 162 A.H., Ibn Abdul Wahid came out of the fort and went to a village and two persons among his companions assassinated him and took his head to Abdur Rahman. Thus came to an end the mischief that had disturbed Abdur Rahman for so long.

Before the assassination of Ibn Abdul Wahid, Abdur Rahman bin Habib known as Saqlabi built a force in Africa in 161 A.H. and planned to invade Spain. The two forces were arrayed against one another in the field of Tadmir. Many Berbers of Spain joined his campaign. Abdur Rahman bin Habib then sent word to Sulaiman Yaqazan, the ruler of Seville to either obey the Abbasid caliphate or be ready to face attack. On refusal, Abdur Rahman bin Habib attacked Sulaiman but was defeated and driven away. On being informed Abdur Rahman the Umayyad marched from Cordova. With the news of the approach of Abdur Rahman, he (Abdur Rahman bin Habib) fled to the hills. On the announcement of a reward for Abdur Rahman bin Habib, one of his companions cut off his head and presented it to Abdur Rahman the Umayyad and got his reward.

Shortly after that, Dihya Ghassani took refuge in fort of Almeria in 163 A.H. and raised his standard of revolt. Abdur Rahman sent Shaheed bin Isa to punish him who defeated and killed the rebel. After a short while the Berbers raised their heads in revolt under Ibrahim bin Sajrah, Abdur Rahman sent Badr to deal with him. Badr killed Ibrahim and dispersed the Berbers. During the same days, a Commander named Salama escaped to Cordova and rose in revolt after seizing Toledo. Abdur Rahman sent Habib bin Abdul Malik to punish Salama. Habib surrounded Toledo and Salama died during the siege and his companions dispersed.

Reasons behind the Revolts

Abdur Rahman could not rule peacefully and the reasons are not hard to find. The Muslim population of Spain had in those days developed a taste and temperament for rivalries and insurgence. They also could not obey anybody sincerely. They could not tolerate the reign of Abdur Rahman because his dynastic rule had perished in the East. The main reason behind the worries of Abdur Rahman was that the Abbasid caliphs were continually hatching plots against him. The Abbasid caliphs had chosen Baghdad to be their Headquarters, which was far from Abdur Rahman and a large sea kept Baghdad and Spain apart.

They would hear about the power and strength of Abdur Rahman's rule but were unable to do away with him due to the great distance between them. Twice they tried to invade but every time their commanders were killed and the Abbasid campaigns had to face ignominious defeat. Failing to achieve military victory, they made use of the same secret planning against Abdur Rahman that they had already used to bring about the ruin of the ancestors of Abdul Rahman the Umayyads. They began to propagate their favor among Arab tribes and men of treasonous nature and to win their support for the Abbasid caliphate. Thus, most of the Arab chiefs and the Berbers who had recently accepted Islam stood by the Abbasids. They rose in revolt repeatedly and every time they incurred a setback, but they did not receive any help from Baghdad.

The shortsighted rebellious chiefs kept Abdur Rahman engaged in dealing with their insurgent activities and provided the Christians of Asturias with an opportunity to get stronger.

Alfonso's son Fruela had enough time to gather Christians around him and to think of ways to develop plans for the future. The forces of Cordova on the other hand did not have an opportunity to extend any help to the Muslims occupying southern France. If Abdur Rahman had dispatched his forces to take on the French, he could not have saved Spain.

Now, in view of the constant revolts by the Abbasid supporters, the French invaded and besieged the city of Narbonne. The Muslims of the city faced the rigor of the siege for six years without any help from outside. But, at last, southern France slipped out of their hands after being under their possession for forty years.

After Abdur Rahman bin Habib, the Commander of the Baghdad caliphate had been killed two persons named Husain bin Asi and Sulaiman bin Yaqzan were left to carry out the subversive activities of the Abbasids. They ruled in Saragossa and its surrounding areas. They entered into correspondence with the Caliph Mahdi who was very pious. However, human nature demanded him to hate the Umayyads. They got the support of Baghdad and then they urged Charlemagne, the king of France to invade Spain and assured him that Mahdi Abbasi also supported the proposal of doing away with Abdur Rahman and his rule. Charlemagne could not have got a better opportunity to win Spain for nothing could have added more to his glory and dignity. Since Muslim bravery and determination were well known to him, he made no haste in making an attack. Besides making large-scale military preparations, he collected information of all kinds through the insurgents and the traitors. Together they made it a point to bring about the release of Abul Aswad, the son of Yusuf Fihri from a fort adjoining Cordova so that broader Muslim support could be expected. It has already been mentioned how Abul Aswad escaped by declaring himself blind. Charlemagne prepared to fight with several hundred thousand troops and the expulsion of the Muslims from Spain and the foundation of Christian rule were advanced as the two-fold purpose of the invasion. The insurgents of Saragossa took up arms before the invasion of Charlemagne. Abdur Rahman was not fully aware of the moral impact of the Baghdad Caliphate, plots hatched by the Muslims of Spain and the huge Christian preparations. Abdur Rahman sent his Commander Thalba bin Ubaid to punish the insurgents of Saragossa. After a series of battles Sulaiman bin Yaqzan arrested Thalba and sent him to Charlemagne to convince him of his power and support. Thalba's troops fled the battlefield, joined Abdur Rahman in Cordova and informed him of the power of the insurgents.

Shortly after the king of France, who was lying on the other side of the Pyrenees, moved ahead. The number of troops was so large that they had to go through two separate passes to meet under the fortification of the city of Saragossa . When the Muslims of Saragossa heard of the huge Christian army and their plan to wipe out all Muslim signs and traces from the face of Spain, they reproached Sulaiman bin Yaqzan. Husain bin Asi too shuddered to think of such a consequence and shut the door of Saragossa. When Charlemagne felt that the Muslims would withdraw their support from him and join the camp of Abdur Rahman, he returned to France without achieving any success.

While Charlemagne was marching to Spain, the Christian State of Asturias had extended its support to him considering him the savior of the Christians. When he began to march back to France because of fear of the Muslims, the Christians of the hilly state started raiding the rear of the Christian force. By the time it had reached the northern part of Spain some of the renowned Commanders and a large part of the force had been killed.

On the return of Charlemagne Husain bin Asi assassinated Sulaiman bin Yaqzan and took over the leadership of the insurgents. Meanwhile, Abdur Rahman also reached Saragossa from Cordova at the head of a strong force and laid siege to the city. Husain bin Asi sought peace at the cost of his obedience and Abdur Rahman conceded to it. Now, in consequence of the French King's march on Spain Abdur Rahman proceeded to France and reached the French plains. During this march, Abdur Rahman ignored the Christians occupying the hilly areas.

Abdur Rahman ravaged the southern part of France and demolished forts and the fortifications of several cities. Charlemagne escaped to the northern part of France and did nothing to save the southern provinces. However, Abdur Rahman could not stay in France for long because he was well aware of the state of affairs in his country. He had hardly passed a few months in Cordova when Husain bin Asi rose in revolt in Saragossa. Abdur Rahman sent Ghalib bin Tammam bin Alqama to put down the revolt. They fought against one another for about a year without any result. Now Abdur Rahman himself marched to Saragossa in 166 A.H. and killed Husain bin Asi and put a large number of rebels to death. During all these years of turmoil and turbulence Abul Aswad kept aloof from court politics and was left to keep the banner of rebellion flying. However, the relatives of those killed by Abdur Rahman were burning with anger and shock. Finally, they persuaded Abul Aswad in Talun to take up arms and they gathered around him. But Abdur Rahman fought and drove him away. He took refuge in the mountains. Abul Aswad came out once again in 169 A.H. but fled again leaving behind four thousand men dead and lost. Abul Aswad died in 170 A.H. His companions who were still leading a life of robbing and plundering elected his brother Qasim bin Yusuf their chief and very soon a large number of troops came under his banner. Abdur Rahman attacked and killed him.

In the same year, 170 A.H. Harun Rashid came to the throne. Charlemagne, in order to gain peace, sought an agreement with Abdur Rahman and offered his daughter in marriage. The Muslim ruler while granting his peace offer declined to marry his daughter. Historians have explained this refusal in a number of ways. Charlemagne knew very well that the Caliph of Baghdad was the enemy of Abdur Rahman. Although he expected no help from Harun Rashid, but anticipating his campaign against Abdur Rahman he sent emissaries to Baghdad to seek his friendship. He was very hopeful of the success of his mission because he had once led his force to Spain in response to the request of Mahdi, the father of Harun Rashid. Charlemagne was right. Harun Rashid greeted his emissaries warmly and sent to Charlemagne a watch as a gift. Charlemagne, in fact, had in mind the destruction of Muslim rule in Spain. Harun Rashid also had his own interest in view. But neither one of them could achieve their purpose.

Death of Abdur Rahman

Following the peace agreement with Charlemagne, Abdur Rahman had very little to threaten him. He was completely and firmly in control of the situation after putting down all opposition internally and externally. However, in 171 A.H. his slave Badr and some of his relatives joined hands to seize the throne of Spain. Abdur Rahman uncovered the plot and banished them to Africa. He died in 172 A.H. at the age of 58 or 59 after ruling his country for 33 years and 4 months. In accordance with his will, he was succeeded by his son Hisham.

An Assessment of Abdur Rahman's Life

Twenty years of his early life he passed in study and the assemblies of the scholars. Swordsmanship was a must for a youth in those days. After twenty years of a comfortable life, he passed through a period where he had to hide himself like a thief and everyone appeared to be thirsty for his blood. He had neither bread to eat nor clothes to wear. After wandering for years in forests and deserts and from one country to another, he became the king of a country. However, this power proved to be a crown of thorns. Had he been anyone else they would have perished right from the beginning but he was lion-hearted and irrepressible. He came to Spain a stranger with no sympathy and no support from any quarter but he turned the tide in his favor by virtue of his far-sightedness and wisdom.

He proved his mettle as a commander and a swordsman although he had no such experience before arriving in Spain. His performance as a commander was beyond criticism. He achieved success in campaigns where his renowned and seasoned commanders met with failure. On no occasion did he lose hope or courage despite revolts and sufferings of the worst nature. No one of his contemporaries could ever fathom the depth of his courage and fortitude.

His life was full of campaigns and adventures but his love for art and learning remained undiminished. He opened educational institutions all over his country to spread learning and wisdom to the masses.

Abdur Rahman fortified all the cities of his state and built mosques wherever they were needed. The Grand mosque of Cordova has no parallel in grandeur and magnificence. Although Abdur Rahman could not complete it in his lifetime the foundation of the mosque revealed the lofty ambitions of the Muslim ruler. The beauty, magnificence and dimensions of the mosque brought men of weak faith to consider it on par with the Ka'bah in glory and sanctity although all mosques deserve an equal respect. His fondness for constructing buildings was greater than that of Shah Jahan of India and in prudence, he excelled Aristotle. For him, to found his rule in Spain was far greater than all the victories of Tamerlane and Napoleon put together.

In patronage of the arts and learning even the Caliphs Harun Rashid and Mamun Rashid did not surpass him. Moreover, the Abbasid dynasty did not produce, after Harun and Mamun, such rulers who could value the real worth of the arts and learning as the children of Abdur Rahman did, with the result that Cordova surpassed Baghdad in fame and glory.

Ibn Hayyan writes that Abdur Rahman was very kind, courteous and cultured. He spoke very eloquently; his understanding was deep and insight sharp. He never formed an opinion about matters in haste but once it was formed, he stuck to it firmly and strongly. However, he would consult his courtiers and advisors on all important issues. Abdur Rahman was brave and attacked his enemy first. His face was awesome for friends and foes alike. He delivered the Friday sermon in the grand mosque himself, attended the sick and joined public assemblies and marriage parties.

During his rule his guards and caretakers were changed one after another and they included Tammam bin Alqama, Yusuf bin Bakht, Abdul Karim bin Mahran, Abdur Rahman bin Mughith, and Mansur, the eunuch. Although Abdur Rahman appointed some persons as his minister but he never acted blindly on their advice. He had formed a committee of nobles and notables, which advised him in administrative affairs. This consultative body consisted of Abu Uthman, Abdullah bin Khalid, Abu Ubaida, Shaheed bin Isa, Thalba bin Ubaid, and Athim bin Muslim.

His Features and His Children

Abdur Rahman was a handsome man having a commanding stature and little flesh, fair complexioned and gray haired. As per some historians, he had a weak sense of smell. He left behind nine daughters and eleven sons, Sulaiman being the eldest. However, he appointed his second son Hisham as his crown prince. Sulaiman was the son he had fled with from the bank of the Euphrates. However, he knew Hisham was more able and was more worthy of throne.

Order and Discipline

As per the statements of a western historian, Abdur Rahman was kind and benevolent but the rebels and traitors compelled him to deal with them harshly. He was inclined to learning and literature but his situation made him an alert and experienced commander. Abdur Rahman passed the earlier part of his life in luxury and faced adverse conditions happily and courageously. Before consolidating his position as a ruler he called the Umayyads and their associates to Spain at his own expense and offered them high posts and positions according to their caliber and abilities. Abdur Rahman could put up with trouble and suffering silently and even his opponents admitted and admired this.

Abdur Rahman had divided his country into six provinces and put a commander in each of them. Every commander had under him two administrators and six ministers and each official was assisted by a *Qadi* (judge) and other officials. Abdur Rahman would always consider the welfare of his people. He enacted laws to what brought prosperity to the masses and granted them freedom to possess property without fear of interference.

Abdur Rahman was very fond of spreading knowledge and education. He constructed roads throughout Spain, set up a postal system and kept horses at every halting point to carry news and information to the capital from all over the country.

Abdur Rahman did away with the robbers and bandits with a heavy hand and the Berbers who used to create disturbances every now and then were kept silent. He would tour extensively around his country to assess the situation and gain first hand knowledge of the performance of his Governors and officials. Wherever he went he started welfare schemes for the needy and the masses as a whole.

Abdur Rahman's benevolence was for one and all and everyone was benefited by it. Although he built mosques and other buildings in large number to serve as welfare centers throughout the country, he showed exemplary interest in and fondness for making the capital, Cordova, the most beautiful and magnificent city. He planted a date palm tree in the courtyard of his royal palace and it was the first date palm tree in Spain. He held the scholars and intellectuals in esteem and he provided the best of education for his sons and ordered them to take part in all royal and legal affairs.

In order to create in the common people a love for learning he would organize meetings of poets to recite their poems and he rewarded them. He personally would often attend these meetings. Regardless of the luxurious surroundings and abundance of wealth, he never lost his military character nor did he ever lack in piety and abstinence. The most suitable spot for building the world famous mosque of Cordova was owned by the Christians. Abdur Rahman refrained from acquiring it by force. He accepted it only when the Christians sold it to him. Furthermore, he allotted to them lands at several other places in the city to build churches. Abdur Rahman had all the qualities of head and heart needed to be a successful king. The day Abdur Rahman came to the throne, Spain became free from the control of the Eastern Islamic caliphate. But Abdur Rahman was wise enough not to claim the caliphate for himself. He included his name in the weekly addresses only after ten years of his rule. He knew very well that there was a section in Spain, which disliked the Umayyads and loved the Abbasids and they recognized the Islamic center of the East only. Had Abdur Rahman claimed the caliphate for himself a large number of Muslims would have taken up arms against him. However, he gradually, brought about the change and turned it in his favor to be called the caliph of the Muslims and Commander of the Faithful. One historian said he spoke eloquently and effectively and was very sober, shrewd and a great administrator. He never liked to pass his time in fun and sport nor took rest without need. He liked white clothes and ate with the poor and needy if any such person would turn up at meal times.

Abdur Rahman was one of those great men who brought a nation to life and changed the course of history.

Hisham bin Abdur Rahman

Since Abdur Rahman was called Caliph, his son Hisham and his descendants can be known as Sultan or Caliph.

Birth

Sultan Hisham bin Abdur Rahman was born in Shawwal 139 A.H. after the entry of his father into Spain. Hisham's mother, Halal, was presented as a gift to him by the former ruler Yusuf Fihri after finalizing a temporary truce. Abdur Rahman married her after freeing her and he loved her intensely.

Accession

Hisham became the ruler of Spain at the age of 32 or 33 years of age as per the will of his father. He had been in Merida as Governor when his father breathed his last. He ascended the throne there and his name was reiterated in the Friday sermons throughout Spain. His Brother Abdullah was in Cordova and he lost no time in occupying the royal palace and the capital Cordova. His brother Sulaiman was at the time Governor of Toledo. Hisham marched on Cordova and arrested Abdullah after a short engagement.

He forgave his brother and gave him a large estate and included him among his ministers and advisors.

Brother's Revolt

Spain was inhabited by people of varied nature and they could easily rise in revolt following the death of Abdur Rahman. But the deceased ruler had broken the back of these elements so violently that they could not muster courage to take up arms against the new ruler. However, Hisham's brothers began to create troubles for him. Sulaiman, the Governor of Toledo revolted and declared his sovereignty. Abdullah on the other hand escaped to his brother Sulaiman. Sultan Hisham pardoned the fault of his brothers and expected their return to correct behavior.

Battle

Ghalib Ghafqi was the minister of Sulaiman in Toledo and had been very loyal to Abdur Rahman. He advised the two brothers to keep from rebelling against the center of the government but they became angry and put him to prison. On being informed of this event, Hisham wrote to them against the imprisonment of such a loyal and trusted old servant. Sulaiman and Abdullah turned violent and reacted by killing Ghalib Ghafqi in the presence of Hisham's emissary and saying this was the reply to his letter. In consequence of such a harsh reply, Sultan Hisham marched to Toledo at the head of a twenty-thousand man army and the two forces clashed at a little distance from Toledo. Sulaiman and Abdullah suffered defeat and took refuge in the fort of Toledo, which was well known for its strength. The fort being hard to conquer Hisham laid a siege around Toledo. Leaving his son and Abdullah in Toledo, Sulaiman took a company of soldiers and marched on Cordova. Abdul Malik, the Governor of Cordova came out and greeted Sulaiman with swords and arrows. Sulaiman fled to Murcia and took to plundering. Hearing this Sultan Hisham deputed a Commander to continue the siege of Toledo and proceeded to Cordova to keep an eye on the movement of Sulaiman.

Brothers pardoned

Fed up with the long siege Abdullah entrusted himself to Sultan Hisham without seeking the safety of his life. Hisham not only forgave his brother's fault but also showed him love and respect and allotted him an estate in Toledo to settle in.

Sulaiman collected a large number of men in Murcia. Hisham sent by young son Umar at the head of an army, which defeated Sulaiman and drove away the rebels. After wanderings for two years, he sought the forgiveness of Sultan Hisham who not only granted him forgiveness but also gave him a respectable position in his court. Sulaiman then expressed his desire to settle in Africa. Hisham granted him permission and purchased his estate in Spain. Sulaiman settled in Africa but took to playing the role of an Abbasid agent and kept the people of Spain incited against Sultan Hisham.

Attack on France

After dealing with his brothers successfully Sultan Hisham led a forty-thousand-man force against France and conquered the entire south of France and regained control of Catalonia province. He collected an unimaginable amount of wealth and possessions from these campaigns. The Christians of the Pyrenees made an attempt to intercept the retreating army as they had done with Charlemagne's army in the past.

Punishing the rebellious Christians

Having reached Cordova in 175 A.H. Sultan Hisham sent his minister Yusuf bin Bakht to punish the Christians who had established themselves as an independent force in the hills. He invaded the State of Asturias and ravaged it thoroughly. Its ruler Bermundo was arrested. Since the territory was not worthy of living in it was restored to its ruler in return for his loyalty and tribute.

Construction of the Cordova Mosque

The Muslims received an enormous amount of spoils of war from the campaign in southern France and the Christian provinces. One-fifth of it was presented to Sultan Hisham, which amounted to 45 thousand gold coins. The Sultan spent all of this for the construction of the Cordova Mosque.

Insurgence in Cataluna put down

During the campaign Abdul Malik, the Governor, issued a strange order. He had a large number of Christian prisoners from Galicia, Asturias, Catalonia and south France. As a price for their liberty, he ordered them to demolish the fortifications of Narbonne and carry the stones to Cordova. They did it with much difficulty and the Sultan released them all. Those stones were used for building a part of the eastern wall of the Cordova Mosque. Moreover, the Christian States were restored to them after they promised to obey the Muslim rule. It was done because the Arab chiefs disliked the cold climate of those northern hilly states. This is the reason that the Muslim population in the southern provinces was far larger than in the north, with the result that the Christians in the southern part embraced Islam more than in other parts.

Cordova Mosque completed

Sultan Hisham paid exclusive attention to the completion of the Cordova Mosque whose foundation was laid by his father Abdur Rahman bin Muawi'yah. Sultan Hisham appointed his son, Hakam as the Governor of Toledo in 175 A.H. The bridge, over the Guadalquivir river (from the Arabic Wadi al-Kabir) in Cordova, was rebuilt in 176 A.H. The bridge was first constructed by the governer Samh during the caliphate of Umar bin Abdul Aziz. Sultan Hisham made it wider, stronger and more beautiful. Abbasid agents kept making secret plans in Spain. Sulaiman, the brother of Sultan Hisham kept misleading both the Muslims and the Christians in Africa (Morocco) and Charlemagne in the north had established friendly relations with Caliph Harun Rashid of Baghdad against Sultan Hisham and the new-born Christian State of Galicia began to show signs of revolt. Sultan Hisham sent Abdul Karim bin Abdul Wahid bin Mughith to Galicia without delay. Muslim troops reached Galicia and returned only after punishing the insurgents and making them obey the Muslim rule. Meanwhile, the Berbers gathered together and took up arms against Sultan Hisham. Abdul Qadir bin Aban bin Abdullah was sent to deal with the insurgents who killed a large number of Berbers and drove away the rest. The event took place in 178 A.H. The people of Galicia rose against the Muslim rule once again with the French supporting them. Sultan Hisham sent Abdul Malik bin Abdul Wahid bin Mughith at the head of an army with the instructions to make inroads into France after punishing the people of Galicia and to meet the Muslim troops advancing into France from the other side. Sultan Hisham had sent another army to France. Being informed of the advance of the Muslim forces, the Christian chief deserted the city and kept fleeing ahead of the invading troops. The Muslim commander then turned to France, he met the other Muslim force and ravaged most of the French cities and forts and returned victoriously.

Death

Sultan Hisham bin Abdur Rahman died in Safar, 180 A.H. at the age of 40 years and 4 months after ruling for 7 years and some months.

Assessment of Hisham's Life

Abdur Rahman had spent 80 thousand dinars on the foundation of the Cordova Mosque, while Sultan Hisham expended one hundred and sixty thousand dinars for the construction and completion of the mosque. Hisham would, like his father, wear white but very simple cheap garments. He was fond of hunting but not at the cost of the state's administration and his religious duties. He had abandoned all this during his last days. He always kept his court open for the poor and the needy and they could find access to him without any hindrance. He sacrificed even his rest and sleep for the peace and welfare of his people and felt pleasure and satisfaction in patrolling the streets and lanes of the city to be acquainted with the problems and sufferings of his subjects. What was charged as a fine from offenders was spent on public welfare instead of being placed in the public treasury. If any of the Muslims were taken captive by the Christians, they were liberated by paying their ransom from the public treasury.

During the period of Sultan Hisham, rich people of Cordova built beautiful and magnificent buildings, which added to the beauty of the city. Although academic centers and assemblies were strong during the tenure of Abdur Rahman, Sultan Hisham further promoted learning by declaring Arabic compulsory in all Madrasas. The result was that the Christians of Spain learned Arabic and became able to learn the Qur'an and Islam directly and they accepted Islam in large numbers. Now the Muslims were no longer a terror to them, they became so close that the Muslims began to marry Christian women. And the Christians chose to dress like the Muslims. In habits, traits and style of life Sultan Hisham resembled Umar bin Abdul Aziz to a great extent. The entire population of Spain addressed him as "Sultan, The Just."

Sultan Hisham was more pious and religious-minded than his father, Abdur Rahman. While Abdur Rahman's court was dominated by religious and spiritual men, Muslim jurists and scholars grew in power and influence during the reign of Sultan Hisham.

It was during his reign that the four different schools of Muslim jurists were brought into practice. Imam Malik bin Anas was very famous in

Madinah at that time and his doctrine was largely practiced by the people of Hijaz. A group of Muslims from Spain came to Imam Malik, stayed with him for sometime and then returned to Spain. Being acquainted with the style and functioning of Sultan Hisham, he expressed his love and respect for him. He used to say that Hisham bin Abdur Rahman alone deserved to be called Caliph of the Muslims. He was right. In devotion and piety, wisdom and bravery, fighting qualities and leadership Hisham was like his father but in devotion and practice he even excelled his father.

These utterances of Imam Malik caused irritation among the Abbasids and they, in turn, began to put the Imam in trouble. During the early period of Hisham some Muslim jurists of Spain like Firaun bin Abbas, Isa bin Dinar and Sayeed bin Abi Hind met Imam Malik on the occasion of Hajj. They benefited enormously from the company of the Imam and they returned to Spain and began to preach his legal system. Under the influence of their preaching Abu Abdullah Zaid, the Chief Justice of Spain also accepted Imam Malik's doctrine. Sultan Hisham too became a devotee of the Imam and ordered the treasurer to bear all expenses of those who wanted to go to Imam Malik for learning Fiqh and Hadith. Now all legal judgments were delivered according to Imam Malik's school of law.

The Crown Prince

Sultan Hisham appointed his son, Hakam as his crown prince and took the oath of allegiance for Hakam from the courtiers. On this occasion Hisham said to Hakam:

"You must not make any difference between the poor and the rich. Treat your subordinates with kindness but punish any atrocious governor heavily. Keep full control over your forces and see that these forces are used for serving the country not destroying it; fulfill your promises; make every effort to keep your subjects happy for angry people pose a threat to the stability of the administration.

Never ignore the farmer. Be careful that their crops are not destroyed nor their meadows. Behave well and the people will

invoke blessings on you. In the case that you put this advice
into practice you will be put in the category of the most
successful kings."

Sultan Hisham passed his whole tenure fighting and invading his
enemies. But his religious, moral, academic and social deeds lead us to
disbelieve that his military character was the most dominant. The
reason behind the foundation of Umayyad dynasty in Spain and its
survival for three hundred years was that its founder was Abdur
Rahman and his successor was Hisham. Even though Hisham had a
short tenure of seven years and eight month his son, Hakam became
an able and sensible ruler.

Hakam bin Hisham

Hakam bin Hisham succeeded his father in 180 A.H. But he had to
begin with insurgencies and revolts.

Sulaiman and Abdullah Rebel

Sultan Hisham's brother Sulaiman had been staying in Africa
(Morocco). He was engaged in creating disturbances in Spain.
Abdullah, another brother of Hisham was then stationed in an estate
adjoining Toledo. With the news of Hisham's demise Abdullah went
to his brother Sulaiman. The latter had a large number of Berbers and
bandits at his command. The two brothers decided to capture
Cordova and become the rulers of Spain. Sulaiman was already in
contact with Charlemagne, the King of France and other frontier
chiefs. It was suggested that Abdullah should make a personal visit to
Charlemagne and invite him to invade Spain and lend support to the
revolt they were going to launch. Charlemagne agreed to the proposal
and sent his son at the head of a strong army. Abdullah then came
back, instigated the Governor of Toledo to rise in revolt and he captured
the city. Sulaiman on the other hand reached Valencia province and
declared his sovereignty as the true successor of the dynastic rule.

Close on the heels of Sulaiman and Abdullah's revolt the son of
Charlemagne set his foot on the plane of Spain after crossing the
Pyrenees seized a number of cities and besieged Barcelona. The

Governor of Barcelona offered his allegiance to Charlemagne but refused the Christian army's entry into the fort. Sulaiman and Abdullah on the other hand captured important central cities and provinces. The Christians launched a massive attack on northern Spain and ravaged it. Spain was about to slip out of Muslim hands.

Defensive Measures of Hakam

Sultan Hakam bin Hisham, first of all, took action against Toledo and besieged it. Abdullah rose in defense. Hakam was still engaged there when he heard of the Christian invasion of Spain. Considering the Christian attack more dangerous he raised his siege of Toledo and rushed to the north. Having heard of Hakam's arrival Charlemagne's forces vacated Barcelona and its suburbs in haste and made no halt until they reached France. Sultan Hakam then turned to Huesca and Lerida but the Christian forces fled the territory. Hakam after getting the Christians out of Spain marched ahead and ravaged the southern part of France and wrested Narbonne from the Christians. Having heard of Hakam's engagement in France Abdullah and Sulaiman began dislodging Hakam's Governors and occupying Spanish cities. The two brothers marched ahead conquering city after city and met at the river Tagus. At this point, they discontinued their march. They began to wait for the consequences of Hakam's campaigns in France. They had a plan to occupy all of Spain in case Hakam was killed in France. Hakam's Governors were also waiting restlessly the result of his hasty invasion of France. They were mentally prepared to obey Sulaiman and Abdullah in case Hakam was killed in France for; after all, they were the sons of Abdur Rahman. But awe-stricken and frightened French forces, instead of facing Hakam took to their heels everywhere. Hakam returned to Spain to face his enemies in Spain instead of consolidating his position in the occupied territories of France.

End of Sulaiman and Abdullah

Making Ubaidah bin Umairah the Governor of Toledo Sulaiman and Abdullah moved ahead to stop Hakam on the way. Hakam's triumphant march had already frustrated their ambition. They faced defeat and fled to the eastern mountain range of Spain. Sultan Hakam deputed his Commander Amr bin Yusuf to besiege Toledo and he himself marched in pursuit of Sulaiman and Abdullah. After several months of hide-and-seek campaigns, they came face to face on the plane of Murcia. During fierce fighting, an arrow hit Sulaiman and he dropped dead on the spot. With the end of Sulaiman, his forces fled the field along with Abdullah who took refuge in Valencia and sought forgiveness from Hakam. Granting the petition of his uncle immediately Hakam asked him to send his sons Asbah and Qasim as ransom and go to Tabkhiv in Morocco to settle there. Abdullah carried out the conditions without loss of time. Hakam treated both his cousins with love. He married his daughter to the elder and appointed the younger as the Governor of Merida city. At a time when Sultan Hakam was chasing Sulaiman and Abdullah, Umar bin Yusuf conquered Toledo and killed Ubaidah bin Umayr. He later made his son Yusuf bin Umar the Governor of Toledo and appeared before the Sultan with the head of Ubaidah. Following this Saragossa rose in revolt. Umar bin Yusuf went there and punished the insurgents. The series of revolts, which started in 181 A. H., came to an end in 184 A. H. and peace and safety prevailed over the whole of Spain.

An Organized Conspiracy of the Christians

It has already been mentioned that the Christian forces could not withstand Hakam's invasion of France and fled for safety. Three years of Hakam's engagements with his insurgent relatives offered the Christians an opportunity to look into their weaknesses and find out ways and means of guarding themselves against Muslim invasions in the future. They had the state of Asturias in the western part of the Pyrenees joining the border of France, Galicia and the Bay of Biscay, another very strong State that was founded by the chiefs of the Goths after their expulsion from Spain. A large part of France was ruled over by Charlemagne. Moreover, rebellious Christians dominated the population of Barcelona, Aragon, Catalonia, and Galicia.

Finding Sultan Hakam preoccupied with the task of putting down internal rebellions the Christians held a large scale consultative meeting in Talur city. As a result of these deliberations, a massive united front came into being against the Muslims. Waves of peace and friendship rose to bring together Christian rulers who had been opposing one another.

New State Founded against the Muslims

Charlemagne, the King of France formed a small State on a piece of land in the south France and appointed a chief named Borrell as its ruler. The State was named "Gothic March" and one of their chiefs was appointed as the ruler with the instruction that he should make the Pyrenees impossible to pass for the Muslims and keep ever ready to stop any advancing march. Strong forts were built at different places at the foot of the Pyrenees and friendly relations with the Governors of northern Spain were established with a view to set them against their ruler. The Caliph of Baghdad was kept informed of their intentions and preparations and Caliph Harun Rasheed also showed encouraging friendly gestures by sending them precious gifts. The new Gothic State also occupied the eastern and southern parts of the Pyrenees and the Christians of northern Spain extended all help and facilities. In short, "Gothic March" rose as a strong State on the pattern of Asturias and the bishops declared all-out help and support to it a religious obligation. Disgruntled Christians from various States came to settle in the new State and this deserted territory turned into a strong, well-populated and splendid piece of land.

Treacherous Muslim Governors encouraged

Hakam had hardly won peace during the last days of 184 A.H. when the Christians stormed northern Spain in 185 A.H. And at such a crucial moment, the Governors of the northern cities lent support to Charlemagne considering him a friend and ally of the Caliph of Baghdad. Moreover, the spies employed in Spain by the court of Baghdad played a very active role in setting the governors against Sultan Hakam who refused to obey Hakam and accepted the King of France as their ruler.

Similarly, the Governors of Galicia and Biscay including the ruler of Saragossa declared their allegiance to the Christian rulers and rose against Hakam. But, despite these disturbances Sultan Hakam did not move from Cordova for the atmosphere in the capital was not at all peaceful. However, he sent his commander Ibrahim to save the northern part of the country. Ibrahim invaded Galicia and Saragossa first and wrested the territories after fierce fighting. The rebel governors fled to Charlemagne along with the Christian forces and common people and persuaded him to invade Spain. Encouraged by the Muslim governors, consultations were held in France. It was decided that the port of Barcelona should also be annexed to the "Gothic March" State. The Governor of Barcelona, Zaid was already in correspondence with King Charlemagne and Count Louis and had offered his allegiance to them. Thus, in 188 A.H., Christian forces along with the troops of Gothic March reached Barcelona plundering the northeastern parts of Spain. But Zaid shut the doors and refused to hand over Barcelona to the Christians. Thereupon, the Christian forces laid a siege around Barcelona and tightened it gradually. Since Zaid received no help from any quarter, the Christians occupied Barcelona on the condition that the Muslim population would be allowed to vacate the territory safely. A Christian Governor took over the Governorship of the city. The newly conquered territory became a part of the Gothic March State. Now the Islamic forces had to face two fronts in northern Spain, the State of Asturias and Galicia on one hand and the Gothic March and Barcelona on the other. Both the fronts were receiving help from France.

In 189 A.H., rebel Muslim Governors of Spain persuaded the Christians to invade Toledo. The Christians marched from Barcelona and the northern cities to Toledo. Yusuf bin Umar attempted to defend the city. They, at last, surrounded Toledo. The Christian population of Toledo city and its suburbs extended all help and facilities to arrest Yusuf bin Umar and capture Toledo. When the news of the fall of Toledo reached Umar bin Yusuf, the father of Yusuf bin Umar, he marched from Saragossa to Toledo and conquered it and he freed Yusuf driving away the Christians. Although the Christians of Toledo deserved heavy punishment from Umar bin Yusuf, he, in view of the demand of the situation, accepted their excuses and restored peace to them.

Causes of Opposition to Hakam

Sultan Hakam was a brave young man but right from the day he came to the throne he remained engaged in constant fighting. Some parts of

Spain slipped out of his hands. The Christians were getting stronger and the Muslims were losing ground. Hakam's relatives, on the other hand, left no stone unturned in opposing him militarily. They resorted to secret planning and instigating the Christians against Hakam. Moreover, the Christian world had become united to weaken the Muslim rule. The antagonistic activities of the Abbasids were encouraging Hakam's relatives and the hostile Christians at the same time against him. The religious scholars and guides of the Malik School had also turned against Hakam. They were quite influential during the period of Hisham but Hakam had cut them down to size. Since they still had their influence over the masses their criticism of Hakam's style of governance made an important difference. They started issuing verdicts against Hakam and he could not withstand their onslaught. All these factors jointly made the hostile Christians very bold and strong enough to make a challenge to the Muslim rule in Spain.

The religious leaders decided to carry out their plans in 190 A.H. The Chief Justice, Yahya bin Yahya and the jurist Talut assembled and held consultations regarding the deposition of Hakam. Following this, a deputation headed by Yahya called on Qasim bin Abdullah, the cousin and son-in-law of Hakam and expressed the desire to bring him to the throne of Spain. Qasim asked them to let him know the names of those whose support could be relied upon. He then asked them to turn up the next day with the list of such powerful and reliable persons who would be able to depose Hakam. Qadi Yahya, along with his party went to Qasim bin Abdullah who had already had Sultan Hakam hiding behind a screen. When Qadi Yahya began to dictate the names to the clerk of Qasim. The clerk of Hakam also began to write down those names sitting beside Hakam. Since Hakam's clerk was afraid of the revelation of his own name, he was simply running his pen on the paper without writing anything. But the pen began to produce a writing sound. Thus with the very thought that somebody else was also writing down those names behind the screen they started leaving the room one by one. But many of them were caught and killed. Following this, the opponents raised their standard of revolt openly. They lived in localities towards the south of the river Guadalquivir (Wadi al-Kabir). They surrounded the palace of Sultan Hakam but Hakam put down the revolt after a short and bloody encounter.

The same year, in 190 A.H. Sultan Hakam established peaceful and friendly relations with the newly formed sovereign Idrisid State in Morocco. Thus, the freedom of the Idrisid rule from the Baghdad caliphate proved a blessing for Spain and Sultan Hakam made no delay in extending the hand of friendship towards the Moroccan rule. Shortly after curtailing the influence of the religious leaders of Cordova and forming friendly relations with the Moroccan rule, Sultan Hakam turned to the northern provinces.

Eradication of Rebels

After a good deal of thinking Sultan Hakam arrived at the conclusion that Toledo was the center of all the Christian conspiracies. Because of being strong and tumultuous, the Christians of Toledo had become the focus of Christian as well as Muslim attention. Sultan Hakam held consultations with Umar bin Yusuf and as per his advice, he replaced his son Yusuf bin Umar in Toledo. Taking over the administration of Toledo Umar bin Yusuf began to show favor and kindness to the people of Toledo. After winning their confidence, the new Governor told some of the nobles that the Umayyad dynasty must be dislodged from power. The people of Toledo expressed great joy at this and promised their whole-hearted support to the plan. After knowing the minds of the citizens, Umar suggested the construction of a strong fort adjoining Toledo as the first step in the way of destroying the Umayyad rule. With control of such a fort, Sultan Hakam would not be able to besiege Toledo. This proposal added much to the jubilation of the people and they contributed largely to the fund. Shortly after the construction of the fort, the frontier Governor, according to their plan, sought military help from Sultan Hakam against Christian threats. Hakam sent his son Abdur Rahman at the head of a huge army. When the force reached Toledo, Umar bin Yusuf came out to greet it and had the prince stay in the new fort as an honorable guest. Umar asked the people of Toledo to show their hospitality to Abdur Rahman, the crown prince to win his heart and make him careless about them. They liked the suggestion, and all those who were willing to put an end to the Umayyad dynasty sought permission to appear before the crown prince to offer their salutation. The prince granted them permission with pleasure and called them all at a fixed time. When all the corrupt elements entered the fort, they were all caught and put to death. Their corpses were thrown into a trench dug for this purpose, which was leveled with earth. In this way, all sorts of disorder and disturbances came to an end in Toledo. Others also lost heart in making a revolt in view of the consequences of these antagonists.

Skirmishes with the Christians

After getting rid of the hostile elements in Toledo, Hakam sent a small company against the Christians who were in occupation of northern Spain up to Barcelona. He did not choose to launch any forceful attack with the result that fighting between the Muslims and the Christians lingered on for seven or eight years. During this period, both the parties tasted victories. Hakam by this way provided the Christians of Gothic March, Asturias and Galicia an opportunity to vent their desire for military exercises on the battlefield with a minimized impact. He could not use another strategy because he could not trust the people of Spain.

Fresh Recruiting Drive

During this period Sultan Hakam made concerted efforts to build a strong military force. He, very cautiously, recruited those Christians who had settled in the southern territories of Spain and had nothing to do with the insurgent Christians of the north. Thus, the Christians of the south were considered more loyal and reliable than the Muslims of doubtful nature. Since the recruited Christian forces were not enough to keep the entire of Spain under control and crush the insurgents, he started purchasing slaves and prisoners from Abyssinia, Middle Africa, Asia Minor and other Asian countries. Now he had a strong slave-based force. Since Arabic was unknown to these soldiers they were called non-Arab and they knew nothing except to obey and fight for their master and ruler. They could neither establish friendly relations with others nor enter into any secret planning against the administration. Sultan Hakam was the first ruler to devise such a means to keep his rule safe and strong. Later, the Ayyubid dynasty followed in the footsteps of Hakam and in this way the Mamluks of Egypt founded a strong rule. Being satisfied with the performance and fighting capabilities of the newly built force Sultan Hakam turned to dealing with the insurgent Christians of the northern territories and invaded the French. However, internal insurgencies had not yet ended.

Asbah bin Abdullah, the ruler of Merida, led by some misunderstanding, took up arms against Hakam. Asbah bin Abdullah was the cousin and brother-in-law of Sultan Hakam. Hakam himself rose to face the offence and arrested him but Hakam's sister removed the misunderstanding and gained liberty for her husband. He was then forgiven and allowed to live in Cordova.

Malkites' Opposition

The Maliki religious scholars raised their heads once again in 198 A.H. When the Sultan began to build his force out of the Christians and the non-Arabs, the Muslim religious leaders began to issue verdicts against the new policy of the Sultan and held it a curse on Cordova. The last conspiracy against Hakam was hatched under the leadership of Qadi Yahya. Since the people of Spain held him in high esteem, Hakam neither charged nor punished him. But he did not mend his ways and kept misleading the Muslim religious leaders and their followers against the administration with the result the people of Cordova hated the non-Arabs and would kill them if one were found alone.

Flames of Antagonism reach the Royal Palace

One day a non-Arab came into a clash with a Malkite supporter. With this news, all the Malkites living across Guadalquivir (Wadi al-Kabir) sprang into action and raided the royal palace and pronounced the deposition of the Sultan. They broke into the gates and advanced up to the threshold killing the bodyguards. The entire palace was engulfed in strife and panic. In such a turbulent state, the Sultan called out to his servant Hasan and asked him to bring perfumed hair oil. After Hakam had applied the oil to his head, the servant mustered enough courage to ask him the reason for applying hair oil in such a violent and disorderly situation. The Sultan replied, "Foolish one had I not used oil how could the rebels have known that it was the head of a king while cutting it off?."

Hakam's Presence of Mind

Historians have quoted this narrative to establish the firmness of his mind in such a treacherous situation. He then called his cousin Asbah and ordered him to go out and set the southern locality on fire. Asbah left the siege and sent word to a military camp of Cordova to go to the southern locality fully armed and set fire to that locality. Meanwhile a force from the military camp arrived at the scene. When the insurgents besieging the royal palace noticed flames and columns of smoke rising from their locality, they rushed to save their burning houses. Taking advantage of the situation Sultan Hakam hurried to the spot at the head of his bodyguards, while Asbah bin Abdullah joined him from another side and put many of them to the sword. Following a large-scale massacre, he ordered the killing to stop and start catching the culprits. The Royal forces from other camps also appeared on the scene and captured thousands of rebels.

Exile of Malkites

Taking stock of the situation Sultan Hakam issued orders for the Malkites to leave the territories of Cordova and its suburbs. However, the Sultan pardoned Qadi Yahya for his faults once again with the purpose of benefiting from his wide knowledge and erudition. It looked rather strange that Qadi Yahya was allowed to join the royal court and become Hakam's trusted adviser. About eight thousand exiled Malkites having wives and children with them showed an interest in going to Morocco to settle there. The ruler of Morocco, Idris welcomed them to settle in the city of Fez and add to its beauty. Fifteen thousand of them reached Alexandria (Egypt) on board ship and occupied the territory but they were driven away from there too. They later occupied Carat Island and founded their rule, which lasted for about a century.

Hazm bin Wahab revolted in Beja but was defeated and he sought forgiveness and Sultan Hakam pardoned him.

Invasion of France

Twenty years had passed since Hakam's enthronement and the whole period had been spent in putting down revolts and he could not, therefore, find time to invade the Christians. Finding the situation relatively peaceful, Sultan Hakam sent a force headed by Abdul Karim towards the north to attack the Christians. He led the force straight to France and took it by storm. The expedition was dispatched to France in 200 A.H. Sultan Hakam and his commanders had committed a blunder by keeping their invasions confined to Charlemagne's armies. They almost always ignored the Gothic March and never tried to wipe it out or reduce its size. They remained satisfied with the submissive attitude of the newly formed Christian State. They so often invaded France to gain permanent peace by subjugating it to their rule. Moreover, the hilly States also created trouble for Sultan Hakam by joining hands with the king of France. Had he put an end to the two hilly States (Asturias and Gothic March) Spain would have remained peaceful.

It was during the tenure of Sultan Hakam that a bishop of Asturias informed the people that the grave of St. James was in the forest bordering Galicia province and he was given a sign of the grave in a dream by a saint. Following this, the ruler of Asturias built a church at that site. This church became a place of pilgrimage not only for the Christians of Galicia but also from far away places of Europe. Gradually it became a populated city and seat of power and brought the whole of Galicia under its influence.

A few years later, Commander Abdul Karim returned from France safe and sound. His campaign was successful and the French were thoroughly punished and beaten. But nothing was done against the States of Gothic March and Asturias. The Muslims conquered France more than once but no Arab Commander ever agreed to settle in France because of its cold climate. They remained satisfied with what they captured as spoils of war and what they received in the form of tribute from the wealthy sections of the country.

Disasters of Famine and Drought

Sultan Hakam enjoyed a period of peace and order after 203 A.H. because there was no serious force to invade Spain or to create disorder and disturbances in the country. However, at the time when everything seemed all right, famine and drought overtook Spain. The famine proved utterly disastrous and distressing and the afflicted part of the country was overwhelmed by a spell of theft and armed robbery. Sultan Hakam faced the situation with his usual courage and determination. He opened houses for the destitute in every city and town and arranged food supplies from abroad. He also deployed special police and military squads to keep the situation under control. In most cases, Hakam himself rose to silence the disturbing elements. In short, he served his people so kindly and gracefully during the terrible famine that they began to love him, and the waves of hate raised by the Muslim religious leaders against him subsided.

Death of Hakam

Sultan Hakam is so often described as a man of the sword and a bloodthirsty Muslim ruler. He killed many, no doubt, but it is an undeniable fact that they all deserved nothing but death. Sultan Hakam died on 25 Dhul Qada 206 A.H. at the age of 52 years and some months and left behind twenty sons and twenty daughters. His son Abdur Rahman II succeeded him.

Assessment of Hakam's Character

Sultan Hakam was brave, benevolent and far-sighted. He was an enemy of the hypocrites and subversives but he was very generous and gracious to his friends. He valued religious scholars and spiritual leaders highly and was a great patron of the poets. He remained firm and determined on the battlefield and forgave faults whenever he expected something good from it. He was a great and magnificent king of Spain. His devotion and sense of divinity can be judged from the fact that once, in a state of violent anger he ordered the amputation of his servant's hand. Ziyad bin Abdur Rahman, a great scholar came in and said addressing Sultan Hakam "Malik bin Anas has narrated from the Prophet ﷺ that whoever controls himself in a state of violent anger will be given peace by Allah Almighty on the Day of Judgment". As these words were uttered, the Sultan's wrath disappeared and the servant was forgiven.

Sultan Hakam's 27-year reign was fraught with strife, turbulence and insurrection. He boldly faced these situations, which were not of his own creation. Had there been on the throne of Spain a man of unstable mind and infirm determination the Umayyad dynasty would have been wiped out of Spain.

Abdur Rahman II

Sultan Abdur Rahman II was born in Toledo in Shaban 176 A.H. and succeeded his father in 206 A.H. At the time of his accession, there was an atmosphere of peace on the surface but he had to deal with internal disturbances created by his own relatives.

Opposition from Family Members

As already mentioned, Abdullah, the uncle of Sultan Hakam had settled in Morocco. Although old at the time of the demise of Sultan Hakam, he reached Spain and proclaimed himself as the ruler of the country. Abdullah's three sons were then the governors of three different provinces of Spain. He had therefore, expected active support from his sons but that was his sheer folly. Royal forces took on Abdullah who fled to Valencia after being beaten thoroughly. His sons sided with Abdur Rahman II and asked his father not to oppose the Sultan any more. At last Abdullah sought forgiveness from his grandson Abdur Rahman II, who not only pardoned him but appointed him as the ruler of Murcia where he died after ruling for three or four years.

Ali bin Nafe honored

In 206 A.H., the very first year of Abdur Rahman's accession, Ali bin Nafe, the disciple of Ibrahim Musali and known as Farabi came to Spain. He was well versed in music and was an erudite scholar of Arabic disciplines. Sultan Hakam had invited him to visit Spain for he was not given proper recognition in Syria and Iraq. But the Sultan had died before Ali bin Nafe reached Spain. When Sultan Abdur Rahman II became aware of the standing invitation, he issued orders to all his Governors to accord a fitting ovation to the visiting guest of honor and present him slaves, horses and precious gifts. Thus, the well renown scholar and musician arrived in Cordova and became close to the Sultan.

Reforms in Mode of Life

Ali bin Nafe brought about many strange reforms in the life style and mode of living which gained wide popularity very quickly. With his efforts, water pipes were set up all over Cordova and then in other cities of Spain. He also originated many sumptuous foods and fashionable garments. His inventions and creations became popular not only in Spain but found popularity with the Europeans as well. Eating with a knife and fork is one of his inventions and the Europeans learned it from the Muslims of Spain. Even though Ali bin Nafe was very close to the Sultan, he never interfered in political affairs. He kept his attention exclusively focused on reforms in the mode of living. Due to this position, he had no one oppose him. The people of Spain learned from him not only the ways and modes of living but music too. In other words, Ali bin Nafe made an all out effort to change the martial life of the Muslims of Spain into pleasure-loving Muslims fond of a luxurious life.

Progress of Malkite School of thought in Spain

It has already been mentioned that Qadi Yahya bin Yahya Maliki had launched a very serious revolt in Cordova during the rule of Hakam. As a result of which one-fifth of the southern locality had become under populated because twenty to twenty five thousand people were exiled from Spain. Later the Qadi joined the courtiers and advisers of Sultan Hakam. Following the accession of Sultan Abdur Rahman II he had been so close to him that he once offered him the post of Chief Justice but the latter refused to accept it, with the result that he was considered higher than the Chief Justice. The people of Spain were immensely devoted to him and he had the last word on religious matters. The Qadi had penned a large number of books and had the distinction of being the student of Imam Malik. He learned Islamic sciences from the Imam for some years. During the rule of Sultan Abdur Rahman, he brought about the complete change in his style and function. He was now making full use of his abilities. His recommendations and intercessions were never rejected. As a result of this, all those religious scholars who wanted a post in the judiciary would bring Malkite doctrine into practice resulting in the influence of the doctrine all over Spain. Since Sultan Abdur Rahman II was deeply involved in the political and administrative affairs of his country, he had gained a lot of experience and was able to take cautious steps in the matters related to the religious scholars and spiritual leaders.

Rebellion Curbed

At the time of the accession of Abdur Rahman II the entire northern territory of Spain including the southern coast of the Bay of Biscay and the southern foot of the Pyrenees were under the occupation of the Christians. But all these Christian chiefs paid tribute to the Islamic State and accepted the supremacy of the Cordova court, which was satisfied with that much. Barcelona too was under the possession of the Christians and a Viceroy of the Gothic March State ruled there. A part of the eastern and northern coast of Spain was under the occupation of the Christians. Asturias State had now stretched up to Leon and Galicia and the new city of Castile had become its capital. Although the Muslims did not want to do away with this State, they followed a policy of keeping it terrified so that it would never be able to invade Spain with the support of France. The city of Ilbira lay to the north where the Governor was appointed by Cordova.

When the governor of Ilbira committed atrocities on the people and entered into secret planning with the Christians, Sultan Hakam had him killed and seized his possessions. However, a short time after Sultan Hakam passed away, on the accession of Abdur Rahman II the frontier Christians drove the force and the people back to Cordova. They made a demand for all their seized possessions saying that they all belonged to the people, which were forcibly taken by the governor killed by Hakam. These people rose to protest at the gate of the royal palace of Cordova in 207 A.H. Royal guards were sent to punish them with the result that many of them fell fighting and the rest fled for safety. In this way, the Christians made an opportunity to create more disturbances on the borders.

The same year, 207 A.H. Modaria and Yamania, two Arab tribes clashed in Tadmir. Royal forces were sent to keep peace. On the return of the royal forces, they again resumed fighting, and once again the royal forces were sent. Their fighting lingered on for about 7 years. The Arab character of the days of Ignorance once again came to the fore. In 208 A.H., the Christian States of Asturias and Galicia refused to pay tribute and rose in open revolt. They later made inroads into Islamic territories and plundered some cities. Sultan Abdur Rahman II sent his renowned commander Abdul Karim bin Abdul Wahid bin Mughith at the head of an army and he drove the Christians away after beating them repeatedly. Abdul Karim pulled down Christian forts and forced them to obey and resume paying tribute to the Islamic State. After attaining success in his mission, Abdul Karim came back. Again, the same force under the same Commander was dispatched to Barcelona from where news of war preparations was received. The Royal Army conquered the entire territory and forced the enemy to flee to the hills. However, the conquered territory was restored to them after their total submission.

Emissary of the Caesar of Constantinople

In 209 A.H., an emissary from the Caesar of Constantinople called on Abdur Rahman II to establish friendly relations with Spain. Baghdad already had cordial relations with France and the latter was constantly persuaded to invade Spain. Cordova knew it well.

Constantinople was under constant attack and had, therefore, sought the friendship of the Sultan of Spain because of his courage and bravery. Sultan Abdur Rahman was naturally sympathetic to Constantinople for Caesar was an enemy of Baghdad. Abdur Rahman accorded a warm welcome to the envoy from Constantinople. The envoy presented him precious gifts and tried his utmost to convince Abdur Rahman that he with a massive military power at his back would be able to take back the lost territories of Syria, Iraq, and Arabia from the Abbasids. Abdur Rahman acted very wisely and promised that he could help Caesar only when he was having peace at home. However, he sent back the envoy with many precious gifts along with his emissary, Yahya Ghazalah.

Abdur Rahman's Sense of Islamic Honor

Yahya al-Ghazalah went to Constantinople and inspected everything carefully and returned after assuring Caesar of Abdur Rahman's friendship. But, in fact, Sultan Abdur Rahman was not in favor of helping a Christian ruler against a Muslim Caliph. Although a little military and monetary help to Caesar could not make any difference to Abdur Rahman II but his sense of Islamic honor did not allow him to do so.

Portuguese Revolt

The same year the Christians of the southwest territories of Spain, now called Portugal rose in revolt under the leadership of the people of Merida city. Ubaidullah bin Abdullah was sent to punish the rebels who returned in 210 A.H. after beating them and pulling down their fortifications. They again raised their heads and Ubaidullah had to go there once again to bring the situation under control. Behind these revolts were the clergymen who would come from Galicia and Castillia to generate hostile feeling among the citizens. The Christian priests knew well that their advantage lay in internal troubles and infighting among the Muslims. The People of Merida were crossing all limits in their hostile moves against the Muslim rule. They had expelled the Governor from the city and had fought with the Royal forces twice. When Sultan Abdur Rahman ordered to throw the stones of the demolished fortifications of Merida into the river, the people once again rose in revolt, expelled the Governor again and seized the city. They rebuilt the fortifications and readied themselves against attacks. It is amazing that the Muslims formed the greater part of the insurgents and Mahmud bin Abdul Jabbar, a Muslim was their head. Royal Commanders repeatedly advanced into their territory but failed to eradicate the hostile activities.

At last, Sultan Abdur Rahman himself led his army against Merida in 218 A.H. No sooner had he besieged the city when he had to return to

Cordova. However, the city was conquered in 221 A.H. and a governor was sent there. The revolt of the people of Merida was the worst ever in Spain. The city had forty thousand armed warriors and received help from Asturias and Galicia. After the conquest of the city in 220 A.H. Mahmud bin Abdul Jabbar fled Merida to take refuge in the state of Asturias where he died serving as the garrison commander.

There were two main causes that set the Christians against the Muslims. First, the Christian wives of the Muslims who were left free to practice their faith and second, the Christians of the northern States who were supposed to be sympathetic to the Muslims and who had free access to Muslim circles could propagate their faith easily and openly. It was once rumored that the new tax imposed by Sultan Abdur Rahman II in addition to *Zakat* was an attempt on his part to capture the public's wealth and property. This poisonous propaganda enraged the Muslims and this rage and dissatisfaction led to the worst consequences.

Revolt in Toledo

Since the curbing of revolts in Merida took time and the Muslim rebels had put the royal force to much difficulty, antagonistic elements once again began to raise their heads. Toledo, where the Christians were in majority, took up arms under the leadership of Hashim Zarab, and the Muslims joined them as well. They jointly expelled the governor and consolidated their position in Toledo. Seeing Hashim in a commanding position another frontier Governor Muhammad bin Wasim also joined him. Sultan Abdur Rahman II sent his son Umayyah at the head of a huge army but his campaign proved fruitless. Umayyah came out of Toledo and the retreating Royal Force clashed with the rebels. The Royal force lay in ambush and when the people of Toledo passed through the area the Royal Force launched a surprise attack and they after incurring heavy losses, fled back to Toledo and took refuge in their fort. The city however, could not he conquered despite repeated sieges.

At last, Sultan Abdur Rahman sent his brother Waleed in 222 A.H. at the head of a huge army. Waleed laid siege around Toledo and cut off all supplies, with the result the people of Toledo laid down their arms. Hashim Zarab died in the action and Muhammad bin Wasim fled into the city. He collected a group of insurgents and occupied Toledo after a surprise attack on the city.

In 224 A.H., Sultan Abdur Rahman himself marched on Toledo at the head of forty thousand troops, invaded Toledo, punished the rebels with a heavy hand and brought peace. From there, he sent a force headed by Ubaidullah bin Abdullah to Alva and Alcala. He punished the insurgent Christians and forced them to obey. Ubaidullah had not yet completed his mission in the northern territories when the French army on the borders made inroads into the city of Salem in the Islamic State and plundered it. Ubaidullah took the Governor of the territory with him and attacked the Christian forces and beat back Larziq, their commander and the King of France.

In 225 A.H., Sultan Abdur Rahman II invaded Galicia and forced them to obey. He also came down heavily on the Christians of Asturias State, had them obey and pay tribute. He then set up his military camp inside the State of Asturias and dispatched his forces to France both from the land and sea routes. After accomplishing his military missions, Abdur Rahman returned to Cordova with a large amount of booty and prisoners of war.

The Next Emissary of Caesar of Constantinople

The same year the Caesar of Constantinople sent another emissary to Cordova of the same nature as was sent in the past. Abdur Rahman welcomed them as warmly as he had done in the past. This time the Caesar of Constantinople was under tremendous pressure from the Caliph of Baghdad and very insistently sought help from Abdur Rahman and had very high expectations. Possibly, Abdur Rahman II could have extended help to Constantinople but, during the same period, the Normans of Northern Europe who still worshiped fire and idols and were not yet Christians had made inroads into southwestern Spain. They had left Germany in their boats and reached the Spanish coast by crossing the English Channel. Sultan Abdur Rahman II dispatched his forces from the land route and sent orders to the ports of the eastern coast to send warships towards the Strait of Gibraltar so that the invading warships would be seized and the escaping enemy soldiers blocked. When the Norman invaders found out about the movement of the fifteen warships to block their route they retreated in their boats.

The Revolt of Commander Musa bin Musa

Close on the heels of the end of the Norman raid Musa bin Musa, the renowned Commander of Abdur Rahman II guarding the northern frontiers revolted and joined the Christian camp. Harth bin Badi'a was sent to punish him. Musa bin Musa came out along with the Christian force to atttack on the Royal Force. But Harth defeated and drove him away. Musa stayed in Toledo while Harth halted at Saragossa. After a long-drawn battle, Musa left Toledo and shifted position and Harth occupied Toledo. Following this, the Christian King Garcia came to reinforce Musa's troops, which gave rise to new encounters. At Alva Harth was captured and sent to the King of France in 218 A.H. Abdur Rahman was terribly shocked at this news. He sent his son Mundhir at the head of a strong army. By that time, Musa had seized Toledo. Mundhir killed the ruler of Navarre in a battle in 229 A.H. who had come to help Musa. Musa sent his son as a hostage for gaining peace. Mundhir granted peace and appointed Musa as the ruler of Toledo.

Revolt of the Christians of the Northern Frontier

In the presence of the disturbances on the northern frontiers the Christians of the northeast started large-scale preparations to rise in revolt. The people of Barcelona made inroads into the Islamic territory and began to plunder it. Killing many Islamic forces they advanced towards southwestern areas. Sultan Abdur Rahman II sent his famous Commander Abdul Karim bin Abdul Wahid bin Mugith to Barcelona in 231 A.H. Abdul Karim cracked down on the rebels of Barcelona and its suburbs and ravaged the Spanish March State, but restored it to them after obtaining their submission. He then advanced into French territories and stormed all the areas up to Gerona but the Islamic forces did not stay in France for long and returned after a tremendous show of force.

The Christians and the enemies of the Umayyads tasted defeat despite all their secret planning. When all the uprisings subsided and normalcy returned, the Christians of France and the northern frontier

States of Spain called a meeting to ponder over the prevailing situation. The clergy of Galicia took it upon themselves to keep the frontiers safe from the onslaughts of Cordova. They did this so that the Christian countries could find time enough to make joint efforts in military preparations, building forts, bringing the northern Governors to their side and striking at the Islamic State to bring about its end. This attempt was declared a religious struggle. A very zealous bishop was deputed to arouse among the Christians of Cordova and other cities a sense of sacrifice and the faith of Christ. The Muslims of Spain had conferred on the Christians complete liberty of practicing and preaching their faith. Religious matters were examined and decided by Christian judges and church expenditures were met by the royal treasury. Muslims and Christians took part in one another's festivals and both peoples had equal rights in commercial and agricultural spheres and there was no material reason to set the Christians against the Muslims.

Fresh Mischief of Christians of South Spain

Nevertheless the Christians of the northern part and their supporters had spread into the south of Spain. They had made it a practice to abuse Muhammad (ﷺ) openly in markets and public gatherings. They also put the Qur'an to disgrace and created among the Muslims a deep sense of provocation. At first, some of the foul-mouthed Christians were arrested and produced in the court of law. But there too they uttered blasphemous words. When one was put to death, another one appeared in the law court and abused the Prophet of Islam and also met his doom. It was discovered that these Christians would come to the courts only to have a sacred death and dignity among men of their faith. After meeting such a death, they were supposed to have received a very lofty spiritual status and their graves were made a place of worship, deep love and respect. In view of this, the Sultan and the Qadi took to overlooking and forgiving their faults. However, Sultan Abdur Rahman was in a fix and could not find a way out. Finally, the bishops, distinguished Christian leaders and the clergy of Cordova and Seville convened a huge religious assembly. The issue discussed was whether abusing the Prophet of Islam and desecrating the Qur'an was an act of reward in

Christianity and should those laying down their lives in this manner be taken as martyrs or not. Bishops and priests made fervid speeches on the topic and declared such an act totally against the Christian faith and principles. However, in a strange decision, it was announced that those who already had been killed must be considered as martyred but those killed in future would be taken as offenders committing a major sin. The decision taken by the council impressed the Spanish Christians. But the clergies of the northern States who thought they had attained a high spiritual position by this device did not abandon their practice. The Muslims were growing opposed to the Sultan for his soft attitude towards the offending Christians, with the result they were encouraged to revolt. The illiterate section of the Christians started reproaching their religious leaders who had declared the Christian martyrs offenders. In the wake of all this, the cordial relations between the Muslims and the Christians began to deteriorate.

Death of Abdur Rahman

Abdur Rahman II died in Rabia al-Thani 238 A.H. after ruling for thirty-one years and some months and his son succeeded him.

Assessment of Abdur Rahman's Rule

Although Sultan Abdur Rahman's reign was not free from fighting and disturbances he never neglected the welfare of his subjects and other progressive works including the arts and literature. Abdur Rahman was an erudite scholar, philosopher and well versed in the Islamic sciences. He added a number of new chambers to the Cordova Mosque and constructed many other mosques, bridges, forts, citadels, and new roads. He provided many other facilities for the spread of education and left no town and village without a madrasa (school). In every city and town, he built magnificent buildings for the Governors and Magistrates to run their administration and also constructed public bathrooms everywhere.

Sultan Abdur Rahman II was very fond of adornment and magnificence. He seldom appeared before the public but was very kind and merciful. He was not inclined to use harsh punishment and killing. During his tenure, the public treasury had become much richer. He brought more beautiful coins to the public and planted some fruit gardens on both sides of the river Guadalquivir (Wadi al Kabir near Cordova) and made them a public trust. He had books of Greek philosophy translated and set up academic councils. Locust swarms once ate up all the crops and failure of rain brought famine to vast areas of the country. The Sultan extended immense help to the masses and made it a practice to purchase large quantities of food with funds from the royal treasury to be kept in stock for such eventualities.

Heir Apparent

Sultan Abdur Rahman had a wife named Tarub whom he loved. She bore a son for the Sultan and had a desire that her son Abdullah be declared crown prince. But his son Muhammad was more deserving because of his intellectual and spiritual qualities. She had once attempted to his murder him. In order to carry out her plot against Muhammad she took a, *kha'ja sara*, eunuch, named Nasr into her confidence who contacted the court physician who was treating Muhammad. He was attracted by the lure of large profits to mix poison with Muhammad's medicine. The royal physician outwardly agreed but informed the Sultan of the secret planning. When the cup of poison was brought, the Sultan asked Nasr to drink it. He drank it and died on the spot. Thus, he fell in the ditch he had dug for Muhammad. A few days after Sultan Abdur Rahman passed away, Prince Muhammad came to the throne with the support of the Royal Guards. Land revenue during the period of Abdur Rahman I amounted to three hundred thousand dinars, which reached up to six hundred thousand dinars however, the total amount of revenue came to one million dinars during the reign of Abdur Rahman II. The total income was divided into three parts; one part was spent on the salaries of the armed forces, another on the salaries of the officials and courtiers and the third was deposited in the royal treasury to be spent on public welfare and construction works. Abdur Rahman II had added to his revenue by taxing the merchandise and this action of his turned the people against him.

It is said that the number of Abdur Rahman's children was more than a hundred. His people called him "al-Muzaffar" (the victorious). He was wheat-complexioned, long-bearded and a tall person with deep eyes. He colored his beard with henna. 45 of his sons were alive when he died.

During the rule of Abdur Rahman II Christians were appointed as heads of important posts. They generally spoke Arabic and could, therefore, manage administrative affairs well. Thus, the Muslims served as soldiers while official responsibilities were entrusted to the Christians.

Accession of Muhammad bin Abdur Rahman II

During the Rule of Sultan Abdur Rahman II the Christians had dominated administrative affairs. The Muslim Jurists observed these developments rather silently. However, they were annoyed at the growing power and mischief of the Christian officials.

Muhammad's First Step

Succeeding his father in Rabia al-Thani, 238 A.H. Sultan Muhammad began to appoint Muslims in charge of high posts and deposed those Governors and officials unworthy of running the administration well. This first action of Sultan Muhammad was highly appreciated by the Muslim religious scholars and spiritual leaders. During the same period, the Hambali School of thought entered into Spain through those Muslim spiritual leaders who had visited Syria and Arabia during the Hajj (pilgrimage). This started many religious debates and dialectics between the Hambali and Malki spiritual leaders of Cordova. The situation deteriorated to the extent that they were ready to take up arms against one another with the result that Sultan Muhammad bin Abdur Rahman II had to intervene in these disputes and decide the issue. In order to divert their attention from contentious issues, he launched a recruitment drive for *jihad* and a strong army was built and sent to campaign against the northern Christian States.

During this time, the ruler of Asturias or Castile State had seized some Muslim cities. Other Christian rulers were making advances in their own way. The newly built Muslim force was headed by Musa bin

Musa, a Goth who had converted to Islam. Other converts like him were appointed as commanders and governors. But this army achieved almost no success worth mentioning and returned empty-handed. However, the Sultan sent the same force to Barcelona for the Christians there had also overstepped their limit. Also, from there the force came back with very little booty.

Rebellions Curbed

In view of the dominance of the Muslim jurists in Cordova and the killing of the Christians as per the resolution passed by the Christians of the north, the people of Toledo began to make preparations against Muslim rule in 239 A.H. As an initial step, they arrested the Governor of Toledo and sent word to Cordova to send back those made hostages by Sultan Abdur Rahman II otherwise the Governor would be put to death and they would declare their sovereignty.

Sultan Muhammad accepted to their demand and sent the hostages back. However, the people of Toledo instead of adopting the right course according to their promise rose in open revolt considering this kind gesture as a weakness. They fortified Toledo strongly and sought help from the northern Christian States. Strangely, in spite of repeated revolts in Toledo no Muslim king ever thought of demolishing its forts and fortifications. The sole reason was the benevolence of the Muslim rulers, which held them back from such an action against the northern Frontier States.

Sultan Muhammad himself marched in 240 A.H. from Cordova to Toledo at the head of a strong force. Sultan Muhammad had not yet reached Toledo when the forces of Asturias State and warriors from the hills marched into Toledo to lend their help. Finding the conquest of Toledo an uphill task Sultan Muhammad hid a large part of his troops behind the hills, mounds and bushes and advanced with a small force. The people of Toledo seeing a small army mustered their courage to go ahead and attack the Muslim force. When the actual battle started, the Muslim force in large numbers rose from all sides and the Christians fled in fear and confusion but the Muslim troops surrounded and killed twenty thousand Christian forces, which destroyed the defenses of the people of Toledo. Sultan Muhammad occupied Toledo easily and established a small military presence therein.

The Christians of Toledo had suffered such a crushing defeat that they did not repeat their action against Muslim rule. However, they had now formed relations with the Northern Christian States. At this time, many Commanders of the Royal Force and Governors had secretly entered into correspondence with the rulers of Asturias, Gothic March, Galicia, and France they then hatched a conspiracy against their own ruler. They once again rose in revolt in 242 A.H. Sultan Muhammad invaded Toledo again and returned after punishing the rebels. However, they took up arms again under the leadership of a Christian chief. Sultan Muhammad had to go there yet again. At last, in 248 A.H. Sultan agreed to confer sovereignty on the people of Toledo after their submission to Muslim rule. They were given freedom to choose their own Governor who should send a fixed annual amount to Cordova. Toledo was left free to manage its own affairs. By acceding to this condition Sultan Muhammad showed not only his weakness but allowed the Christians to lay the foundation stone of Christian rule in Spain once again. He, in this way, dug a hole into the very foundation of Muslim rule in Spain, which led to its end. The people of Toledo wanted to appoint the son of Musa bin Musa as Governor. Sultan Muhammad gave it his approval. Following this Christians from the northern hilly States and warring Christians began to join the state of Toledo in large numbers and they started uprooting Muslims from there. The city of Toledo turned out to be another model based on the Asturias State. Musa bin Musa had, on the other hand, entered into a secret pact with the Christian States and this family of traitors played a fundamental role in weakening the Islamic rule although they were overtly considered a Muslim family.

The same year the Normans descended on the western coast of Spain and made inroads into the coastal areas but the ships of Sultan Muhammad captured fifty of their boats and they fled without inflicting much loss.

In Rajab, 251 A.H. Sultan Muhammad sent his son, Mundhir towards the north to Alva and Alcala to punish the insurgent Christians and he himself set out behind him towards Galicia. Father and son both were crowned with victory. But the insurgent Christians were fully aware of the war policy of the Muslim rulers. Facing an attack of a strong Muslim force, they escaped to the hills and then sought forgiveness and recaptured their lost territory on the return of the invading troops. This was repeated once again, as the Royal Force retreated to Cordova, the Christians made their advances. Prior to this, the Christian attacks were meant for plundering Muslim territories but now, in view of the inherent weakness of the Muslim rulers of recent times, they would appoint their Governors to manage the affairs of the occupied land and carry out expansionist activities. They were restless to descend on the eastern coast after capturing Barcelona and they kept occupying the western coast and brought the Portuguese territory under their control. Although Sultan Muhammad built a war fleet and dispatched it to attack Galicia, it was overtaken by a violent storm and returned after incurring heavy losses. Following this the very thought of a sea campaign was abandoned.

Insurgencies rose in a number of cities and every city with a large Christian population claimed sovereign rule. Sultan Muhammad never had total peace.

New Religion Invented

Abdur Rahman bin Marwan also took up arms against Sultan Muhammad. He had already revolted more than once but was still holding a high post in the area of Merida as a concession. Sultan Muhammad invaded the territory and after three months of encounters, Abdur Rahman bin Marwan, instead of leaving for Baghdad, invented a new faith in Spain. The new faith consisted of tenets of both Islam and Christianity. Many vagabond elements amongst the Muslims and the Christians joined it. Since the wind of willfulness and anarchy were blowing throughout the country, a large number of misguided people joined Abdur Rahman bin Marwan and in this way, a strong force came into being in the area of Galicia and Portugal under the leadership of Abdur Rahman. Sultan Muhammad sent a force headed by his Prime Minister, Hashim bin Abdul Aziz. Abdur Rahman deluded Hashim by running away in front of him and led the pursuing Muslims to a place where his force was lying in ambush, which surrounded them on all sides, and killed all the troops and captured Hashim. Abdur Rahman bin Marwan was already in correspondence with Alfonso, the ruler of Asturias. He sent Hashim to the Christian ruler to make a show of his strength and thus strengthening his friendly ties with him. Sultan Muhammad wrote Abdur Rahman bin Marwan to release Hashim. Abdur Rahman bin Marwan demanded a sum of one hundred thousand dinars. After corresponding for a few months Sultan Muhammad agreed to Abdur Rahman bin Marwan's rule over Badajoz (Arabic: Batalyaws) and its environs without paying any tribute and after receiving ransom for the release of Hashim. When Hashim came out of captivity, he found Abdur Rahman bin Marwan a strong and sovereign ruler. According to Ibn Khaldun Prime Minister Hashim was released in 265 A.H. after passing two and half years in prison.

In short, Abdur Rahman bin Marwan, an ordinary insurgent chieftain now considered himself a ruler equal in position to Sultan Muhammad. He also strengthened his friendly relations with the Asturias State. This event resulted in a series of revolts in almost every part of the country and the fear of the Umayyads rule went out of their minds.

Musa bin Dhun'nun, governor of Shant Briah revolted and invaded Toledo but was defeated. He attacked once again and the trial of strength continued. Asad bin Harth bin Badi'a raised his standard in revolt. Sultan Muhammad sent Prince Mundhir to take on Musa bin Dhun'nun. Mundhir conquered a number of cities and came back to Cordova. In short, Sultan Muhammad could not get even a day's respite from these engagements.

At this crucial period Umar bin Hafsun, a Christian from the Spanish peninsula organized a group of bandits in the southeastern hills. Making his fortress in a difficult hilly place as his center Umar bin Hafsun started his plundering and robbing activities. Governors of the nearby cities and towns invaded the area a number of times but suffered defeats. Finally, a strong army was sent from Cordova in 267 A.H. to punish him but he sent a petition seeking peace and promising normalcy in the area and the hilly fortress was left under his control.

In 268 A.H., Sultan Muhammad sent his son, Mundhir at the head of a huge army to punish the insurgent Christians of the northern parts. Prince Mundhir first went to Saragossa and put the insurgents in order and then marched to Alva and Alcala. He also restored peace in Lerida and returned after appointing Ismail bin Musa as the administrator there but with the return of Mundhir the ruler of Barcelona attacked Ismail but Ismail latter defeated him.

In 270 A.H., Umar bin Hafsun raised his head again and broke the peace of Malaga. Hashim bin Abdul Aziz, the Prime Minister of Cordova marched from Cordova to punish Umar bin Hafsun. After some initial encounters, Hashim contacted Umar bin Hafsun and tried to bring him to reason and made him agree to accompany him to Cordova. Prime ·Minister Hashim was very happy with the bravery of Umar bin Hafsun. He took the matter to Sultan Muhammad and had him appoint Umar bin Hafsun the Commander-in-chief of the Royal Force.

In 271 A.H., Prime Minister Hashim took Umar bin Hafsun and marched to the North at the head of a strong army. The people of Saragossa had once again raised their heads and Asturias was also threatening the peace. Umar bin Hafsun won much acclaim during these campaigns and both of them returned with a large amount of booty.

Umar bin Hafsun was not content with the leadership of Islamic forces since, in his present state, he could not hope to establish a Gothic state. He broke away from Hashim on the way back and went straight to his old fort. His old friends and supporters joined him there and Umar bin Hafsun proclaimed his sovereign rule in Malaga. Abdur Rahman bin Marwan, on the other hand, started plundering Seville and its suburbs. Sultan Muhammad sent his son Mundhir and Prime Minister, Hashim to Seville at the head of an army. Because of these attacks and the Sultan's being kept busy in other areas Umar bin Hafsun found time to strengthen his power. Seville and its suburbs remained under the shadow of strife and fighting for about two years. Finally, peace was bought from Abdur Rahman bin Marwan in 272 A.H. by giving away some more territories.

Following this Prince Mundhir was sent to Umar bin Hafsun. Umar bin Hafsun had now become more civilized and far-sighted. He had learned a lot from Cordova and Prime Minister Hashim and he was no longer a robber and bandit. He had now donned the mantle of a ruler. As his first step, he eradicated theft and robbery from the bounds of the territory under his control and took to punishing offenders and criminals very harshly. His people enjoyed perfect peace and safety and extended their support to their ruler.

Death of Sultan Muhammad

Sultan Muhammad had sent his crown prince Mundhir bin Muhammad to punish Umar bin Hafsun. During early encounters Umar bin Hafsun suffered setbacks and he was about to be arrested or killed for he was wounded and his troops had fallen in disorder. Umar was about to lay down his arms when Mundhir was shocked to hear the news of his father's death and he rushed to Cordova. Thus Umar bin Hafsun was saved from total disaster.

Sultan Muhammad was born in 207 A.H. and he died in 273 A.H., after ruling for 34 years and some months, his son succeeded him.

Assessment of Sultan Muhammad's Rule

The entire tenure of Sultan Muhammad was overtaken by conflict and disturbances and he did not enjoy peace even for a single day. The never-ending revolts and external threats and conspiracies kept him engaged and troubled all the time. During the rule of Sultan Muhammad, the Umayyads had lost much of their power and prestige and even ordinary men took up arms against the throne. The Christians reaped the most benefit from the weakness and disruption in the Muslim ranks. They had now started envisioning setting up their rule once again in Spain.

Sultan Muhammad was brave and prompt but internal disturbances and rebellions of Muslim commanders had sent the country into chaos and untold miseries. Christian countries and the Abbasid Caliphs were playing their roles in creating discord and disunity among the Muslims. Moreover, the Muslim jurists also contributed in dividing the Muslims on doctrinal lines. Prior to the situation during his rule, Christians in large numbers had come to the fold of Islam and despite the discouraging propaganda of the Christians of the Northern States, sensible sections of them felt attracted to the Islamic character and way of life.

However, during the period of Sultan Muhammad the religious spiritual leaders and jurists issued verdicts, which went against the legal Islamic rights of the Christians. Those Muslims converted to Islam also felt unsafe, with the result, that apostasy raised its head and many converts began to revert to Christianity. Nothing was more unfortunate than Muslim spiritual leaders and jurists causing a large group of new Muslims to be categorized as apostates, this proved very dangerous and that danger was right in the heart of Cordova. Due to the tight grip the Muslim spiritual leaders and jurists held over the proclamation of legal verdicts and the competition between rival groups of scholars, justice one of the outstanding attributes of Islam, suffered tremendously and the people reacted in kind.

During the last days of Sultan Muhammad different groups emerged with different purposes in view:

(1) Pure Arab race: they were disunited and had different groups like Syrians, Yemenites, Hijazi, and Hadramis (people from Hadramaut, southern Yemen) and they had in most cases accepted their superiority as a given fact.

(2) Mixed: those who were from Arab fathers and Christian mothers from Spain and Berber fathers and Spanish mothers.

(3) The new-Muslims: those who were Christians before their conversion to Islam. Their offspring were also called new-Muslims and they would follow Islam strictly.

(4) Pure Berbers: they were originally North Africans and were found in large numbers.

(5) The Magi: They were the progeny of those who were bought as slaves from various countries and were not large in number.

(6) Jews: They were old citizens of Spain. They were traders by profession and kept aloof from insurgent activities.

(7) Christians: They followed their faith freely and they were in large number.

(8) Apostates: They were those who had reverted to Christianity during the period of Sultan Muhammad. Along with them, there was a group that followed no faith and lived on plundering and robbery.

The first four Muslim groups were considered the real Islamic force. The ruler as well as the Muslim spiritual leaders and jurists should have given equal treatment to all but Sultan Muhammad made a grave mistake by treating the Mixed group as inferior, although they were larger in number. The emerging discord among the religious leaders and their doctrinal differences dampened the spirit of the new-Muslims. The Berbers too were affected. All this resulted in the loss of spirituality and the weakening of the morality of the Muslims of Spain as a whole. The spirit of *Jihad* was almost lost. The swords that were unsheathed in the way of Allah were now serving personal causes and self-interest. Special interest groups began to appear. The more the Sultan added to the power and influence of the Muslim jurists the more he lost the confidence of the people. This loss of confidence led the people to lose love for Islam and prefer a materialistic approach to life.

While Muslim rule was on the decline in every respect, the Christian States had expanded to equalize the Muslim State and were progressing rapidly. Alfonso, the ruler of Asturias was planning to drive away the Muslims from the bounds of Spain. Portuguese Christians were ready to establish their separate rule. Seville was under the rule of Ibn Marwan while Malaga was under the control of Ibn Hafsun. Toledo had expanded its territories up to the surroundings of Cordova, Galicia, and Aragon the state of Toledo had power from the Pyrenees to the western coast of Spain. In short, Sultan Mundhir had come to the throne at a very tumultuous time.

Accession of Mundhir bin Muhammad

Mundhir bin Muhammad was born in 229 A.H. He succeeded his father in Safar, 273 A.H. His entire life had been passed in fighting. He had served as Commander several times during the tenure of his father.

Deeds

Shortly after his accession to the throne he did away with Hashim bin Abdul Aziz, the Prime Minister of his father who was condemned to death by the religious leaders. Getting rid of Hashim, he attacked Umar bin Hafsun and went ahead conquering forts and driving off enemy troops. Ibn Hafsun sought peace and Mundhir accepted it. But Sultan

Mundhir was yet to arrive in his capital when he heard of Ibn Hafsun's revolt. He turned back right from there and surrounded the city. Ibn Hafsun begged pardon very humbly and agreed to accompany the Sultan to Cordova. Sultan Mundhir took him to the capital with honor.

Sultan Mundhir had decided to invade Toledo shortly after reaching Cordova and only would considered something else after conquering Toledo. He was wise enough to understand the importance of Toledo with respect to its situation while his predecessors had failed to recognize this fact. Toledo was situated in the middle of Spain and was strong enough to curb the territorial ambitions of the Northern Christian States. Although Sultan Mundhir had decided to utilize Umar bin Hafsun's abilities in some suitable job, Ibn Hafsun thought of the fate of Hashim bin Abdul Aziz and fled away by hiding from Mundhir's men. He once again went straight to his fort and took refuge therein and his people rejoined him.

Death of Sultan Mundhir

Sultan Mundhir turned back once again and besieged the fort. Umar bin Hafsun put up a strong fight with the result the siege dragged on. The fort was yet to be conquered when Sultan Mundhir died in 275 A.H. at the age of 46 years after ruling for less than two years. He had no male child so the nobles made the oath of allegiance to his brother Abdullah.

Accession of Abdullah

Abdullah recognized the rule of Umar bin Hafsun. He then took the funeral bier of his brother and moved towards Cordova. Arab commanders started criticizing him on the way and their condemnation rose to such an extent that all but less than a hundred soldiers deserted him by the time Abdullah stepped in Cordova with the body of Sultan Mundhir.

First Weakness of Abdullah

The first mistake committed by Sultan Abdullah bin Muhammad shortly after accession was that he immediately recognized Umar bin Hafsun as a ruler, although he could have won much support if he had conquered the fort.

Condition of the Umayyads during the Rule of Abdullah

At the time of the accession of Abdullah the condition of the Umayyad dynasty in Spain had touched a new low. The treasury was empty. The annual revenue, which had once gone up to one million dinars had now come down to one hundred thousand dinars annually. Apart from the Christian States Cordova had given birth to two strong rivals, which were equal to the central rule. On one side was Umar bin Hafsun and Ibn Marwan on the other. Ibn Hafsun was wiser and his style of governance had attracted a larger number of people and they liked to be governed by him. But since he was declared an apostate, many Muslims withdraw their support from him and turned towards his rival Ibn Marwan. Ibn Hafsun had no truck with the Christians despite his being labeled an apostate but Ibn Marwan, despite being a Muslim had friendly relations with Alfonso, the ruler of Asturias and others. Some Arab chiefs had their estates in the environs of Seville and had settled there. But in view of the turbulent situation, they rose in revolt and occupied Seville. The same types of feudal rulers seized Granada. Thus, two more power bases rose as Ibn Hafsun and Ibn Marwan's rivals. These four all took up arms against each other and Cordova had no power to punish any of them. He sometimes played the role of a peacemaker because each of them recognized Abdullah bin Muhammad as his king, although they were all independent in practice paying no tribute to the king. But since the Arab chiefs did not treat the new-Muslims well they in large number left to join Ibn Marwan.

During the same period, two Governors of the Northern cities inflicted a heavy setback on the Christian plans to end the Muslim occupation of Spain. Governor Lab bin Muhammad of Talsuna with a small band drove away the forces of the king of Asturias when he moved towards the south. Abdur Rahman bin Marwan on the other hand sent word to his friend, the king of Asturias that he would be the first man to take him on in case he overstepped his bounds. This warning silenced the Christians for sometime for they knew well that their invasions would help to bring the warring Muslim powers together.

Ibn Hafsun very cleverly corresponded with Aghlabid dynasty of Africa and requested to make the Abbasid Caliph issue him credentials for ruling Spain. Although Umar bin Hafsun failed in his attempt, Cordova was shocked to hear this news and it invaded Ibn Hafsun. Sultan Abdullah knew very well that any such credentials from the Abbasid Caliph would turn the people to him. Sultan Abdullah could not gather together more than fourteen thousand troops while Ibn Hafsun had thirty thousand soldiers under his command. When the rival forces came face-to-face, Sultan Abdullah displayed extraordinary valor, defeated and drove Ibn Hafsun and his troops back to hills. This victory brought some prestige to Cordova.

Abdullah's Action

During the same days Abdur Rahman bin Marwan made peace with Ibrahim bin Hajjaj the sovereign ruler of Seville and tried to strengthen his power. Sultan Abdullah thought it necessary to break the back of Ibn Marwan. He then sent his Prime Minister Ahmad bin Abi Ubaidah to take on Ibn Marwan who sought help from Seville. Ibrahim bin Hajjaj rose to help him but Ahmad bin Abi Ubaidah defeated the joint forces following which Ibrahim bin Hajjaj offered his allegiance to Abdullah who appointed him as the Governor of Seville. This victory added even more to the prestige and power of Cordova. Following this event Abdur Rahman bin Marwan died and his sons began to rule Toledo. But Ibrahim bin Hajjaj annexed some of their territories. On the return of the Sultan, Umar bin Hafsun came out of the hills and began to increase his power once again.

Alfonso the king of Asturias clashed with his brother and sought to renew his peace treaty with Sultan Abdullah who welcomed the offer. The Sultan made peace on the condition that both sides would honor each other's territorial integrity. This peace treaty was however, in favor of Alfonso for he now enjoyed peace and safety from the Muslims who claimed the territories under his rule.

The people had become fed up with all the frequent disorder and began to express themselves against rising in revolt or supporting the rebels. Thus, all the various rulers enjoyed peace for a time in their respective States. However, all of them would show due respect to Cordova.

Children

Sultan Abdullah had eleven sons and out of those Mutrif and Muhammad were mature enough to take part in the administrative affairs of the State. However, with the passage of time they felt enmity towards one another. Most of the able and sensible men had already shifted to Seville because scholars and intellectuals were held in esteem there. Cordova's treasury had run out. The emerging State of Seville under Ibrahim bin Hajjaj had become enviable even to Cordova. The low-spirited courtiers and nobles left no stone unturned to aggravate the enmity between the two brothers. Mutrif did a lot to poison his father's ears against his brother Muhammad and his supporters among the courtiers confirmed his allegations. Circumstantial compulsion made Muhammad escape from Cordova and join Umar bin Hafsun. Shortly thereafter, he felt his mistake and sent a message to his father that he was ready to return to Cordova provided he was given safety of life. Abdullah acceded to his request. Now Mutrif had an opportunity to turn his father against Muhammad even more than before, with the result Abdullah confined his son to a portion of his palace. Sultan Abdullah had to leave Cordova for a few days. He appointed Mutrif as the ruler of Cordova to look after the State affairs during his absence. Mutrif took advantage of the opportunity and had Muhammad assassinated. Abdullah was shocked at this event. He then began to raise Muhammad's son Abdur Rahman with much love and care. After sometime Mutrif assassinated the Prime Minister Abdul Malik bin Umayyah under some trumped up charges. Sultan Abdullah grew furious and had Mutrif killed in retaliation.

Death

Sultan Abdullah died on 1 Rabia al-Awwal 300 A.H. at the age of 42 years after ruling for 25 years. His whole period of rule was passed in dealing with riots, strikes and disturbances, which weakened his rule. Evidently, there was no hope of restoration of the past glory. His grandson Abdur Rahman succeeded sultan Abdullah.

Chapter 5
Abdur Rahman III

Accession

Abdur Rahman succeeded his grandfather Abdullah on 1 Rabi-al-Awwal 300 A.H. at the age of 21 years. The country that had been conquered by Tariq and Musa and the rule founded by Abdur Rahman al-Dakhil was torn into pieces and was on the verge of going to the Christian fold. But divine decree had decided to give some more time. The young Sultan had a number of uncles who claimed the throne by virtue of their age and rights. Either because of their noble sentiments or their being disinterested in ruling a rotten and wretched State they kept silent.

First Order

Shortly after succession the young Sultan issued orders that all sorts of taxes and duties levied on the people by his predecessors particularly Sultan Abdullah to fill the public treasury be curbed. And those against the Islamic code were abrogated. This proclamation produced a good effect and the Sultan was lavishly praised for this action.

Following this he proclaimed that those obeying the rule and promising firmness in their loyalty would get his past faults pardoned without any distinction of faith. Since the people had become fed up with anarchy and civil wars, strife and disorder almost all the rulers of the small States adjoining Cordova appeared before the Sultan to confess their loyalty to him. The public revenue rose to fill the treasury and mitigate the losses of the canceled taxes.

Two Rival Forces

Now only two mighty powers were left who could challenge Cordova and both were not far away. On one hand was Umar bin Hafsun, the ruler of Malaga, Rayyu and Bashter who wanted to destroy the rule of Cordova with the support of the Fatimids of North Africa and he would also receive help from the northern Christian rulers. The Christians liked him because of his reversion to Christianity. The Arabs on the other hand, ruled Seville and its power and grandeur had excelled the Court of Cordova. Abdur Rahman, first of all, turned to Seville and pressed it to confess loyalty to him. Many chiefs of Seville offered their allegiance to his central rule.

First Campaign

When Sultan Abdur Rahman III felt safe concerning Seville, he sent his freed slave Badr to Umar bin Hafsun at the head of a strong army. Badr started conquering Umar bin Hafsun forts one after another. After losing a large part of his plains, he took refuge in his hilly forts. Badr returned safe and sound and this victory attracted a large number of people to join Abdur Rahman's army.

Revolts Curbed

Sultan Abdur Rahman III invaded Seville to punish the disobedient Ibn Maslama. Ibn Maslama sought help from Umar bin Hafsun who promptly came to his aid. When the royal force advanced towards Seville, Umar bin Hafsun's force moved from the rear. However, Abdur Rahman beat it back and defeated Ibn Maslama too who was captured. Sultan Abdur Rahman III sent his own governor to Seville. He was able to do it without any difficulty because the relatives of Maslama and his courtiers also wanted Seville to be annexed by Cordova. One of the famous Commanders of Seville named Ishaq bin Muhammad came to Cordova and after judging his worth Sultan Abdur Rahman III, made him Prime Minister of Cordova and on his death the post was given to his son Ahmed bin Ishaq.

At this point, the greatness and glory of Cordova touched a new high and Sultan Abdur Rahman built his force to deal with Umar bin Hafsun. He invaded his territories in 304 A.H. Umar bin Hafsun sought help from the Fatimids but Sultan Abdur Rahman intercepted their warships with his own and didn't allow them to reach Ibn Hafsun. All the ships were captured at sea. Ibn Hafsun lost all hope and sent a petition to the Sultan seeking pardon and promising his submission and loyalty to Cordova in the future. The Sultan seized all his green and fertile lands and left Ibn Hafsun a small territory. Achieving peace and success, he returned to Cordova.

Following this, the Sultan sent a force under the command of Prime Minister Ishaq bin Muhammad to punish Murcia and Valencia. Ishaq brought the insurgents to order and invaded Carmona and removed its ruler Habib bin Suwarah and annexed it to Cordova. The same year the freed slave Badr invaded Lablah, captured the rebel chief Uthman bin Nasr and sent him to Cordova. In 306 A.H., he conquered the fort of Sambarah and forced the rebels to obey.

Conspiracy Against the Sultan

In 308 A.H. Muhammad bin Abdul Jabbar bin Sultan Muhammad in collaboration with Qadi bin Sultan Muhammad, hatched a plot to assassinate Sultan Abdur Rahman III and capture the throne. However, one of the plotters informed the Sultan of the situation. The Sultan, instead of taking any hasty steps, kept investigating the matter and killed both of them only after the charge was substantiated. Since their crime had become known, nobody raised any objection to their punishment.

Tarsawi Fort was conquered in 309 A.H. The same year Ahmad bin Adkhi Hamdani who had occupied Jama and was defiant offered allegiance on his own and sent his son to Cordova as a hostage. The other chiefs who had established their independent rule were one by one either made to obey or killed. The territory of Cordova expanded and the condition of the country considerably improved. Now the country that had been divided into scores of fragments rose again as a mighty Islamic state.

Details of the occupied Christian Territories

A hilly area adjoining the southeastern coast occupied by Ibn Hafsun had turned Christian. Ibn Hafsun's wide experience had made it a strong Christian State. However, it had made peace with the central rule of Cordova. Toledo was a strong and formidable city, which had become a sovereign state during the period of Sultan Abdullah. The state was situated in the middle of Spain. There were Christian States in Barcelona and Catalonia and Navarre also had a strong State adjoining Catalonia, which was ruled by the French. Asturias had risen as a very large State stretching into the plains of Spain having Galicia, Leon and Castile under its sway.

In addition to these, several small Christian States were established on the Portuguese coast on the Atlantic Ocean and were subordinate to Galicia. These conquered Christian territories fell within the bounds of Spain. Besides those mentioned, there were Christian states of southeastern France, western France and northern France, which were bent on opposing Spain. The only corner of Muslim rule stretching out towards the north was Saragossa, which was ruled over by a Muslim governor. He had friendly relations with the Christians and nobody objected to it for Sultan Abdullah and Alfonso III themselves had signed a peace treaty, which was violated by none.

Getting rid of all the rebels within a few years Sultan Abdur Rahman III invaded Toledo. Before the invasion, the Sultan sent word to the people of Toledo to obey him and join his camp. Toledo gave a bitter reply and started making military preparation of large proportions besides asking the Christians everywhere to rise up to save Toledo. Sultan Abdur Rahman marched on Toledo with the utmost care and caution. The Sultan conquered Toledo after a concerted effort, striving and fighting for about one year. He treated the conquered kindly and softly and returned to Cordova after putting the administrative affairs of Toledo right. Since the Fatimids of Northern Africa were torn by internal strife, they posed no danger to Cordova. Spain was now safe because Morocco also came under the occupation of Sultan Abdur Rahman III.

The Governor of Saragossa (Sarcat) revolts

Internal feuds of the Christian powers came to an end in 322 A.H. The Christians then had Muhammad bin Hisham as the Governor of Saragossa rise against the central rule and promised him all their help. Now the whole territory from Barcelona to Galicia rose up against Sultan Abdur Rahman III. The annexation of Morocco had infuriated the Christians and so they decided to break the back of Abdur Rahman by setting the Governor of Saragossa against the Muslim ruler.

Abdur Rahman turned to the north to chastise the Governor and found the Christians ready to take him on. He won a decisive victory and arrested Muhammad bin Hisham while the Christian forces fled to their respective territories. Abdur Rahman singled out each of them and made them the target of his attack and made each of them to submit. Sultan Abdur Rahman returned to Cordova after serving a warning to the Christians, punishing Muhammad bin Hisham thoroughly and appointing Umayyah bin Ishaq as the governor of Saragossa.

Battle of Trenches

In 327 A.H. a brother of Umayyah bin Ishaq was charged with hatching a plot and the Sultan put him to death. Umayyah bin Ishaq was shocked and distressed at this action. The Christian powers extended their sympathy to Umayyah and set him against the Sultan. The Christian king Ramiro was very clever and experienced. Umayyah revolted and shifted to Galicia with as much treasure and force as he could take away with him. Forces from other Christian States rushed to join him. This was in fact the greatest demonstration of Christian might in Spain, which was joined by a Muslim governor with all the power at his command. Besides, he gave some secret information and significant advice. The presence of Umayyah bin Ishaq was very encouraging. On hearing this new development, Sultan Abdur Rahman III declared *jihad* with the result that people in large numbers joined his camp.

The number of Muslim troops rose to fifty thousands. As the Muslim force advanced towards the north, the Christian troops concentrated in Simancas. The Christians fortified the city and made a trench in front of it along with having a huge army. Ramiro was the Commander-in-chief of the allied Christian forces and Umayyah bin Ishaq was his supporter and adviser. The Muslim army initiated the attack and the Christian troops came out to meet the challenge. The Christians were defeated in every engagement. A few days after the initial engagements, the Christian force was besieged in the fortifications of Simancas. The Muslim force advanced into the fortifications and they conquered three walls one after another. But as they crossed the last wall, the Christian troops snipped at the surrounded Muslim army and they could not move ahead or go back and they fell into the trenches only to die. Only 49 fighters were able to save their lives and Abdur Rahman III was the 50th person to remain alive. He was pulled out of the trench with much difficulty. Ramiro wanted to send a squadron in pursuit of the fifty men including Sultan Abdur Rahman III but Umayyah bin Ishaq advised against this risky step for the Muslim force might attack from an ambush. Abdur Rahman suffered an immense setback. Never since the first Muslims had set foot on the soil of Spain had the Muslims suffered such a heavy setback. The battle was known as the Battle of Trenches.

When Umayyah bin Ishaq at the end of the bloody battle witnessed the battlefield filled with the dead bodies of fifty thousand Muslims, he was shocked to the core and repented his mistake and his conscience reproved him for what he had done. He sent a petition to the Sultan seeking pardon for his fault and he deserted the Christians. Having returned to Cordova Sultan Abdur Rahman built a huge army and sent it to the Christian countries. It went on beating and defeating the Christian forces and deprived them of taking advantage of the Muslim setback of the Battle of Trenches. The Muslim force reached to the French territories and returned with a large amount of booty.

The Abbasid Caliphate suffers

The same year, 327 A.H., the Abbasid Caliph Muqtadir was assassinated and the Fatimids laid their claim to the caliphate. In view of the absence of any threat from the Abbasid caliphate and the Fatimids unpopularity among the Sunni Muslims, Sultan Abdur Rahman adopted the title of *Amir-Al-Mominin* (Commander of the Faithful) and chose for himself the appellation of *"Nasir-Ledinillah"* (The Victor for Allah's Religion). Nobody objected to this and, in fact, in the entire world of Islam he alone deserved to be called Caliph of the Muslims. Shortly after this, Abdur Rahman turned to constructing palatial buildings and beautifying Cordova. However, for the next eight to ten years he kept sending forces against the northern Christian States every year. The Christians were thus subdued to such an extent that they came to the Muslims for peace, safety and security.

The events mentioned so far bring to surface one glaring mistake of Caliph Abdur Rahman III that in spite of gaining full control over the situation he neglected the most necessary task of annihilating the northern Christian States for their insurrections. It was also, perhaps, because that in those days no one could think that the descendants of the Muslims of Spain would ever be so poor and weak and would not be able to withstand the Christian onslaughts of the future and they would get wiped out without leaving any trace behind.

Navy and Army Strengthened

From 328 A.H. starts by and large the period of peace for Abdur Rahman III and nothing was apparently able to threaten him. During this period the Muslim ruler paid his exclusive attention to the strengthening of his navy and army, he built warships and his fleet became the strongest of all time. The Caliph's supremacy on the Mediterranean Sea was recognized by everyone. He built a magnificent building adjoining his old royal palace and added to the beauty and adornment of the Cordova Mosque. Academic discussions were held and facilities given to traders who began to go to far off places with their commodities.

Worldwide Glory of Abdur Rahman

Very soon the fame of Caliph Abdur Rahman encircled the World. In 336 A.H., Constantine the king of Constantinople sent his emissaries to Cordova with precious gifts. In this way, he attempted to display his wealth and grandeur on one hand and win the friendship of Caliph

Abdur Rahman on the other. When Caliph Abdur Rahman came to know of the approaching emissaries, he issued orders to decorate the entire city of Cordova. His forces in glittering uniforms stood in two rows. And the emissaries were left in amazement at the work of golden embroidery on the curtains hanging along the doors and walls and the other kinds of decoration and began to look down upon the presents brought by them. Passing through the marble pillars and mosaic floors the emissaries entered the magnificent palace where Caliph Abdur Rahman III was sitting on his throne with his nobles, scholars, poets and commanders standing in order. The emissaries were astonished to witness such an exhibition and awesome scene. However, they recovered from their state of wonderment, made obeisance to the Caliph and handed over the letter from their king. In a sky blue cover with some thing written in gold letters was wrapped a small box with a heavy golden seal, on one side of the seal was engraved the image of Christ and that of Constantine on the other. There was a smaller crystal box within the small box with golden and silver floral designs engraved on it and inside of it was a beautiful silken envelope in which was a letter written in letters of gold on a sky blue thin skin. On the top, the Caliph Abdur Rahman was addressed with glorious appellations. The Caliph had the letter read out. Following that he suggested that Muhammad bin Abdul Barr should make an improvised speech for which he was famous. The jurist spoke a few words but the splendor and awe of the assembly overpowered his mind so much so that he fell down unconscious. He was followed by Abu Ali Ismail bin Qasim who rose to speak but could not say a word after glorifying Allah Almighty. He appeared overpowered by anxiety. Witnessing this an ordinary religious leader Mundhir bin Sayeed stood up and began to speak without any fear or hesitation. The speech was so pleasant, fervid and suitable to the occasion that it attracted loud applause. The Caliph became so pleased that he appointed Mundhir bin Sayeed Chief Justice of the caliphate. The court was then adjourned and the emissaries were treated as honored guests. After enjoying the royal hospitality for a few days, the ambassadors took leave accompanied by Hisham bin Hudhayl who was sent to the king of Constantinople by Caliph Abdur Rahman as his emissary. He was instructed to bring a friendly agreement from Constantine. Hisham did it successfully and came back to Cordova.

Following this, the envoys of Italy, Germany, France and Sicily came to the Caliph one after another to have good relations and friendship with Cordova. Every ruler of Europe vied with each other to win the support of Cordova to keep safe from their enemies.

Caliph Abdur Rahman made his son Hakam his heir apparent. Another son Abdullah was inclined to religious practices and was called "the pious". A Muslim jurist of Cordova tempted him to take the throne by assassinating the Caliph. Abdullah in collaboration with Abdul Bari, the jurist, hatched a plot to assassinate the Caliph and the crown prince. Many others were made to join the conspiracy. But the plot was unearthed on 10 Dhul Hijjah, 339 A.H. and both Abdur Rahman and Hakam were saved. Abdullah and the jurist Abdul Bari were put in jail. On the first day of their imprisonment, the Caliph executed his son Abdullah and Abdul Bari committed suicide in the prison.

On the death of Ramiro the king of Galicia in 334 A.H., his son Ordono succeeded him and sent his envoy to Cordova to seek permission for his accession. The Caliph acceded to his petition and granted him permission to rule in Galicia. In 345 A.H., Ferdinand the ruler of Castile sent a petition recommended by Ordono IV to the Caliph to grant permission for ruling and he was also given permission.

Sancho had occupied his ancestral State Leon and his maternal grandmother Tota was the ruler of Navarre State. Sancho became victim of fatness to such an extent that he was unable to even walk. Ferdinand and Ordono dislodged him from Leon. Sancho came to his grandmother in Navarre State where he also had a maternal uncle. However, his grandmother ruled the State because of her abilities and experience and played her role as the guardian of her son, Sancho's maternal uncle. Queen Tota sent precious presents to the Caliph and entreated his help for the restoration of Leon and Galicia, which was forcibly occupied by Ferdinand and Ordono and also to send a physician for treating fatness. The Caliph promptly responded to the entreaty and sent at once a physician to Navarre. However, the restoration of the lost State of Leon was put off to some other date. Sancho responded to the treatment and was cured and he regained his health and was able to be active again.

Three Petitioners in the Court of the Caliphate

In 447 A.H. Queen Tota decided to personally visit Cordova to persuade the Caliph to restore Leon. She left along with her son the King of Navarre and her maternal grandson, Sancho the King of Leon. These three Christian rulers set out from the French territories to appear before the Caliph. It was a very absorbing scene. People thronged the route they were traveling to have a glance at the passing royal party. On reaching Cordova, they were accorded a warm welcome. On entering the palace, they were subdued by the awe and grandeur of the Caliph and his court. The Caliph was so deeply moved by their visit that he sent with his guests some troops to restore Leon and Galicia back to Sancho, which they did. Ordono fled to Castile to be with Ferdinand. In view of the consequences of what happened to Ordono, the King of Barcelona and the chief of Tarragona sent their envoys to Cordova to confess that they were but the slaves of Cordova. They considered their ability to rule as an endowment from the caliphate and they were ready to fulfill all the conditions of their rule with a deep sense of obedience and loyalty. The Caliph granted them permission to rule in their respective territories.

Patronizing of Scholars

Caliph Abdur Rahman III made it a point to call those who excelled in every walk of life to his court with the result that scholars and men of skill from Baghdad, Constantinople, Cairo, Damascus, Madinah, Makkah, Yemen, Iran, and Khorasan joined the court of Cordova. They all belonged to different faiths and nationalities.

Construction Works

Caliph Abdur Rahman III occupies the same position in Spain, that Shah Jahan enjoyed among the Mughal kings of India. Even though the construction work of the Mosque of Cordova was started by Abdur Rahman I and was completed by his son Hisham, every succeeding ruler added to the beauty and grandeur of the mosque. Caliph Abdur Rahman III also spent in the millions on it. The length of the mosque from the east to the west was five hundred feet while its arches were based on one thousand four hundred marble pillars. Close to the main arch lays a high pulpit of pure ivory and of thirty six thousand wooden pieces of different colors and designs and studded with jewels of all kinds. The pulpit had taken seven years to be completed. Caliph Abdur Rahman III had a new minaret erected for the mosque eight hundred feet high after removing the old ones and the new minaret had one hundred and seven ascending and descending steps. The mosque contained ten thousand big and small chandeliers for providing light out of which three of the biggest all were made of pure silver and the rest were of brass. The big chandeliers each had one thousand four hundred eighty lighted cups. Three hundred employees maintained the mosque.

Caliph Abdur Rahman III built for his Christian wife Zahra a magnificent palace at the foot of *Jabal-al-Urus* four miles away from Cordova. The building was so broad-based that it came to be called *Madinat-al-Zahra* (Zahra city) instead of *Qasral-Zahra* (Zahra palace). The expanse of the palace can be understood from the fact that its walls had fifteen thousand high steel doors. The palace was four miles long and three miles wide. The foundation stone of the palace was laid in 325 A.H. and it was completed in 350 A.H. Ten thousand masons and architects and four thousand camels and donkeys were brought to serve daily during the construction period. The palace had four thousand three hundred and sixteen towers and was supported by thousands of pillars made of marble and other precious stone. Some of the pillars were presented to Caliph Abdur Rahman III by the kings of Constantinople and France. Marble in large quantity was brought from Africa by royal engineers like Abdullah Hasan bin Muhammad and Ali bin J'afar. The biggest golden fountain had a very beautiful floral pattern and embellishment brought by Ahmad the Greek and the priest Rabi'a from Constantinople. A fountain of green stone was brought from Syria. It was filled with twelve birds and animals having faces of gold and jewels. From the mouth and beak of every animal and bird would shoot out fresh water and the workmen displayed such skill and handicraft in the construction of the fountain that it left all those who viewed in wonder.

(*Qasr al-Khulafa'a*) Palace of the Caliphs was a part of this palace and was an amazing sight. Its roof was made of pure gold and transparent marble that one could look at like a mirror. A beautiful and jewel studded fountain was installed in the middle and upon its head was set the famous pearl presented to Abdur Rahman III by the king of Greece. Besides the fountain, a fountain-like tray was kept in the middle filled with mercury. The palace had around it very beautiful mirrors framed in ivory. Jewel studded doors of different kinds of woods were set in marble and crystal. When the doors were opened the house would be illuminated with the sun's rays, they were so bright that you could not look directly into them. The mercury would be set in motion in such a way that it looked as if the entire palace was moving and those unaware of its secret would experience fearfully the sensation that the palace was moving.

Thirteen thousand seven hundred and fifty servants and thirteen thousand three hundred eighty two Christian slaves were employed to serve and maintain this palace. Six thousand women served in the harem and twelve thousand loaves of bread in addition to other food were dropped in the reservoir just to feed the fish. "Zahra City" was such a unique palace that travelers from far off places and distant lands would visit this wonderful building to see the expanse of marble palaces within a palace, the splendor of the royal court, the orchards and beautiful settings where thousands of fountains, lakes and reservoirs flowed. The Arabs had turned the palace into the exhibition of their skills, construction work and handicraft. Unfortunately, when the Christians occupied Cordova, they razed Zahra palace to the ground, pulled down its mosques, demolished the tombs and even dug up its graves.

Piety

Chief Justice Mundhir bin Sayeed has been referred to above. An event related about him is worth mentioning. Caliph Abdur Rahman III wanted to buy a house in Cordova. The house belonged to some orphan children who were entrusted to Justice Mundhir. When he was asked to sell the house to the Caliph, he refused point-blank to do so and sent word to the Caliph that the house could not be sold unless three conditions were fulfilled:

1. In case of dire need.

2. If destruction of property is feared.

3. If the property brings profit to the orphans.

But at present none of the three conditions are being fulfilled for the price offered by the royal officials was too little. The Caliph kept silent. Justice Mundhir feared that the Caliph might take the house and so he had the house pulled down. Afterwards, the official bought the land at double the price. When the Caliph came to know of this, he sent for the Justice and inquired about the reason for demolishing the house. He replied that when he had ordered demolition of the house he was thinking about the Quranic verse: So they both proceeded, until, when they embarked the ship, he (Khidr) scuttled it. Musa (Moses) said: "Have you scuttled it in order to drown its people? Verily, you have committed a thing *Imr* (a *Munkar* — evil, bad, dreadful thing)." (Q. 18:71)

Hearing this the Caliph kept silent and from that day, he began to show more respect for Justice Mundhir. This event brings to light the sense of piety of both the Caliph and the Chief Justice. The Justice died in 355 A.H. five years after the Caliph. The Caliph Abdur Rahman III died on Ramdan 2, 350 AH. at the age of seventy-two and some months at the Zahra palace.

Land Revenue

During the tenure of this Caliph twenty five million four hundred and eighty thousand dinars came to the royal treasury as land revenue while seven hundred and sixty-five thousand dinars were received through other sources. The whole income was spent on public welfare. The amount received by way of tribute and poll-tax collected from the Christians and the Jews was deposited with the main royal treasury out of which one-third was fixed as expenses for the Sultan and the rest was spent on construction of buildings, bridges, and roads.

Death of the Caliph

Following the death of the Caliph some memoirs were found in his papers where he had penned the account of some days during the fifty years of his life as a ruler when he had free time, they totaled only fourteen days. He left eleven sons at the time of his death Hakam bin Abdur Rahman was the crown prince.

Assessment of Abdur Rahman's Rule

The period of Caliph Abdur Rahman III was the golden period of Islamic rule in Spain. The country enjoyed complete peace and trading activity was at its peak. The people of Spain had set up trade centers in far off places of Africa and Asia. The naval force was matchless and all the seas were practically ruled by the Caliph's navy. The Caliph never let his commanders and officials share royal powers and looked after all important administrative affairs himself. He gradually limited the powers of the Arab commanders and jurists and enhanced the powers and position of his sincere supporters and sympathizers. He built a squad of security guards from his personal slaves. Nothing remained out of his sight and he kept his eyes on everything big or small.

The most significant performance of the Caliph was the annihilation of feuds and group conflicts. Every party and group enjoyed the rights they deserved and none of them were hostile to the central rule. This was the secret of his success as a ruler and it is because of this that the entire world looked upon the Spanish Muslims with respect.

During the tenure of this Caliph, the non-Muslims, Christians and Jews, were treated very kindly and gently. The Christians living within the territorial bounds of Caliph Abdur Rahman III loved him no less than the Muslims.

He reminded the narrow-minded and rigid Muslim spiritual leaders of the kind treatment the Prophet of Islam (ﷺ) would give to the non-Muslims and he forced them to be aware of and put into practice the true spirit of the Qur'an and the Hadith. The Caliph succeeded in his mission.

The Caliph was not lacking in waging *jihad* and fighting against the enemies of Islam. His military actions were remarkable. In the fields of public welfare, social reforms, building construction and development of agriculture and economic progress and promotion of arts and literature he was unique.

During his period, not only Cordova but all of Spain had become a model of paradise. Not a piece of land was left uncultivated and there was an abundance of beautiful gardens, which turned the country into a bed of flowers. No city or town or village was lacking in beautiful and towering buildings. The Spain, which was the seat of anarchy and disorder turned into a center of peace and prosperity with his advent to the throne. The palatial buildings of Cordova and other cities far exceeded the splendor of Baghdad and Damascus. In comparison to Spain, all of Europe looked like a desert without a trace of culture or manners. The revenue of all the European kings put together did not equal that of Caliph Abdur Rahman III. The number of his registered troops reached one hundred and fifty thousand but the might of his paramilitary force was unknown. The personal security force of the Caliph consisted of eight thousand horsemen and four thousand infantry.

There was a network of roads and highways throughout the Spanish peninsula. Police posts were set up at short distances from each other to give protection to the wayfarers and a large number of police were deployed on patrol duty. Messengers would deliver the mail using a postal service based on a system of fast running horses. News from one place to another reached with amazing speed. Numerous towers were built to keep a watch over enemy activities. Construction of these buildings used large amounts of money from the royal treasury because they were constructed for the public welfare and safety. Such construction also provided jobs for both the skilled and unskilled laborers. As a result, the territories under Muslim occupation had the largest number of palaces, forts and bridges. Official houses were provided for the sick and destitute and they were taken care of by official expenditure. The entire country had orphanages where the orphans were brought up and educated and the Caliph personally bore their expenses.

The population of Cordova had reached one million during Caliph Abdur Rahman's rule. Neat and clean roads and streets, beautiful houses of marble, admirable drainage systems were some of the distinctive marks of his remarkable administrative acumen. He had set up a special department, which worked day and night, for keeping the city clean. Attractive and graceful gardens dotted the city and the countryside. The city had approximately one hundred and thirteen thousand houses excluding palaces and citadels of the Caliph, Ministers and Nobles. Besides, the city had eighty thousand and four hundred shops, seven hundred mosques, nine hundred public baths and four thousand and three basement warehouses for preserving merchandise and commercial commodities. Cordova had men, garments and coins of from all countries. The city was twenty-four miles long and six miles wide and stretched along the banks of Guadalquivir (Wadi al Kabir). The main city was strongly fortified and covered an area of fourteen square miles. If anyone covered ten miles in a straight direction passing through the bazaars, he would find his path completely lighted by glittering lamps. No one could draw a parallel between Cordova and any other city on the earth. No other city had handwritten books and manuscripts in such large numbers, as Cordova possessed. Fresh mountain water entered the city through pipes, which covered a distance of two and half miles. A network of water pipes spread throughout the city. Every madrasa, mosque and inn had a separate set of pipes at their gate. Seven big gates of the city were kept locked. The city was divided into five parts within the fortifications each of them had their own separate fortification. Among those five parts, one was the royal palace. It had its own citadel where the caretakers of the royal administration lived. Not only in Cordova but all over Spain there were no beggars asking for alms. Sultan Abdur Rahman III had shifted to Zahra city during the last days of his rule. This city near Cordova had assumed a separate position and left Cordova behind in beauty and grandeur. Spain then abounded in fruits of all kinds, which were very cheap in the markets.

A large number of schools and colleges were running in the capital. Poetic symposia, intellectual gatherings and academic discussions were held in many places. These gatherings were patronized and attended by the princes, nobles and the Caliph himself. The presence of astronomers, physicians, philosophers, jurists, scholars of Hadith and commentators of the Qur'an enlightened Cordova. Boarding and lodging expenses of all the pupils were paid for from the royal treasury. During the last days of his life, Caliph Abdur Rahman III had entrusted a greater part of the administration to the crown prince and began to devote most of his time to prayers.

Caliph Abdur Rahman III finally departed from Spain at a time when bordering Christian rulers had after the struggle and failure of a hundred years come to serve and obey the Islamic rule of Spain, even those Christian rulers who were far off from Cordova tried hard to win the pleasure of the Caliph. Abdur Rahman III passed away at a time when Morocco, the Mediterranean Sea and all other oceans were ruled by the royal fleet and the country was internally peaceful and safe.

Accession of Hakam bin Abdur Rahman III

The third day after the demise of his father Caliph Hakam came to the throne of Spain at Zahra Palace on 5 Ramadan 350 A.H. at the age of forty eight years. Ministers, Commanders, Nobles and the pillars of the administration appeared before the new Caliph to offer their allegiance. They took the oath of allegiance after the Chief Justice and other judges followed by the Caliph's brothers and princes. The servants and slaves took the oath last of all. The accession of Hakam was celebrated with great pomp and show. Hakam adopted the appellation of (*Mustansir Billah*) "The one who is victorious by Allah."

A Review of the Administration

Caliph Hakam took a review of all the administrative departments minutely. He visited the office of each minister, examined military registers and made himself aware of the number of soldiers serving the royal forces. He tried to gain knowledge about everything in his administrative organization although he was already aware of what was going on. Following this, he issued letters confirming every official and thus established his prestige as a shrewd and timely ruler.

Revolts of Bordering Christian States

Caliph Hakam was extremely fond of reading books and acquiring knowledge since his childhood. When he ascended the throne of Spain, he was already mature and wise. Even great scholars and spiritual leaders felt embarrassed when speaking before him. No country perhaps has ever had on its throne such a learned and erudite king. Since his love of learning and scholarly attitude had gained fame far and wide before he came to the throne, the Christian rulers thought that he would not be able to be a brave commander and so they began one by one to rise up in revolt against him.

The king of Castile began to make inroads into the bordering Islamic cities. Hakam led his forces against Castile and delivered a smashing defeat to the Christians and took the battle deep into Galicia.

But the audacious Castilians forgot the punishment and rose up again. Caliph Hakam sent his freed slave Ghalib at the head of the royal forces and directed him to chastise them harshly. Ghalib found the enemy forces much larger than his own however, he launched a fierce attack relying on Allah Almighty. The Christian forces were defeated and driven away and Ghalib came back after ravaging a greater part of Castile and pulling down their citadels.

Shortly after this event news about a revolt by Sancho and the Christian forces from Leon, Navarre and Castile concentrated their efforts to help him. Caliph Hakam directed Yala bin Muhammad, the ruler of Saragossa to punish the rebels. He took on the allied Christian forces all alone and defeated all of them and appeared before the Caliph with the captured booty. Yala bin Muhammad was still in Cordova when news about Barcelona's rebellion and also of war preparations by Castile reached Cordova. Caliph Hakam sent Ghalib to Barcelona and deputed Hudhayl bin Hashim to punish Castile. The Christians suffered a heavy setback and they had to confess their allegiance once again.

When Caliph Hakam gave his enemies a number of defeats during the very first phase of his rule that they all felt dejected and lost hope. They understood that Caliph Hakam II was not lacking in courage and determination. Frontier Christians showed open defiance but Yala bin Muhammad and Qasim bin Mutrif put them in order. The same year the Normans invaded the western coast of the Spanish peninsula and plundered the city of Lisbon. The Caliph ordered his Navy Commander Abdur Rahman to block the pirates and he himself marched at the head of an army against them. But the citizens of the city had driven away the pirates from the land and sea before the Caliph and the Navy Commander appeared on the scene.

Awe-Struck Christian Rulers

Ordono the cousin of Sancho and son-in-law of Ferdinand, the ruler of Castile was the ruler of Leon. When Caliph Abdur Rahman III restored Leon to Sancho, Ordono had gone to Ferdinand. Now Ordono along with twenty men from Galicia reached Salamanca city in 355 A.H. on the way to Cordova. But Ghalib, the caretaker of the northern borders stopped him because he was visiting Cordova without permission of the Caliph. Ordono, the former ruler of Leon argued that he considered himself an ordinary slave of the Caliph and was, therefore, going to appear before his master and needed no permission. However, Ghalib held him in Salamanca and informed the Caliph about Ordono. The Caliph granted him permission and sent a commander to welcome him to Cordova.

On entering Cordova, Ordono went to the tomb of Caliph Abdur Rahman III, got down from his horse, kept praying for a long time and moved ahead after offering his prostration to the departed Caliph. The Caliph allowed him to appear in the court in a white garment, which was considered a sign of honor among the Umayyads. Abdullah bin Qasim, the bishop of Toledo and Waleed bin Khairun, the magistrate of the Christians of Cordova had accompanied him. Appearing before the Caliph, Ordono was astonished and awe-stricken by the splendor and magnificence of the court and took off his cap in a state of bewilderment. However, his Companions escorted him towards the throne and he fell down in prostration before facing the Caliph. He then raised his head and moved ahead on his knees and lay prostrate once again. He reached the spot fixed for him lying in prostration repeatedly. At last, he sat in the chair put for him. Even though he made several attempts to utter something, he failed to be able to speak. The Caliph in view of his state of bewilderment kept silent for sometime and gave him time to collect himself. At last the Caliph broke his silence and said:

> "O Ordono, I am happy to see you here. My royal favor will do the needful for you."

Having heard this remark from the Caliph, Ordono rose in a fit of joy and then fell down in prostration once again. He could say only this much "O my master, I am an ordinary slave of yours". Thereupon the Caliph said "I reckon you among the well-wishers of my rule and grant your petition. Do submit it if you have any desire". Hearing this Ordono fell down in prostration once again and lay in this state a little longer and then raised his head and submitted with all the humility at his command: "Sancho is my cousin. He appeared before the former Caliph in this very place. He had none to help him. His subjects were unhappy with him. The late Caliph granted his petition and made him king. I did not go against the order of the Caliph and left the country although the subjects were happy with me. I have now appeared with my heartfelt passion and a sense of respect for you and entreat you to grant my rights and restore my lost rule". Having heard this the Caliph said, "I understand your object. If your right to the throne is more than that of Sancho, you will be restored to your country. Hearing this Ordono fell down in prostration yet again. The Caliph adjourned the court and ordered an escort for Ordono to the guesthouse. On the way to the guesthouse, he saw a throne, which was used by the Caliph sometimes. Ordono bowed down before the vacant throne as if the Caliph was sitting upon it. Following this, the Prime Minister J'afar offered him a costly royal garment on behalf of the Caliph. After a few days, the Caliph sent Ordono back in the company of his commanders to have him seated on the throne. Shortly after that, Sancho and the heads of Zamora and Galicia sent petitions to the Caliph with costly presents to confess their loyalty. The rulers of Barcelona and Tarragona also followed suit.

Following this, the rulers of France, Italy and other Christian States started sending their emissaries to express their loyalty. The Christian ruler of western Galicia who had then grown powerful sent his mother to the Caliph to seek credentials for the rule of her son. The Caliph treated her honorably and conferred on her what she sought.

Revolt of the Moroccan Rule

The Idrisid ruler of Morocco deputed by the Caliph rose in revolt in 361 A.H. The Caliph sent Yala bin Umayyah to Morocco. On hearing of the invasion, the Moroccan ruler sought help from Muizz Ubaidi, of the Fatimid Dynasty, and he offered his allegiance to him. The fight between the two forces was fierce and Yala bin Muhammad was killed in action and the campaign suffered a setback.

Cordova was shocked to hear of this setback. The Caliph sent Ghalib to Morocco. With the arrival of Ghalib Hasan, the ruler of Morocco advanced to take him on. After a number of encounters, Ghalib forced Hasan to shut himself in a citadel and then he surrender. The ruler of Morocco was then arrested and sent to Cordova. The Caliph treated him honorably and kept him as a guest with a daily allowance. After a short stay, he was sent to Alexandria as per his desire. Ghalib stayed in Morocco and fortified the administration and returned to Cordova in 363 A.H. with a large number of prisoners of war. He was accorded a warm royal welcome.

Crown Prince

The Caliph appointed his son Hisham as crown prince in 365 A.H. and took from the nobles, ministers and courtiers their oath of allegiance for him.

Death

Caliph Hakam II died of paralysis in Cordova on Safar 2, 366 A.H. at the age of sixty-four years after ruling for sixteen years. His son Hisham was then 11. He came to the throne the next day. Muhammad bin Abi Amir was made his Prime Minister as per the proposal of Caliph Hakam II.

Assessment of Caliph Hakam's Rule

Caliph Hakam II of Spain was reckoned among the most eminent scholars. Had there been more engagements and campaigns, he would have established himself as a commander of the first rank. His forces quickly put down the few encounters and disturbances that did occur.

He passed the greater part of his time in academic engagements. His Prime Minister J'afar was equal to the Prime Minister of Caliph Harun

Ar-Rashid in ability and fame, J'afar Barmaki. Moreover, the Caliph had spared much of his time by increasingly entrusting important administrative affairs to his Prime Minister. During this period, religious fanaticism was absent and every person enjoyed complete freedom and the court of Cordova was free from narrow mindedness and low ideals. He was very particular about maintaining justice with the result that all his subjects were happy with him.

The Caliph observed Quranic injunctions strictly and made the Muslims keep to them. Prior to his administration, a section of the Muslim Spaniards had indulged in drinking but he had put a complete ban on making, selling and the using of wine. He spent a large amount daily on giving alms. Every city had schools and colleges. Students from foreign lands were treated as royal guests for the period they would be studying and acquiring knowledge. The Caliph appointed his brother Mundhir as the Head of the Education department.

Hakam's Love of Learning

Caliph Hakam II was well versed in all the sciences. His agents kept moving in Damascus, Baghdad, Constantinople, Cairo, Makkah, Madinah, Kufa, and Basra and at places of learning and literature would purchase any or every good book for the Caliph that became known. Authors were persuaded to send their books to the Caliph and he encouraged scholars to come to Cordova and they were elevated to a high position and a place of abundant wealth. In every city, copyists were appointed to copy books for the Caliph. The Caliph had friendly relations with almost all the kings and rulers of the world and they had given facilities to Hakam's copyists and translators to provide rare books to him in any form.

The Caliph of Cordova gained fame far and wide as a great patron of the arts and learning. Even writers in Baghdad and Basra dedicated their books to the Caliph and sent them to him. Hundreds of scholars were deputed to translate books of Greek and Hebrew. The Caliph had created such an academic atmosphere all over the country that every house had a private library.

Not only Cordova but also every big city had a government library. Anyone who had a desire to be honored by the Caliph came to him with a rare and useful book.

Personal Library of Hakam

The personal library of Caliph Hakam was in no way inferior to the royal palace in grandeur and magnificence. The building was made of marble with marble grounds and mosaic work of marble and black stone. Bookshelves were made of Sandalwood, ebony and other precious wood. Every bookshelf had written in golden letters the subjects of the books. The royal library had thousands of bookbinders and calligraphers. The numbers of books were more than six hundred thousands.

Catalogue of the Library

The catalogue of the library books consisted of forty-four volumes. The catalogue had simply the names of the books and their authors. There was in the library hardly any book, which hadn't been gone through by the Caliph. Almost every book had marginal notes from the Caliph and the first page of each book had the names of the book and the author and the genealogy of the author in his handwriting. He had an extraordinary power of memory. He was a critic of the first rank and could write prose and poetry of all kinds with amazing ease.

Hakam's Books

The Caliph was particularly very fond of history. He had himself penned the history of Spain but it was destroyed with the passage of time. Cordova had become the center of arts and learning during his tenure.

Honoring Scholars and Accomplished Persons

Abu Ali Qali of Baghdad had come to Spain during the period of Abdur Rahman III. Sultan Hakam never allowed him to leave his company. Abu Bakr al-Arzaq, a renowned spiritual leader belonged to the family of Salmah bin Abdul Malik bin Marwan. He had reached Cordova in

349 A.H. and died in Cordova in 385 A.H. at the age of 58 years and was buried in Cordova. Caliph Hakam showed him great respect. Ismail bin Abdur Rahman bin Ali belonging to the family of Ibn Zam'a had come to Spain from Cairo and joined the circle of scholars. Thaqr al-Baghdadi and Qayas bin Amr were famous calligraphers and were held in esteem by the Caliph. Hakam had once sent one thousand Dinar each to Abul Farh Asfahani and Abu Bakr Maliki. Muhammad bin Mafraj was an accomplished scholar of Fiqh and Hadith. Ibn Mughith, Ahmad bin Abdul Malik, Ibn Hisham Al-qawi, Yusuf bin Harun, Abul Waleed Yunus and Ahmad bin Sayeed Hamdani were eminent poets. On the order of Caliph Hakam, Muhammad bin Yusuf Durrani wrote the history of Africa along with its geography. Isa bin Muhammad, Abu Umar Ahmad bin Faraj, Yaeesh bin Sayeed were famous historians and scholars in the court of Caliph Hakam.

Favoring Scholars

An episode regarding Caliph Hakam's fondness of knowledge is worth mentioning. One day a fakih named Abu Ibrahim was delivering a sermon in the Abu Uthman Mosque. A royal mace-bearer came and asked the fakih (Jurist) to accompany him to the Caliph without loss of time and he was waiting outside. The fakih told him to tell the Caliph that he was engaged in a divine task and could not, therefore, go to him. The mace-bearer was astonished to get such an answer and conveyed to the Caliph the reply from the fakih with the utmost sense of fear. The Caliph asked the mace bearer to go and tell the fakih that he became happy to hear the reply and wanted him to visit the court only when his divine duty was over and until then he would be waiting for him in the court. Abu Ibrahim asked the mace-bearer to tell the Caliph that his old age allowed him neither to go riding nor on foot through the far off gate called Saddah Gate. However, if the nearby Sana Gate was opened for him he could make his entry into the court. That gate was usually kept closed and was opened only on special occasions. Abu Ibrahim resumed his sermon while the mace-bearer returned to him with the Caliph's answer, the mace-bearer politely sat through the sermon. When the sermon was over, the mace-bearer told him that Sana Gate was opened for him and the Caliph was awaiting his arrival. When Abu Ibrahim arrived at the gate, he found the ministers and nobles there to accord him welcome. He went into the court, talked to the Caliph and came back honorably through the same gate.

Distinctive Characteristics of Hakam's Rule

Hakam II may rightly be called the greatest Caliph of Spain. It is because during his period there was peace and order throughout and power, wealth, agricultural and commercial development was at its peak. But the progress of arts and learning had left everything else behind. During Hakam's tenure, the sun of learning had reached its meridian, even the Caliphs Harun, Mamun, or Mansur did not share this exclusive achievement. Caliph Hakam was fortunate enough to preside over a glittering assembly of scholars kings, and those powers patronizing the arts and learning. However, in spite of his amazing wisdom and learning he was overpowered with love for his son whom he appointed as his successor although he was only eleven years old at the time of his demise. One would have expected of Hakam II alone to have done away with the practice of hereditary rule but, unfortunately, he too could not break the malaise.

Caliph Hakam's brother Mughira would have been a better successor with his abilities to run the administration. But appointing his son, a minor as his crown prince and depriving Mughira of the throne, Hakam II gave the throne to the last Muslim Caliph of Spain. Although the Umayyad dynasty dragged on for sometime after the demise of Hakam II, it virtually came to an end with the end of his life.

Hisham II bin Hakam II and Mansur Muhammad bin Abi Aamir

At the time of Caliph Hakam II's demise in 366 A.H. and the accession of his son Hisham II, the following persons held powerful positions in the Islamic Caliphate of Spain.

1. J'afar bin Uthman Mustafi, the Prime Minister. He held the post from the period of Caliph Hakam II. He was able, learned and respectable.

2. Queen Sabah, the Christian wife of Hakam and the mother of Hisham. She had much influence in the administration and was deeply loved by the Caliph.

3. Ghalib, the Commander-in-Chief of the Spanish forces. He was the freed slave of Hakam II and commanded the love of the troops and the citizens alike.

4. Muhammad bin Abi Aamir bin Muhammad bin Abdullah bin Aamir bin Muhammad Waleed bin Yazid bin Abdul Malik Ma'afri. His ancestor Abdul Malik Ma'afri had come to Spain in the company of Tariq bin Zeyad, the Conqueror of Spain.

5. Fa'iq, the (*khawaja sara*) eunuch and Commanding officer of the guards of the royal palace and inspector of the wardrobe.

6. Jodhar, the (*khawaja sara*)eunuch and caretaker of all the bazaars of Cordova. These two eunuchs were so powerful that even distinguished nobles feared them and tried to earn their pleasure.

Consultations among the Leaders of the Court

Fa'iq and Jodhar were present when Caliph Hakam passed away. On the death of the Caliph, both of them were unanimous that the accession of prince Hisham was not safe and therefore Hakam's brother Mughira should be put on the throne for he alone could bear the burden of the caliphate. Jodhar was of the opinion that Prime Minister J'afar Mustafi should be assassinated so that the accession of Mughira might not be obstructed. But Fa'iq was in favor of taking Prime Minister J'afar Mustafi into confidence and if he differed with their opinion he would be put to death. J'afar was called in. When the news of Hakam's death was broken, he was informed of their point of view. The Prime Minister understood their intentions and promised to act according to their opinion. However, he pleaded for the participation of some other important persons as well. In this way, he deluded them and came out safely. Shortly after that, he called the leaders of the caliphate and informed them of the demise of the Caliph and the opinion of Fa'iq and Jodhar. He further advised to kill both Mughira and Hisham to put an end to all the controversies. All those present supported the decision but none of them rose to assassinate a boy of such a tender age. Finally, Muhammad bin Abi Aamir stood up and went to the house of Mughira who was sleeping unaware of the death of his brother Hakam. When he woke up and heard of the demise of his brother, he grew very sad and expressed his intention to offer his allegiance to his nephew Hisham. When Muhammad bin Abi Aamir informed J'afar Mustafi of the loyalty of Mughira for Hisham, he suggested imprisonment for Mughira instead of assassination. J'afar threatened that he would send some other person to carry out his order if he (Abi Aamir) was unable to do the job. Having heard this Muhammad bin Abi Aamir assassinated Mughira.

Accession

Hisham was then put on the throne. Fa'iq and Jodhar failed in their mission. They rose to create a stir among the people and drew their attention to the assassination of Mughira and a feeling of dissatisfaction overtook the country. Because of this, Christian tributaries of the northern frontiers attacked the Islamic areas furiously. In such a turbulent situation, Prime Minister J'afar did not prove his worth and embarrassed himself.

Muhammad bin Aamir as Adviser

At last, at the instance of Queen Sabah, Muhammad bin Abi Aamir was made to share the administrative responsibilities with J'afar. In a few days Muhammad bin Abi Aamir prevailed over the administration and took over power from J'afar.

Muhammad bin Abi Aamir's life

Muhammad bin Abi Aamir was born at Tarkash in Spain in 357 A.H. where his family was living. His ancestor Abdul Malik M'afari was a Yemenite soldier and most of his children received a military education. Muhammad bin Abi Aamir was still in his mother's womb when his father died in Tripoli on the return journey after performing Hajj. The young Muhammad bin Abi Aamir came to Cordova and joined a government madrasa. After completing his education, he adopted the profession of letter and petition writing in a rented shop adjoining the royal Palace. This was his only source of income. By chance, Queen

Sabah, the mother of Hisham needed a clerk to write down the accounts of her own property. A certain eunuch mentioned the name of Muhammad bin Abi Aamir and he was called to join the task. His skill and the recommendation of the Queen led him to be appointed as the collecting officer of Seville. Since he remained far away from Cordova, he approached the Queen to recommend his name to Caliph Hakam to have him appointed in Cordova. He was then appointed as manager of the mint. Muhammad bin Abi Aamir preformed well in this high office. He also kept Queen Sabah happy with presents and drew sympathy from the Prime Minister and other nobles as well. In short, he earned so much confidence that Caliph Hakam made him the instructor of his son Hisham before his death.

Deeds of Muhammad bin Abi Amir

When Hisham came to the throne after the death of Caliph Hakam and the assassination of Mughira the entire administration came under the control of Prime Minister J'afar Mustafi. Ghalib was apparently considered a rival to J'afar. Queen Sabah was very deeply involved in the affairs of State. Everyone respected her and she was more sympathetic to Muhammad bin Abi Aamir. Muhammad bin Abi Aamir, first of all, broke the back of the eunuchs by persuading J'afar and Ghalib to take action against them. Fa'iq was exiled to Mallorca and he died there an unknown. Jodhar was forced to resign and their group was destroyed. It was in this situation that news came that the Christians of the North had refused to pay tribute and invaded the Muslim's territory. Prime Minister J'afar sent Muhammad bin Abi Aamir at the head of an army to punish the Christians. He gave a series of defeats to the Christians and returned safely. This victory enhanced the prestige of Muhammad bin Abi Aamir. The people of Cordova accorded him a warm welcome and his influence was strengthened. He joined hands with Ghalib and had Mustafi deposed and disgraced by putting him into prison where he died.

Since Ghalib was popular throughout the military, it was not easy to challenge him. Muhammad bin Abi Aamir launched a recruiting drive and admitted Christians of the northern hill areas and the Berbers from Morocco and Tripoli. Ibn Abi Aamir was now the unchallenged Prime Minister of Spain. However, he showed great respect for Ghalib and married his daughter. He was not in danger of losing anything to Ghalib. Since Muhammad bin Abi Aamir was a very ambitious person, he did not want to share power with anybody else. As a matter of planning, he removed a part of the old army and the rest were deployed to unimportant fronts to disintegrate the organized power of the forces. He then gradually increased the number of forces and made new rules and regulations. In this way, he very cleverly weakened the position of Ghalib. Following this he also removed Ghalib from his way without any protest. Ibn Abi Aamir and Ghalib once exchanged hot words, which developed into an armed clash, with the result Ibn Abi Aamir received a minor wound and Ghalib fled to the Christian king Leon. On getting rid of his rivals, he put an end to the power of Queen Sabah and interned Hisham II in a part of the palace.

Hisham could not go out of the palace but he was provided with all the pleasures and luxuries of life. Nobody was permitted to see Hisham. Ibn Aamir then turned to his forces and won their love and support by giving them unparalleled facilities.

Jihad against the Christians

He then waged *Jihad* (holy war) against the Christian States, annexed some of them while some others were punished so harshly that his name sent them into a state of terror. The matter became so serious that some Christian rulers and commanders joined his force and played an active role in ravaging the Christian States and started to pull down churches on their own. However, Abi Aamir stopped them from desecrating the churches and destroying them. He then turned to Africa and expanded the Spanish territories there. He waged *Jihad* fifty six times and won every battle. During the last days, he adopted the appellation "Mansur" and came to be known as Mansur the Great.

Death

While returning from the last *Jihad* in Castile in 394 A.H., he died in Salamanca after ruling for twenty-seven years.

Assessment of Muhammad bin Abi Aamir's Rule

Mansur the Great preferred to be called the Prime Minister of Spain even though he acted as a sovereign ruler in all the affairs of the country. He built a palace at a distance of few miles from the Cordova palace, which was like a citadel. He carried all his offices and treasures to this stronghold. Addresses were delivered in the name of Hisham along with Muhammad bin Abi Aamir. Nobles and the leaders of the caliphate showed him the same respect as they did to the Umayyad Caliphs.

Ibn Abi Aamir's presence was a blessing to Spain and the Muslim rule in Spain. He made Leon and the principalities around it a part of the Cordova caliphate. He succeeded in making Barcelona, Castile and Navarre tributaries of Cordova. Once an emissary of Ibn Aamir visited a Christian State whose leader was called Garcia. Garcia accorded him a warm welcome and led him on a tour of his whole country. During the tour, the emissary found out that a Muslim lady was being kept prisoner by some monks. On his return while relating to the Caliph the condition of the State visited by him, he referred to the woman in confinement. Mansur the Great led an army against that state immediately. When he reached near Garcia's territory, Garcia came out submissively and begged to know whether he had committed any wrong. Mansur told him that in spite of his promise that his state would not keep any Muslim prisoner a Muslim woman was in confinement in a certain church. Garcia released the woman at once and pulled down the Church.

Mansur the Great marched to Coria city on 24 Jamad al-Awwal 387 A.H. and after conquering it entered into Galicia. The Christian Commanders rushed to seek employment. He took with him those newly employed Christian Commanders and marched along the coastal areas punishing the audacious elements and demolishing their citadels and conquered some small islands in the Atlantic Ocean. After conquering the coastal cities of France and demolishing the buildings functioning as the centers of conspiracies he came back to Cordova. This was his forty eigthth Jihad.

Showing Regard to Learning

Mansur the Great was very fond of learning like his predecessor Caliph Hakam II. He was himself a scholar and held scholars in esteem. His childhood class fellows grew jealous of his glory and grandeur. They hatched a plot against their Caliph and charged him with being inclined to philosophy and atheism. But Mansur denied the allegation by convening a meeting of the religious scholars. He built a number of bridges, extended Cordova mosque and added to the welfare and prosperity of his subjects. He led his forces where no Muslim ruler had ever reached. His name sent terror into the hearts of the Christians more than anybody else's did. He rose to the pinnacle of power and glory. He commands a place of highest distinction among the most respectable and ambitious men in history. When he died in 394 A.H., the Umayyad dynasty was taking its last breath due to the ineptitude of Caliph Hisham II but its glory had touched a new high.

When the news of Mansur's demise reached Cordova, the well wishers and supporters of the Umayyads grew happy to think that Caliph Hisham II, virtually a pawn, would now be able to take his place as the sovereign ruler. Some of them called on Hisham to give him the "good news" of Mansur's death but Hisham was shocked and frustrated. When Mansur's elder son Abdul Malik came to Cordova to bury his father, Hisham called him and made him Prime Minister of the Muslim State and conferred on him the title of "Muzaffar", the victorious. Muzaffar followed in the footstep of his father and died in 399 A.H. after ruling for six years. Muzaffar invaded the Christian countries eight times and every time he came back victorious. The arts and learning flourished during his period and the power and awe the rule established during the tenure of his father was not diminished in the least.

On the death of Muzaffar his brother Abdur Rahman bin Mansur also known as Abdur Rahman Sanchuelo, became the Prime Minister and adopted "Nasir" as his appellation. Even though both Muzaffar and his father Mansur were the real sovereign rulers of Spain, they liked to simply be called the Prime Minister of the state. However, in view of the wide support for Nasir in the court, with the commanders and the friends of his father, he proclaimed his sovereignty and began to show slackness in paying his respect to the Caliph.

Following this Nasir forced Hisham to proclaim him as the successor of the caliphate. Thus, Hisham put his signature on a paper prepared by Nasir who circulated it among the Governors of all Muslim provinces. The royal proclamation described Nasir as a man from a respectable family commanding qualities of mind and spirit. The proclamation was made in the Grand Mosque of Cordova as well. Although Nasir was very happy with this development in his favor, this elevation in his position as the successor of the Caliph proved fatal for him.

Hisham's Deposition

In the very first year of his tenure Nasir, following the practices of his predecessors, led his forces against the frontier Christians. The Quraish and the Umayyad felt aggrieved at the transfer of power from the Umayyads to another family. Due to this, they secretly began to arouse the people in support of the Umayyads. When Nasir was fighting on the northern frontier along with his forces, they killed his military officers in Cordova. They installed Muhammad bin Hisham bin Abdul Jabbar bin Caliph Abdur Rahman III, the great grandson of Caliph Abdur Rahman III with the title of "Mahdi Billah". Installing Mahdi, they deposed Caliph Hisham II. Nasir marched to Cordova but as he came near to it most of his Commanders and Berber soldiers deserted him and joined the camp of the Caliph Mahdi. When Nasir was left with a very small number of troops, one of his companions put him to death. His head was sent to Caliph Mahdi. Thus, the rule of Bani Aamir ended and Spain fell prey to anarchy.

Mahdi bin Hisham bin Abdul Jabbar

In view of the desire of the people Hisham II undertook his deposition in writing for the second time. Muhammad bin Hisham addressed as Mahdi interned him in a part of the palace, brought to the throne his cousin Muhammad bin Mughira and appointed another cousin Umayyah bin al-Haaf as the police chief of Cordova. Following this he sent his forces towards the city of Mansur the Great and his palace. The citizens opened the gates of the city without any resistance. Caliph Mahdi's forces razed the palace and the other buildings to the ground. This event took place in 399 or 400 A.H. Following the event of Nasir's assassination and the end of the rule of Ibn Abi Amir's dynasty and as the fourth Islamic century and three centuries of Islamic rule in Spain approached its end the doors of anarchy opened.

Military Rule

The Berber troops had played a major role in the deposition of Caliph Hisham II and the installation of Caliph Mahdi. They were involved with the Quraish and the Umayyads in the process of the change of power and they dominated the scene in the administrative affairs of Caliph Mahdi. The reins of actual power came to the military, which began to perpetrate a reign of terror on the people. Finally, the people lodged a complaint to the Caliph. However, the Caliph paid no heed to their grievances for fear of the displeasure of the military. Thus, even those who played an active role in bringing Mahdi to power turned hostile against him and began to find ways and means of getting rid of his passive rule. Being fed up with the atrocities of the Berbers the people killed a few of them and Caliph Mahdi killed the killers in retaliation. The situation became worse, with the different factions looking for any Umayyad prince to be the figurehead of their faction to lend authenticity to their claims.

The Plot against Mahdi

Caliph Mahdi was devoted to breaking the back of the Berber's power. However, they got wind of the secret planning of the Caliph against them and as a counter measure, they set prince Hisham bin Sulaiman bin Abdur Rahman III against Mahdi by tempting to give him the throne if he helped in deposing the Caliph. When the plot was unearthed, Caliph Mahdi arrested Hisham bin Sulaiman and his brother Abu Bakr and killed them in order to curb the trouble.

Flight from Death of Sulaiman bin Hakam

On hearing the news of the assassination of these two relatives one Umayyad prince Sulaiman bin Hakam fled Cordova for safety. The

Berbers were looking outside Cordova to find a person to replace the present Caliph. When Sulaiman bin Hakam approached, they grew very happy. They lost no time in proclaiming him as the Caliph under the title "Musta'in Billah" and persuaded him to launch an attack on Cordova. Sulaiman bin Hakam counseled against any hasty steps and pleaded in favor of increasing their military strength. With this plan in mind Sulaiman, bin Hakam, known as Musta'in went to Toledo and appointed Ahmad bin Naseeb as his Prime Minister.

Civil War

Musta'in took troops from Toledo and marched to Salamanca. Mahdi sent his slave Qaisar at the head of a squadron of horsemen to help Wadah Aamiri, a commander of the northern provinces and the freed slave of Mansur bin Abi Aamiri. Qaisar was killed during the fight and Wadah closed himself inside the fort.

Sulaiman & Mahdi both seek Help from the Christian King

In view of failing to win the battle and the shortage of provisions Musta'in wrote the Christian king Ibn Alfonso to supply food and forces so that he could conquer Cordova and take the Caliphate. On hearing this news, Mahdi also sought help from the Christian king with the promise of handing over all the frontier forts and cities to him. However, the Christian king preferred Musta'in and sent him one thousand oxen, fifteen thousand goats and other necessary provisions accompanied by Christian forces. Now Musta'in marched to Cordova instead of fighting with Wadah. Wadah also marched behind Musta'in but he committed a blunder by attacking Musta'in's force. In the wake of a bloody battle, Mahdi's army was defeated losing twenty thousand of his men. He fled to Toledo with the rest of his troops while Musta'in entered Cordova victoriously. Since the victory was won with the military support of the Christians, they were warmly welcomed although a large number of Muslim scholars and intellectuals were killed by these savage Christian troops. Caliph Mahdi once again wrote to the Christian king from Toledo and sought his military help. This was an excellent opportunity to set Muslim against Muslim and weaken their power and unity. Mahdi attacked

Cordova with the help of some Christian troops. After a bloody battle, Musta'in was defeated while Mahdi entered Cordova victoriously and regained his throne. The Christian forces, which had been with Musta'in, joined the camp of Mahdi. This battle took a heavy toll on the Muslims. Musta'in left Cordova and stormed through the rest of the country. The Christian troops on the other hand let loose a reign of terror against the Muslims of Cordova, while Mahdi fell into a life of pleasure and luxury. Thus Spain, which had been enjoying peace and order, became a center of looting, arson and anarchy.

Deposition of Mahdi

Wadah Aamiri was an ally of Mahdi but when he noticed the country was in jeopardy he indulged in extensive consultation with the influential persons of Cordova about the deposition of Mahdi and the restoration of the throne to Caliph Hisham II. They had Mahdi assassinated by a slave in the open court and Hisham II was taken out of prison and put on the throne once again.

Peace with the Christian King

Wadah Aamiri, the freed slave of Mansur bin Abi Aamiri, became the Prime Minister. Wadah sent the head of Mahdi to Musta'in and wrote to him that Caliph Hisham had come to the throne once again and it was proper for him to offer his allegiance to the Caliph. But Musta'in rejected the message with contempt and Musta'in invaded Cordova with the help of the Christian king Alfonso. Cordova was surrounded after the adjoining areas were ravaged.

Being fed up with the long siege and in order to bring about a separation between the Christian king and Musta'in, Hisham II gave away two hundred citadels and a few big cities adjoining the Christian kingdom. He signed a peace treaty with the Christian king who broke his relations with Musta'in. But Musta'in continued the siege with the result that the stress of the trial of strength began to show on both sides. Sometimes the citizens of Cordova would drive away the Berbers and at times, the Berbers would make progress into the city. The Christian powers took advantage of this disturbing situation and took away a number of States from Cordova.

End of Hisham

At last Musta'in occupied Cordova in Shawal in 403 A.H. Hisham II
was either killed or had disappeared without leaving any trace
behind. Wadah Aamiri had already been killed a few days prior.
Musta'in thus came to the throne of Cordova.

Musta'in Billah

Musta'in was now the Caliph of Cordova. But various provinces had
become independent of the central rule of Cordova. Ibn Ubad began
to rule in Seville, Ibn Aftas in Badajoz, Ibn Abi Aamir in Valencia and
Murcia, Ibn Hud in Saragossa and Mujahid Aamiri in Denia and
Alzira. The northern Christian states took full advantage of the
turbulent situation. Every Christian State annexed the territories
adjoining it. The era of anarchy took hold of the Islamic caliphate,
which was torn into pieces.

Assassination of Musta'in

Musta'in ruled Cordova and its suburbs till Muharram, 407 A.H. and
after ruling nominally for a period of three years and a few months
Musta'in was arrested and killed shortly after being defeated on a
battleground adjoining Seville. This led to the end of the Umayyad rule.

End of the Umayyad Rule

Although the rule of the Umayyad dynasty had come to an end in 407
A.H. with the assassination of Musta'in some of the Umayyads tried
to regain power and in some cases gained nominal success, by 408
A.H. the end was complete. Ali bin Humud came to the throne in 407
A.H. after killing Musta'in. He and his brother ruled Cordova until
413 A.H. Ibn Jumud's rule ended in 413 A.H. and Abdur Rahman bin
Hisham bin Abdul Jabbar, the brother of Mahdi came to the throne in
Ramadan 414 A.H. with the support of the people of Cordova. He
adopted the title of "Mustahzhir". Within two months Muhammad
bin Abdur Rahman bin Ubaidullah bin Abdur Rahman won the
throne of Cordova and began to rule with "Mustakfi" as his title.

Yahya bin Ali bin Humud attacked Cordova in 416 A.H. and Ali bin Humud fled to the North and died there. Yahya bin Ali bin Humud continued to rule in Cordova until 417 A.H. But Prime Minister Abu Muhammad Jamhur bin Muhammad bin Jamhur took the oath of allegiance from Hisham bin Muhammad the Umayyad in his absence. Hisham bin Muhammad was with Ibn Hud in Lerida. Having heard of the allegiance to him, he shifted to Bidant. He stayed there for three years and adopted the title "Mutamid Billah'. When the nobles clashed with one another, Hisham bin Muhammad was brought to Cordova and they installed him as their ruler. But the troops rose against him in 422 A.H. and deposed Hisham bin Muhammad. Hisham came to Lerida and died in 428 A.H. with the end of Hisham bin Muhammad ended even the nominal caliphate.

Assessment of the Umayyads

Abdur Rahman I had laid the foundation of his rule in Spain in 138 A.H. This rule lasted for two hundred ninety years and met its end in 428 A.H. with the death of Hisham bin Muhammad. Among the progeny of Abdur Rahman I there were a few ambitious and adventurous rulers who made Spain the pride of all countries. They not only made the country advanced and prosperous but developed arts and learning to such an amazing extent that the whole world praises them even to this day. Europe owes most of its progress in the realm of arts and learning to Muslim Spain. The Spanish Caliph had burnt the candle of learning that enlightened all of Europe. The might and grandeur of the Muslim rulers of Spain had made them a terror to the Europeans who would go down to any level to win the pleasure of the Muslim Caliphs. The sole reason behind the annihilation of the Muslim rule in Spain was the rulers making a distance between themselves and the Islamic Code and the sublime teachings and character of the Prophet (ﷺ). Islam was totally against the concept of dynastic rule. However, the Muslims later made the transfer of the rule to be hereditary, as was the practice before Islam. The Prophet (ﷺ) had done away with this practice but the Muslims later embraced this evil practice with the result inept and unworthy persons came to power. A negligent way of following the injunctions of the Qur'an and the Code of Islam resulted in disunity in Muslim ranks and constant infighting, which strengthened the powers hostile to the Muslims.

Chapter 6

Bani Hamud's (Hammudid's) Rule

The Idrisid dynasty referred to above was founded in Morocco during the caliphate of Harun Rashid Abbasi and it had already become extinct. Two full brothers, Ali and Qasim, accompanied the Berbers who had come to Spain from Morocco during the period of Ibn Abi Aamir. These two were the sons of Hamud bin Maimun bin Ahmad bin Ali bin Ubaidullah bin Umar bin Idris. Ali and Qasim were descendents of the founder of the Idrisid dynasty and they joined the services of Ibn Ali Aamir's forces. They fought valiantly against the Christians and Ibn Abi Aamir was very happy to appoint them as officers in the army. As high-ranking officers of the Berber regiment, they enjoyed support and satisfaction of the soldiers particularly because their dynasty in Morocco had been very influential. These two brothers played a pivotal role in uprooting Ibn Abi Aamir's rule and made Musta'in the Umayyad Caliph of Spain. On coming to the throne in Cordova Musta'in appointed Ali bin Hamud the Governor of Tangiers and other provinces.

Ali bin Hamud

Since various provinces had been proclaiming their independent rule
during the short tenure of Musta'in, Ali bin Hamud also declared
himself a sovereign ruler of Tangiers. He later forged an alliance with
Khairan, the Governor of Almeria and sent a force to Spain. He
deputed his son Yahya in Tangiers and he marched to Cordova and
spread the rumor that he had come to avenge the blood of Caliph
Hisham II. Musta'in fought Ali bin Hamud on the battlefield of
Malaga. In Muharram, 407 A.H. Musta'in suffered a smashing defeat.
Ali marched ahead and captured Cordova, killed Musta'in and sat on
the throne with the title "*Nasir-Li-Dinillah*'. Since Ali bin Hamud
enjoyed the support of the Berbers, he had no opposition. The earlier
part of Ali bin Hamud's rule was graceful for he tended to keep justice
but later he turned his people against himself. He started levying tax
after tax on the people with the result that both the military and the
civilians turned against him. In view of this development, Khairan the
Governor of Almeria recognized Abdur Rahman bin Muhammad as
the king of Spain.

Assassination of Ali bin Hamud

Ali bin Hamud had some Saqlabi among his special slaves. These
slaves were supported by Khairan who was from the Saqlabi
(former slaves) and they killed Ali bin Hamud in the bathroom in
408 A.H.

Qasim bin Hamud

The people generally rejoiced at the assassination of Ali bin Hamud.
In spite of this, the Berbers called Qasim bin Hamud the brother of Ali
bin Hamud to Cordova from Algeciras and put him on the throne.
However, the Berber regiment was in favor of Yahya the son of Ali.
Khairan Saqlabi on the other hand toured the country along with
Abdur Rahman bin Muhammad and the people started favoring
Abdur Rahman but a few days later the Governor of Granada, a
Berber Commander killed Abdur Rahman bin Muhammad on the
battlefield.

Yahya bin Ali, the Governor of Malaga, had a brother named Idris bin Ali bin Hamud. After winning the support of his brother, he entered the territory of Spain by ship and staked his claim to the throne in opposition to his uncle. Khairan Saqlabi joined Yahya even though Idris, the brother of Yahya brought to his attention the mischievous nature of Khairan but Yahya ignored it saying that he could benefit from his help at the time. Yahya marched on Cordova with his army and Qasim fled from there and took refuge in Seville with Qadi Ibn Ubad.

Yahya bin Ali bin Hamud

Qasim fled from Cordova on 1 Jamad al-Awwal 410 A.H. and Yahya bin Ali sat on the throne unopposed with "Mut'ali" as title. Yahya made himself to be the ruler of Spain after coming on the throne of Cordova although nobody recognized him as the ruler outside of Cordova because everyone else had already declared their own sovereignty. The negligence and stupidity of Yahya led the people to rise up against him and many commanders of the Cordova forces went to Seville to persuade them to invade Cordova. Upon being aware of these developments, Yahya grew so afraid that he fled to Malaga.

Qasim Re-Enthroned

With this news Qasim came to Cordova in 413 A.H. and began to rule it. Yahya began to rule in Malaga. But his brother wrested power from him and he (Yahya) shifted to Tangiers. Thus Cordova came to be ruled by Qasim, Malaga by Idris and Tangiers by Yahya bin Ali.

Massacre of the Umayyad

The Berber chiefs grew displeased with Qasim before long. The people of Cordova on the other hand began to think of an Umayyad prince they could put on the throne. But Qasim started killing and arresting the Umayyads without discrimination. The people raised their voice against these atrocities. Qasim used the Berber force to put down the insurgence of the citizens. The citizens rose up as one man and drove away Qasim and his troops by defeating them openly. The Berber troops conceded defeat and fled to Malaga while Qasim went to

Seville. Qasim had made his son the Governor of Seville and appointed Muhammad bin Ziri and Muhammad bin Ubad as his advisers. When they heard of Qasim's return after his setback they shut the doors of Seville and decided to fight him. Qasim stayed outside the city and sent word to the chiefs to send his son out so that they could leave for anywhere else. They sent out his son and his other relatives. Qasim took his relatives along with his Negro slave and took refuge in Sarish Fort but Yahya bin Ali conquered the Sarish Fort in 415 A.H. and put Qasim in prison. In 427 A.H., Qasim was killed by the order of Yahya.

Abdur Rahman bin Hisham

When Qasim left for Seville after his defeat, Cordova remained without a ruler. During this period, three princes staked their claim to the throne. The people of Cordova elected Abdur Rahman bin Hisham to the throne with "Mustazhir" as his title. On coming to the throne, he set Abu Imran, a Berber free against the will of his ministers and appointed him as his Commander. But a plot hatched by Abu Imran led to Mustazhir's assassination on 3 Dhul Qada 414 A.H.

Muhammad bin Abdur Rahman bin Abdullah Mustakfi

Muhammad bin Abdur Rahman bin Abdullah sat on the throne with "Mustakfi" as his title. Yahya bin Ali bin Hamud who had already arrested his uncle, Abul Qasim and conquered Sarish, Malaga and Algeciras marched on Cordova. Mustakfi grew so terrified that he fled to the northern borders and died there on 25 Rabia al-Awwal 416 A.H. Yahya entrusted Cordova to an officer named Ibn Ataf and left to Malaga and started military preparations to conquer Seville. Shortly after that, the people of Cordova drove away Ibn Ataf and his troops from Cordova.

Among the people of Cordova was one very influential person named Abu Muhammad Jamhur bin Muhammad. Advised by this person the people of Cordova accepted Hisham bin Muhammad staying at Lerida as their Caliph. He was not able to arrive in Cordova for three years. However, he came to Cordova in 420 A.H. and ascended the throne with "Mutamid Billah" as his title. Two years after the people and troops of Cordova deposed and drove him away in 422 A.H. and he went back to Lerida and lived there until 428 A.H. Yahya bin Ali surrounded Seville and kept Cordova under threat. On the departure of Hisham from Cordova, the people declared their allegiance to Yahya. Yahya made Seville obey him in 426 A.H. Thus, Yahya bin Ali became one of the stronger leaders in this state of anarchy. Abu Qasim bin Ubad, the ruler of Seville died the same year. His son Mu'tazid succeeded him. Seville took up arms once again and Yahya bin Ali attacked Seville but was killed. This event took place in 427 A.H. With the killing of Yahya bin Ali, his supporters shifted to Malaga the center of his power. Idris bin Ali ascended the throne with the title "Mu'taid Billah." Abu Muhammad Jamhur set up a democratic rule and the members of the Council elected him as its president and Cordova came back to peace and order. Idris bin Ali formed an alliance with the Governors of Carmona and Almeria and invaded Seville. This campaign covered a period of three or four years during which Idris bin Ali passed away in 431 A.H. Some of the Commanders made an attempt to bring his son Yahya bin Idris to the throne of Malaga while others accepted the claim of Husain bin Yahya, the governor of Ceuta. Finally, the latter came from Ceuta and ascended the throne under the title "Mustansir". But Husain's cousin the daughter of Idris poisoned him to death. From that time, Malaga was ruled by the slaves and servants of their family.

Idris bin Yahya Hamudi

At last Idris bin Yahya bin Ali bin Hamud occupied the throne of Malaga in 443 A.H. Granada and Carmona States offered their allegiance to him. Idris bin Yahya adopted "Aali" as his title and entrusted Ceuta's rule to his father's slaves Sukut and Zarqullah. Muhammad bin Ali bin Hamud revolted in 448 A.H. and Idris bin Yahya suffered a defeat and fled to Carmona. Muhammad bin Idris ascended the throne in Malaga under the title of "Mahdi" and appointed his brother "Sanai" his successor. Muhammad bin Idris died in 449 A.H. and with his death, Idris bin Yahya ascended the throne again. He died in 450 A.H.

Muhammad Asghar-the Last King of Hamud Dynasty

After this Muhammad Asghar bin Idris bin Ali bin Hamud sat on the throne of Malaga. Baris bin Habus, the king of Granada invaded Malaga and dislodged Muhammad Asghar from Malaga. Muhammad Asghar came to Almeria and stayed there in a state of frustration. On the request the people of Melilla (Africa) he went there and ruled until 460 A.H. Muhammad Asghar was the last king of the Hamud dynasty who ruled Malaga until 451 A.H. Qasim bin Muhammad entitled "Wathiq Billah" ruled over the province of Algeciras until 450 A.H. He also belonged to the Hamud family. Mu'tazid bin Abul Qasim bin Ubad, the ruler of Seville occupied Algeciras in 450 A.H. and arrested Muhammad. This was the end of Hamud dynasty in Spain.

Chapter 7
State of Anarchy

Banu Abbad, Banu Dhun'nun, Banu Hud etc.

The rule of the Umayyads came to an end with the end of the fourth century Hijrah. We have covered a period up to 450 A.H. while dealing with the Hamud dynasty although Hamud only ruled some small territories of the Spanish peninsula. There were other contemporary dynasties, which had sovereign rule over separate parts of the peninsula. Since their coverage will not consume much space, we are mentioning them as a whole. We have chosen only those who exemplify the realities of the era and maintain the continuity of the historical events. The separately ruled states had their beginning when the Northern Christian powers were making a total effort to expand their territories and took advantage of the situation by setting one Muslim ruler against another.

Seville and Western Spain (Banu Abbad or Abbadids)

Among the Abbad was a man named Muhammad bin Ismail bin Quraish of the town of·Tashana who would lead the prayers. His son Ismail was appointed minister in the court of Seville in 413 A.H.

Ismail bin Muhammad's son Abul Qasim Muhammad became the Qadi and Minister of Seville. When Qasim bin Hamud came to Seville, Abul Qasim Muhammad the Qadi of Seville and Muhammad bin Zubairi blocked his entry into the city.

Abul Qasim Muhammad

Shortly after that, Abul Qasim Muhammad turned Muhammad bin Zubairi out of Seville and occupied Seville on his own. Qasim bin Hamud left for Carmona where Muhammad bin Abdullah Barzali had set up his sovereign rule in 404 A.H. After a short time Qasim bin Hamud left for Fort Sarish and Muhammad bin Abdullah continued his rule in Carmona.

Abu Umar Abbad

Abu Umar Abbad ascended the throne of Seville after his father Abul Qasim Muhammad and called himself "Mu'tazid". Mu'tazid fought several battles with Muhammad bin Abdullah, the ruler of Carmona. Ismail bin Qasim bin Hamud killed Muhammad bin Abdullah and captured Carmona. Shortly after that Ismail went to Algeciras and Carmona was occupied by Muhammad bin Abdullah's son Aziz known as Mustazhir. A short time later Mu'tazid conquered Carmona, Sarish, Arcos, and Ronda. Abdul Aziz Bakari was the sovereign ruler of Adinah and Silves. Mu'tazid, the ruler of Seville invaded his territories but Ibn Jamhur, the Prime Minster of Cordova intervened and brought peace between the two. Soon after the death of Ibn Jumhur, Mutazid conquered Adinah and Silves and sent his son Mu'tamid to rule over the annexed territories. Muzaffar, the ruler of Setubal died in 422 A.H. and Mu'tazid annexed Setubal too in 443 A.H. by dislodging Muzaffar's son.

Abul Abbas Ahmad bin Yahya had set up his rule in Lablah in 414 A.H. He died in 433 A.H. and was succeeded by his brother Muhammad bin Yahya. Mu'tazid invaded Lablah. Muhammad bin Yahya left Lablah and joined his nephew Fath bin Khalaf bin Yahya in Cordova. Mu'tazid occupied Cordova too in 445 A.H. He also wrested Almeria from Rashiq and Martelah from Ibn Taighar and gradually expanded his territories and thus established the rule of the Abbads. Badis bin Habus had set up his rule in Granada. But Badis bin Habus and Mu'tazid clashed with one another and the matter was still undecided when Mu'tazid died in 461 A.H.

Mu'tamid bin Mu'tazid bin Ismail

He was succeeded by his son Mu'tamid bin Mu'tazid bin Islamil. Mu'tamid too, like his father, started expanding his territories. Badis bin Habus conceded to the supremacy of Mu'tamid. Ferdinand, the Christian King of Castile and Leon because of the fighting among the Muslims took advantage of the opportunity and attacked Seville with full force. The Muslim rulers had in order to overpower their Muslim rivals agreed to pay tribute to Ferdinand and seek his help. Mu'tazid also agreed to pay tribute to the Christian king to avoid his expected attack. Ferdinand I died in 458 A.H. He was succeeded by his son Alfonso VI. He was very arrogant. Mu'tamid fortified his military strength by 468 A.H. and stopped paying tribute to the Christian king.

Alfonso's Plunder of Islamic Cities

Besides Banu Abbad in western Spain some chieftains were also having territories under their sovereign rule. Those independent of Banu Abbad had gone under the influence of the Christian king. Alfonso VI had grown very strong by plundering Islamic cities and receiving tribute from the Muslim Chiefs. He built a huge force and wrested Toledo from Qadir, the last king of Bani Dhun'nun in 478 A.H. He then became a source of trouble to all the Muslim States.

Alfonso demanding Tribute

Alfonso's Jewish emissary Ibn Shalib called on Mu'tamid and demanded tribute. Mu'tamid gave it immediately. But the emissary sent it back to Mu'tamid saying that he would not accept silver coins and wanted the tribute in gold ones. On receiving this message, Mu'tamid called the emissary and punished him by driving nails into his hands and feet. Finding himself on the point of death, he entreated that in case he was forgiven he was ready to give him gold equal to his weight. But Mu'tamid paid no heed and killed the emissary and arrested those accompanying him. Mu'tamid was now sure of Alfonso's invasion. Alfonso grew very furious when he found out about the death of his emissary. The Muslims on the other hand were so strife-torn that they could not save Spain from Christian occupation.

Mu'tamid Seeks Yusuf bin Tashfain's Help

In view of the looming disaster Mu'tamid told Yusuf bin Tashfain, the ruler of Morocco that without his help Islamic rule in Spain would meet its doom. Yusuf bin Tashfain was a renowned and victorious king. On the request of Mu'tamid, he rushed to Spain and reached Seville. Alfonso also marched to Seville from the other side.

Historical Battle with the Christians

On the Battleground of Zallacca both forces came face to face in 480 A.H. (October 23, 1086 C.E.). The joint army of Yusuf bin Tashfain and Mu'tamid went up to twenty thousand while the Christian army had sixty thousand troops ready to fight. This battle is reckoned among the most significant battles of Spain because it fortified the Muslims power in Spain for several hundred years and they became a terror for the Christians once again. The dimensions of fighting may be measured from the simple fact that, according to Ibn Athir (The famous historian), Alfonso VI escaped from the battlefield with not more than three men while the rest fell fighting. In the wake of such a major victory the Muslims gained an opportunity to put their ranks right but this hope was not to be realized. Shortly after the return of Yusuf bin Tashqain to Morocco, large-scale infighting started among the nobles and chiefs of Spain once again. Even though Mu'tamid was fond of learning and was a patron of the scholars with the conquest of Zallacca his style of life took a change for the worse. Yusuf bin Tashfain came to Spain once again and instructed his governor in Spain to keep an eye on the troublemakers and later he annexed Spain. He arrested Mu'tamid and confined him at Aghmat in Morocco where he died after four years in 488 A.H. Thus came the end of Bani Abbad's rule.

Banu Aftas Rule in Badajoz

In the wake of Spain being taken over by disorder Abu Muhammad Abdullah bin Maslama, commonly known as Ibn Aftas, occupied Badajoz and declared his sovereignty. After his death, his son Abu Bakr Muzaffar succeeded him. He was involved in fighting with Banu Dhun'nun and Banu Abbad and had to remain confined to his fort. At last, Ibn Jamhur brought peace between the hostile parties. Muzaffar died in 660 A.H. and was succeeded by his son Abu Hafs bin Muhammad known as Sajah with "Mutawakkil" as his title.

Yusuf bin Tashfain's Occupation of Badajoz

Yusuf bin Tashfain captured Badajoz in 489 A.H. and did away with Mutawakkil and his progeny. He was punished very harshly for his entering into secret correspondences with the Christians to invade Spain and to put an end to the influence of Yusuf bin Tashfain on the country.

Ibn Jamhur's Rule in Cordova

Jamhur bin Muhammad with Ibn Hazm as his filial name came to the throne of Cordova with the support of the people. He formed an executive committee under his leadership and ruled with common consent. He also disliked being called a king or Sultan. He was a pious and virtuous man and his rule was commendable. He would attend patients and join public assemblies. He died in 435 A. H. and was buried in his house.

Abul Waleed bin Jamhur bin Muhammad

Jamhur bin Muhammad was succeeded by his son. Abul Waleed Muhammad bin Jamhur with the unanimous support of the people of Cordova. He also valued scholars and religious divines like his father. On his death, he was succeeded by his son Abdul Malik, who the people began to hate.

Abdul Malik bin Jamhur

Banu Dhun'nun invaded Cordova. Abdul Malik sought help from Banu Abbad. Abbadid forces drove away Dhun'nun but they occupied Cordova and put Abdul Malik in prison. This was the end of the Jamhur dynasty in 461 A.H. Mu'tazid Abbadi appointed his son Sirajuddaula as the Governor of Cordova however, he was poisoned to death shortly after being appointed. Following this Mu'tazid seized Cordova and began to rule.

Ibn Habus's Rule in Granada

At the time Banu Hamud set up their rule a Berber Chief Zadi bin Ziri Manad had founded his rule in Granada. When Spain was overtaken by civil war, chief Zadi deputed his son in Granada and he went to the king of Qairwan in Africa. In his absence, his brother Maks bin Ziri seized Granada and dislodged his nephew. Maks bin Ziri died in 429 A.H. His son Badis known as Ibn Habus succeeded him. Ibn Habus clashed several times with Dhun'nun and Ibn Abbad. He had a Jew named Ismail as his Prime Minister. Ibn Habus died in 467 A. H. He was succeeded by his grandson Abu Muhammad Abdullah bin Balkin bin Badis with "Muzaffar" as his title. He appointed his brother Tamim as Governor of Malaga as per the will of his grandfather. Yusuf bin Tashfain's of the Almoravids (from the Arabic Murabitun those serving at the frontier out posts) deposed and exiled both the brothers to Aghmat in Morocco.

[*Editors Note:* The name Almoravids is a corruption of the Arabic: Murabitun (from the Arabic root for rabat or outpost), which was made by orientalist historians and remains in this corrupted form in the history books of the west until today.]

Banu Dhun'nun's Rule in Toledo

At a time when Spain was stormed by riots and violence, Ismail bin Zafir bin Abdur Rahman Sulaiman bin Dhun'nun seized Aqlanteen Fort. Yaeesh bin Muhammad bin Yaeesh, the Governor of Toledo declared his sovereignty. When he died in 427 A.H. the commanders of the forces of Toledo called Ismail from Aqlanteen Fort to seize Toledo. Thus, Ismail occupied Toledo without any resistance and began to rule successfully. Ismail bin Zafir died in 429 A.H. and was succeeded by his son Abul Hasan Yahya with "Mamun" as his title. Mamun became a very strong ruler in a state where there was nothing but anarchy in the atmosphere. He fought several battles with the Christian chiefs. Among the offspring of Mansur the Great was a man named Muzaffar, who had occupied Valencia province. Mamun dislodged him in 435 A.H. and annexed Valencia. Mamun then invaded Cordova and took it away from the Banu Abbad. Following this, his son Abu Umar was killed by the people of Cordova. Mamun was also poisoned to death in 467 A.H. Then Toledo came under the control of his grandson Qadir bin Yahya bin Ismail. Alfonso, the Christian king of Castile invaded Toledo. Qadir bin Yahya vacated Toledo but sought Alfonso VI's help in the occupation of Valencia. Valencia was then under the control of Qadi Uthman bin Abu Badr bin Abdul Aziz. When the citizens of Valencia, came to know of Alfonso's possible attack on Valencia they deposed Uthman bin Abu Bakr and brought Qadir bin Yahya to power. Qadir passed away in 481 A.H.

Banu Hud's Rulers in Saragossa

When Spain was overtaken by riots and violence at the end of the Umayyad Dynasty, Mundhir bin Mutrif titled Mansur proclaimed his independent rule in Saragossa. He entered into a pact with the Christian rulers. Mansur died in 414 A.H. and was succeeded by his son, Muzaffar. Toledo was then under the rule of Abu Ayub bin Muhammad bin Abdullah (the freed slave of Abu Hudayfa). Sulaiman bin Muhammad bin Hud who was a commander in the Northern territories, overpowered and killed Muzaffar and seized Saragossa and also took the title Musta'in. Muzaffar's son Yusuf then began to rule in Lerida and set out on a new series of battles.

Sulaiman ibn Hud, known as Musta'in died in 437 A.H. and was succeeded by his son Ahmad with Muqtadir Billah as his title. Muqtadir Billah sought help from the Christian rulers of Southern France and the Basque country and they came to his help. Yusuf fought valiantly and surrounded both Muqtadir and the Christians in Saragossa. This event took place in 443 A.H. Yusuf met with failure in this siege and the Christians returned to their respective lands. Muqtadir died in 474 A.H. after ruling in Saragossa for 37 years.

His son succeeded him in Saragossa with "Mu'tamin" as his title. He was well versed in mathematics. He wrote a number of books on this subject. He died in 478 A.H. the same year the Christians wrested Toledo from Dhun'nun. His son Ahmad with Musta'in II as his title succeeded Yusuf Mu'tamin. During his tenure, the Christians surrounded Huesca. Ahmad Musta'in marched from Saragossa in 489 A.H. and took on the Christians at Huesca but was defeated leaving ten thousand

Muslims dead. Ahmad Musta'in returned to Saragossa and continued to rule. Since the victory at Huesca had encouraged the Christians, they built a strong army and attacked Saragossa in 503 A.H. Ahmad Musta'in came to out of Saragossa to take on the enemy and was killed in the battle.

Ahmad Musta'in was succeeded by Abdul Malik in Saragossa with Imaduddaula as his title. But the Christians seized Saragossa in 512 A.H. and dislodged Imaduddaula. He took refuge in the citadel of Rueda and died in 513 A.H.

His son Ahmad ascended the throne in the citadel with Saifuddaula as his title. He tried his level best to restore his ancestral country from the Christians but failed in his efforts. At last, he sold the Rueda citadel to the Christians and began to live in Toledo along with his relatives and died in 536 A.H.

Islands of Eastern Majorca, Minorca, and Sardinia

Isam Khulani conquered Majorca in 290 A.H. and was appointed the Governor of the territory by the Sultan of Spain. Isam was succeeded by his son, Abdullah, as the Governor of Majorca. He ruled until 350 A.H., Caliph Nasir then appointed his servant Muwaffaq the Governor of the island. Muwaffaq waged *jihad* on France several times. He died in 359 A.H. His servant Kauser was appointed the Governor of the island. He passed away in 389 A.H. Mansur then sent his slave Muqatil to the island as the new Governor. He died in 403 A.H. Following him Mujahid bin Yusuf bin Ali Aamiri was appointed the Governor of Majorca. Abdullah became the Governor after him and he conquered and annexed Sardinia in 415 A.H. A man named Mubash'shir became the Governor in 468 A.H. until then the islands of Majorca, Minorca and Sardinia were governed by anarchy however, Mubash'shir brought them together to make a united country and waged *jihad* against France. At last, the Christian rulers of Barcelona and France surrounded Majorca on all sides. Mubash'shir sought help from Ali bin Yusuf bin Tashfain. Ali sent his warships without loss of time and drove away the Christians. Following this, the Almoravids began to rule the islands and then shifted to the Almohads and during their last days, the Christians seized these islands.

Chapter 8

Christian Brutality in Spain

Almoravid Rule

The Almoravids take their name from the Arabic Al Murabit and in Arabic, they were called the Murabitun. The name is derived from the Arabic for those dwelling in frontier fortresses. We will have to go back to bring about the continuity of events. When the Muslim kingdoms were over taken by chaos and disorder, the Christian states of the northern frontiers began to see the opportunity for advancement and prosperity. They first tried hard to aggravate anarchy and internal fighting in the Muslim ranks. Alfonso VI built his force to fight the Muslims. He persuaded all the Christian States bordering Muslim Spain to attack and achieved success in his mission. He took Toledo from the control of Qadir Billah and annexed it. He asked the Christian clergy to convert the Muslims to Christianity through sermons but in the wake of a total failure in this mission, Alfonso VI began to perpetrate atrocities against the Muslims and could not stop himself from demolishing mosques and converting grand mosques into churches.

The Christian king of Aragon massacred Muslim forces pretending that they were going to invade Valencia. Rodmir, the Christian king wrested Saragossa from the Muslims and did not hesitate in the least from pulling down mosques. It is worth mentioning that the Muslim powers had so many times defeated the Christians and entered into their cities victoriously but never showed any brutality nor killed innocent Christian women and children.

After conquering Toledo Alfonso made an attempt to step into the territory of Barcelona. Mu'tamid bin Mu'tazid Abbadi, the king of Barcelona was then engaged in fighting with the king of Almeria so he sent tribute to Alfonso to avert trouble. Alfonso sent word to Mu'tamid that he wanted to keep his pregnant wife in the Cordova Mosque until she delivered and so he should make arrangements for the delivery and Zahra Palace should also be vacated for him. Cordova was then under the control of Mu'tamid but Mu'tamid rejected the petition point blank and killed his envoy as a punishment for his impertinence of requesting gold instead of silver, as already mentioned. Hearing this Alfonso VI marched ahead and made the demand, after encamping on the bank of Guadalquivir, that the city and its palaces be vacated for him. Mu'tamid replied on the back of his letter that he would not take much time in teaching him a lesson. This brief answer sent terror into the heart of Alfonso and he held back from attacking. However, he spread the rumor throughout that Mu'tamid had invited Yusuf bin Tashfain from Morocco to help him. He did this because the Muslim chiefs of Spain disliked the entry of the Moroccan king into their country and considered it a matter of utter disgrace, yet they felt no shame in paying tribute to the Christians. In the wake of such a rumor, the Muslim rulers wrote letters decrying such an injurious step taken by Mu'tamid. Mu'tamid wrote back the following to one and all:

"I prefer watching the camels to favoring the pigs"

What he meant was that if Alfonso captured him he would make him serve his pigs while Yusuf bin Tashfain would take him to Morocco and ask him to graze his camels if he occupied Spain. He would, therefore, never like to become the prisoner of Alfonso. Following this Mu'tamid sent an ambassador to Yusuf bin Tashfain to seek his help against the Christians. Yusuf bin Tashfain rushed to Spain. Alfonso also started preparations to face such a formidable enemy and collected sixty thousand brave and seasoned warriors from various sources. Then looking at his huge army, Alfonso remarked with the utmost arrogance that even the angels from heaven could not defeat his force. Following this, he wrote a letter to Yusuf bin Tashfain who was with Mu'tamid in Seville. Referring to his large army and military strength he hurled a stream of abuses at him. Yusuf asked his secretary to write a reply. He drafted a lengthy well formatted letter in reply. Yusuf rejected it saying that such an ornamentation of style was not needed and wrote with his own pen on the back of Alfonso's letter;

"One who remains alive will see"

Alfonso grew terrified with the brief reply. Both forces faced each other on the battleground of Zallacca. The Muslim force was not more than twenty thousand in number. When the Muslim force moved ahead on Wednesday, Rajab, 479 A.H. Alfonso sent word that he requested to go to war on Saturday. Yusuf and Mu'tamid granted his petition. However, Alfonso had actually deceived the Muslim army and he launched a sudden attack while the Muslims were in a state of complete unawareness. However, they rose very cautiously and courageously to stop the invading Christian force and began to fight valiantly. Three horses fell dead under his thighs but he felt no terror and as Yusuf bin Tashfain made his charge the Christians sustained heavy losses of men. Alfonso VI received deep injuries and fled the battlefield of Zallacca on Rajab 20, 479 A.H. with only a few hundred soldiers. Muslim forces stayed on the battleground for four days. Mu'tamid asked Yusuf about the distribution of the spoils of war, he replied that he had come to help not to secure spoils of war. Both Yusuf and Mu'tamid went together to Seville. Yusuf took a rest for several days and then returned to Africa. Alfonso lost his senses after this smashing and disgraceful defeat however, the Muslim chiefs didn't take advantage of the terrible setback of the Christians and continued to engage in mutual conflict and feuds. In view of the plight of the Muslims the Christians began to muster courage once again and began to conquer Muslim cities including some of the citadels of Seville.

In response to the petitions of Spanish Muslim nobles, Yusuf bin Tashfain came to Spain once again. Muslim discord had risen to such a height that they even started quarrelling in the presence of Yusuf bin Tashfain. He grew so disappointed that he left for Morocco without doing anything.

Two years after that Yusuf bin Tashfain came to Spain again in 483 A.H. to punish the audacious Christians. The Spanish Muslim rulers had already acknowledged him as their patron. This time Yusuf bin Tashfain reached near to Toledo pushing back and defeating the Christian forces and besieged it. During the siege he asked the nobles of Spain to come to his help to make the siege a success. However, nobody paid any heed to his call, particularly, Abdullah bin Balkin, the king of Granada. Therefore, Yusuf bin Tashfain raised the siege and returned from Toledo, the capital of Alfonso VI. Then he decided to set the nobles of Spain in order, he arrested Abdullah, the ruler of Granada and his brother Tamim, the ruler of Malaga and sent them to Africa.

Following this, in Ramadan, 483 A.H., Yusuf bin Tashfain left his nephew and commander Sair bin Abi Bakr bin Tashfain with the force in Spain to punish the Christians and went back to Africa. He attacked Alfonso and wrested a few places from him. It was essential for the Muslim rulers of Spain to reinforce the Moroccan Commander but they refused flatly to do anything for him. Paying no attention to the unworthiness of the inept rulers of Spain, he kept marching against the Christians and took large amounts of territory including Portugal and forced some Christian rulers to obey him. When he consolidated his position in the conquered territories, he informed Yusuf bin Tashfain of his conquests along with fact that the Muslims of Spain extended him no help and they actually kept friendly relations with the Christians in a situation when the very integrity of Islam was at stake, he asked the Moroccan ruler to issue orders for his next step.

Yusuf bin Tashfain wrote him to keep waging *Jihad* on the Christians and make fresh attempts to seek the help of the rulers of Spain. If they take part in his mission, he should not oppose them. However, in case they lend support to the Christians against him, it is better that he should occupy their territories. He should make it a point to first occupy the Muslim states bordering the Christians so that those territories could not join the Christians. This instruction was implemented in letter and spirit and Sair bin Abi Bakr first turned to Ibn Hud, the king of Saragossa. At the time, Saragossa was under the control of the Christians. The Muslim king of Saragossa was then staying in Rueda and ruling over the surrounding areas. Sair conquered Rueda rather easily. He then wrested Murcia from Abdur Rahman bin Tahir in Shawwal 484 A.H. and sent him to Africa. Shortly after that he annexed Almeria and Badajoz and conquered Carmona, Baiha, Bhalat, Malaga, and Cordova. Mu'tamid, the king of Seville then started preparations against the Almoravids. He was at the time the strongest of all kings in Spain and he also sought help from Alfonso. Alfonso sent a force to reinforce Mu'tamid. Having heard of the approaching Christian help Sair bin Abi Bakr besieged Seville on one hand and sent a commander to stop the Christian force on the other. The stated commander defeated and drove away the Christians. Sair bin Abi Bakr conquered Seville and arrested and sent Mu'tamid along with his family to Africa where he lived in detention and died in Rabia al-Awwal 488 A.H.

Yusuf bin Tashfain Occupies Spain

The entire Islamic Spain came back under the control of Yusuf bin Tashfain, and the state of anarchy ended. Spain was ruled by Yusuf bin Tashfain, king of the Almoravid's Viceroys and Governors. The strife-torn country of Spain, which was about to go to the Christian fold, was saved by a Muslim king. All hopes entertained by the Christians of taking back Spain were dashed to the ground. Although the Christians were in control of the northern areas of the Peninsula, a large part of the populated and fertile area was under Muslim rule. Muqtadi Bi'amrillah, the Caliph of Baghdad sent him a garment and a standard and conferred on him the title of "Amir-ul-Muslimin" (Commander of the Muslims).

Yusuf bin Tashfain's Death

From the time of his occupation of Spain Yusuf bin Tashfain remained alive for fifteen years and died in 500 A.H. It was a peaceful time in Spain. The citizens of the Arab race disliked the Almoravid rule because they hated the Berbers ruling over them but this was their mistake. Had the Berber Muslims not been ruling over them the Christians surely would have.

Abul Hasan Ali bin Yusuf bin Tashfain

Abul Hasan Ali bin Yusuf bin Tashfain succeeded his father at the age of 33 years. He surrounded Toledo in 503 A.H. The city could not be conquered owing to its strong fortifications and its situation. But Ali conquered Hijarah valley and its surrounding cities. The same year he wrested Lisbon and the remaining cities from the Christians. Ali bin Yusuf appointed his brother Tamim bin Yusuf as the viceroy of Spain. When Tamim heard of the military preparations of Alfonso I bin Ramirez, the king of Barcelona he attacked and stopped their advance and conquered and annexed Saragossa. The king of Barcelona sought help from the king of France and besieged Saragossa in 512 A.H. The Muslims could not withstand the invasion of the very large Christian force and in the face of the scarcity of food, they opened the gates of the city of Saragossa. The Christians conquered other cities and citadels also. The news of the fall of Saragossa came as a shock to Ali bin Yusuf. He lost no time and rushed to Spain in 513 A.H. and passed through Barcelona and Cordova on route to Saragossa and conquered all the areas won by the Christians and returned to Morocco in 515 A.H. after punishing the Christians and obtaining their submission. Alfonso VI who had made Toledo his capital died in 513 A.H. But Alfonso I of Aragon was still alive and was known as Ibn Ramirez. With the return of Ali bin Yusuf to Morocco Ibn Ramirez attacked the Islamic occupied areas with the support of the Christian citizens of Toledo and they were committed to the invasion of Granada. Ramirez advanced with a large army but Tamim bin Yusuf bin Tashfain gave them such a crushing defeat that he fled to Barcelona after losing half of his troops. A large number of Christians inhabited Grenada and its environs and they kept plotting against the Muslims. In the wake of such a situation Ali bin Yusuf came to Spain in 516 A.H. and sent a large number of Christians inhabiting Granada and its surroundings to Africa and scattered others in various places throughout Spain.

Abu Tahir Tamim bin Yusuf appointed his son Tashfain bin Tamim bin Yusuf bin Tashfain as the viceroy of Spain. Ali bin Yusuf died in Rajab, 537 A.H. after ruling for thirty-six years and seven months.

Abu Muhammad Tashfain

Ali son Abu Muhammad Tashfain succeeded him. Ali bin Yusuf had come to Spain for the last time in 516 A.H. He became involved in the controversy regarding Muhammad bin Abdullah known as Mahdi, the Promised in Morocco. The strife became aggravated to such an extent that even Ali's son Abu Muhammad Tashfain could not escape it after coming to the throne and could not pay attention to Spain.

Tashfain bin Ali

When Tashfain bin Ali succeeded his father in Morocco in 537 A.H. He appointed Yahya bin Ali bin Ghania as the viceroy of Spain. Yahya did his level best to save Spain and reduce the power of the Christians. The Almoravid rule on the other hand showed signs of weakness and decline and at last, Tashfain bin Ali died in 539 A.H. in a state of frustration after sustaining a defeat from Abdul Mumin, the leader of the Almohads and follower of Muhammad Abdullah.

Effect of the End of the Almoravid Rule On Spain

In view of chaos and anarchy prevailing in the seat of power of the Almoravids the rulers of various Spanish territories declared their sovereignty as had happened following the end of the Umayyad dynasty. Muslim Spain was then so terribly fragmented that every city and town had its separate rule and every ruler had his own chosen title. But the worst was their unfriendly and hostile attitude of one towards another and the entire Muslim Spain was engulfed by strife and fighting. The Christians had an opportunity to seize the whole Peninsula. Yahya bin Ali, the Viceroy of Spain, had joined the anarchists by seizing Cordova. He was not the strongest of all. In such a turbulent atmosphere Abdul Momin, the ruler of the Almohads dislodged the Almoravids from Morocco and deputed his own commander in Spain and occupied it in 542 A.H. and after a short period of anarchy, Spain joined the Almohads rule.

During the Almoravid rule, Muslim jurists were very strong. Both the kings, Yusuf and Ali followed the Maliki doctrine and valued the jurists very highly. The highly learned and pious rulers had gone to the extent of being labeled as the enemy of philosophy and scholastic philosophy. Qadi Ayadh had made the royal court issue orders against the works of Imam Ghazali and any body possessing any piece of his work was subject to capital punishment.

Chapter 9

Almohads (Al-Mowahad) Rule in Spain

Muhammad bin Abdullah Tumart

Muhammad bin Abdullah bin Tumart, known as Ibn Tumart, was born in the village of Sus in Morocco. He belonged to the Berbers of Mauritania. He later claimed to have descended from Ali bin Abu Talib carrying his pedigree from Hasan bin Ali.

In 501 A.H. he left his territory in quest of knowledge and stayed in the eastern countries for about 14 years. He took lessons in Fiqh from Abu Bakr Shashi and learnt Hadith from Mubarak bin Abdul Jabbar and other scholars. He achieved the honor of drinking from Imam Ghazali's fountain of knowledge. He turned towards his motherland halting at Alexandria. Even in this short duration he campaigned against practices foreign to the Islamic *Shari'ah,* which led to his expulsion from the city. However, he feared none in spreading good and eradicating evil. He was, by all standards, a pious and righteous person. Ibn Khaldun reports his piety and purity in clear and strong words. He lived a life of utmost simplicity in food and clothes. He commanded grace and dignity and showed a cheerful disposition. But his creed regarding the attributes of Allâh was a mixture of Ashairah, Sheiates and Philosphers. He could speak Arabic fluently and the Berber language was his mother tongue. In 515 A.H. he returned to his motherland and plunged heart and soul into preaching to his countrymen.

Declaring Himself as Imam Mahdi

He claimed for himself the status of Imam Mahdi and formed various classes of his followers. He called the first as Muhajirin and the second *Muminin*. There were seven or eight classes in total. When the number of his followers increased he brought them under the command of Abdul Mumin and asked him to wage a war against the Almoravid Rule. In the first encounter Abdul Mumin's Army was defeated and later due to a power struggle among the Almoravids it gave them a hold over a considerable part of Morocco. Ibn Tumart had started military activities in 517 A.H. and died in 524 A.H. after 7 years of hectic military activity. He appointed Abdul Mumin as his successor with the title of "Amir al-Muminin'. By this time Ibn Tumart's dynasty had become a formidable power and a rival of the Almoravids.

Abdul Mumin

At the same time, Abdul Mumin, a man from the Berbers came to him and joined his circle of disciples. In his thoughts and feelings he was very much like Ibn Tumart. The ruler of the country showed dislike for Tumart's thoughts and activities and decided to do away with him. However, Ali bin Yusuf stood in the way and argued that he saw no reason for his elimination. Following the insistence of the Muslim jurists, he was expelled from Morocco. Ibn Tumart set up his headquarters in the High Atlas Mountains and shifted there with his followers. A large number of Berbers came and joined his camp.

His father's name was Ali who belonged to Kaumia Clan among the Berbers of Mauritania. He was born in 487 A.H. Shortly after the demise of Ali bin Yusuf bin Tashqain in 537 A.H. the whole of Morocco came under the sway of Abdul Mumin. Since the main message of the teachings was belief in the perfect oneness of God his followers came to be called Mowahads [(from the Arabic root of the word one: wahid) those who believe in perfect oneness, the name was corrupted to be Almohads by orientalist scholars and remains in this form in the western history books until today, we continue to use this corrupted name in this volume for the sake of easy reference for the reader.*]*

Abdul Mumin's Conquest of Spain

After taking charge of Morocco Abdul Mumin sent General Abu Imran Musa bin Sayeed to Spain in 536 A.H. He first conquered Tarifa. He then marched to Saltes and Seville and then brought Cordova under his control. In 541 A.H., Abdul Mumin decided to come to Spain but the news of uprisings on his eastern borders stopped him. However, he sent his sons to Spain. Thus Abu Sayeed bin Abdul Mumin won Alzira and Cordova fell to Yahya bin Maimun, a general of Abdul Mumin, in 545 A.H. Abdul Mumin laid the foundation for the city of Rabat (camp or outpost) and named it Al-Fath (Victory), this is the present day capital of Morocco. It was there that he quartered troops for the jihad on Spain. Abdul Mumin crossed the Strait of Gibraltar and made inroads into Spain. It was from there that the chiefs and rulers of a number of territories thronged to extend their loyalty to him. Thus the flag of Islam fluttered over Spain.

In 555 A.H. Abdul Mumin appointed his son, Abu Sayeed, the Governor of Granada and viceroy of Muslim Spain. However, Abu Sayeed had to go to Morocco in response to a call from his father. During his absence, a man, Ibrahim by name, captured Granada and declared his independent rule. Abu Sayeed proceeded to Spain along with his brother Abu Hafs. Ibrahim came out with his troops and gave a fierce battle, which resulted in the defeat of Abu Sayeed and the death of Abu Hafs. Abu Sayeed took refuge in Malaga. He kept his hope intact and built a large army to avenge his defeat. Abdul Mumin dispatched his third son Abu Yaqub and General Abu Yusuf bin Sulaiman to assist Abu Sayeed. The Almohads became victorious after extensive bloodshed. Ibrahim conceded defeat and sought forgiveness, which was granted. After winning peace all around Abdul Mumin began to build a huge army to advance further into European territories. At last he was able to raise 5 hundred thousand fighters from Africa, Spain and Morocco. He was about to move forward with his massive army when he passed away in Jumad al-Thani 558 A.H.

Abu Yaqub

His son, Abu Yaqub Yusuf came to the throne as his successor, he failed to fulfill his father's dream because of some internal problems and impediments. The Christians, on the other hand, captured some of the western districts of Spain. Abu Yaqub moved forward at the head of ten thousand men and retook the territories captured by the Christians. He than laid siege around Toledo but raised it to go back to Morocco. In 580 A.H. the Christians of Santaren city rose once again against the Muslim rule. Abu Yaqub Yusuf rushed to Spain and besieged Santaren. During the siege that took over a month he fell ill and died in Rajab, 580 A.H.

A Review of Abu Yaqub's Reign

Abu Yaqub was good-natured, enlightened and a great lover of learning. Abu Bakr Muhammad bin Tufayl, a leader in Philosophy was his courtier and adviser, another scholar, Abu Bakr bin Sane, known as Ibn Maja was among his main advisers. At the insistence of Ibn Tufayl, Abu Yaqub called Abul Waleed Muhammad bin Ahmad bin Muhammad bin Rushd from Cordova and enlisted him among his honorable courtiers. He is the same Ibn Rushd who was a renowned philosopher and critic of Aristotle's philosophical thoughts. He very ably highlighted the inherent weak points in the philosophy of the Greek scholar. During the reign of Abu Yaqub all the countries from Morocco to Tripoli and the entire Spain including the Island of Sicily and other Mediterranean Islands came to the fold of Islam.

Abu Yusuf Mansur

After Abu Yaqub, his son, Abu Yusuf took the throne at the age of 32. He was born of a Christian mother named Sahira. During his reign in Spain, Muslim power and welfare remained the dominant factor. In his qualities of mind and spirit Mansur was similar to his father. He held the religious scholars in high esteem and was fond of books. He passed his life mostly in Spain. In 585 A.H. he eliminated Christian influence from the western parts of Spain. Alfonso, the King of Castile, was eager to sign a peace treaty for five years with him. Mansur granted his entreaty. Being safe from Muslim invasion he embarked on his plan of building a strong army from all the Christian lands including Spain.

Since Mansur had a very strong navy, Salahuddin Ayubi sent his envoy and poet Abdur Rahman bin Munqad to Mansur with a letter requesting him to reinforce the Muslims with his warships against the Christian forces and help him guard the coastal areas of Palestine. Since Sultan Salahuddin Ayubi recognized the Caliph of Baghdad as the Caliph of the entire Muslim *Ummah*, he did not address Mansur with a title. This attitude of Salahuddin Ayubi enraged Mansur. Although, he greeted the poet and emissary he paid no heed to the request of Salahuddin and simply kept delaying the matter.

Alfonso II of Castile, enjoying peace with the five-years no war-pact, plunged himself heart and soul in making massive military preparations against the Muslims. He gave the ensuing war the air of a Crusade and thus attracted active help and support from the entire Christian community. At last, he arrived at Alarcos in Badajoz along with several Christian rulers and their forces in Rajab, 591 A.H. The two forces clashed on the battlefield of Alarcos. Although the Muslim fighters were much less in number, the Christians suffered a crushing defeat and fled the field leaving behind one hundred and forty-six thousand killed and thirty thousand captives. It was a great victory indeed. The volume of preparations made against the Muslims can be gauged from the fact that the fleeing Christian fighters left on the battlefield one hundred and fifty thousand tents, eighty thousand horses, one hundred thousand mules, four hundred thousand donkeys and sixty thousand coats of mail of different designs. Mansur very generously distributed among his soldiers all the spoils of war.

Alfonso fled for his life and took refuge in the Alarcos Fort with the rest of his troops. But Mansur moved forward at his back and laid siege around the fort, Alfonso escaped and went to Toledo. He was so overwhelmed with grief and anger that he had his head and beard shaved and vowed while holding the Cross that he would not enjoy comfort and luxury unless he avenged the killing of the thousands of Christians by the Muslims. When Mansur came to know of this, he rushed to Toledo immediately, besieged the city and began to destroy the fort, its walls and ramparts with his war machine. In this grim situation Alfonso II, acted very disgracefully by sending his mother, wife and daughters to the court of Mansur. They came bareheaded, and Alfonso's mother begged forgiveness for her son. She cried and bewailed so pitiably and Mansur was moved so deeply by the scene that he not only forgave his sworn enemy but also treated the ladies honorably and sent them back laden with costly gifts. He then raised the siege of Toledo and went back to Cordova. The thirty or forty thousand Christian prisoners languishing in confinement were sent to Morocco to settle there.

Mansur was good-natured, pious and a staunch follower of the *Sunnah,* the practices of the Prophet Muhammad (ﷺ). Following his order, the persons leading the Muslims in prayer would recite *Bismillahir Rahmanir Rahim* aloud preceding *Al-Hamd* in prayers. He died in Safar, 595 A. H. after reigning for fifteen years. King Richard of England died the same year.

Abu Abdullah Muhammad

His son, Abu Abdullah Muhammad came to the throne in Safar 595 A.H. at the age of 17 with Nasir Ll-Din-Allah as his appellation. With the beginning of his reign, the eastern parts of Morocco faced insurgence and disorder and some of the chiefs of the Almoravids started capturing territory. Nasir had to stay in Morocco to put down the uprisings. The Christians, after being defeated by Salahuddin Ayubi in Syria and pates time fled back to Europe burning with anger. They worked out a plan to invade Spain and Morocco to avenge their crushing defeat in Syria and Palestine. They gave a call to the Christian world to join the crusade against the Muslims. The Archbishop of Rome proclaimed a crusade against the Almohads. At the same time the nobles rose against John, the King of England and the Archbishop proclaimed the King excommunicated from Christianity. John sent a three-member deputation to Nasir in Morocco. They met Nasir and gave his letter to the Muslim ruler, which sought his military help to put down the insurgencies in his country. He had also written about his readiness to embrace Islam by renouncing Christianity. Bishop Robert was the leader of the delegation. He also spoke strongly in support of the letter. Nasir grew doubtful of the letter and their intent and greeted them rather coldly. He thought that they wanted to change their religion for worldly gains. He was sure that the King of England would proclaim his acceptance of Islam despite his cold attitude if Islam had actually entered his heart.

Nasir was a man of polite nature and hated unnecessary bloodshed. His army, which was very strong, active and spirited during the reign of his father, had now lost much of its vitality and fighting spirit. Besides, his predecessor would give each of the soldiers a quarterly reward in addition to their monthly salaries but Nasir abandoned the practice, which led to the frustration of the troops and their Generals. King Alfonso set up a military camp in Toledo where Christians from Europe and other countries rushed to join. Spain was nearer to Europe in comparison to Syria and Palestine and they could mobilize their military might much easier.

When Nasir heard of the military preparations of the Christians, he mobilized his troops from Morocco and Spain and declared *Jihad* against the Christians. About six hundred thousand Muslim fighters gathered at Seville while Alfonso's forces encamped at Al-Uqab near Salem. Nasir's troops also reached Al-Uqab. The Christians were growing mad with rage and their defeat in Syria had ignited the fire of revenge against the Muslims. The state of the Muslim Army was the opposite. Almost the entire fighting machine was in a state of revolt and they presented a scene of disorder. The soldiers had received no salary for some months not to speak of gifts and rewards. The commanding officers intended defeat as the only course left to win the attention of their ruler to gain their rights and welfare.

When the battle line was drawn between the rival forces, some of the Generals left the battlefield with the troops under their commands. In the midst of fighting a large number of Muslim fighters buried their spears in the ground instead of piercing them into enemies' bodies, while others threw their swords towards the enemy's rows. Others refused to obey the orders of Nasir. Thus those sincere and spirited fighters lost their courage when they watched others indulge in activities injurious to the Muslim cause and the very safety of Islam. The miserliness of Nasir coupled with disgraceful deceit and disloyalty of the Muslim soldiers inflicted an untold loss to Islam and its followers. Never in the whole history of Islam had Muslim forces taken the field in such a large number and had the bulk of the Muslim troops not been treacherous the Christian Army would have tasted the most smashing and ignominious defeat. They would have been crushed more relentlessly then what they experienced in Syria and Palestine. How pitiful it is that six hundred thousand men conceded such a shameful defeat and only one thousand of the whole army remained alive to mourn the disaster. Nasir fought gallantly but his sword could not change the defeat into victory. Almost all the soldiers of the defeated Muslim army were either killed in the battlefield or slaughtered in captivity.

Nasir came back to Seville, defeated and frustrated. The Christians went wild and started plundering cities and killing Muslim men, women and children in as many numbers as they could. When Alfonso noticed the Christians' large-scale indulgence in loot, arson and massacre he tried to bring the situation under his control. But it resulted in their opposition to the King. Moreover, the Christians from other countries began to leave for their respective countries. Alfonso saw this development with a sense of satisfaction. The damages caused by the Christians brought the decline of the Muslim rule in Spain. Many towns, villages and settlements had a deserted look and none of them could escape from death. In Shaban, 610 A.H. Nasir came to Morocco from Seville and died shortly after that.

Yusuf Mustansir

Nasir was succeeded by his son Yusuf on Shaban 11, 610 A.H. and adopted the title of Mustansir. He was only 16 when he ascended the throne. He died after ruling the country for a decade. He was lacking in courage and spirit and lived a very luxurious life. Most of Spain was captured by the Christians during his rule. During his entire tenure of ten years not even once did he leave Morocco and he never went to Spain after becoming king.

Abdul Wahid

His brother, Abdul Wahid came to the throne after Mustansir. After a short tenure of nine months he was dethroned and assassinated by his nobles and courtiers.

Abdul Wajid Adil

At that time another son of Nasir and the brother of Abdul Wahid was the Governor of Murcia, a province of Spain. He staked his claim to the throne when he heard the news of Abdul Wahid's assassination and he came to the throne in Murcia with the title of Adil.

The same year 621 A.H. the Christians attacked him and he was defeated in the battle. Following this he appointed his brother Idris as his deputy in Seville and went to Morocco. The people of Morocco had enthroned a young boy of 16, Yahya bin Nasir and gave battle to Adil. Adil was arrested, knowing of this Idris came to the throne with the title of Mamun. It was at the time when the Almohads had lost their power and influence all over Spain and Morocco. Banu Marin were taking over the lead in Morocco while the nobles of Spain refused to accept men from Morocco and Berbers to rule their destiny. They also feared that weak Moroccan rulers would surrender their country to the Christians leaving them to pass the rest of their lives as slaves. Thus a person from Bani Hud named Muhammad bin Yusuf, rose to the occasion and laid the foundation of his rule.

End of the Almohads' Rule

Thus was erased the name of Almohads from the face of Spain by 625 A.H. Mamun set up his center in Ceuta fort and died there. His son, Rasheed succeed him. Bani Marin were gradually and steadily developing their might with the result they captured Morocco completely ending the Almohad Rule.

Chapter 10

Anarchy again in Muslim Spain

As has already been mentioned, many sovereign states emerged out of the ruins of Banu Umayyad and the Christian Kings took advantage of their constant rivalries. They expanded their territories by taking Muslim lands. Later the Almoravids came to power in Muslim Spain and small Kingdoms united under one Muslim rule. Almohads established their rule on the debris of the Almoravid dynasty. The Christians' gains from the prevailing anarchy were not insignificant and whatever the Almohads had established as a result of the united Muslim front was lost on the battlefield of Al-Uqab. It was an opportunity for the Christians to wipe out all traces of the Muslims from the face of Spain but the corrupt practices of the Christian fighters invited hatred and opposition to the Christians in Spain. When the Almohad Rule came to its end, more than half of the northern part of Spain and all the western provinces had already come under Christian control. Muslim Spain was overtaken by anarchy once again. Muslim rule was again broken into small fragments each at war with another. Every Muslim chief invited the Christian troops against another and offered them some cities and forts in return for their military help. This depravity of the Muslim rulers was very pleasing and encouraging for the Christians.

Banu Hud State

Muhammad bin Yusuf

In 503 A.H., Ahmad Musta'in bin Abu Amir Yusuf Mutamin bin Abu J'afar bin Hud was martyred fighting against the Christians. During the last days of the Almohad dynasty he passed a life of luxury and comfort. When he noticed cracks in the structure of the central rule, he joined a band of robbers and within a short period became its chief. He first set himself to the task of increasing his strength and then attacked Abul Abbas, the Governor of Murcia and captured the province. He conquered Granada, Malaga, and Almeria and then captured Cordova by expelling King Mamun from Spain. By 625 A.H. the entire Muslim Spain came under his control. The same year the Christian King of Barcelona expelled the Almohad Governors following his conquest of Majorca and Minorca islands. Following in the footsteps of Muhammad bin Yusuf several other ambitious leaders raised their heads and set up their own independent states. When Muhammad bin Yusuf felt that it was next to impossible to subdue the chiefs and bring their subjects around to his policies, he wrote a letter to the Abbasid Caliph of Baghdad saying: "I have conquered the whole of Spain in your name and established my government here. I request you with the utmost regard that I be appointed as the ruler of this country and a royal certificate authorizing me for the throne of Spain be issued. The Caliph of Baghdad thought it to be an event from the unseen and conferred upon him the certificate along with royal garments. As a follow-up action, Muhammad bin Yusuf ordered the people to assemble in the Grand Mosque of Granada and appeared in the royal attire with a black standard in his hand. He then read out the edict from Caliph Mustansir Abbasi and greeted the Muslims as a whole. This device left a positive impact on the nobles and the people in general gave him support. It was however just a passing event. The nobles could not continue with Muhammad bin Yusuf for long. Their old antagonistic activities came to the surface once again. The result was internal disturbances and civil war. The Christians found an opportunity to capture Muslim cities one after another. In 627 A.H., they captured Merida city, the biggest city after Cordova. On being informed Muhammad bin Yusuf came with his army and attacked Alfonso, the Ninth. After a fierce encounter he was defeated. He came back frustrated and chose Murcia as his ruling center. In 629 A.H., Ibn al-Ahmar staked his claim on Spain and captured a number of cities. About the same time a chief, named Abu Marwan captured Seville. Ibn al-Ahmar developed a friendship with Abu Marwan and increased his military power. In 632 A.H., Ibn al-Ahmar stepped into Seville as a friend but captured the territory by assassinating Abu Marwan. The people of Seville expelled Ibn al-Ahmar from Seville and showed their obedience to Muhammad bin Yusuf. The Muslim ruler appointed Ibn Al-Ramimi as his Minister and entrusted most of the official work to him. He was later appointed as the Governor of Almeria where he rose against the central rule. Muhammad bin Yusuf proceeded to punish the rebel when Ibn Ramimi's spies strangled him to death while he was sleeping in his camp. Following this Ibn Ramimi declared himself the sovereign King of Almeria. However, Murcia remained under the children of Muhammad bin Yusuf who showed their obedience to Ibn al-Ahmar. Finally, the dynasty saw its end in 658 A.H.

In addition to Banu Hud, Ibn al-Ahmar, Ibn Marwan, Ibn Khalid, and Ibn Mardiansh established their separate rules and Ferdinand played a fundamental role in setting one State against another. The King of Barcelona began to invade the Muslim States one after another. The Christians would extend military help to one against another and then fought against the one, which was once given help. Their sole purpose was to expand the Christian territories. In Shawal, 636 A.H., the King of Castile conquered Cordova, the capital of the central rule and established their government by ravaging the grandeur of this magnificent city. It was indeed the end of Islamic splendor. In this era fraught with sufferings and disturbances one wise step taken by Ibn al-Ahmar was to make peace with Ferdinand and to strengthen his own power under the shadow of peace won in lieu of some cities and forts. This spell of peace he utilized to win victories over Granada, Malaga, Lorca, and Jaen. Thus he established a strong rule over one-fourth of Spain, a rule which spanned over 250 years. The capital of Muslim Spain had changed to Granada from Cordova.

Chapter 11

Granada

Ibn Al-Ahmar

Nasr bin Yusuf, known as Ibn Al-Ahmar, had captured Granada and Malaga in 632 A.H. after befriending Ibn Khalid, the ruler of Seville. In 643 A.H., the ruler of Almeria extended his obedience to him and the people of Lorca accepted him in 663 A.H. as their King. Until that time he had the support of Ferdinand. However, when the Muslim States began to fall one after another, the Christians thought of usurping the State of Ibn Al-Ahmar but Ibn al-Ahmar was wise enough to have already established friendly relations with King Yaqub Abdul Haq of Bani Marin. King Yaqub had become the ruler of North Africa and Morocco after the end of the Almohad's dynasty. Thus, whenever, he was threatened by the Christian powers, he received help from Yaqub Marini without delay. By this device, Ibn al-Ahmar defeated the Christians repeatedly and saved his small State. Ibn al-Ahmar laid the foundation of Al-Hamra Palace in Granada, which is still considered as one of the Seven Wonders of the World and a relic of the declining years of Muslim grandeur. However, it bears no comparison with the Zahra Palace of Cordova, which was pulled down by the savage Christians. Ibn al-Ahmar was on his way back to Granada after giving a disastrous defeat to the Christians when his horse stumbled near his fort and he fell down. Even though he had not sustained any deep injury, he succumbed to it on 29 Jumad al-Thani 671 A.H.

Abu Abdullah Muhammad

His son, Abu Abdullah Muhammad, succeeded him. He was 38 when he came to the throne. In accordance with the will of his father, he kept friendly relations with Bani Marin and devoted himself whole-heartedly to campaigning against his enemies. In 673, the Christian forces invaded Granada, Muhammad asked Yaqub bin Abdul Haq Marini for help. He immediately sent his son to Spain at the head of a strong army and he followed him with another force, Algeciras was taken from a rebel Chief and turned it into his military cantonment. Muhammad, on his part, offered Zarifah Fort to Yaqub to set up his own cantonment. Sultan Muhammad and Sultan Yaqub launched a joint attack on the Christians and gave them a crushing defeat on Rabia al-Awwal 15, 673 A.H. Following this defeat the Christians built a strong army and launched another attack on the Muslims but were defeated again. In Muharram, 695 A.H. the King of Castile began to concentrate his army on the borders of Granada. Being informed Sultan Muhammad stormed into Qajata and its surroundings and conquered the military base of the Christians. In 699 A.H., Sultan Muhammad wrested some frontier forts from the Christians. Sultan Muhammad died on Shaban 8, 701 A.H. after an eventful reign of about 30 years. He is also known as Sultan Muhammad Faqih for he was very fond of books.

Muhammad Makhlu'a

Muhammad was succeeded by his son Muhammad Makhlu'a. He handed over all powers to his Minister, Muhammad bin Muhammad Hakam Lakhmi. In 703 A.H., Abu al-Haj bin Nasr, the ruler of Gaudix rose against Muhammad Makhlu'a, which was suppressed with a heavy hand and the rebel was put to death. The majority of people were angry with the Minister and they persuaded Muhammad Makhlu'a's brother Nasr bin Muhammad to rise in revolt against the government, plunder the house of the Minister and arrest and depose Muhammad Makhlu'a after which Nasr bin Muhammad was enthroned.

Sultan Nasr bin Muhammad

Nasr bin Muhammad came to the throne and appointed Nasr, the son of the assassinated Abul al-Hajj, to his administration. The event of enthronement had taken place on the Eid Day in 708 A.H. The next year the King of Castile invaded Algeciras. Although this city remained unconquered Jabl-i-Tariq (Gibraltar) was captured by the Christian King. The same year the King of Barcelona attacked Almeria and King Nasr dispatched his army to save Almeria. The battle was still on when Abu Sayeed, the nephew of Ibn al-Ahmar and the ruler of Malaga rose against him. Abul Waleed, the son of Abu Sayeed conquered both Almeria and Malaga. Thus started a civil war in Granada and the rule over Granada was divided into two. The situation was still out of control when Nasr fell ill and his condition turned almost hopeless. They attempted to enthrone Muhammad Makhlu'a in place of Nasr but King Nasr recovered and killed Muhammad Makhlu'a in prison. Following this Abu Sayeed and his son, Abul Waleed started ruling the occupied territories by making Malaga their capital. In Muharram 713 A.H., Abul Waleed proceeded with his troops and camped near Granada. Nasr came out from Granada with his own army but was defeated by Abul Waleed on Muharram 13, 713 A.H. and he took refuge in Granada. He then started a peace process but the peace treaty was still to be finalized when the citizens of Granada held him back from signing any treaty and persuaded him to take over Granada completely. When he found some chiefs of Granada sympathetic to him, he became ready to attack. The two forces clashed at Sardonia and Abul Waleed achieved victory. Nasr took refuge in Al-Hamra Palace. At last he abdicated the throne in favor of Abul Waleed.

Abul Waleed

After coming to the throne of Granada he gave Nasr permission to settle in Ash valley. Abul Waleed took over the administration of

Granada and began to run it skillfully. The Christians who were until then happy over the civil war among the Muslim states grew worried at the firm rule of Abul Waleed. They now engaged themselves in preparing to go against Granada. The King of Castile attacked and captured some border areas of Granada. Abul Waleed faced the challenge with firmness and determination and drove away the Christians from his land. In view of Abul Waleed's supreme military operations the Christians declared it a holy war and roused the entire Christian world against the Muslim rule. Bishops and clergies ignited in their people the fire of anger and revenge against the Muslims as a whole. The Archbishop personally took part in the Christian campaigns. Christian forces were concentrated in Toledo and their number rose to two hundred thousand. They seemed determined to wipe out all Muslim signs and traces from the face of Spain. Crown prince Batardah of the Castile dynasty was given the command of a huge Christian force. About twenty-five Christian rulers from Europe joined the holy war. The Archbishop spread his hand over the head of every general and the bishops all over Europe supplicated for the annihilation of the Muslims.

The Battle of Albirah

The Muslims of Granada grew anxious to hear of the massive military preparations by the Christian world. Abul Waleed sent a call for help to Abu Sayeed but his call received no response with the result that the Muslims of Granada felt even more anxious. They were expecting their extinction. Abul Waleed could muster only five thousand and five hundred troops from all over Granada, which was virtually insignificant in comparison to the huge Christian army of several hundred thousand. However, Abul Waleed marched out of Granada at the head of a handful of men relying wholly and solely on the help and support of Allah Almighty. He sent General al-Ghazat as the vanguard with five hundred troops under his command and he himself marched at the head of five thousand troops. They covered the entire route discussing ways and means of winning victory over such a large Christian army. However, the vanguards of both sides clashed at first and the result was a reverse for the Christians. Abul

Waleed then hid one thousand cavaliers behind the brush adjacent to Albirah. He then sent General al-Ghazat ahead with a column of five hundred soldiers with instructions that they should retreat after coming face to face with the Christians troops so that the chasing Christians would be suddenly attacked by the hidden Muslim troops. Abul Waleed himself was waiting at a suitable place with only three hundred horsemen under his command. The rest of the troops were given to another General to lead slowly towards the enemy. Following the plan general al-Ghazat moved near the Christian troops early in the morning of Jumad al-Awwal 6, 719 A.H. The Christians found the Muslim side very poor in number and made no delay in attacking them. General al-Ghazat began to move back while the sea of Christian forces pursued the retreating troops with a desire to crush the Muslims. When the Christian troops moved in front of the bush, the one thousand strong Muslim column sprang from behind the thick bush and fell on the Christian troops. In the meantime, General al-Ghazat fought back the embarrassed Christians while Abul Waleed launched his attack from the third side. The rest of the troops also caught the enemy unaware. Although the Muslim troops were no match for the Christian army their tactics and the supreme sacrifice of lives paid them rich dividends. The four-pronged fierce attack of the gallant Muslim troops tore off their battle-lines and made them flee from the scene of their death and destruction leaving behind one hundred thousand dead. It is quite amazing that the number of Muslim martyrs did not exceed 13. This event is, indeed, one of the marvels of the history of war. The Commander-in-Chief of the Christian army along with his twenty-five guards was also found among the dead. His wife and son were among the seven thousand captives of war. It was a backbreaking defeat for the Christians. It now dawned upon them that the annihilation of the Muslims from Granada was not an easy task. Abul Waleed thanked Allah Almighty for the unexpected victory and then conceded to the peace offer made by his enemies. When he returned to Granada victoriously, his nephew treacherously assassinated him. The assassin was also killed in *qisas* (punishment by retaliation) and the throne was given to Muhammad, the son of Abul Waleed.

King Muhammad

Sultan Muhammad appointed Abul Ala Uthman as his minister. But when Uthman consolidated his power beyond all limits and his activities proved injurious to the throne, Muhammad had assassinated him in 729 A.H. In 733 A.H., Sultan Muhammad cleared Gibraltar of the Christian military. The Christians launched an attack with Army and Navy but failed to save Gibraltar. On his way back to Granada, the sons and relatives of Abul Ala Uthman assassinated him.

Sultan Yusuf

Sultan Muhammad was succeeded by his brother Yusuf who was then 16 but he was very wise, brave and God-fearing. He held together vital components of his government with caution and prudence and avenged the blood of his brother. Meanwhile, the Christian powers began to raid Gibraltar and its surrounding areas. Sultan Yusuf drew the attention of Abul Hasan Marini, the King of Morocco towards this. Abul Hasan sent his son towards Gibraltar with a detachment. Sultan Yusuf reached there from another side. The Christian troops tasted defeat in the encounter. When the Moroccan army was on its return journey, the Christians sniped at it and inflicted heavy casualties. In 740 A.H. Sultan Abul Hasan marched to Spain at the head of sixty thousand fighters while Sultan Yusuf came from another side to lend his support to Abul Hasan. A huge and well-equipped Christian army gave a heavy blow to the Muslim forces and captured a part of Granada. After this Sultan Abul Hasan went back to Morocco and Sultan Yusuf took refuge in Granada.

In 749 A.H., Sultan Yusuf appointed Lisanuddin Ibn al-Khatib as his Prime Minister and set himself to preparing for avenging his defeat. In 755 A.H., when Sultan Yusuf was quite ready to take on the Christians a stranger killed him with his spear while he was performing the Eid prayer and was in prostration.

Sultan Muhammad Ghani Billah

His son, Muhammad with the appellation of Ghani Billah, succeeded Yusuf. Sometime after coming to the throne he sent Lisanuddin Ibn al-

Khatib to Abu Salim bin Abul Hasan Marini, the King of Morocco to seek his help against the Christians. Abu Salim dispatched a detachment. No large-scale encounter took place and no purpose was served. Ridwan, the caretaker of Sultan Muhammad's government made inroads into his thoughts and feelings and was at the helm of all administrative affairs. Because of this, Ismail, the stepbrother of Sultan Muhammad captured the Granada Fort when Muhammad was away from the city at Generalife, the name of the garden resort for the Sultans of Granada (corrupted from the Arabic Jannat al-Arif and is considered part of the Al Hamra palace). When King Muhammad heard about this, he went straight to Gaudix and began to build his Army. He also sent a letter to the King of Castile requesting him for his help. He had not yet received any satisfactory reply from the Christian King when Abu Salim bin Abul Hasan Marini, the King of Morocco, sent Abu al-Qasim bin Sharif as his envoy to Sultan Muhammad and requested him to come to Morocco. He went to Morocco and was greeted with honor.

Sultan Ismail

Sultan Ismail also entered into correspondence with the King of Castile asking for his hand of friendship. Since the Christians were at war with the King of Barcelona at that time, they considered this offer of peace and friendship as a sign from providence. However, on 4 Shaban 761 A.H. Abu Yahya, the brother of Sultan Ismail killed Ismail and his coterie and captured the throne. On 27 Shawwal, Sultan Muhammad returned to Spain with the help of the King of Morocco and captured parts of Granada. Abu Yahya Abdullah, finding himself too weak to face the onslaught of Sultan Muhammad, rushed to the King of Castile for help. The Christian King had him and his Comrades killed at Seville on 2 Rajab 763 A.H. and captured all their possessions.

Sultan Muhammad Makhlu'a, on the other hand, captured Granada and came on the throne. For several years the Government of Granada had become a tributary of the Christian rule of Castile. Sultan Muhammad captured Granada and made all efforts to consolidate his position. Luckily, civil war started among the progeny of Abu Salim of

Morocco after his demise. The King of Castile was locked in battle with his own brother. Sultan Muhammad took advantage of these civil wars. He captured Gibraltar and refused to give tribute to Castile and the Christian powers could do nothing except keep silent. During Sultan Muhammad's rule, Granada flourished in every field and he became a terror for the Christian forces.

Sultan Yusuf II

Sultan Muhammad died in 793 A.H. and was succeeded by his son, Yusuf II. He was peace loving and wise and he finalized a peace treaty with the King of Castile. Among his four sons Yusuf, Muhammad, Ali and Ahmad, Muhammad was the cleverest one of them.

Sultan Muhammad VII

Yusuf II died in 798 A.H. Muhammad came on the throne by passing his elder brother Yusuf. Since a number of men in the family were given "Muhammad" as their name, Muhammad bin Yusuf the second is known as Muhammad, the seventh. A few days after the enthronement of Muhammad VII, clashes with the Christians took a fresh start. It resulted in the defeat of the Christians and the Muslims captured a number of Christian territories. During this time the King of Castile passed away leaving behind his suckling son John. After the baby was put on the throne, his Uncle Ferdinand took charge of the operation of affairs and acted as regent. The Christian troops were much greater in number so Muhammad the Seventh kept the Christian troops engaged on the battle front and invaded Jaen city with the rest of his army. This caused the Christians to send a considerable number of their men to save the city and the pressure on both fronts was so heavy that Ferdinand was forced to sign a peace treaty with Muhammad VII. By this technique the fighting between the two ended. However, in 803 A.H. a fresh encounter between the rival forces broke out and no side was able to subdue the other. The Christians once again requested peace and a peace treaty was signed, which served its purpose for only eight months. The terms of the treaty were still to be completed when Sultan Muhammad fell ill and died. His interned brother Yusuf, the third, succeeded him.

Sultan Yusuf III

Immediately after coming to the throne Yusuf III sent general Abdullah to Ferdinand to extend the term of the peace treaty for two years. When this two-year peace term was about to end, Sultan Yusuf III sent his brother Ali to the King of Castile as his envoy requesting him for a further extension. The Christian King thought his seeking peace was due to Yusuf's weakness and he told Ali that the request for an extension could be granted only with the payment of tributary. Ali rejected the conditional peace terms and left for Granada. Close on the heels of this rejection Ferdinand invaded Granada with a huge army and after a heavy encounter, the Christians took a part of Granada. The battle was going on when a detachment from Morocco launched an attack on Gibraltar under the command of Prince Abu Sayeed. Hearing of the onslaught Yusuf III sent his brother Ahmad at the head of an army to save Gibraltar. But the two princes entered into peace instead of fighting. Abu Sayeed then came to Granada as a guest of Ahmad. In the meantime the King of Morocco and elder brother of Abu Sayeed wrote Yusuf III to kill Abu Sayeed while he was in Granada. Yusuf III gave the letter to Abu Sayeed and told him that his brother had asked him to invade Gibraltar simply as a plot to kill him. Abu Sayeed was shocked at the nefarious plan of his brother. He then set himself to making preparations in Spain and then attacked Morocco with the help of Sultan Yusuf III. He dispossessed his brother and came to the throne. He thanked his benefactor, Sultan Yusuf III for his help and support.

The same year 820 A.H., King John of Castile took over the reign and deposed his uncle Ferdinand. He made peace with Yusuf III on the advice of his mother. Yusuf III was a lover of justice and most of the Christians would make him their mediator in personal disputes and would agree to his decision. Yusuf III passed away in 822 A.H.

Soon after coming to the throne Sultan Muhammad VIII, the son of Sultan Yusuf III renewed the peace and friendship treaty with Castile and Morocco and appointed Amir Yusuf as his Minister. Unfortunately, after sometime Muhammad VIII joined the company of the people having low and base conduct. Finally, Muhammad IX captured

Granada and Muhammad VIII fled for his life and went to the King of Tunis in the guise of a poor boatman. He greeted him with honor and promised him help.

Sultan Muhammad IX

After coming to the throne Sultan Muhammad IX made the nobles his supporters. But he committed the mistake of antagonizing the minister, Yusuf who began indulging in activities injurious to the administration. Yusuf, the minister, left Granada with one thousand five hundred men and came to Murcia and went to the King of Castile with his permission. He then tried to have John, the King of Castile lend his support to Muhammad VIII. The Christian King thus had an excellent opportunity to set the Muslims against each other. He advised Yusuf to send a deputation of selected persons to the King of Tunis and seek his help as well. The King of Tunis gave five hundred cavaliers and a substantial amount by way of help and sent Muhammad VIII on board his ship to Spain. When Muhammad VIII landed on the coast of Spain, he found the inhabitants of Almeria supporting him in the wake of efforts made by Yusuf. Muhammad IX sent his army to take on Muhammad VIII. When the rival forces came face to face a greater part of Muhammad IX's army changed sides and joined the rival camp. The rest fled back to Granada. Muhammad VIII advanced towards Granada and conquered it in 833 A.H. Muhammad IX was arrested and put to death.

After regaining the throne Muhammad VIII changed his ruling style on the advice of Yusuf and set himself to the task of bettering the lot of his subjects. He also attempted to make permanent peace with the Christian King but he agreed only on the condition of tribute, which Muhammad VIII declined. However, the King of Castile was himself facing disturbances in his territories and he could not challenge the Muslims. He invaded Granada in spite of his troubles. Both sides were engaged in a long drawn out battle in which victory and defeat came to both of them. The battle was still going on when Yusuf bin al-Ahmar, a close relative of Muhammad VIII rose in revolt against him. He staked his claim on the throne of Granada and entered into correspondence with the Christian King of Castile. He promised to pay annual tribute to the Christian King if he captured Granada besides helping him with his army. The Christians took it as a gift from providence. The King of Castile then sent his forces to reinforce Yusuf's men. Muhammad VIII launched an attack and a heavy battle broke out. The King of Castile was himself present at the battle but the battle remained undecided. At last the King of Castile returned to Cordova along with Yusuf Ibn al-Ahmar and Muhammad VIII left for Granada.

The King of Castile held his court in Cordova and appointed Yusuf Ibn al-Ahmar as the King of Granada and promised all possible help. He then dispatched Yusuf at the head of an army to capture Granada. He reached Granada and stormed the city with the active help of the local Christians. The Christians were satisfied that the two Muslim sides were set against each other inviting death and destruction upon themselves. Sultan Muhammad VIII sent his Minister Yusuf to punish Yusuf Ibn al-Ahmar but the latter killed the former. On hearing this news the people of Granada felt disturbed and they expressed themselves against Muhammad VIII. Muhammad VIII saw the writing on the wall and left Granada for Malaga along with all his treasures and possessions.

Yusuf bin Al-Ahmar

Yusuf bin al-Ahmar captured Granada and sent a letter to the King of Castile expressing his loyalty to him. He then started preparing to send an army to Malaga to arrest Muhammad VIII but he had not even sent the army when he passed away after ruling for only six months.

Immediately after hearing the news of Yusuf Ibn al-Ahmar's demise Muhammad VIII hurried to Granada and sat on the throne for the third time. He appointed Abdul Haq as his minister and Abdul Barr as his Commander-in-Chief. The Christians invaded Granada once again but the Commander-in-Chief fought them back. This defeat brought about discouragement in the Christian community and the rule of Granada became formidable once again. Unfortunately, civil war broke out at a time when there was an opportunity to improve the lot of the Muslims and strengthen their military power. Ibn Uthman, the Governor of Almeria and nephew of Sultan Muhammad VIII revolted against him and instigated the people of Granada against their administration. When they favored his plan, he came to Granada, took over as the chief of the insurgents and captured Al-Hamra Palace and put Muhammad VIII in prison after dethroning him for the third time. Abdul Bar, the Commander-in-Chief fled from Granada, collected the well wishers and began to think of ways to release Sultan Muhammad VIII. He knew that if he brought to the surface any demand for the release of Muhammad VIII he would be done away with. With this in mind he incited another nephew of Muhammad VIII named Ibn Ismail to stake his claim to the throne. Ibn Ismail agreed to the proposal. He met Abdul Bar after exchanging letters with the King of Castile and after getting permission from him to take over. It was an opportunity for the Christians to make a political gain. Thus Sultan Ibn Uthman's territories faced a two-pronged attack from Ibn Ismail and the King of Castile. The campaign continued for a long time. In 852 A.H., the King of Aragon and King Arbonia (Catalonia) both Christians waged a war against the King of Castile. When he himself suffered a setback, he pulled back his army from the Muslim front. Because of this, Ibn Ismail also kept silent until the end of the civil war. When Sultan Ibn Uthman came to know that the King Aragon and King of Arbonia (Catalonia) formed an alliance against the King of Castile, he sent his envoy to both the Kings and extended his hand of friendship besides ensuring them of his help when needed. Thus Sultan Ibn Uthman attacked Castile in 854 A.H. and forced the Castilian troops to flee. He ravaged Murcia province and came back to Granada with huge spoils of war. The next year he launched an attack on Andalusia and plundered it like he did to Murcia. He could have captured Cordova but he paid no attention to it. Ibn Uthman continued to help the two Kings against the King of Castile until 858 A.H. The Christian King of Castile then dispatched Ibn Ismail to attack Ibn Uthman the next year. Since Ibn Ismail enjoyed the support of the majority of Muslim nobles Ibn Uthman was defeated. He fled and took refuge in the mountains while Ibn Ismail came to the throne of Granada.

Sultan Ibn Ismail

Shortly after the enthronement of Ibn Ismail, John, the King of Castile died and was succeeded by his son. After John, his sons and grandsons resumed the battles against Ibn Ismail and the fighting lingered on until 870 A.H. During this series of battles Ibn Ismail's son, Abul Hasan achieved much renown. Ibn Ismail died in 870, and was succeeded by his son, Abul Hasan.

Sultan Abul Hasan

Since Sultan Abul Hasan was also an experienced Commander, he continued to fight the Christians adequately. But the doom of Muslim rule was not far away. Ferdinand, the young King of Castile was married to Isabella, the princess of the Kingdom of Aragon and with this marriage Aragon and Castile joined to make a mighty Christian state. Both Ferdinand and Isabella were great fanatics and hated the Muslims as a whole. They, therefore, decided together to wipe out Muslim rule from Spain. Unaware of what was going on against him Abul Hasan felt it expedient to make peace with the Christians. But his friendly gesture was rudely responded to with the demand of annual tribute from him. Abul Hasan not only rejected the demand rather disdainfully he also wrote back that his (Abul Hasan's) mint was minting swords instead of gold coins so that the heads of the Christians could be cut off. This bold reply sent terror into the heart of Ferdinand and he didn't invade the Muslim territory for several years. Abul Hasan had made a firm resolve to live a life of freedom and sovereignty and preferred death to being ruled by the Christians.

Having heard of the Christian preparations Abul Hasan himself made an advance and took the Sakhra Fort from the Christians. Ferdinand was shocked to hear of the loss of the fort. By way of retaliation, he invaded Al-Hamma Fort treacherously and captured it rather easily for there was no garrison to put up any resistance. Muslim fighters had inflicted no harm on the Christians while invading the Sakhra Fort but the Christian troops mercilessly massacred Muslim men and women. When the sad news of the fall of Al-Hamma Fort reached Granada, there arose a tremendous outcry. Sultan Abul Hasan sent an

Arab chief to recover the fort and he went and besieged it. Hearing of this the ruler of Cordova set out at the head of an army to save Al-Hamma Fort. Being informed of this, the Arab chief left a part of his troops to continue the siege while the rest of them he took with him to stop the advancement of troops from Cordova. When the two forces clashed, the ruler of Cordova fled the battlefield. However, the ruler of Seville, another Christian chief, appeared with a huge army. Since the number of troops outside the fort was very few, the Muslim troops raised the siege and returned to Granada and the fort was not restored. Since Al-Hamma Fort was very strong and lay near Granada it was a heavy loss for the Muslims.

In Jumad al-Awwal 887 A.H., Sultan Abul Hasan found out that Ferdinand was moving towards Granada at the head of a huge army. Abul Hasan also came out of Granada with his troops and both the armies clashed at Loja on the border of Granada. Ferdinand was defeated and the winning side collected heavy spoils of war. Unfortunately, Abu Abdullah, the son of Abul Hasan revolted against his father. Thus, close on the heels of his victory over Ferdinand, he was informed that his son had pronounced himself sovereign after capturing Almeria, Alpujarras and Granada. Abul Hasan had to remain at Malaga while Granada and half of the eastern areas came under the sway of Abu Abdullah Muhammad. However, the other half of the western part remained with Sultan Abul Hasan. Thus the division of this small Islamic state attracted the greedy eyes of the Christian rulers and Abu Abdullah Muhammad set himself to making preparations for taking the other half from his father. Thus, the allied Christian forces of Seville, Ecija (known as Estadja by the Arabs) and Sarish first attacked Malaga but they were defeated and the rulers of Seville and Sarish were arrested along with two thousand troops. The rest were either killed or forced to flee for their lives. When Abul Hasan returned to Malaga he found his son ready to capture Malaga too. Thus the father and the son faced each other and the fate favored the father. The son, Abu Abdullah Muhammad fled to Granada. When Abul Hasan entered Malaga victoriously, he became paralyzed and lost his eyesight. With this news, Abu Abdullah Muhammad felt safe from his father and attacked the Christian territories. He stormed into Lucena but the commander of the Christian forces played a trick on the inexperienced Muslim ruler. He attacked the Muslim troops from an ambush while they were going back carelessly laden with booty. All the troops were put to death and Abu Abdullah Muhammad was captured and sent to the King of Castile. Now the people of Granada invited Abul Hasan to take over the administration of Granada. The Sultan declined the offer due to his disability and asked his brother Abu Abdullah Zaghal to sit on the throne of Granada and he himself abdicated the throne and took to a life of seclusion.

Sultan Abu Abdullah Zaghal

Having come to the throne Abu Abdullah Zaghal embarked on his plan to regularize and improve his administration. But a huge Christian army attacked Malaga province and captured the forts lying mismanaged and neglected. They also besieged Baqwan Fort and shelled it so heavily that one wall of the fort gave it. The besieged Muslims although few in number came out and fought so gallantly that the huge Christian army suffered a heavy loss. At last the brave Muslim fighters succumbed to their injuries one by one, and the fort went to Christians. On Shaban 19, 890 A.H., Sultan Zaghal left Granada to manage the affairs of the bordering areas and was camping in a field when a Christian army caught them unaware and began to kill Muslim troops. When the fighting and killing began to advance towards Sultan Zaghal, the Muslim fighters stood in the way and charged at the enemy so violently, that the Christian fighters took to their heels leaving behind thousands of dead and injured. The Muslims gave them chase and captured their artillery. King Ferdinand was also moving forward with a huge army when he came across the runaway defeated Christian soldiers. When he heard that the Muslim fighters had captured their artillery and had strengthened the fort with it, he decided to return.

Despite some successes, here and there Ferdinand was utterly convinced that the annihilation of the Muslims, as a whole was not an easy proposition. Even though the area of the Islamic state was much reduced they could have won the whole of Spain with their swords if they had made a joint venture and fought like one man as they had done during the times of Tariq and Musa. The wisdom and farsightedness of Ferdinand stopped him from further campaigns against Muslims. He thought it better to use tricks and deception. Abu Abdullah Muhammad bin Abul Hasan the prisoner of the battle of Lucena was in his possession.

He called Abu Abdullah Muhammad before him and talked to him in very polite words and instilled in his mind that he was the rightful heir of the Granada rule and his uncle Zaghal had usurped his right to rule. He also assured him all help in case he was able to take Granada from Zaghal. He tried to bring home to him that his only interest lay in a good Islamic State enjoying peace and prosperity behaving like a good neighbor. Abu Abdullah came straight to Malaga highly excited and intoxicated with the sense of ensuing success in his mission. He met the people and asked them to follow him to victory and safety from Christian invasions. Since they were desperately in need of peace and safety they made no delay in extending their support for him. He easily became the ruler of Malaga. Even though Zaghal attempted to put down the insurgence, active support from the Christians inhabiting the Muslim territories caused his mission to fail. Abu Abdullah then asked his uncle, Zaghal for the important center of Loja and promised a joint attack on Ferdinand in lieu of this coveted gift. When Zaghal found most of his people inclined to the demand of Abu Abdullah, he gave away Loja to his nephew but Abu Abdullah very treacherously handed over Loja to Ferdinand. Abu Abdullah then left to besiege the forts of Albirah, Maslin and Sakhra and he gave away all these forts to Ferdinand after capturing them with the active help of the Christian King. Thus what was a Herculean task for Ferdinand became easier with the support of Abu Abdullah. Now the eyes of the Muslims opened and they charged him as an agent of the Christian King who captured cities and forts and handed them over to the King of Castile. Now the people of Malaga renewed their loyalty to Sultan Zaghal and removed all signs and traces of Christian rule. Ferdinand attacked Malaga with a huge army and sent warships to the coast of Malaga as well. Zaghal came out from Granada to arrive at Malaga but Abu Abdullah Muhammad captured Granada in his absence. Zaghal moved towards Granada leaving Malaga under the siege of Ferdinand. When he heard that Abu Abdullah Muhammad captured Granada, he stopped in Guadix. The people of Malaga checked the advances of the Christian troops with exemplary courage and determination and requested the rulers of Morocco, Tunis, Egypt and Turkey to save them from the jaws of the Christian monsters. However, none of them paid heed to their entreaty, and in a state of utter disappointment, they handed over Malaga to the Christians. When they met their doom as a result of their disunity and discord and felt it deeply, they extended their hand of friendship towards the Christians but they rejected the request scornfully and demanded the key of the city. When the Christian ruler subdued Malaga, he ordered the arrest of every Muslim and seizure of their wealth and property. They enslaved fifteen thousand Muslims and the rest were banished from Malaga without goods and chattels and many of them died of starvation. Some of them reached the African coast and settled there. Ferdinand then ravaged the surrounding areas of Malaga and destroyed the cities and forts and drove away all the Muslim population. The Christian ruler was set to obliterate all signs of Muslim rule from Spain. He then arrived in Gaudix and extended his hand of friendship towards Zaghal and tempted him with the rule of Granada. Zaghal welcomed the friendship of Ferdinand for he wanted to see Abu Abdullah Muhammad's disaster. Thus, he gave away Gaudix to Ferdinand and accompanied him. Ferdinand won Almeria without any difficulty with Zaghal on his side. Abu Abdullah Muhammad was happy to find his uncle, Zaghal in the clutches of Ferdinand. Sitting in the magnificent al-Hamra Palace he was dreaming of his exclusive rule in Granada. At last calamity knocked at Abu Abdullah's door. He received a letter from Ferdinand ordering him to hand over Granada. Shocked and stunned he read out the calamitous letter to the influential people of Granada. He then said to the people that Zaghal had persuaded Ferdinand to take possession of Granada and al-Hamra Palace and also to fight with him. The people of Granada were fully aware of the depravity of Abu Abdullah Muhammad in destroying the Islamic rule and his role as a stooge in serving the nefarious design of Ferdinand at the cost of Muslim honor and unity. They favored fighting with the enemy. Abu Abdullah Muhammad had to bow before public opinion. Consultations were still going on when Ferdinand of Castile arrived with a huge army and laid siege around Granada. The citizens rose with courage and determination and fought gallantly against the Christians. Aware of the bravery and resolution of the Muslim fighters the shrewd Ferdinand decided to put off his campaign against Granada for the time being. He raised the siege and went back, Abu Abdullah took advantage of the respite and marched to some of the forts that had already been captured by the Christians. He recovered those forts and put a large number of Christian fighters to death. He then came back to Granada, strengthened his troops and came out again for further attacks. During his fresh campaigns, he captured some of the towns in Alpujarras and restored the Andarsh Fort and unfurled the flag of Islam atop by throwing away the Christian one. The entire population of Alpujarras showed their loyalty to the Muslim ruler.

Abu Abdullah's uncle Zaghal was also staying somewhere in Alpujarras. He felt terrified with the rising power of Abu Abdullah and informed Ferdinand that the growing strength of Abu Abdullah could prove menacing for the Christian rule if not checked right away. Zaghal utterly ignored the cause of Islam and rose to resist the advancement of Abu Abdullah's forces with the help of Christian troops. The courage and bravery of the people of Granada filled Abu Abdullah with so much enthusiasm that he pounced upon Hamdan, Mankab, and Shalobania. Before the victory of Shalobania Abu Abdullah came to know that Ferdinand of Castile was proceeding to Granada and so Abu Abdullah turned towards Granada. Putting aside Granada Ferdinand reached Gaudix and committed a large-scale massacre of the Muslims and banished the rest. He also razed the Andarsh Fort to the ground and returned after rampaging through the cities and forts that came in his way.

On the way back to Castile, Ferdinand told Zaghal rather rudely that he was no longer in need of him and the maximum he could do for him was to allow him to go out of the bounds of his country. With this order, Zaghal left Spain and went to Africa and passed the rest of his life at Tlemcen (city in Northwest Algeria) in obscurity. Ferdinand practiced utmost patience and endurance in implementing his plans of gradually wiping out all signs and traces of the Muslims from the face of Spain. The people of Granada also lost courage with the constant news of the massacre of Muslims and the devastation of their cities.

End of Islamic Rule in Spain

On 12 Jumad al-Awwal 896 A.H., Ferdinand reached Granada along with Queen Isabella at the head of huge army with heavy artillery. With his arrival he embarked on a rampage ravaging greenery, gardens, crops and the populated areas and set a river of Muslim blood to flow. He set up a military cantonment in front of Granada and besieged the city. Discouraged and disheartened, the Muslim population once again broke the siege and plunged into fighting against the surrounding troops sacrificing their lives. The siege continued for eight months and this was the last Muslim population in the whole of the Spanish peninsula. When winter set in and snow capped the mountains and obstructed supply routes, they told Abu Abdullah to go to war with the Christians. They showed their determination to go down fighting on the battlefield rather than to die of starvation. They reminded him of Tariq bin Zeyad when he crushed one hundred thousand well-equipped Christian soldiers with a handful of troops, and their Muslim fighters numbered nearly twenty thousand so they had no reason to fear one hundred thousand Christian troops. Abu Abdullah was now fully convinced that the surging flood of his people, if ignored, would result in open revolt against his rule. He convened an emergency meeting of his ministers, nobles, religious scholars and celebrities of the surrounded city at al-Hamra Palace. Abu Abdullah could not say addressing them that the Christian forces would never raise their siege without capturing the city what could then be done to tackle the problem? Abu Abdullah was so depressed than nothing more could be expected of him at that moment, and then the entire audience said in one voice, "It is better to sign a peace treaty with the King of Castile". Commander Musa bin Abul Ghassani got up in zeal and said, "There is still hope of success. We must not lose hope and fight to the finish. I hope we shall be able to drive the Christians away and force them to raise the siege". Although the citizens had the same opinion that Musa had expressed none among the audience supported his advice. They expressed fear that in case they lost the battle none of the Muslims would be left alive. They wanted peace and safety for their lives and property. Since the subjects and soldiers had expressed themselves in favor of giving battle to the enemy, Abu Abdullah Muhammad sent his minister, Abul Qasim Abdul Malik on a secret mission to buy peace from Ferdinand. Since the Christians also were tired of the long-drawn siege of the Muslim city and they wanted some honorable course to arrive at a final decision, they welcomed the peace proposal and readily agreed to sign it. In order to keep the peace talks a secret Abul Qasim would go to the Christian camp in the darkness of night. The peace treaty was, however, signed by Abu Abdullah Muhammad and Ferdinand after some initial differences.

Peace Treaty with the Christians

The peace document contained the following conditions:

1. The Muslims will enjoy the liberty of either living in the country or leaving it. No harm will be caused to the life and property of any Muslim.

2. The Christians will not seek to interfere in religious affairs of the Muslims.

3. No Christian will intrude into mosques.

4. Mosques and trusts will remain intact.

5. Muslim affairs will be decided by Muslim judges according to the Codes of *Shari'ah*

6. Prisoners on both sides will be set free.

7. A Muslim intending to go to Africa will be sent on board ship.

8. The converted Christians will not be forced to abandon Islam.

9. The spoils of war possessed by the Muslims will not be recovered.

10. No tax other than the existing ones will be levied on the Muslims.

11. No tax will be realized from the Muslims for a period of three years; they will also remain exempt from the existing tax for this period.

12. The Government of Al-Bashrat will be handed over to Sultan Abu Abdullah.

13. After sixty days from the signing of the treaty Al-Hamra Palace and the artillery and other means of warfare, which it contains, will be given to the Christians.

14. Within sixty days from signing, the treaty will be completed with all its conditions.

15. Granada city will be left free for one year. After one year the Christians will capture it fulfilling the conditions mentioned above.

The treaty was signed on 1 Rabia al-Awwal 897 A.H. The event could not remain a secret from the people of the city and the Army. There was widespread discontent and Abu Abdullah was charged with destroying the Muslim state. He grew extremely anxious and handed over Al-Hamra Palace to the Christians for fear of public insurgence. Ferdinand asked Mandhurah, the Archbishop of Spain to first step in the city and set a cross atop of the highest tower of Al-Hamra Palace pulling down all Islamic signs so that the King along with his queen can watch the change before making their entry into the city. When Abu Abdullah noticed the arrival of Mandhurah in the Palace, he came out at the head of fifty chiefs on horseback. The entire city looked deserted and its people grief-stricken and deeply distressed. Abu Abdullah then moved forward to the King of Castile and handed over the keys, saying: "O Mighty King! We are now your subjects and entrust this country of ours to you for it was the Will of Allah. We trust that you will treat your subjects gently and generously". Ferdinand wanted to utter some consoling words but Abu Abdullah went ahead and left for al-Bashrat after meeting Queen Isabella. His relatives and goods and chattels had already been sent ahead. Meanwhile the silver cross glittered atop the tower in the sunshine and the Christian King stepped into al-Hamra Palace with royal grandeur. When Abu Abdullah reached a mountain top, he turned towards Granada and recalled his past magnificence and burst into tears. His mother who accompanied him remarked:

"When you could not save your country despite being a brave soldier what is the use of shedding tears like women now?"

Christians' Atrocities on the Muslims' of Spain

Soon after capturing Al-Hamra Palace the Christians forgot all the conditions mentioned in the peace treaty. They captured Granada and bought Alpujarras from Abu Abdullah for a paltry sum of money, with the result Abu Abdullah went to Morocco and became an employee of the King of Morocco and died after serving the King for many years. Ferdinand set up a Christian law court throughout the country where Muslims were brought on untrue and fabricated charges and were burnt to death as punishment enjoined by the law court. Actually, they were punished for being Muslims.

A general order was issued in 904 A.H., to confess Christianity or face death, with the result that the Muslims escaped to the hills and accepted a miserable life instead of renouncing Islam. Some of the Christians who had already converted to Islam were baptized. But they, however, kept sticking to Islam and worshipped Allah inside their houses.

Those Muslims who opted for migrating to Africa were provided with ships and they boarded the ships with their books and other valuables. However, many of the ships were sunk in the sea before reaching the African coast.

Finally, not a single Muslim was to be found in the whole of Spain. They were all put to the sword or burnt or drowned.

A Glance at the Islamic Rule in Spain

Even though Arabian rule in Spain was autocratic like the righteous era it was, however, dominated by a democratic temper. The command of Caliphs and the Codes of *Shari'ah* were applied equally to all and sundry. A certain Christian lodged a complaint against Abdur Rahman II of the Umayyad dynasty in a law court and the ruler lost the case and had to fulfill his obligations like a slave. The judge in the Muslim courts had full power to punish the Caliph. Police administration was at its best. Government officials roamed about the market-place checking business transactions and the prices of commodities. They had set up hospitals and dispensaries and a network of roads and canals all over the country. Caliph Hisham had built a giant bridge across the river, Wadi al-Kabir. In the art of warfare Muslims were the most civilized of all. The Muslims of Spain were the first to invent tools for dismantling forts. During their 800-year rule Muslim rulers taught savage Christians a lesson on how to behave in a civilized and humane manner in the wake of victory. While the Christians behaved wildly and violently massacring Muslim men, women and children, the Muslim conquerors spared the Christian population following their victories. Moreover, they brought about peace and prosperity to the Christian lands in the wake of their victories. They developed agriculture to the extent that it became a perfected art. They turned hundreds of thousands of square miles of barren and deserted land in Spain into gardens of fruits, trees and greenery. Spain and the entire European continent came to know of rice, cotton, saffron, pomegranate, and peach through the Muslims. They produced olives and dates in Andalusia and Seville and grapes in Sarish, Granada and Malaga, besides other agricultural development. They were the first to find mineral deposits in Spain and explore mines of gold, silver, iron, mercury, copper, ruby, and sapphire. Granada was the last sign of Muslim rule in Spain but even that small rule left magnificent monuments of Muslim glory and grandeur. The Muslims of Spain invented cement of such an amazing quality that Al-Hamra Palace is still an object of wonder for the tourists of the world. It was built by the Muslim rulers of Granada on a very high mound under the shade of the snow-clad peaks of the Sierra Nevada. It had within its walls such beautiful and green gardens and fruit trees that the like of which was never witnessed by the sky. During their rule, the Muslims established all over the country universities, schools, laboratories and magnificent libraries, which contained resources for academic research of all kinds. In the universities of Cordova, Seville, Malaga, Saragossa, Lisbon, Jaen, and Toledo students from Italy, France, Germany, and England would come to receive education in various sciences and arts. The Muslim scholars translated books on Greek philosophy into their own languages. Ibn Rushd too was a Muslim, of Spain who was superior even to Aristotle. Muslim scientists set up such laboratories and developed Astronomy to such an extent that the entire Europe followed them. The astrolabe, the soul of all laboratories, was invented by none but the Muslims of Spain. In medical science and surgery they made such progress that until recent times the whole of Europe benefited from their books. They made advances in Zoology and Botany and they developed separate gardens and factories for this purpose. Manufacturing paper out of cotton and jute was their remarkable achievement. In terms of modern warfare Alfonso XI has written:

> "Muslims of the city would hurl resounding objects and apple-sized iron shells. These shells covered such a long distance that they hit the enemy ranks directly and at times fell beyond the lines."

This statement makes it clear beyond a doubt that when the Muslims used artillery and gunpowder the Christians were unaware of all these things. The writer of Senin al-Islam writes that some of the Muslims of Spain had discovered America as far back as 441 A.H. but this discovery was not made famous. It was Columbus who later achieved fame as the man who discovered America.

It was the Muslims' deep love for knowledge and their great fondness for the arts, literature and philosophy that opened the doors of art and science for the Europeans. For eight hundred years the Muslims were the teachers of the Europeans. Christian nobles, during this long period, took pride, in learning from and following the Muslims in language, style, expression and other things of this kind. They wrote Arabic prose and poetry purely in Muslim style. In French and Italian languages most of the words related to shipping and naval activity come from Arabic. And this provides ample proof that they learned about shipping activities from the Muslims. Most of the words concerning hunting and recreation are Arabic in origin while names of medicines and astronomical terms that are current in European languages belong to Arabic.

It is worth-mentioning here that when Muslim fighters conquered Spain in the first century Hijra they didn't force a single person to accept Islam. They would embrace Islam because of its inherent traits and superiority. But, when, the Christians captured Muslim territories they put all kinds of pressures upon the Muslims to confess Christianity and when they failed in their mission they massacred hundreds of thousands of Muslims, burned them alive and drowned them.

Chapter 12

Morocco and North Africa

Some historians are of the opinion that the progeny of Ibrahim عليه السلام Bani Israel settled in Morocco. Roman and Greek dynasties also ruled these territories. The world-renowned Carthage belonged to North Africa. The Goths had also taken Morocco by storm as they did in Iberia (Spain). The Berbers inhabited Morocco and its adjoining eastern territories and were formed, in fact, from the totality of the Arabs, Syrians, Egyptians, Greeks, Persians, and Romans. Territorial conditions and climatic influences carved them out as a people distinct from all others in respect of taste, temperament and disposition which made them inclined to harshness, cruelty and barbarity and they remained so until they embraced Islam. Whenever they forgot their Islamic discipline their old sense of enmity, rivalry and feuds rose again.

Morocco was conquered by Uqba bin Nafe. Even though it revolted against the Muslim rule each time it was subdued. Musa bin Nusayr, Governor of Africa and Morocco had entrusted the rule of Morocco to Tariq bin Ziyad. Tariq and Musa bin Nusayr then conquered Spain. Shortly after the conquests of Morocco and Spain, the Berbers started insurgent activities. In Spain they were easily crushed but their uprising in North Africa lingered on for a longer period. Such a disturbing situation drew the attention of forces antagonistic to Islam towards this country.

Idrisia Rule

Idris

We have already made mention of Imam Muhammad bin Abdullah and his family while dealing with the Abbasid dynasty and how they were ruined in Makkah. A member of the same family named Idris reached Morocco along with his servant. He settled in Prolila whose chief Abdul Hameed greeted him honorably. Gradually Idris become popular among Zawagha, Lawata, Zanata, Sadrota, Meknes and the Ghanaza clans of the Berbers. With the efforts of Ishaq bin Muhammad bin Abdul Hameed most of the Muslim clans among the Berbers took the oath of allegiance to Idris's Caliphate. In a very short period Idris built a strong army and waged *Jihad* on those Berber clans, which still were outside the circle of Islam. After subduing them he managed to teach them Islam and Idris became their Caliph or Sultan.

Idris attacked Tlemcen and the Governor of the province expressed his loyalty to him. Idris made it his capital and built a mosque there. He strengthened his military power very rapidly. His quick progress and expanding area of power and influence made Caliph Harun Rashid anxious. However, he sent his slave Sulaiman bin Jarir to do away with Idris. Sulaiman appeared before Idris as an opponent of Harun Rashid. Idris believed him and eulogized him among his courtiers.

His Death

Sulaiman gave Idris a kind of tooth powder, which choked him to death and Sulaiman escaped safely.

Idris II

Soon after the death of Idris his slave Rashid brought to the notice of the people that a Berber slave-girl named Kanzah was pregnant by Idris and they should, therefore, make the oath of allegiance to the child after its birth. In this way, Rashid was able to keep intact the country ruled by Idris. The Berber slave-girl gave birth to a male child. Rashid asked the people to take *ba'it* at the hand of the child and the people did accordingly. They made *ba'it* when he was weaned and once again when he was a boy of twelve. The same year Ibn Aghlab, the Governor of Africa incited the Berbers against Rashid and he was killed. However, this did not break the *ba'it*. The boy was also named Idris and came to be known as Idris II or Idris Junior. After Rashid, Abu Khalid bin Yazid bin Ilyas Abdi was appointed as his instructor.

Conquests

Being aware of the art of statesmanship Idris II appointed Mus'ab bin Isa Azdi as his Minister. He then gradually expanded his territories and captured almost the whole of Morocco. Men in large numbers from Arabia, Spain, Africa, Egypt, Syria and other far off places came to Idris II in search of peace and prosperity and added to the splendor and activity of the country. Idris shifted his capital from Prolila, a small town Fez where he laid the foundation of a new city, which flourished very quickly. After initial conflicts with the Berbers Idris succeeded in dominating every tribe and Morocco become a country wholly and solely ruled by Idris II, independent of the Abbasid Caliphate.

Muhammad bin Idris

Idris II or Junior died in 213 A.H. and was succeeded by his son Muhammad. It so happened about the same time that Sulaiman bin Abdullah bin Hasan bin Muthana bin Hasan bin Ali bin Abi Talib, the full brother of Idris I reached Tlemcen via Egypt and Africa. The Berbers took the oath of allegiance at his hand he was able to found his rule in Tlemcen.

Kanizah, the mother of Idris II and the grandmother of Muhammad bin Idris put forward a suggestion that Muhammad alone should not rule the entire country and his brothers should also be given various parts of the country to set up their independent rule. Her proposal was accepted. Accordingly, Muhammad was given Fez and its surrounding areas while among his brothers, Qasim got Tangier, Sayut received Taitwan, and Umar was given Tabkisyan, Targha and the rule of Dahajah and Ghamrah tribes. Daud received Hamarah, Matalsol, Tazi and Meknes and Gheyatha tribes. Abdullah got Baghwat, Nafis, Jibal, Madamdah, Lamata, Saus, al-Aqsa. Yahya got Basila, Ara'ish, Darogha and Isa was given Shala, Sala, Azmur and Tamasna and Hamza got Walila and its outskirts. Those who were still young boys were put under the care of their grandmother, Kanizah. Tlemcen was already captured by Sulaiman bin Abdullah. Thus, the mighty Empire of Morocco was cut into pieces by acting upon the suggestion of a woman. After a short time Isa of Azmor attacked his brother Muhammad bin Idris. Muhammad asked his brother Qasim to help in the fight but he refused to obey. He then sent Umar to face Isa and the former defeated the latter and attacked the occupied territories. Muhammad then asked Umar to punish Qasim who had defied his order.

Umar attacked Qasim and Qasim was defeated after a bloody encounter. Qasim passed the rest of his life in seclusion, practicing piety and purity of life. Umar attacked the territory of Qasim and thus added to his strength and power yet he remained loyal to his brother, Muhammad. When Umar died in 220 A.H. Muhammad made his son Ali bin Umar his father's successor.

His Death

Seven months after the death of Umar, Muhammad bin Idris also died in 221 A.H. He had appointed his 9 year old son, Ali as his successor and crown prince before his death.

Ali bin Muhammad

After Muhammad the courtiers and the powerful section of the society were pleased to pledge their support to Ali bin Muhammad. He set himself to rule his country properly. He kept peace throughout his thirteen-year rule. He died in 234 A.H. and appointed his brother Yahya bin Muhammad as his successor at the time of his death.

Yahya bin Muhammad

Yahya bin Muhammad added much to the power and splendor of his rule. During his tenure the Idris Caliphate came to be counted among the most magnificent states in the world. The population of Fez flourished, trade reached its peak and religious scholars and intellectuals came to join his court.

Yahya bin Yahya

Yahya bin Muhammad was succeeded by his son Yahya bin Yahya. His misconduct displeased his people and they rose in revolt against him under the guidance of Abdur Rahman bin Abi Suhail and deposed Yahya bin Yahya and banished him from Fez. Ashamed and dishearten he died shortly after that. Ali bin Umar was still the ruler of his state and after the shameful exit of Yahya bin Yahya he came to Fez and ascended the throne. Shortly after that, Abdur Razzaq Kharji rose in revolt and captured most of their territory and the Idrisi dynasty passed though a precarious state.

Yahya bin Idris bin Umar

Yahya bin Idris bin Umar bin Idris Junior became strong enough to capture Morocco in 292 A.H. and restored the lost splendor of Idrisi dynasty. He is considered the greatest King among the Idrisi leaders. At that time, the Ubaidite (Fatimid) ruled over Africa. The Ubaidite army invaded Morocco in 305 A.H. Yahya bin Idris came out to give battle but was defeated after fierce fighting. Yahya came back to Fez and made efforts to buy peace. He was given peace on condition that he would show obedience and pay some money annually in cash as a token of loyalty. When Talha bin Yahya bin Idris, the son of Yahya bin Idris became the ruler he was captured by the Ubaidite troops. He had to pass two years in captivity and settled in Mahdiya after being released and died there in 331 A.H.

By 309 A.H., Morocco and Fez came under the rule of the Ubaidites (Fatimids). In 313 A.H., Hasan bin Muhammad bin Qasim bin Idris rose against Raihan Katami, the Ubaidite Governor of Fez and established Idrisite rule once again in Fez. But the Ubaidite commander, Musa bin Abi al-Aliya invaded and captured Fez and Hasan was put to death. Most of the small districts of Morocco were still ruled by the Idrisities. They at last turned towards the Sultan of Spain who captured Morocco and drove away the Ubaidites. Morocco become a province of the Cordova rule.

End of Idrisite Rule

Sulaiman bin Abdullah, already mentioned, was brother of Idris senior or Idris I. He had established his rule in Tlemcen and Tiaret. Muhammad bin Sulaiman succeeded his father but civil war broke out among Banu Sulaiman with the result the country broke into small pieces.

The Aghlabs of Africa

During Umayyad dynasty the viceroy of the Berber countries of Northern Africa lived in the Qairwan city of Tripoli and the governors of Morocco and Spain were appointed on the advice of the Viceroy of Qairwan. During the Abbasid rule, when Spain and Morocco broke away from the central government, the status of the Viceroy of Qairwan was reduced to Governor. Since this territory was also like Morocco with respect to the political climate and the Berbers that inhabited it, changing of Governors and revolts had become common.

Ibrahim bin Aghlab

In the wake of frequent changes of the Governor, Muhammad bin Muqatil took over the province, once again he had to face the displeasure of the citizens. They wrote Ibrahim bin Aghlab to request the Caliph for the province. Following this message Ibrahim bin Aghlab submitted to Caliph Harun Rashid that he spent one hundred thousand dinars from the Egyptian revenue to run the administration of Tripoli while the province gave nothing in return. After this statement he promised to send forty thousand dinars annually from Tripoli without asking for a farthing from the central government if the province was given to him. Caliph Harun Rashid agreed and issued Ibrahim bin Aghlab a letter of authority to take over the administration of the province. Since the change was in the public interest peace prevailed in the entire territory. Ibrahim bin Aghlab took over the rule of Tripoli and founded a new city adjacent to Qairwan and named it Abbasia.

Battles

A person named Hamdis rose against the Abbasids. Ibrahim bin Aghlab sent Imran bin Mujahid at the head of a strong army to put down the revolt. Hamdis was crushed after a fierce battle and ten thousand insurgents lost their lives. Following this Ibrahim bin Aghlab paid constant attention to the far west. Idris had already died in Morocco and Rashid was running the administration in the name of Idris Junior. Ibrahim Aghlab attracted the Berbers with costly gifts and rewards with the result that a party of the Berbers beheaded Rashid and sent his head to Ibrahim bin Aghlab in Qairwan. But, during this period, the citizens of Tripoli rose in revolt against Sufyan bin Muhajir, the Governor of Ibrahim bin Aghlab and forcibly drove him out of the province. Ibrahim sent troops to Tripoli and regained his lost territory. Imran bin Mujahid rose strongly against Ibrahim in Tunis in 195 A.H. and captured Qairwan. Ibrahim bin Aghlab dug trenches around Abbasia and took refuge in his guarded city. Imran besieged the city for a long period of nearly one-year. Although a number of encounters took place between them, neither one of them gained any advantage. Ibrahim informed Caliph Harun Rashid about the state of affairs and requested money, which the Caliph sent without delay. Ibrahim bin Aghlab then attracted a large number of Imran's troops by the lure of large sums. Imran grew anxious with the deteriorating condition of his military power, raised his siege and went to Zabin, Ibrahim then sent his son, Abdullah, to Tripoli in 196 A.H., but a few days after assuming power he suffered a serious military revolt with the result he was surrounded in his palace. He was given peace only on the promise of leaving Tripoli. Abdullah came out of Tripoli but stayed on the outskirts where he began to collect some Berbers around himself by the power of the purse. He then invaded Tripoli and captured it. A few days after this event Ibrahim bin Aghlab deposed Abdullah from Tripoli and appointed Sufyan bin Mudar as Governor. The people of Tripoli revolted again and forced him out of Tripoli and Sufyan went straight to Ibrahim in Abbasia. Ibrahim sent Sufyan again to Tripoli along with his son, Abdullah and after a large-scale blood bath peace came to Tripoli but for a very short time. It was actually a lull before the storm. Abdul

Wahab bin Abdur Rahman bin Rustam then invaded Tripoli at the head of a strong Berber force and killing and bloodshed broke out.

His Death

Ibrahim bin Aghlab passed away in Abbasia in 196 A.H. When the news reached Tripoli, Abdullah made peace with Abdul Wahab He gave the outskirts of Tripoli to Abdullah and kept the city of Tripoli under him. He then went towards Qairwan.

Abdullah bin Ibrahim

Ibrahim bin Aghlab appointed his son Abdullah as his crown prince before his death and exhorted his second son Ziyadatullah to obey his brother. Abdullah bin Ibrahim bin Aghlab arrived at Qairwan in 197 A.H. and took over the administration and succumbed to a wound to the ear in 201 A.H., after ruling for five years. His brother, Ziyadatullah, succeeded him.

Ziyadatullah

Ibrahim Aghlab had received the authority of ruling the country on contract from Caliph Harun Rashid. After coming to the throne Ziyadatullah received a letter from Mamun Rashid ordering him to invoke for Abdullah bin Tahir from the pulpit. Ziyadatullah felt this to be problematic and while bidding farewell to the messenger of the Caliph he sent some valuable gifts along with a few dinars bearing the stamp of Idrisite rule making clear that he could at anytime, build up his relation with the Idrisite government.

Revolts

Shortly after that Zeyad bin Sahl, one of his military officers, revolted against him and besieged Bajah city. Ziyadatullah sent his army, which captured Zeyad and put him to death. Mansur Tirmidi revolted in Tanjah (Tangier) and invaded Tunis and Ismail bin Sufyan, Governor of Tunis was killed in the encounter. Mansur captured Tunis. Ziyadatullah sent his cousin and Minister Aghlab bin Abdullah at the head of an army and told him at the time of departure that he would kill him if he came back defeated. Mansur defeated Aghlab bin Abdullah. On the way back to Qairwan his troops killed him out of fear for their lives and joined Mansur. Mansur became powerful and captured Qairwan. Ziyadatullah took refuge in Abbasia. After a siege of forty days Ziyadatullah became victorious and Mansur fled to Tunis. Various generals of his Army captured different parts of the country and only a very small part remained under the possession of Ziyadatullah. However, he gradually subdued all other rulers and annexed their territories.

Conquest of the Island of Sicily

The Caesar of Constantinople ruled over Sicily where his governor carried out his orders. Caesar sent a crusading General, Qaseal to replace him and he appointed a Roman named Femi as Admiral of the Navy. Femi took the African coast by storm and established himself as a force to be feared on the sea. At this time, Caesar wrote to the Governor of Sicily to arrest and send the Admiral to him. When the Admiral came to know of this order, he went into Sicily and captured the city of Martusa. Fierce fighting took place between the Governor and the Admiral in which the former was killed. Admiral Femi then captured the whole of the Island and declared himself the sovereign ruler. He then put a person named Blat as the administrator of part of the Island. Mikhail, the cousin of Blat ruled over another part of the Island. These two brothers jointly rose against Femi. After a number of encounters they captured Syracuse. Femi took refuge with his fleet, and then came to Ziyadatullah for help. He sent Asad bin Furat, the Qadi of Qairwan with him at the head of a detachment.

The island of Sicily was first invaded by the Muslims during the Caliphate of Muawiyah bin Abu Sufyan and was led by Abdullah bin Qays Fazari it was done as a strategy to destabilize the Romans and this happened in 33 A.H. Musa bin Nusayr, the Viceroy of Africa, invaded the Island in 85 A.H. and the Island was attacked again by a commander of Caliph Yazid bin Abdul Malik in 102 A.H. Bishr bin Safwan Kalbi attacked it in 109 A.H., during the Caliphate of Hisham bin Abdul Malik. The Muslims won victories in all these encounters and brought large amounts of booty and many captives. Mustanir bin

Harth, the General of Ubaidah bin Abdur Rahman Qaisi, the viceroy of Tripoli launched an attack on Sicily but it failed due to a storm at sea and the sinking of his ships. In 122 A.H., Ubaidullah bin Hijab, the Governor of Africa sent Habib bin Ubaidullah along with his son, Abdur Rahman bin Habib to Sicily. Abdur Rahman bin Habib got off at the coast and started winning victories and made his way into Sicily up to Syracuse, its capital. The ruler of Sicily agreed to hand over the Island to Abdur Rahman bin Habib but the Island was taken out of Islamic rule before long. The ruler of Africa once again made an assault on Sicily in 135 A.H. but the Muslim powers could not look towards Sicily until 212 A.H.

Femi came to Ziyadatullah and persuaded him to conquer the Island. Ziyadatullah sent the Qadi of Qairwan, Asad bin Furat with a fleet of one hundred ships besides the ships of Femi. He instructed the commander to annex Sicily and set up a permanent Islamic Government after winning it and obliterating all signs and traces of the Romans. The war fleet left in the middle of Rabia al-Awwal 212 A.H. and reached the coast of Sicily after the third day. Blat, the ruler of Sicily sent an army to face the Muslim invaders. A battle between the two forces broke out and the Muslim troops moved ahead crushing the Christian fighters. Even though Femi was accompanying the Muslim army, he was growing sad and dejected with the winning spree of the Muslim fighters. He started sending secret information and advice to the Christians, which proved injurious to the Muslim strategy. However, the forward march of the Muslim troops could not be checked and it resulted in the death of Blat. Femi also met his doom when the Christians of Sicily appointed another man as their ruler in place of Blat and kept fighting the Muslim army. Qadi Asad bin Furat laid a siege around Syracuse but he died during this siege in Shaban, 213 A.H.

The Muslim troops elected Muhammad bin Abul Jawari in place of Qadi Asad bin Furat. Close on the heels of this development ships laden with troops were sent from Constantinople. But, after fierce fighting the fresh reinforcing troops were fought back. Unfortunately an epidemic broke out among the Muslim troops, which proved more injurious than the Christian attacks. It took a heavy toll of Muslims lives. Because of this they raised their siege and decided to go back to the occupied cities and regroup to comeback and conquer the Island. While they were moving back, they found the warships from Constantinople surrounding the area and the Christian forces proceeded to attack the retreating Muslim soldiers and surrounding them in their camps. Muhammad bin Abul Jawari died during the attack.

The Muslim troops immediately chose Zuhayr bin Auf as their commander. The Muslims were besieged for some time when by chance, a fleet of Muslim warships from Spain was sailing in quest of waging *Jihad* and happened to be in the Mediterranean Sea. When the besieged Muslims of Sicily found out about this, they contacted the fleet and brought to their attention the precarious state of the Islamic forces. Responding to the call for help three hundred boats were directly sent to the coast of Sicily. They landed on the coast and started fighting the Christians and forced them to raise their siege and flee. After their freedom, the Islamic forces resumed their conquests. The Spanish fleet after doing the needful took leave. The African Islamic forces besieged Palermo and set up their government over the occupied territories again and in the meantime, reinforcements from Africa in the form of military boats arrived.

The army that had come with Asad bin Furat numbered ten thousand and seven hundred in all, ten thousand infantry and seven hundred cavalry. Palermo had not been conquered when Muhammad bin Abdullah bin Aghlab, the cousin of Ziyadatullah arrived after becoming Governor of Sicily. Palermo was ruled by the Romans. The southern half of Sicily was under Muslim rule while the northern part was controlled by the Christians and they received constant help from the Caesar of Rome. However, the Muslim were continuously expanding their territories and after the conquest of Palermo, Sicily virtually became a province of the Aghlab rule and a Muslim Governor presided over it.

The greatest accomplishment of Ziyadatullah's rule was the inclusion of Sicily to the Islamic lands. Muslim rule continued on the island for almost three hundred years. Civil war among the Muslims caused it to be lost to the Christians and they wiped out all the Muslims from Sicily as they did in Spain.

His Death

Ziyadatullah died in 223 A.H. and his brother Aghlab bin Ibrahim Aghlab succeeded him.

Aghlab bin Ibrahim Abu Iqal Aghlab

He kept his subjects happy and any revolts were quickly dealt with. He died in 226 A.H., after a peaceful rule of two years and seven months. His son Abul Abbas bin Ibrahim bin Aghlab succeeded him.

Abul Abbas Muhammad

Abul Abbas also ruled like his father. But Abu J'afar, the brother of Abu Abbas rose in revolt in 240 A.H., and deposed Abul Abbas and set up his own rule. Abul Abbas rebuilt his army and drove him out of Egypt and regained the throne in 242 A.H. Abul Abbas died and was succeeded by his son Abu Ibrahim Ahmad bin Abul Abbas.

Abu Ibrahim Muhammad

After coming to the throne Abu Ibrahim brought about an increment in the salaries of his fighters built forts at various places. He also continued fighting with the Romans of Sicily.

In Shawwal, 247 A.H., the Muslims won a great victory over the Romans and a large number of captives were brought to Africa. They were sent to the Caliph Mutawakil in Baghdad from the Aghlab family despite having their own independent rule, they were attached to the Baghdad Caliphate's authority. Abu Ibrahim Ahmad died in 249 A.H. and was succeeded by his son Ziyadatullah who gained fame as Ziyadatullah the Younger.

Ziyadatullah

Ziyadatullah's rule was similar to his elders but he did not rule for more than one year when his brother, Muhammad bin Abu Ibrahim entitled Abul Gharaniq came to the throne.

Abul Gharaniq

Abul Gharaniq came to the throne in 250 A.H. following the death of his brother, Ziyadatullah. He was fond of fun and sport. During his period the Romans conquered a part of Sicily. However, shortly after that the Muslim forces took it back from them. He built a number of forts along the border of Morocco and in the coastal areas. He died in 261 A.H. after ruling for eleven years and was succeeded by his brother Ibrahim bin Abu Ibrahim.

Ibrahim bin Ahmad

Ibrahim bin Ahmad was a wise person. He began well and made his administration strong and stable and minimized the possibility of insurgence. Egyptian forces invaded Africa in 267 A.H. but Ibrahim's troops repelled the attack. An interval of insurgence broke out in 269 A.H. and took a heavy toll of Muslim lives before coming to an end. The Khawarij attack against the government in 280 A.H. took the entire country by storm. Ibrahim faced the disturbance with exemplary courage and determination and put down the uprisings by sending his troops to every corner of the country. Following this event he recruited Sudanese fighters for his forces and horsemen from the Sudanese slaves rose to thirty thousand. Ibrahim came to Tunis from Qairwan in 281 A.H., built a palace and settled there.

News came from Sicily in 287 A.H. that the people of Palermo had revolted. Ibrahim sent his son, Abul Abbas Abdullah at the head of a fleet consisting of one hundred and sixty warships. Abul Abbas reached Sicily and gave repeated reversals to the Christian insurgents and brought peace to the entire island. He then moved ahead with his boats and invaded the coastal areas of France and returned after a long campaign of one and half years. On his return, Ibrahim himself attacked the coastal areas of France and the French feared him much. He was still besieging some areas when he passed away in 289 A.H. and was buried in Palermo. During the rule of Ibrahim a Shi'ite named Abu Abdullah Husain bin Muhammad began to preach love for the *Ahl-e-Ba'it* (members of the Prophet's family) in Kutama city towards the south of Mount Atlas lying between Morocco and Africa. He gained much popularity and strength and started putting pressure on the Aghlab rule after capturing Kutama. On the death of Ibrahim Aghlabi, his son Abul Abbas Abdullah came to the throne.

Abul Abbas

Abul Abbas chose Tunis as his capital. He sent his son Abul Khul at the head of an army who massacred the followers of Abu Abdullah the Shi'ite. Abu Abdullah again built his army and launched an attack on Abu Khul. After a day and night encounter Abu Khul was defeated and came back to Tunis. He collected fighters again and proceeded to attack Abu Abdullah, the Shi'ite but the latter sniped at his army, which fled in disorder. He built his army once again and marched on Abu Abdullah's territories. Unfortunately, his brother, Ziyadatullah bin Abul Abbas hatched a conspiracy with the servants of his father and did away with Abul Abbas and came to the throne in Shaban, 290 A.H. On getting news of the event Abu Khul came back to Tunis but was arrested and killed. Ziyadatullah killed his other brothers and uncles too. His appellation was Abu Mudir.

Abu Mudir Ziyadatullah

After Abu Mudir Ziyadatullah's accession to the throne Abu Abdullah, the Shi'ite captured Setif city and his power expanded greatly. Abu Mudir passed a life of luxury and lacked courage. He left Tunis and settled in Raqqadah, and sent his General, Ibrahim bin Habeesh to take on Abu Abdullah the Shi'ite, Ibrahim bin Habeesh marched with an army of forty thousand men and stayed in Ksar el-Kabir for six months. During this period, he collected fighters from far and near, which at last rose to one hundred thousand. He then advanced towards Kutama but was unexpectedly defeated and fled back to Qairwan.

Abu Abdullah conquered and killed the Governor, Fath bin Yahya. The victories won by Abu Abdullah stirred the people of Qairwan and other cities. Ziyadatullah spent money like water to restore peace and order and kept the recruiting process going but Abu Abdullah continued moving ahead, capturing one city after another until he conquered Qamudah.

End of Aghlabia Dynasty

In the wake of the fall of the city of Qamudah Abu Mudir Ziyadatullah left Raqqadah by ship laden with goods and chattels and moved towards the east. He first wanted to land in Alexandria but the Governor did not allow his entry. He then landed on the Syrian coast and settled and died in Riqa. This virtually was the end of Aghlabia dynasty. Abu Abdullah, the Shi'ite then captured all the territories of the Aghlabia dynasty and took an oath of allegiance from the people for Ubaidullah Mahdi and this was the beginning of Ubaid (Fatimid) dynasty. It was the same year that Abu Ubaidullah, the Shi'ite captured Qairwan and Raqqadah and sent Hasan bin Khazir Katami as the Governor of Sicily. However, the people of Sicily put Hasan bin Khazir in captivity in 299 A.H because of his rudeness and evil disposition and requested Ubaidullah Mahdi to replace him with someone else.

Chapter 13

Ubaidullah Dynasty in Egypt and Tripoli

Abu Abdullah

With the beginning of Abbasid Caliphate, the Alwis (type of Shites) started antagonistic activities against the Abbasid administration. The Alwis tried repeatedly to disrupt the Islamic caliphate and each time they met with failure. Abdullah bin Saba, the Jew had sown the seeds of discord among the people and conspiracies against the central administration. Their nefarious plan was aided and abetted by the Magians, Jews, and Berbers who carried out their activities in the garb of new Muslims. When the Abbasid dynasty showed signs of weakness, some Jews and Magians tried to present themselves as Alwis to benefit from the situation of their increased power. Since Berber territories were far from Baghdad, the center of the ruling power, they took advantage of this situation. A person named Muhammad Habib who lived in Salmia near Homs, Syria towards the end of the third century Hijra came on the scene claiming descent from Imam J'afar Sadiq's elder son Isma'il. He tried to take advantage of his relation with the Imam. Imam J'afar Sadiq's influence had spread throughout Yemen, Africa and Morocco. He used all his means, devices and force to get the people ready to expect the arrival of Imam Mahdi in the immediate future and indoctrinated them with the idea that he would be from among the Alwi Fatimid. Habib sent one of his confidants Rustam bin Hasan bin Hoshab to Yemen to convince the people there of the arrival of Imam Mahdi in the near future and he performed his duty with the utmost care and tact.

Following this a man named Abu Abdullah Hasan bin Muhammad bin Zakariya, a Shi'ite by faith, and a staunch supporter of the Alwis came to Habib. Habib found him promising and sent him, after the necessary instructions, to be in the company of Rustam bin Hasan for a short time and learn from him the art of preaching and then to go to the Berber territories to perform his duty. Muhammad Habib also told Abu Abdullah that his son, Ubaidullah was Imam Mahdi and that he was being sent as one of those inviting people to him. Abu Abdullah arrived in Yemen, took lessons in preaching and reached Makkah in the Hajj season. He came close to the wealthy and powerful people of Kutama, from North Africa, who were in Makkah for Hajj and accompanied them to Kutama when the Hajj was over. He plunged himself into preaching and influenced a large section by exhibiting his piety and dedication to the prayers. Abu Abdullah, the Shi'ite came to Kutama on 15 Rabia al-Awwal 288 A.H. and began to convince the people of the advent of Imam Mahdi without experiencing any difficulty. The people of Kutama built a house for Abu Abdullah and he set up his preaching center there. He was able to convince the people around him that the place where Imam Mahdi would appear was to be Kutama and he was very sure that *Kutama* was the place that the Imam would appear. They were told by him that they should keep ready and be alert to welcome, follow and support him.

When Ibrahim bin Ahmad bin Aghlab, the ruler of Africa, came to know of these activities of Abu Abdullah, he ordered him to stop it otherwise he would be punished. By this time, the entire area of Kutama and the surrounding tribes had accepted the doctrine preached by Abu Abdullah. Finding himself strong enough Abu Abdullah showed disrespect to the envoy of the ruler and sent him back with rude and harsh words. The people of Kutama on reflection feared punishment from the ruler and decided to save the situation by turning Abu Abdullah out of Kutama and sent him to Ibrahim bin Ahmad, the ruler of North Africa. However, the religious leaders opposed this proposal and united to help him. With their efforts Harun Ghassani, the Governor of the province invited him to Touggourt. The people of Kutama also reversed their stand and extended their strong support to Abu Abdullah and his power and influenced increased to a great extent. With all the help and support and favorable circumstances Abu Abdullah gathered so much strength that he became the ruler of the western part of the country and it all happened within a short period of one and half years.

When Ibrahim Aghlabi's son Abul Abbas Abdullah bin Ibrahim came to throne, he sent his son, Abu Khul to take on Abu Abdullah. At first Abu Abdullah lost the battle to Abu Khul but later Abu Khul was killed and Abu Abdullah's problem was solved. When Ziyadatullah, the last ruler of the Aghlabi dynasty came to power, Abu Abdullah had ample opportunities to expand his area of influence. He then began to preach with full force that the advent of Imam Mahdi was at hand. Messengers of Abu Abdullah came to him and informed him that his rule had already been established in the western territory and Ubaidullah, then known as Ubaidullah al-Mahdi was requested to take over the administration of these territories. Ubaidullah was accompanied there by the people of Salmia and his son, Abul Qasim and a slave went with him. They proceeded in the guise of a trade caravan and chose a zigzag path instead of straight one. Spies informed the Abbasid Caliph Muktafi that such and such person had left from Salmia to the western territories. Muktafi issued orders to Governor of Egypt, Isa Nawishtri, to arrest the man of such and such features on his way to the western territories via Egypt. The Governor rounded up the caravan but later left Ubaidullah go due to a lack of positive identification. Ubaidullah reached Tripoli and sent word to Abu Abdullah in Kutama of his arrival. The Governor of North Africa, Ziyadatullah Aghlabi, stood in the way of their meeting. The Governor had already been informed that Ubaidullah was heading towards Abu Abdullah, following this alert he posted his men at several places to catch him. The person who had been informed of

Ubaidullah's arrival was Abu Abdullah's brother, Abul Abbas, who was sent along with his men to escort Ubaidullah. Abul Abbas was arrested in Qairwan and Ziyadatullah put him to prison. When Ubaidullah came to know of the arrest of Abul Abbas, he fled to Ksar el-Kabir and then to Sijilmassa where al-Yasa the servant of the Governor, Ziyadatullah Aghlabi, took him to be a tradesman and treated him honorably. When the Governor issued orders to arrest Ubaidullah he was captured by al-Yasa. Abul Abbas and Ubaidullah Mahdi suffered the bitterness of captivity for three or four years in Qairwan and Sijilmassa respectively. During this period Abu Abdullah, the Shi'ite kept conquering territories. By 296 A.H., he collected a huge army of two hundred thousand and took his brother, Abul Abbas, out of the prison after conquering Qairwan in 296 A.H. He then appointed Abul Abbas as Governor of Qairwan and proceeded to Sijilmassa. Various tribes on the way showed their loyalty to him and when he reached near Sijilmassa, he wrote a very soft letter to al-Yasa bin Madra'a seeking peace. When the envoy of Abu Abdullah met al-Yasa, he killed the envoy, tore up the letter and came out to fight with Abu Abdullah. Following a fierce encounter al-Yasa's troops fled to safety and al-Yasa and his men followed suit. Following his conquest Abu Abdullah stormed into the city went straight to the prison and freed Ubaidullah Mahdi along with his son, Abul Qasim. He then had Ubaidullah Mahdi and his son Abul Qasim mounted on horseback and followed Ubaidullah shedding tears of joy and saying: "This is your master. This is your master." He escorted him to camp, had him seated on his throne, took *ba'it* and made the others follow him. Al-Yasa was brought in chains and was ordered to be put to death.

Ubaidullah Mahdi

Abu Abdullah and Ubaidullah set out towards the west after passing forty days in Sijilmassa and Qairwan. Abu Abdullah presented all his possessions to Ubaidullah. *Ba'it* of Caliphate for Ubaidullah Mahdi was administered. His name came to be mentioned in the Friday address and preachers were sent to the Berber territories to teach them the new doctrine. All the people were forced to accept their faith. The people of Kutama had been supporting Abu Abdullah and so gained the upper hand in the army and the administration. Abu Abdullah and his brother, Abul Abbas were active in governmental affairs. It was Abu Abdullah who had brought such a great empire into existence. He was instrumental behind uprooting the Aghlabi dynasty and called Ubaidullah to take charge of the administration.

After coming to the throne and finding himself a sovereign ruler, Ubaidullah wanted to wipe out the influence of Abu Abdullah and his brother, Abul Abbas. At this point Abu Abdullah's eyes opened. The people of Kutama had more faith in Abu Abdullah and they had accepted Ubaidullah as Imam Mahdi with the efforts of Abu Abdullah. Abu Abdullah began to convince the people secretly that the identification of Ubaidullah as Imam Mahdi was his mistake, and that he was certainly not the Imam, the Innocent. He was, in fact, a usurper and a man-eater. The real Imam Mahdi was yet to come. Most of the people of Kutama sided with him and when Ubaidullah came to know of this, he began to kill the people hatching the conspiracy against him. With the mutual consultations of Abu Abdullah and the people of Kutama, Sheikh al-Mashaikh the leading religious leader of Kutama, a very pious and noble person of the city, was sent to Ubaidullah Mahdi. He went and asked him to show any sign of his being Imam Mahdi. Ubaidullah foresaw the lurking danger and he signaled his slave and Sheikh al-Mashaikh was beheaded. The people of Kutama were violently engaged and wanted to kill Ubaidullah.

Abu Abdullah Assassinated

In view of the deteriorating situation Ubaidullah invited two of the most influential chiefs of Kutama named Aruba bin Yusuf and his brother, Habasa bin Yusuf to his special place of retreat and talked to them very sincerely and affectionately. Later, he asked them to kill Abu Abdullah and his brother Abul Abbas. His order was duly implemented and both the targets were attacked and done away with. This event took place in 298 A.H.

Revolts

In the wake of this event the supporters of Abu Abdullah revolted against Ubaidullah who faced the situation and put down the insurgence. After a short time, the people of Kutama rose up against Ubaidullah and he once again put it down with a heavy hand. Since the atmosphere of the country was deteriorating, Ubaidullah stopped preaching the Shi'ite creed. Following this Ubaidullah Mahdi gave Bajah to Aruba bin Yusuf, Barqah (Cyrenaica) to Habasa bin Yusuf and appointed his son Abul Qasim as his crown prince. After a few days, the people of Kutama appointed a youth as their chief and declared him Imam Mahdi and very violently revolted against Ubaidullah. They also declared this youth a Prophet. Ubaidullah sent his son Abul Qasim at the head of a huge army to punish the people of Kutama. Abul Qasim defeated the people of Kutama and ravaged Kutama and the young Mahdi was also captured and killed. The people of Tripoli revolted in 300 A.H. Abul Qasim was sent to face the uprisings and he conquered Tripoli after a long siege.

Abul Qasim led a strong navy and invaded Egypt and Alexandria in 301 A.H. Habasa bin Yusuf also accompanied the navy. Alexandria was conquered. When Caliph Muqtadir Abbasi of Baghdad received the news he dispatched an army under the command of Sabugtagin and Munis, his slave. They were able to force Abul Qasim and Habasa out from the borders of Egypt. The Ubaidite forces returned to Qairwan. Habasa once again launched an attack on Alexandria in 302 A.H. but Munis, the slave forced him to flee after a few encounters. Seven thousand of Habasa's troops lost their lives and Habasa escaped miraculously. Ubaidullah Mahdi killed Habasa the same year. Following the killing of Habasa his brother Aruba revolted against rule of Ubaidullah. The people of Kutama lent their support to Aruba. Ubaidullah chose his slave, Ghalib to punish Aruba. He assaulted Aruba with a huge army and defeated and killed him along with his cousins and comrades. Soon after that Sicily revolted and drove out the Governor, Ali bin Amr from the territory. They then sent word to Caliph Muqtadir Abbasi showing their loyalty to him. Ubaidullah sent Hasan bin Khazir at the head of a war fleet to punish the people of Sicily. Ahmad bin Qahrab defeated and killed Hasan bin Khazir after a fierce encounter. The people of Sicily feared punishment from Ubaidullah so they caught Ahmad bin Qahrab and sent him to Ubaidullah and sought his forgiveness. Ubaidullah killed Ahmad and appointed Ali bin Musa bin Ahmad as the Governor of Sicily.

The Founding of Mahdiya City

Since Ubaidullah Mahdi was an Isma'ili Shi'ite and one who claimed to be Imam Mahdi, he was in constant fear of uprisings against him, particularly when the whole North Africa did not accept his claim. He planned to found a new city for his capital. He visited the coastal areas and chose a narrow rocky peninsula on Cape Ifriqiya and laid the foundation of a city. He named it Mahdiya. The city was strengthened with strong fortifications and iron doors. When the work was completed, Ubaidullah Mahdi said laughingly, "I have today, won peace for Bani Fatima. They are now safe". The same year he set up a boat factory, which built nine hundred boats for his fleet in the first year. He then sent his son, Abul Qasim to invade Alexandria in 307 A.H. Abul Qasim conquered Alexandria and captured the Nile Delta. After receiving this news Caliph Muqtadir of Baghdad sent his slave, Munis, to Egypt. After a number of encounters and trials of strength Munis was victorious. Ubaidullah had sent a fleet of eighty war ships to reinforced Abul Qasim but he had been defeated and forced to flee before the reinforcements arrived. The fleet was unaware of the defeat of Abul Qasim and they continued moving ahead. The fleet met its doom when Munis smashed it, set the boats on fire and killed them all.

The next year 308 A.H. Ubaidullah Mahdi sent Mudala bin Habus to invade Morocco. He came into conflict with Yahya bin Idris bin Amr more than once. Finally, Yahya became subordinate to Ubaidullah Mahdi, and Ubaidullah appointed Musa bin Abi al-Afiya Maknasi as the caretaker of the Moroccan provinces. In 309 A.H., other provinces of Morocco were also annexed under the Ubaidite rule. Fez was then under the rule of Yahya. The same year Musa bin Abi al-Afiya lodged a complaint against Yahya and by the order of Ubaidullah Yahya's part of the territory was also annexed to Ubaidite rule. When the Idrisite rule was no longer in effect, some individuals of the dynasty shifted to Rif (Northeastern Morocco) and Ghumarah (Northwestern Morocco) and established their governments there. After dealing with Morocco Mudala invaded Sijilmassa and handed it over to his cousin by killing family members of the Madrar Maknasi tribes, who were antagonistic to the Ubaidites. Mudala was a great commander who had played a pivotal role in setting up Ubaidullah Mahdi's rule in Morocco. However, his expansionist policy, violence and bloodshed made the Berbers rise up against him. A number of encounters took place and Mudala was finally killed. With his assassination Morocco was overtaken by revolt and it went out of the control of the Ubaidites.

Ubaidullah sent his son, Abul Qasim to Morocco in 215 A.H. When Muhammad bin Khazar, the chief of the Zanata tribes realized Abul Qasim was moving towards him he changed his way and turned to the southern deserts. Abul Qasim proceeded towards the west conquering city after city. He besieged Hasan bin Abi al-Atish in Jerada city (Northeastern Morocco). The siege dragged on and Abul Qasim had to return without any gains. On the way back, he arrested Banu Kamlan, the ruler of the city of Masila and banished him to Qairwan. He then reconstructed Masila, named it Mohammedia and entrusted it to Ali bin Hamdan along with Zab city. He gave the general rule and vigilance to Musa bin Abi al-Afiya but, very shortly, he rose against Ubaidullah Mahdi and accepted the leadership of the Umayyad dynasty of Spain and the name of the Caliph of Spain formed part of all official addresses all over Morocco.

Hearing this Ubaidullah sent Ahmad Maknasi to Morocco at the head of a strong army. After a number of encounters Musa bin Abi al-Afiya moved towards Spain and Ahmad Maknasi went towards Mahdiya after ravaging Morocco.

Death of Ubaidullah

Ubaidullah Mahdi died in Rabia al-Awwal, 322 A.H. after completing twenty-four years on the throne. He was succeeded by his son Abul Qasim Muhammad Mahdi under the title "Qaim Bi Amrillah". He is also known as Abul Qasim Nazar.

Abul Qasim Nazar

On coming to the throne he first put down the uprisings that had broken out in the wake of Ubaidullah's demise. He then turned to Morocco. It was again taken over by Musa bin al-Afiya. By 324 A.H., the whole of Morocco except Fez once again came under the rule of Abul Qasim. Following this Abul Qasim sent a General named Ibn

Ishaq at the head of a massive navy to conquer the northern coastal line, Ibn Ishaq conquered the whole territory up to Genoa followed by the island of Sardinia. Ibn Ishaq then sent his slave, Ziran to Egypt with an army that captured Alexandria. After these events Abul Qasim became involved with the disturbances created by a man named Abu Yazid and continued to be occupied with this.

Skirmishes with Abu Yazid

Abu Yazid Mukhallad bin Kirad belonged to Qastila and would frequently visit Sudan as a part of his trading activities. His son, Abu Yazid was born and brought up in Sudan. The Sudanese were inclined to Kharji creed and opposed the Shi'ite sect. Yazid was also influenced by their religious thoughts. He then came to Nahert and took to teaching. It was the period when Abu Abdullah, the Shi'ite had commenced his preaching work among the Berbers. Abu Yazid continued preaching his thoughts and creed among the people and watched Abu Abdullah's activities silently. Both Abu Abdullah and Ubaidullah were aware of the preaching efforts of the teacher but important administrative affairs and military activities did not give them an opportunity to uproot Abu Yazid's antagonistic ideas. When Ubaidullah Mahdi died and the country was overtaken by disturbances, Abu Yazid started preaching with force and determination and gave himself the title Sheikh al-Muminin. People in large numbers started coming and joining him as disciples. He was able to build a strong army out of his disciples. When the ruler of Bejaia came to know of Abu Yazid's war preparations, he attacked Abu Yazid but was defeated. Abu Yazid moved ahead and besieged Bejaia, which lingered on for a long time and he left in disappointment. Berber tribes lent their support to him and he ordered them to mention the name of Musa bin Nusayr, the Caliph of Spain in addresses from the pulpit. With the help and support of the Zanata tribes Abu Yazid gradually rose to power and city after city went out of Abul Qasim's control. Even though Abul Qasim sent seasoned Generals and Commanders, each one was defeated. Abu Yazid's army captured Qairwan and Abul Qasim was forced to take shelter in his fort. Abu Yazid then spread his troops all over Tripoli and bloodshed and plunder broke out. Abul Qasim wrote to some governors still free from the sway of Abu Yazid. The people of Kutama came to his help. However, the people of Kutama fled the battlefield when the other forces, which took the field on behalf of Abul Qasim, were beaten. After that Abu Yazid led his troops up to the fortifications of Mahdiya city but failed to make progress there. At last, Abu Yazid moved back to Qairwan and Abul Qasim's troops began to snipe at his retreating army.

Death of Abul Qasim

Abu Yazid's son Ayub invaded Mahdiya and besieged it in 324 A.H. During this siege, Abul Qasim died in Mahdiya. Abu Yazid was then laying siege around Susah city.

Isma'il bin Abul Qasim

Isma'il bin Abul Qasim succeeded his father and entitled himself Al-Mansur. Isma'il raised the siege of Ayub bin Abu Yazid and sent a contingent to reinforce the army in Susah. Abu Yazid made an all out effort to obstruct the launching of the enemy fleet but met with failure. The reinforcing troops landed on the coast and took the battlefield against Abu Yazid with the active support of the people of Susah. Abu Yazid was beaten and his military camp was plundered. He moved to Qairwan in distress because of his defeat, the people of Qairwan turned out his Governor from Qairwan and stopped Abu Yazid from coming into the city. At the same time they declared their loyalty to Abul Qasim. Abu Yazid then moved to Sabha. Following this Isma'il bin Abul Qasim came to Qairwan and consoled the citizens. Abu Yazid invaded Qairwan with a massive army in 334 A.H. Ismail faced the invasion but conceded defeat after a number of encounters. However, he rebuilt his army in a very short time by collecting his scattered fighters and defeated Abu Yazid after a fierce attack. Abu Yazid moved to Bejaia, defeated and disappointed and the people closed the door of the city on him. At last, Abu Yazid besieged the city.

Hearing this Isma'il bin Abul Qasim led his army to Bejaia. When Abu Yazid heard of Ismail's arrival, he left Bejaia and besieged another fort. He was unsuccessful for Isma'il also went there as well to support that fort. Abu Yazid continued to wander from here to there and at last Abu Yazid and Isma'il came face to face near the mountain of Kutama. Abu Yazid was injured and escaped leaving ten thousand fighters killed and wounded. Although Abu Yazid plunged himself into the task of collecting troops once again, his Governors and allied tribes joined the camp of Isma'il bin Abul Qasim by seeking his forgiveness. In that way all the territory, which until then was ruled by Abu Yazid, came under the control of Isma'il Abul Qasim bin Ubaidullah.

Abu Yazid's Arrest and Death

When Abu Yazid was captured from Fort Kutama he was badly injured and died of his wounds before long. Isma'il then went to Qairwan. Shortly after that he was informed that the Governor of the western territory, Hameed bin Baslin, had revolted against the Ubaidite dynasty and submitted himself to Umayyad dynasty of Spain. Ismail led his army to punish the rebel Governor and they faced one another at Tiaret. Hameed was beaten and about the same time Fadl bin Abu Yazid, besieged Bejaia. Isma'il turned to punish him but before the occurrence of an event someone beheaded Fadl and sent it to Ismail. After attaining peace for a short period he deposed Khalil bin Ishaq from Sicily and replaced him with Husain bin Ali bin Abul Husain.

Death of Isma'il

In 340 A.H. Isma'il built a massive war fleet and asked Husain bin Ali bin Abul Husain, the Governor of Sicily to be ready to join the fleet. The southern part of Italy was conquered and the victorious army returned to Qairwan and Mahdiya rich with spoils of war in 341 A.H. but Isma'il had already died.

Muiz bin Isma'il

His son, Muiz, succeeded Isma'il. The first year of his coming to the throne some Berber tribes expressed their loyalty to him. In 344 A.H., he sent word to Husain bin Ali bin Abul Husain, Governor of Sicily to invade Murcia, on the coast of Spain. Husain carried out the orders and returned with booty and prisoners. As a retaliatory action, Nasir ad-Dinullah of Spain ordered his slave, Ghalib to lead a fleet to invade the coast of Africa. But Muiz's forces were ready to face them and

Ghalib had to return without attainting any success. However, the Spanish fleet successfully invaded the coast of Africa in 347 A.H. and returned with a large number of captives and huge amount of valuables as booty after completely ravaging the coastal areas and cities.

Following this Muiz turned to building up his military power, regularizing the administrative machinery of the country and expanding his territories. The persons mentioned below governed the following provinces:

Province	Person
Ifkan and Tiaret (Northwestern Algeria)	Yala bin Muhammad
Ashir (North Central Algeria)	Ziri bin Manad Sanhaji
Masila (North Central Algeria)	J'afar bin Ali, the Spanish
Bejaia (Northeastern Algeria)	Caesar of Sicily
Fez (North Central Morocco)	Ahmad bin Bakr bin Abi Sahl
Sijilmassa (Southeastern Morocco)	Muhammad bin Wasal Maknasi

During the last days of 347 A.H., Muiz got the news that Yala bin Muhammad was plotting against his rule. He sent his scribe, Johar of Sicily to punish Yala with the help of J'afar bin Ali and Ziri bin Manad, the Governors of Masila and Ashir respectively. Yala bin Muhammad also accepted the challenge. The Governors of Fez and Sijilmassa also rose up in revolt. After fierce fighting and bloodshed, Yali was arrested in 348 A.H. and Fez and Sijilmassa also fell. Ahmad bin Bakr and Muhammad bin Wasal were also caught and brought to Qairwan.

During the Abbassid rule one of the banished groups from Spain landed on the banks of Egypt and captured Alexandria during the governorship of Abdullah bin Tahir. He surrounded them and promised peace and safety on the sole condition of their departure from Egypt. The banished Spanish group left Alexandria and captured Carat Island and accepted Abu Hafs Bluti as their King. The Christian navy attacked the Island with a fleet of seven hundred warships. After a heavy toll of Muslim lives, the island fell to the Christians, The Caesar of Constantinople and Muiz's navy clashed in 354 A.H., which ended in the defeat of the Christians. Muslim forces marched ahead captured a number of cities and forced the Caesar of Constantinople to pay the *Jizyah* (poll tax) and tribute. A short time after this event Muiz came to know that, following the demise of Kafur Akhashedi, the Governor of Egypt, disorder and disruption had spread all over Egypt.

Conquest of Egypt

Muiz gave his minister and scribe, Johar a huge army in 355 A.H. and ordered him to march to Egypt, he proceeded gradually regularizing the administrative affairs. Akhashedi's troops could not withstand the assault; with the result that Johar stormed into Egypt on 15 Shaban 359 A.H. and delivered an address in the name of Muiz from the Grand Mosque of Egypt. In Jumad al-Awwal 359 A.H. Johar offered his prayer in Grand mosque of Ibn Tulun and ordered them to add, *"Hayya ala Khair il amal."*

This was the first *adhan*, which was pronounced in Egypt with this addition. After capturing the entire country of Mahdia Johar arrested all the relatives of the Akhashedi family and sent them to Muiz in Egypt. He then sent his General J'afar bin Falah Katami to Palestine and Syria at the head of an army. He captured Damascus in 360 A.H. It added to the joy of Muiz who then resolved to make Cairo his capital. He then appointed Balkin bin Ziri bin Manad as viceroy of the western territories and asked him to reside in Qairwan and conferred on him the title of Abul Futuh. In Shawwal 361 A.H. he left his capital Mahdiya and stayed near Qairwan.

Transfer of the Capital to Cairo

Shortly after the departure of Muiz from Mahdiya all his treasures, possessions and belongings were sent to Egypt along with the troops. Balkin bin Ziri escorted him for a stage or two. Balkin was then dispatched to Qairwan and Muiz himself set out towards Barqah and arrived at Alexandria in Shaban 362 A.H. The citizens came out to greet and lead him honorably into the city. He reached Cairo on Ramadan 5, 363 A.H. The journey from Qairwan to Cairo took about one year. Before this Bani Tabghaj ruled over Damascus and they paid tribute to the Qaramatians. When J'afar bin Falah captured Damascus, he refuse to pay tribute to the Qaramatians. The King of the Qaramatians, A'sim, attacked Damascus. J'afar fought the Qaramatians back. They launched a massive attack on Damascus once again in 361 A.H. Although J'afar faced the assault gallantly, he was killed on the battlefield and Damascus fell to the Qaramatians. Their next target was Ramla. After capturing Ramla, they started preparing for the invasion of Egypt. Muiz came to know all this during his journey. When he arrived in Cairo, he was informed that the Qaramatians had besieged Jaffa and their forces were concentrating on the borders of Egypt.

Encounters with the Qaramatians

Shortly after reaching Egypt Muiz wrote a long letter to A'sim, the King of the Qaramatians detailing the submission and subordination of his elders to those of his own and to banish from his mind all thought of fighting. He wrote back:

"Your letter reached me. It is poor in content and lavish in words. We are about to attack you".

A'sim dispatched the letter to Egypt and ordered his troops to get ready for battle. He then led the army himself and entered the borders of Egypt halting at Shams. Hassan bin Jarrah Tai, the Chief of Arabia joined A'sim with a large group from Tai. A'sim and Hassan held talks and then spread small fighting groups to ravage the towns and villages of Egypt. The entire territory was engulfed by blood and fire. Muiz grew afraid of the massive fighting forces of the Qaramatians. The Qaramatians made no delay in attacking Cairo. In view of the advances of the Qaramatians Muiz wrote a letter to Hassan bin Jarrah and promised to give him one hundred thousand dinars if he would desert A'sim's forces on the battlefield and leave the field along with his own troops. Hassan bin Jarrah agreed to take the bribe and complete the treachery. Thus, according to the agreement as Muiz came out and attacked the Qaramatian army Hassan and his troops left the field. A'sim and his fighters lost their nerve. Although they kept fighting, they lost the battle at last. About one thousand five hundred Qaramatians were taken as prisoners of war. Muiz sent his commander, Abu Muhammad at the back of the fugitives and he drove them out of Egyptian territory. ˙

Conquest of Damascus

After this conquest Muiz killed all the Qaramatians prisoners' of war. He then sent Zalim bin Mawhub Aqili as the Governor of Damascus. Zalim reached Damascus, arrested the Qaramatian Governor and sent him to Egypt where he was put in prison. In 362 A.H., the Ubaidite flag was unfurled over Damascus. The same year, the people of Makkah and Madinah accepted Muiz's rule under compulsion and the Friday addresses were delivered there in his name. The people of Damascus were not happy with the Ubaidite rule. In the beginning of 365 A.H., Uftagin, who was among the servants of Izz ud-Daula bin Boya, captured Damascus and turned out Muiz's Governor from there. The people of Damascus were happy with his arrival. When Muiz came to know of this event, he wrote a letter to Uftagin requesting him to keep ruling over Damascus and that he would shortly issue him a letter authorizing him to rule. The one condition was that he should deliver the Friday addresses in Muiz's name and sever his relations with the Caliph of Baghdad. But Uftagin turned down the proposal and kept delivering the addresses in the name of the Caliph of Baghdad. Muiz became angry and marched on Damascus at the head of a strong army.

Death of Muiz and Succession of Aziz

Muiz reached Babbis when he received the message of his death on 15 Rabia al-Awwal 365 A.H. He had to bid farewell after reigning for 23 years. He was the first Ubaidite King who succeeded in conquering Egypt. His son, Nazar under the title, "Aziz Billah", succeeded him. Nazar kept the death of his father a secret for a few months. On Eid al-Adha 365 A.H. he announced his father's death and formally came to the throne.

Aziz bin Ubaidi

Invasion of Uftagin

Having heard of the death of Muiz, Uftagin invaded Egypt and besieged Sadia. Zalim bin Mawhub and other Ubaidite chiefs came out to fight but fled back after being beaten. Uftagin moved ahead and captured Rakka followed by Tabariya. After that he returned to Damascus. Aziz bin Muiz sent his scribe, Johar at the head of a strong army to take on Uftagin and conquer Damascus. Johar besieged Damascus and fighting between the two forces continued for a long time. Being tired of the siege Uftagin wrote to the Qaramatian King A'sim for help. With the receipt of the letter A'sim marched towards Damascus at the head of a strong army. With the news of his arrival Johar raised the siege of Damascus and left the place. Uftagin and A'sim chased Johar jointly. He first went to Ramla and then to Asqalan. When Johar was surrounded at Asqalan, he requested Uftagin to let him go to Egypt and he would have his King, Aziz bin Muiz, send goods in return for the obligation. Even though A'sim advised Uftagin to decline the offer Uftagin did not listen to him and let Johar go. Johar went straight to Aziz and advised him of the impending danger. Aziz reacted very sharply and marched to invade putting Johar in charge of the vanguard.

Arrest of Uftagin and His Ministry

In 367 A.H. Aziz besieged Ramla and sent words to Uftagin to join him by severing ties with A'sim on condition that he would be appointed the commander-in-chief of his army and given the rule of the part of the country he would choose to possess. Uftagin rejected the offer and launched an attack instead. Aziz was about to be defeated when he took to the battlefield firmly and fought back the joint forces of A'sim and Uftagin. Twenty thousand of their fighters fell dead. After winning victory Aziz announced a reward of one hundred thousand dinars for the one who would bring Uftagin to him alive. Someone captured Uftagin deceptively and received his reward. Aziz held Uftagin in high esteem and appointed him as his Prime Minister. He also sent his messenger to A'sim and asked him to meet him. On his refusal Aziz sent ten thousand dinars with the promise that he would be getting the same amount annually. However, A'sim declined the offer and left Tabariya for Ahsa. Aziz went to Cairo along with Uftagin. The former Prime Minister, Yaqub bin Maksi grew jealous of Uftagin and poisoned him to death. Aziz arrested him and put him in prison for forty days and ordered him to pay five hundred thousand dinars as a penalty. After that Yaqub was again given the post of the Prime Minister.

When Uftagin was chasing Johar, he had put a man named Qassam in Damascus as his substitute. However, Uftagin never had an opportunity to get back to Damascus since that time. Qassam in the mean time had consolidated his position there. When Qassam heard of the departure of Uftagin to Egypt, he commenced delivering addresses in the name of Aziz. When Aziz sent Abu Muhammad bin Ibrahim as the Governor of Damascus, Qassam blocked his entry to the territory. Aziz sent reinforcements to punish Qassam. Bakchur, the servant of Saif ud-Daula, who was the ruler of Hims, sent supplies to the Egyptian ruler. Mufrij bin Jarrah, the chief of Arabian tribes also rose to fight. After a series of encounters Aziz appointed Bakchur as the Governor of Damascus. Bakchur turned out the supporters of Yaqub bin Maksi, the Prime Minister of Egypt from Damascus for he had opposed the appointment of Bakchur as the Governor of Damascus. Shortly after that Yaqub turned Aziz against Bakchur. An army was sent from Egypt to dislodge Bakchur who fought with the Egyptian troops but was defeated. Saif ud-Daula invaded Syria and the King of Constantinople, launched an assault on his own. In short, Damascus remained in the grip of large-scale fighting and bloodshed until 385 A. H.

Death of Aziz

On receiving the news of the movement of the Roman forces towards Damascus Aziz himself led an army to Damascus and proclaimed *Jihad* against the Romans. However, he fell ill at Balbis. It is strange that his father too had fallen ill at this very same place and died there. In short, Aziz also succumbed to his illness at the end of Ramadan 386 A.H. and his son Abu Mansur came to the throne.

Mansur Hakam bin Aziz Ubaidi

Mansur entrusted the administration to Hasan bin Ammar Katami. After wielding power in the country the Katamis put the population to great trouble. Some members of the Dailmi family of the east had, being Shi'ite, shifted to Egypt to lend active support to the Ubaidite rule. Moreover, they added to the numbers of the easterners who had already been counted as a force in Egypt. Because of this, a serious conflict broke out between the Eastern and Western sections, which led to civil war of the worst nature. Damascus and Hijaz also showed signs of revolt, in such a state of confusion and disorder Damascus was ruled over sometimes by the Arabs and at times by Turkish slaves and Egyptian chiefs.

Rebellion of Waleed bin Hisham and His Assassination

In the meantime Waleed bin Hisham, known as Arkoh made a bid for power. When after gaining power in Spain, Mansur bin Abi Amir started killing and arresting the princes of Banu Umayyad, Waleed, the son of the last Caliph of the Banu Umayyad of Spain, fled for his life and first reached Qairwan and then to Syria via Yemen and Makkah. Syria was at that time passing through a state of chaos and disorder so he went to Egypt. He gained acceptance at Barqah. At first Hakim Ubaidi paid no attention to his movement. However, the people were unhappy with the reign of Hakim Ubaidi and tribe after tribe clustered round Waleed bin Hisham. Gaining strength and manpower he captured Barqah and invaded Egypt. Now the eyes of Hakim Ubaidi opened. He sent an army to eliminate the threat in its beginning but they met with defeat. The exercise was repeated several times. The entire territory of Egypt and Tripoli was about to fall when Hakim Ubaidi tried another strategy and played a trick and drew some of the Generals of Waleed to his side by the power of his purse. They led Waleed to be arrested treacherously. Hakim Ubaidi had him killed and this was the end of these disruptive activities. In order to bring the people round to his line of thinking he proclaimed liberty for the people to either confess Sunni or Shi'ite faith or pronounce "hayya ala khair al-amal" or not.

Hakim's Death

Hakim Ubaidi believed in the influence of the stars on human life and was greatly inclined to astronomy and astrology. He had built a house on mount Maqtam adjacent to Cairo. He used to go there alone to imbibe the spiritual power of the stars and perform other religious rituals. On 17 Shawwal 411 A.H. he went as usual alone to mount

Maqtam riding on his donkey. His officials and courtiers waited for him for a couple of days and when he did not return, they moved ahead in search of Hakim. After covering some distance the donkey was found dead and then they found Hakim's garments covered with bloodstains. However, his dead body was never found. As per one narration, Hakim's sister had illicit relations with some men and when it come to the knowledge of Hakim he reproached her violently. Then she hatched a conspiracy with some of the Katami chiefs to kill him, because of his blasphemous beliefs and spiritual practices. Confirming Hakim's death the courtiers brought to the throne his minor son, Ali bin Hakim. *Zahir Li-Din Allah* was his appellation and his father's sister was made the caretaker of the administration.

Zahir bin Hakim Ubaidi

Zahir's paternal aunt died and he had to run his Government with the help of the nobles and courtiers. Saleh bin Mirdas captured Syria and Damascus in 420 A.H. and dislodged the Ubaidite rule. Zahir ordered Zariri, the Governor of Palestine to launch an attack and he restored Damascus and Palestine, but Syria remained constantly dominated by fighting and revolts.

His Death

Zahir died in 427 A.H. His son Abu Tamim M'ad with the appellation of Mustansir succeeded him. Abul Qasim Ali bin Ahmad was his Prime Minister. After Mustansir's accession to throne Abul Qasim took over the running of the Government.

Mustansir bin Zahir Ubaidi

During the reign of Mustansir Arab tribes captured Syria and Damascus in 433 A.H. and the country went out of the control of the Ubaidites. Muiz bin Baris raised the banner of revolt in Tripoli and began to deliver addresses in the name of the Caliph of Baghdad. Meanwhile Mustansir deposed his Minister, Abul Qasim and replaced him with Husain bin Ali Tazwari. He then dispatched an Arab army towards Tripoli. It halted at Barqah and did not attack Tripoli. In view of this Mustansir started buying slaves to counter the Arabs and the number of these slaves rose to twenty-three thousands. The Arab tribes now fighting for themselves marched ahead and set up their rule at various places including Tripoli and Atij. The Arab tribe Banu Adiy stormed the whole of Africa. Later these Arab chiefs sent their emissaries to Muiz bin Baris, who received them with warmth and honor, for he hoped they would abandon their life of plunder but they belied his hope and finally Muiz decided to punish the Arab tribes with the help of twenty thousand Berber tribesmen. Although the Arab tribes numbered only three thousand in all, the result of the fierce fighting went against Muiz. Muiz bin Baris fled and took refuge in Qairwan. Muiz collected his Berber fighters once again and attacked the Arabs on Eid al-Adha 10 Dhul Hijjah 446 A.H. but was again defeated. His third attack also ended in failure. The Arabs then chased him out of Qairwan and he went to Mahdiya. Yunus bin Yahya captured Qairwan.

Civil War

In Cairo Mustansir's mother had every order she wanted issued according to her will. Her power and influence had increased beyond all limits. In view of protecting themselves the ministers began to recruit Turkish men. The army was dominated by a few powerful groups the slaves, the Katami clan, the Berbers and the Turkish. Nasir ud-Daula bin Hamdan, a Sudanese rose to the high position of Commander-in-Chief and became the leader and Commander of the Turks. Various administrative wings were being separated from the main body. Power struggles had started among the fundamental parts of the Government, Mustansir and his mother in Cairo. Each of them was trying hard to erode the power of the other. Civil war broke out between the Turks and the slaves and the army was divided into two factions one fighting against another. At last, Mustansir signaled for Badr Jamali ruling in Aakka to come. He came to Egypt with a huge Armenian army and appeared before Mustansir who appointed him as his minister. He also made the Turks understand that Nasir ud-Daula had plunged them into the flames of fighting and killings without any rhyme or reason. The Turks put Nasir ud-Daula to death for their own safety. Badr Jamali then become the chief of the Turks.

He gained tremendous power and influence, regularized the administration and won the confidence and satisfaction of everyone. With his internal peace and strength he was able to force the revolting chiefs to obey him and wrested Tripoli from the Arabs. All the territories of Palestine were annexed under his rule. Damascus was passing through a state of flux and anybody could capture and establish his authority but the Friday addresses were delivered in the name of the Egyptian Ubaidi ruler and the Cairo court was satisfied with that much. In 468 A.H., Badr Jamali was able to put the administration of Mustansir right to a great extent, Amir Aqdas captured Damascus and his address was delivered in the name of the Caliph of Baghdad. In 469 A.H. Atsaz bin Ufaq, the Commander of the Seljuk army attacked Damascus. Badr Jamali dispatched his troops, which besieged Damascus. In 470 A.H., Sultan Malik Shah Seljuk entrusted Syria to Tatish Seljuk and authorized him to take the portion of Syria conquered by him. Thus Tatish made progress into Syria and attacked the city of Halib (Aleppo). When they refused to surrender, he laid a siege around Halib at the same time Atsaz was still under siege in Damascus. He sent word to Tatish that he was surrounded by Egyptian forces and if he failed to extend his help he would be forced to hand over Damascus to them. Tatish marched to Damascus immediately. On getting the news the Egyptian forces raised the siege and fled back to Egypt. Tatish reached Damascus killed Atsaz and captured Damascus.

Following this Halib also came under the rule of Tatish and gradually the whole of Syria. Hearing this Badr Jamali collected a huge army and invaded Damascus but failed to gain victory over Tatish. After this, the Egyptian forces attacked Syria several times but every time they met with failure. In 484 A.H. the Christians took Sicily away from the Muslims. Badr Jamali died in Rabia al-Awwal, 487 A.H. at the age of eighty years. Mustansir also died shortly thereafter. The early period of Mustansir was fraught with troubles and the Ubaidi dynasty was on the brink of being ruined. But Badr Jamali infused new blood and saved it from a certain death. Mustansir had three sons, Ahmed, Nazar and Abul Qasim. Mustansir had appointed Nazar as his crown prince:

Hasan bin Sabbah Takes Ba'it

Hasan bin Sabah came to Egypt from Iraq in the guise of a merchant during the reign of Mustansir. He took *ba'it* at the hand of Mustansir and asked him about the next Imam. Mustansir said that his son Nazar would be his next Imam. Following this Hasan bin Sabah sought Mustansir's permission to go back to Iraq and start preaching in favor of his *Imamat* (Shiite Leadership) and Caliphate. Mustansir granted permission and sent him as his preacher. Hasan bin Sabah came to Iraq and started his work with missionary zeal and gradually captured Al-Mut Fort.

Mustansir had appointed Muhammad Malik as minister after the death of his father Badr Jamali. Muhammad Malik and Nazar were not having good relations at that time so, after the demise of Mustansir, Muhammad Malik made Mustansir's sister declare that Mustansir had appointed Abul Qasim as his successor to the throne. Thus the people pledged their support to Abul Qasim who came to throne with the appellation of "Mustali Billah".

Abdul Qasim Mustali Billah Ubaidi

Three days after Abul Qasim's accession to throne Nazar left Cairo for Alexandria. Badr Jamali's slave Nasir ud-Daula was then the Governor of Alexandria. But, on hearing of Abul Qasim's accession, he rose in revolt and lent his support to Nazar. Accepting his right to the throne he enthroned Nazar in Alexandria and took the oath of allegiance to him and gave him the appellation of "Mustafa Li-dinillah". With this news Abul Qasim's minister, Muhammad Malik rushed to punish Nazar and besieged Alexandria. Being distressed at the long siege the people sought peace at the cost of their city and handed Alexandria over to Muhammad Malik. He arrested Nazar and sent him to Cairo where Abul Qasim had him killed immediately. His minister carried Nasir ud-Daula Uftagin with him to Cairo. Abul Qasim put him to death as well.

It has already been mentioned that Tajuddaula Tatish Seljuk captured the entire country of Syria. Soon after the demise of Tatish his sons

Waqaq and Ridwan fell out with each other, which led to civil war. Waqaq had occupied Damascus while Ridwan possessed Halib. During this period, the Christians of Europe launched a joint attack to take Bait al-Maqdis (Jerusalem) from the Muslim's possession. They laid siege around Antioch (Antakya). Yaghisan, the Seljuk Governor fled for his life and he was killed by an Armenian who cut off his head and brought it to the Christian camp. The fall of Antioch and the assassination of Baghisan stirred Syria. Buqa, a Seljuk chief and ruler of Mosul, advanced towards the Christian invaders and camped at Marj Dabiq. Hearing this Waqaq bin Tatish and Sulaiman bin Ratiq, the ruler of Hims joined Buqa with their forces. All of them jointly marched ahead to combat the Christian troops. Muslim troops numbered much less than the Christian forces and they were beaten after a bloody fight. Thousands of Muslims laid down their lives on the battlefield. The Christian fighters plundered the Muslim camps. Following this the Christians captured Hims and then besieged Aakka. The Turk Seljuks did not give in despite many hardships.

The Christian troops were still besieging Aakka and all the Syrian Muslims had their attention centered on Syria when Muhammad Malik, the minister of Abul Qasim led a strong Egyptian force and invaded Bait al-Maqdis (Jerusalem). This Shi'ite assault benefited the Christians and the Islamic Syrian forces could not withstand the two-pronged attack. Sulaiman and Ilghazi were engaged with the Shi'ite assault on Bait al-Maqdis and could not extend any help against the Christians, with the result that Bait al-Maqdis fell to the Egyptians. Sulaiman and Ilghazi left towards the east. The Egyptians could not keep it in their possession for long. The Christians won Bait al-Maqdis on Shaban 23, A.H. after a siege of forty days. They stormed into the city a committed the large-scale massacre of Muslims. Muslims took refuge in the Arch of Daud (علیه السلام) so that the Christians would hold themselves back from their killing spree but there was nothing to put a check on their madness. Seventy thousand Muslims were put to sword in Al-Aqsa Mosque and Sakhra-e-Sulaiman. All the valuable possessions of the Aqsa Mosque including chandeliers of gold and silver were looted. The rest of the Muslims reached Baghdad in a very wretched state and narrated the tales of sufferings and woes to the Caliph of Baghdad. The Caliph wrote to the Seljuk Kings Barkayaraq,

Muhammad and Sanjar to save Syria but they were engaged in civil wars so deeply that they could not pay any attention to the message, with the result that Syria was reduced to ashes. The Egyptian minister who had provided the Christians with an opportunity to conquer Bait al-Maqdis once again led an army to restore it. However, the Christian forces came out and fought him back and none of the runway Egyptian fighters could save their lives. The minister returned to Egypt in the company of only a few persons.

Death of Abul Qasim

Abul Qasim died on Safar 15, 495 A.H. and was succeeded by his five-year son, Abu Ali with the appellation "Amir bi-Ihkamillah".

Abu Ali Amir Ubaidi

With the accession of Abu Ali to the throne his minister took charge of all administrative affairs, he had wielded power during the reign of Abul Qasim who never took any action without him. The minister built a strong army and sent it against the Christians under the command of his father Badr Jamali's slave S'aduddaula. The Egyptian troops were beaten. With the news of the defeat he dispatched a huge army led by his son, Sharaf al-Ma'ali. The two forces clashed at Ramla and the Christians were defeated. Sharaf al-Ma'ali moved forward and besieged Ramla, which fell to him after two weeks. Four hundred Christians were killed and three hundred made prisoner. The Christian Commander left Ramla for Jaffa and made an advance towards Bait al-Maqdis (Jerusalem) along with the Christian pilgrims from Europe to the sacred city of Jerusalem. Hearing of the presence of the pilgrims Sharaf al-Ma'ali left for Egypt without fighting. The Christians then captured Asqalan without an encounter. However, the Egyptian army made a fresh attack and took Asqalan from the Christians. This event occurred in Dhul Hijjah 496 A.H.

Following this the Egyptian army attacked the Christians once again in 498 A.H. and the Turkish army in Damascus also came to help but the fighting bore no fruit. Among the cities on the Syrian coast Tripoli, Saur, Saida and Beirut were then under Egyptian rule. The Christian war fleets sprang into action and captured Syria after conquering all the cities one by one. They conquered Bait al-Maqdis later and appointed a King for the country built on the debris of the conquered cities and territories. This set up Christian rule in Syria. It continued to gain strength and power because of the constant military and economic help from the European continent. Ubaidite rule remained inactive even though the new Christian country came into being from the Egyptian cities and territories won by the Christians. The Christian army failed to conquer Damascus, which was then under the rule of Seljuk chiefs, nor could they muster courage to invade the eastern parts of Syria. Had the Seljuk Kings and commanders abandoned their internal feuds and civil wars and paid their attention to Christian invaders they could not have stepped into Bait al-Maqdis.

Amir Ubaidi could not put up with the expanding influence and power of his minister and had him killed in 515 A.H., and appointed another man as his minister with the appellation of "Jalal al-Islam." A few years after he grew angry at Jalal al-Islam too and had Jalal killed along with his brother Mu'taman and his well wisher Najibuddaula.

Assassination of Amir Ubaidi

At last, some Qaramatians killed Amir Ubaidi in 524 A.H. when he was getting on his mount. Since he had left no son, his cousin, Abdul Majeed, who adopted "Hafiz Li-Dinillah" as his appellation, succeeded him. The people in general pledged their oath of allegiance to him on the condition that if the pregnant wife of Amir delivered a male child he would be considered as the true successor to the throne.

Hafiz Ubaidi

After accession to throne Hafiz Ubaidi killed many ministers one by one. At last he appointed his son as his minister. He also hatched a conspiracy to wrest the throne from his father. Hafiz Ubaidi then replaced his son by a man named Ridwan who belonged to the Sunni Muslims. He faced joint opposition from the Shiites and Imamites and relinquished his position as minister. Following this Hafiz Ubaidi carried out his administrative business without a minister.

Death of Hafiz Ubaidi

Hafiz Ubaidi died at the age of 70. His son Abu Mansur Ismail who adopted "Zafir billah" as his appellation succeeded him.

Zafir bin Hafiz Ubaidi

Zafir appointed Adil bin Salar, Governor of Alexandria as his minister. Being at the helm of affairs, Adil turned Zafir into a figurehead. The Christian army besieged Asqalan in 548 A.H. The people of Asqalan sent a message for help to the court of Cairo. Adil sent Abbas bin Abi al-Futuh to Asqalan to combat the besieging Christians. Zafir and Abbas jointly made a secret plan to do away with Adil. Abbas himself went away with the army and halted at Balbis. Abbas's young son Nasir killed Adil while he was sleeping. On receiving news of Adil's assassination Abbas returned to Cairo and handed over the ministry to him. During all of this nobody paid any attention to the distress of the people of Asqalan. Finding no way out they surrendered to the Christians.

Zafir's Assassination

Nasir invited Zafir to a feast during Muharram 549 A.H. and then Nasir killed Zafir and his companions and had them buried in that very house. The next day Abbas bin Abi al-Futuh, the minister came to the royal palace as usual and inquired about King Zafir. They expressed ignorance and Abbas left the palace. The court officials then went to Zafir's brother Jibril and Yusuf and narrated to them that Zafir had gone to the house of Nasir and did not return from there. Yusuf and Jibril then advised him to acquaint Abbas, the minister with what was happening. Abbas fell in doubt about Yusuf and Jibril's part in the plot and he had them killed along with both of the sons of Hasan bin Hafiz. He then entered the royal palace and forcibly lifted Zafir's son on his lap and had him seated on the throne and gave him the appellation of "Fa'iz bi-Nasrillah." He then took the oath of allegiance from the people for the boy. Since five members of the royal family were slain the ladies of the royal family sent their envoy secretly to Saleh bin Zarik, the Governor of Athmonin and Nabsa, they acquainted him with all the events and requested him to punish Abbas. Because of this Saleh bin Zarik collected his fighters and marched to Cairo. Knowing that even the people of Cairo had risen against him he took his son, Nasir and friend, Osama bin Manqad and left for Syria and Iraq along with the main body of his forces. On the way he came into a clash with the Christians. During the encounter Abbas was killed, Nasir was held and Osama escaped and reached Syria. Saleh reached Cairo in Rabia al Thani, 559 A.H. after the departure of Abbas. He dug out the dead body of Zafir from Nasir's house and had it buried in the royal graveyard. He then took oath of allegiance to Zafir's son, Fa'iz and gave him the appellation of "*Malik al-Saleh.*"

Fa'iz bin Zafir Ubaidi

Saleh became the minister and started regularizing the administration. He then came into correspondence with the Christians and had Nasir bin Abbas repatriated in return for a settled amount. When Christian officials brought him to Cairo, Saleh put him to death and hung his body on public display. Saleh was a staunch follower of the Imamia sect and a great well wisher of the Ubaidite dynasty.

After getting rid of Nasir he turned towards the rebel chiefs who had the courage to oppose the central government. Two of the most prominent among them were Taj-ul-Mulk Qaimaz and Ibn Ghalib Saleh he deputed Generals and troops to capture them but being informed before hand, they escaped to unknown places. However, his action proved effective so much so that the other Generals submitted to his rule. He also replaced all the old guards and officials with his own men. He then transferred the valuable assets of the royal palace to his own house. Fa'iz Ubaidi's paternal aunt was watching the growing power of Saleh with anxiety and she began to think of how to get rid of him. Saleh came to know of the plot against him and he went to the royal palace and put her to death.

Death of Fa'iz Ubaidi

After a nominal rule of six months King Fa'iz Ubaidi died in 555 A.H. Following this Saleh bin Zarik asked the guards to bring the boys of the royal family before him so that one of them might be chosen for the throne. Thus Abu Muhammad Abdullah bin Yusuf Hafiz Ubaidi was given the throne with the appellation of "Azid Li-dinillah". He was then at the age of puberty. Saleh gave his daughter in marriage to the new King Azid.

Azid bin Yusuf Ubaidi

Since Saleh was the virtual ruler and Azid was considered the nominal one. The nobles and courtiers disliked these developments. The younger paternal aunt of Azid vowed to avenge the blood of her elder sister by putting Saleh to death. At last she persuaded some Sudanese nobles to do away with the culprit. One of them struck Saleh with his lance so that he fell down and died shortly after coming to his house. Before his death he advised Azid to appoint his son as his minister. Azid did accordingly and entrusted the ministry to Saleh's son with the appellation of "Adil". Shortly after assuming charge as minister he killed Azid's paternal aunt and the Sudanese noble with the permission of Azid. As a first step in bringing about the administrative reforms, Azid deposed Shadar S'adi, the Governor of Sa'id and put Amir bin Raq'a in his place. Shadar rose in revolt against Adil and led an army to Cairo. Adil could not face him and fled away. Shadar entered Cairo with his colors flying in 558 A.H. and Zarik Adil was caught and brought to Cairo and was killed. Shadar made no delay in taking over the office of the minister and Azid conferred the post of Prime Minister on him. Nine months after the event Dergham, the Inspector of the Palace grew in power and forced Shadar out of Cairo and took the office of the minister. Shadar left for Syria. Dergham killed Ali, the son of Shadar in Cairo and did away with all the Generals and nobles he feared.

Nuruddin Muhammad Zangi Turns to Egypt

Shadar reached Syria and narrated to Nuruddin Muhammad Zangi what was going on in Egypt. After many deliberations, Sultan Nuruddin asked his commander Asaduddin Sherkoh to accompany Shadar to Cairo at the head of an army. Sherkoh was instructed to appoint Shadar as the minister by deposing Dergham and fight back the forces standing in the way. After dispatching Shadar and Sherkoh to Egypt Sultan Nuruddin himself led an army towards the Christians so that they would not stop the movement of Sherkoh's troops. Sherkoh and Shadar moved smoothly up to Balbis where Nasiruddin and Fakhruddin, the brothers of Dergham challenged them on the way. Sherkoh repulsed their attack and captured both of them and entered Egypt victoriously. Dergham fled for his life but was caught on the way and killed. Similarly, both Nasiruddin and Fakhruddin were put to death. Shadar took over as Prime Minister once again. However, after holding the high post Shadar committed a breach of promise and Sherkoh had to leave Egypt in frustration. Instead of giving thanks to Nuruddin and Sherkoh, Shadar joined hands with the Christians against Nuruddin's rule. In view of the notoriety of Shadar, Sherkoh invaded Egypt in 562 A.H. after seeking permission from King Nuruddin, and captured a number of Egyptian cities.

Egyptians Seek Help From the Christians

Shadar sought immediate help from the Christians. They were already waiting for such opportunity and sent their military help without any loss of time. Asaduddin Sherkoh's comparatively small army of two thousand men was nothing in comparison to the heavy joint forces of Shadar and the Christians. However, Sherkoh took the field in the name of Allah and fought so gallantly that both the forces suffered ignominious defeat. Sherkoh, already some one to be feared by the Egyptians, moved ahead towards Alexandria and the citizens welcomed his arrival by opening the doors of their city. After appointing his nephew, Salahuddin bin Najmuddin Ayub, Governor of Alexandria, Sherkoh marched to Sa'id. As he left Alexandria for Sa'id the Egyptian force concentrated in Cairo started getting ready to attack Alexandria. On receiving this information Sherkoh rushed to help his nephew, Salahuddin. However, in the meantime, Shadar had been able to lure away some of the Generals of Sherkoh who were found fighting rather half-heartedly. In such an anxious moment Sherkoh received a message from Shadar with the request to leave Alexandria after receiving some indemnity from him. After much deliberations and looking into the pros and cons, Sherkoh decided to grant the petition with honor. He took the indemnity, vacated Alexandria and returned to Syria.

Consequences of Indiscretion

Shadar had to withstand the worst of his indiscretion. The Christian force, which had come to Egypt at the call of Shadar, would not agree to leave the country at any cost. They rather laid the foundation for capturing Egypt. They finally put forward a number of conditions for their departure, which Shadar had to concede under circumstantial compulsion. The conditions were the following: (1) The Christian army would remain in Cairo. (2) An administrator would reside in Cairo on behalf of the Christians. (3) The Christians will keep control over the doors of the fortified city.(4) The Egyptian ruler would continue to give to the Christian King one hundred thousand dinars annually.

When the Christians set their feet firmly on Egyptian soil, they started meddling with the administrative affairs of the central government. They annexed Balbis under Christian rule. Their next step was to capture the capital, Cairo. In order to carry out their nefarious design they, with the active support of Shadar, called a large Christian army, demanded two hundred thousand dinars instead of one hundred thousand and large quantities of grain. Azid Ubaidi grew very anxious at these excesses on the part of the Christians.

Azid Turning to Nuruddin Zangi for Help

Azid sent his envoy to Sultan Nuruddin Zangi to help take away the Christian possession of Egypt. On being informed Shadar made an all out effort to hold Azid back from seeking help from Nuruddin and Azid kept silent. Sultan Nuruddin asked his Commander, Sherkoh to march in the company of his nephew, Salahuddin and other Generals. Asaduddin Sherkoh marched to Egypt. He ravaged the Christian camp and appeared before King Azid who held him in high esteem and served him and his army as his honored guests. One day Azid drew Sherkoh's attention to Shadar's friendship with the Christians and his enmity with themselves and proposed to get rid of the scourge. Sherkoh agreed and ordered his Generals to kill Shadar. Shadar's head was brought before Azid in a few days. Being overjoyed and highly satisfied Azid offered the highest office of the Prime Minister to Sherkoh, which he accepted with the permission of Nuruddin Zangi. However, he could enjoy this envious position only for a few months and died in 565 A.H.

Salahuddin Ayubi as Prime Minister of Egypt

Azid appointed Sherkoh's nephew, Salahuddin as Prime Minister. Salahuddin kept his relations with Nuruddin intact. Like Sherkoh, Nuruddin entrusted full authority to Salahuddin. Both Sherkoh and Salahuddin were staunch followers of Imam Shafe'i. Salahuddin took the drastic step of replacing the Shi'ite Jurist and Judges by scholars of the Shafe'i school of thought. He also laid the foundation of Shafe'i and Maliki madrasas (schools). Since 565 A.H. when Sherkoh assumed the post of the Prime Minister, he had not only driven away the Christian troops from Egypt but also stopped paying tribute to them. The Christians grew anxious at the unity forged between Damascus and Cairo for under such circumstances it was impossible for them to keep control over Bait al-Maqdis (Jerusalem). They sent messages to the bishops of Sicily and Spain for immediate help to save Bait al-Maqdis. Following this the bishops and clergies began to deliver sermons on joining the crusade against the Muslims, with the result that the Christian forces from Spain and the rest of Europe started concentrating on the coast of Syria. After gaining strength, as a result of the massive help they received from all over Europe, the Christians marched ahead and surrounded Damyat. The Governor, Shamsul Khawas Mankur informed Salahuddin Ayubi. The Shiites of Egypt were angry with Salahuddin Ayubi, the Egyptian minister. Salahuddin sent an officer named Bahauddin Qaraqush to Damyat at the head of an army. He also wrote Sultan Nuruddin Zangi to keep an eye on Damyat, as he himself could not leave Egypt for fear of the disruptive activities on the part of the Shiites and the Sudanese. Thus Nuruddin Zangi invaded the coastal areas of Syria to divide the power and attention of the Christians. When they raised the siege under compulsion and moved back towards their cities, they were shocked to find them ruined and deserted. After this Salahuddin Ayubi called his father, Najmuddin Ayub to Egypt from Syria. King Azid came in person to greet him and held him in great honor. Azid was a great admirer of the services of Salahuddin and he had practically nothing to do with the administrative affairs. However, the Egyptian Shiites were opposed to the growing power and influence of

Salahuddin. Moreover, the Sunni Muslims were flourishing during his time. However, Ammarah, Yemeni, Zubaidi, Awirash and others made a secret plan to hand over Egypt to the Christians. They also thought of arranging a secret meeting between Azid and the Christian envoy. With this purpose in view they tried, on one hand, to bring Azid around to their own opinion and entered into correspondences with the Christians on the other. Accidentally, one of the letters addressed to the Christian King was intercepted on the way and was produced before Salahuddin. He first tried to find who were the real culprits, he recorded their statements in an open court of law and put all the criminals to death. Bahauddin was appointed as inspector of the royal palace. This event led the Sudanese, numbering fifty thousands, to become angry and they rose against Salahuddin and the Turkish troops. At last, fierce fighting broke out between the Turks and the Sudanese and the Turks won the battle. A large number of Sudanese either fell fighting or escaped. The Turkish soldiers ransacked their houses. However, Salahuddin restored normalcy and rehabilitated the Sudanese and gave them back their houses. Because of these events, the strength and influence of the Sudanese diminished to a great extent. Sultan Nuruddin Zangi wrote to Salahuddin to begin delivering his addresses in the name of Caliph Mustadi Abbasi instead of Azid. At this time Azid was seriously ill and was near to death. In Muharram 567 A.H., the Friday address was delivered in the name of the Abbasid Caliph of Baghdad from the pulpit of the Grand Mosque of Cairo and nobody opposed the change. From the next Friday the addresses were delivered in the name of the Caliph of Baghdad from the pulpit of all the mosques of Egypt.

Death of Azid Ubaidi

King Azid Ubaidi died on 10 Muharram 567 A.H. With his demise ended the Ubaid dynasty and the Abbasid Caliphate staged a comeback. Egypt once again became a part of the Abbasid Caliphate of Baghdad. Salahuddin Ayubi was given from the caliph of Baghdad a royal order to rule Egypt with royal attire and scepter. It was the beginning of the Ayubi dynasty in place of Ubaidites.

A Short Commentary on the Ubaidite Dynasty

Ubaidi dynasty (also known incorrectly as the Fatimids) ruled for two hundred and seventy years. It was first set up in western area of Africa and Tripoli. They later captured Egypt and chose Cairo as their capital. The Idrisite rule of Morocco is generally considered as the Alwis Shi'ite rule. But in fact, Idrisite rule was that of the Berbers and was, therefore only semi-Shi'ite. Idrisites had nothing in their creed and action that could be construed as being superior to the Sunnis, nor did the Idrisite have any enmity with the Sunnis'. However, the foundation of this rule was laid down by Idris who used the Ahlil Bai't (family of the Prophet ﷺ) to succeed in drawing the masses towards him. Except for this, nothing was done as Shi'ite as we know the practices of the Shiites to be. However, Ubaidite rule was Shi'ite, but certainly not the Alwi type of Shi'ite. Ubaidullah's grandfather, writes Sayuti in Tarikh al-Khulfa, was a Magian and a blacksmith. Although Ubaidullah Mahdi claimed to be Fatmid during his visit to the western territory the majority of experts in lineal genealogy decline to accept his claim. Aziz Ubaidi wrote a letter to the Umayyad Caliph of Spain, which contained abuse and satire about the Caliph's family. The Caliph wrote back that he (Aziz) had passed satirical remarks about the Caliph's family because he knew about his ancestors but he (the Caliph) could not do the same and pass such remarks because his (Aziz's) ancestors were unknown to him. Although Aziz was disgusted at these remarks he kept silent. The Ubaid are generally known as Fatimids but this shows sheer ignorance of the realities and this name is only based on a false claim. Ubaid were generally Isma'ili Shiites. They are also called *Batnis*. One of their branches was founded by Hasan bin Sabah, which had Al Mut Fort as its capital. This is also called Fida'is' rule and they also were not Alwi.

Thousands of devout Muslims were killed during the Ubaid dynasty simply because they refused to disgrace the Companions of the Prophet ﷺ. The Ubaidite dynasty did no service to Islam nor did they leave any record of deeds in any field that could make one be proud of and some of our religious scholars have declared them apostate. Some of them including Azid Ubaidi claimed to know the unseen. Wine was also permissible according to them.

Chapter 14

Qaramatians of Bahrain

Yahya bin Faraj Qaramate

Bahrain is a country, which has the Persian Gulf towards the east, Oman towards the south, Yamama towards the west and Basra towards the north. The country is called Bahrain after the name of one of its cities. Sometimes Bahrain is called Hajar after another city. A third city named Hafiriya was ravaged by the Qaramatians and they founded another city named Ahsa. Hence the country is known as Ahsa as well. This city was the center of the territory of Ahsa. Ubaid and Qaramatian dynasties came into being about the same time. Both were Isma'ili Shi'ite and had almost the same creed. In 275 A.H. a person named Yahya bin Faraj appeared on the outskirts of Kufah. He introduced himself by the name of Qaramate and claimed to be the envoy of Imam Mahdi. He passed most of his time in prayers. He charged from his followers one dinar each in the name of Imam Mahdi. When his followers rose in number, he sent some of his disciples as preachers to various parts of the country. Being acquainted with these activities, the Governor of Kufah arrested him. A few days after Qaramate escaped from the prison and disappeared. His disappearance led his disciples and followers to believe that he was undoubtedly the envoy of Imam Mahdi.

Qarmate's (Caramate) teachings were strange. The way of performing Salat (prayer) was quite different and they observed fasts on particular days of particular months instead of Ramadan. He had declared wine lawful and nabeedh unlawful. Wudu (ablution) was enough after sexual pollution. Tail-bearing animals and those having five toes were prohibited. A few days after Yahya bin Faraj, known as Qarmate, appeared again after his disappearance and began to collect people around him by adopting the appellation "Qa'im bil-Haq" (Who stands up with Truth). The Governor of Kufa Ahmad bin Muhammad Ta'i attacked him with his troops and dispersed his men. Following this event, some Arabian tribes became his followers. He again gathered strength and attacked Damascus in 290 A.H. but Balkh the Governor of Damascus, after a series of encounters, killed Yahya and dispersed his party.

Husain Mahdi

Husain, the brother of Yahya appeared on the scene with the appellation of "Mahdi Amirul-Mominin". He collected some people, especially the desert-dwellers and continued plundering the outskirts of Damascus and Syria. Abbasid Generals were deployed to catch them. One of his sons Abul Qasim escaped but "Mahdi Amirul-Mominin" was caught and killed. This event occurred in 291 A.H. Husain's brother also fled the territory and thus saved himself. He later collected a band of desert-dwellers and plundered Tabriya and San'a city and occupied Yemen. They also created disturbances in Yemen, Hijaz and Syria.

Yahya II

Close on the heels of Yahya bin Faraj's escape from the prison a person also named Yahya appeared in the town of Qatif adjoining Bahrain and claimed in 281 A.H. to be the real envoy of the Imam Mahdi. Giving, news that Imam Mahdi was to appear in the immediate future he claimed that he had also brought a personal letter from the Imam Mahdi. Hearing this, Ali bin Mualla bin Hamdan, an extremist Shiite, assembled his community in Qatif and read out to the audience the letter claimed to be brought by Yahya from the Imam Mahdi. The contents of the letter sent the Shiites into great jubilation.

The news spread like wild fire in the outskirts of Bahrain. Among them was an influential and respectable person named Abu Sayeed Hasan bin Bahram Janabi. Shortly after that, Yahya disappeared and reappeared again with another letter from Imam Mahdi enjoining his followers to contribute thirty-six dinars each to Yahya. They did it with all pleasure. Soon after collecting the money he disappeared once again and came back with a third letter from Imam Mahdi ordering each of his followers to deposit with Yahya one-fifth of their possessions in the name of the Imam. This order was carried out as well.

Abu Sayeed Janabi

Since Abu Sayeed Janabi was an influential person, he began his preaching mission in Bahrain too. Gradually, a large number of desert-dwellers turned towards Abu Sayeed. Abu Sayeed trained his followers in warfare and proceeded with his men from Qatif to Basra. When, Ahmad bin Muhammad Yahya came to know of the preparations of Abu Sayeed he finding himself weak, informed the Caliph of the new developments. The Caliph sent orders to Abbas bin Umar Ghanwi, the Governor of Persia to save Basra. Abbas marched to the trouble spot at the head of a two thousand man army. During the encounter, Abu Sayeed captured Abbas and plundered his military camp. Abbas was released shortly but his men were put to death. This initial success encouraged Abu Sayeed and he attacked and occupied Hajr and founded his capital there. He appointed his son, Sayeed as his crown prince. This step angered Abu Sayeed's younger brother, Abu Tahir Sulaiman. He assassinated Abu Sayeed and declared himself the Chief of the Qaramatians.

Abu Tahir

Soon after assuming power, Abu Tahir attacked Basra in 288 A.H. and returned to Bahrain after plundering Basra. Caliph Muqtadir grew very anxious and he ordered the immediate fortification of Basra. Abu Tahir continued to rule Bahrain rather successfully. During this period, he corresponded with Ubaidullah Mahdi (Fatimid Dynasty of North Africa) and the latter expressed his satisfaction over Abu Tahir's way of governance. Abu Tahir attacked Basra again in 311 A.H. and ravaged it totally. The Grand Mosque of Basra was also demolished and was not rebuilt for a long time. The marketplaces were reduced to ashes.

Abu Tahir's Plunder

Abu Tahir came out in 312 A.H. to pillage the caravans of pilgrims (Hajjis). He arrested the royal commander, Abul Haija bin Hamdun accompanying the caravan and looted the Pilgrims completely and went back to Hajr. Abu Tahir then attacked Iraq in 314 A.H. and ravaged the outskirts of Kufa like Basra. Once back in Bahrain he plunged heart and soul in populating the city of Ahsa and doing extensive construction work there. During this period, he built palaces for his fellows and made the city his permanent capital. Abu Tahir attacked Oman in 315 A.H. The Governor of Oman took refuge in Persia and Abu Tahir declared Oman as a province under his rule. He began a series of attacks towards the north in 316 A.H. Caliph Muqtadir Abbasi called Yusuf bin Abi As'saj from Azerbaijan, conferred on him the authority to rule Wasit and then ordered him to fight with Abu Tahir. After a heavy fight, Yusuf was beaten and arrested. This news created quite a sensation in Baghdad. Abu Tahir set out from Kufa to Anbar. The Caliph deployed Generals like Munis khadim, Muzaffar, and Harun but all of them came back to Baghdad after being beaten by Abu Tahir. He then proceeded to Rahba and ravaged it too. Jazirah province experienced the same plight at his hands and nobody advanced to check his wanton excesses.

Invasion Of Makkah

Abu Tahir invaded Makkah in 317 A.H. During his wild action, he killed a large number of Hujjaj, plundered Makkah, uprooted the doors of Ka'bah, pulled off the cover of Ka'bah and distributed its pieces among his army. He also removed the *Hajr al-Aswad* (Black Stone) and carried it with him saying that the next Hajj would be performed in his territory. Many influential chiefs corresponded with Abu Tahir to return the Black Stone and they offered up to fifty thousand dinars for the return of the sacred stone but he did not agree. He continued his ruinous activities and went on rampaging Iraq and Syria. He levied heavy taxes on the people of Damascus too.

Abu Mansur

His elder brother Ahmad succeeded Abu Tahir. He is known by his filial appellation of Abu Mansur. A section of the Qaramatians refused to recognize him as a ruler and acknowledged Abu Tahir's elder son as the real one. In order to sort out the controversy the Qaramatians sent their messenger to Tripoli to put the case before Abul Qasim Ubaidi who was to them all the envoy of Imam Mahdi. Abul Qasim Ubaidi passed his judgment that Abu Mansur should be recognized as the ruler and Sabur ibn Abu Tahir as his successor. They happily agreed to the decision. Abul Qasim Ubaidi died in 334 A.H. and was succeeded by Ismail Ubaidi in Africa. Abu Mansur sent felicitations upon his accession through his envoy. Isma'il Ubaidi wrote to Abu Mansur more than once to send the Black Stone back to the Ka'bah. Abu Mansur finally returned the Stone. During the reign of Abu Mansur, the Qaramatians launched very few attacks on other countries and he paid more attention to internal stability and administrative reforms.

Sabur's Assissination

In 358 A.H., Sabur bin Abu Tahir arrested Abu Mansur and killed his brothers and supporters who had aided and abetted in the crime concerning the Black Stone. Sabur captured the throne but he could not save himself from the opposition of his brothers. They stormed the capital and took out their uncle Abu Mansur from the prison. After coming back to the throne, Abu Mansur assassinated Sabur and banished his supporters to Awall Island. Abu Mansur died in 359 A.H. Abu Ali Hasan bin Ahmad with the appellation of "Azam" succeeded him. On coming to the throne, he banished all the sons of Abu Tahir to Awall Island.

Hasan Azam, The Qaramite

Hasan Azam was moderate in his thought and beliefs. He was not so devoted to the Ubaidi nor did he hate the Abbasid Caliphate. It has already been mentioned that Abu Tahir had levied an annual tribute on Damascus and the rulers of Damascus had to send the amount to the Qaramatian king to avoid the death and destruction of their people. At the time of the enthronement of Azam, J'afar bin Falah Katami had conquered Damascus and established his rule. Azam demanded the tribute from the new ruler but he refused it completely. Azam dispatched an army to Damascus. Mu'iz Ubaidi was moving from Qairwan to Cairo when news came to him of this development, he wrote to the Qaramatians to hold back Azam from such an action, otherwise, he would proclaim the deposition of Azam by declaring the sons of Abu Tahir the rightful heirs to the throne. When Azam knew of this, he rose against the Ubaidi and started delivering addresses in the name of Abbasid Caliphate in all his territories. The army dispatched at first by Azam to Damascus was defeated by J'afar Katami in 360 A.H. Then Azam himself led an army in 361 A.H. and captured Damascus by killing J'afar Katami on the battlefield. He brought peace to the people of Damascus and then marched to Egypt.

During the time when Azam the Qarmate was engaged in Syria and Egypt, Mu'iz Ubaidi wrote to the sons of Abu Tahir, who were then confined on Awall Island that they should go ahead and capture Ahsa. He himself pronounced in Bahrain that he had bestowed the rule of Bahrain on the sons of Abu Tahir by deposing Azam. As a result of this, the sons of Abu Tahir ravaged Ahsa. Having seen this, Ta'i Abbasi, the Caliph of Baghdad wrote a letter to the sons of Abu Tahir not to create any disturbances and they should obey his orders. Azam was not paying attention to the events, when finally he came back to Ahsa and put them right. Meanwhile Mu'iz Ubaidi's troops captured all of Syria in 363 A.H. Then Azam came back to Syria at the head of his army, beat and pushed out the Ubaidi forces from Syria and made progress into Egypt up to Balbis. Mu'iz Ubaidi lured away a large part of Azam's army and a number of Generals. In this way, Azam was defeated and he went back to Ahsa, and different Arab chiefs occupied Syria. Some Turkish Generals were also trying to capture Damascus at the same time. Mu'iz Ubaidi himself set out to Damascus in 365 A.H., but died on the way. Azam conquered Syria once again in 366 A.H. Since Azam had offered his allegiance to Abbasid caliphate and he strongly hated the Ubaidi, the Qaramatians felt frustrated by being alienated from their natural allies the Ubaidi and aligned with their historical enemies and they rose up against him. The revolt succeeded in great part because Azam was then engaged in Syria far away from his capital. When Azam returned from Syria, he found everyone antagonistic to him and his cavalry also joined the insurgents. They arrested Azam and replaced him jointly by J'afar and Ishaq. Azam and his relatives were banished to Awall Island. Abu Tahir's progeny were already passing their lives in banishment on the island, and they killed the newcomers to the island right away without delay.

J'afar And Ishaq

J'afar and Ishaq took hold of the Qaramatians and immediately after assuming power they turned away from the Abbasids and acknowledge the Ubaidites (Fatimids). They started delivering addresses in the name of the Ubaidite king. They then attacked Kufa and occupied it. Izz ud-Daula bin Boya dispatched an army to punish the Qaramatians but was thoroughly beaten and chased up to Qadsiyah. Then enmity arose between J'afar and Ishaq and each of them attempted to destroy the other to rule alone. It resulted in weakness and frustration among the Qaramatians. Other Qaramatian Generals also staked their claims to kingdom, with the result that Asgher bin Abul Hasan Taghlabi captured Bahrain and Bani Mukarram occupied Oman. They offered their allegiance to the Abbasids and Taghlabid dynasty wiped out all signs of the Qaramatian from Bahrain by 375 A.H.

Chapter 15

Kingdom Of The Qaramatians
Batinians Of Persia

Soon after the destruction of the empire the Qaramatian creed underwent a drastic change. Even though the belief of Azam, the King of the Qaramatians' of Bahrain were different from other Qaramatians and he vehemently hated the Ubaidite king of Egypt, the Qaramatians in general looked upon the Ubaidite ruler with love and respect and accepted him as their king. Now when the Bahrain ruler slipped out of their hands and they had already lost Iraq and Syria as a shelter, they took to forming their own groups, and even though they kept mixing with the Muslims, they continued their preaching mission secretly. Like the Ubaidites, they appointed their preachers for different places. These preachers kept their activities a secret. They would go to people in the guise of devotes and divines and make their disciples from among them. And among these disciples, they entitled those as "Rafiq" (comrade) whom they found of kindred spirit. They then taught such people their own lessons. They created two classes, the preachers and the "Rafiqs" (comrades). These preachers spread all over Syria, Iraq, Persia and Khurasan (northeastern Iran, southern Turkmenistan, and northern Afghanistan). The Ubaidite king helped and patronized them. These preachers used to get all kinds of help secretly from Egypt. In this way, the Ubaidites imperceptibly spread the net of the Qaramatian preachers into various Islamic countries. The Seljuks kept occupying Islamic countries and were unaware of their secret enemy. After the fall of the Qaramatians in Bahrain, the Qaramatian teachings and the entire congregation turned into a group of preachers. The Ubaidite rule, therefore, felt no need to send its members from Egypt to Iraq as they were constantly supporting the clandestine activities of the Qaramatian preachers. At times, these preachers would turn into robbers and bandits with the help of their "Rafiqs." They had taught their disciples and followers to kill anybody outside their creed without any sense of crime. The Muslims in general had to suffer too much as their rage multiplied. They made it a regular feature of their operations to kill Muslim chiefs, generals and commanders whenever they found an opportunity. However, they kept quiet wherever they found the ruler alert and vigilant, but they flourished in the territories of weaker ones. Since the Qaramatians had donned the attire of piety and divinity and deceiving a Muslim was an act of virtue and reward to them, they found opportunities to secure positions of power in various Muslim courts. A certain person from their group was once appointed as a garrison commander. He made the fort a center to let loose a reign of terror, banditry and looting on the entire surrounding area. Since the party carried out its activities clandestinely, it came to be called *Batiniah* (hidden). These Batiniahs gradually became strong enough to seize the Shahwar Fort of Isfahan. One of the Batiniah preachers was a man named Attash who was a distinguished personality among his people. He was the man who had taught his creed to Hasan bin Sabbah and had virtually made him his pupil.

Ahmad Bin Attash

Attash had a son named Ahmad who commanded respect among his people like his father. Ahmad took leave of his group, he had the appearance of a wealthy young man and he met the garrison commander of Shahwar Fort and became employed there. Within a few days, Ahmad showed such an example of duty and responsibility that he was appointed as a deputy to the garrison commander and was entrusted with all the powers in decision making. Shortly after that the garrison commander died Ahmad secured the same post for himself. Being at the helm of affairs Ahmad bin Attash released all the prisoners of the Batiniah group who fell under his jurisdiction. Soon after being released, they went on a rampage in Isfahan, looting and killing people throughout the territory. During the same period Hasan bin Sabbah was spreading his conspiratorial net all over the areas of Taliqan and Qazwin.

Hasan Bin Sabbah

Hasan bin Sabbah was the classmate of Nizamul Mulk Tusi the prime minister of Malik Shah bin Alp of the Arsalan Seljuks. He first tried to find access to the royal court through Nizamul Mulk but later changed his mind and came to the service of Abu Muslim, a relative of the Nizamul Mulk who was a garrison commander. As an aide to him, he began to spread the net of his plots. Meanwhile, Abu Muslim came to know that spies from the Ubaidite ruler of Egypt would come to Hasan bin Sabbah. He interrogated Hasan bin Sabbah about the matter and when Hasan bin Sabbah saw that his secret was disclosed he escaped the territory and went to Mustansir Ubaidi in Egypt who showed respect to him. Hasan then offered his allegiance to Mustansir, who became happy and sent him on a preaching mission to Persia and Iraq by conferring on him the post of Head of the Preachers. He was entrusted with the task of inculcating in people the spirit to support Mustansir's leadership and caliphate. Mustansir Ubaidi had three sons named Ahmad, Nazar and Abul Qasim. On the eve of taking leave Hasan bin Sabbah asked Mustansir who would be chosen as Imam after him. "My son Nazar", Mustansir replied. Nazar was virtually made crown prince by Mustansir. But, the Minister and the sister of Mustansir, after the demise of the king, joined hands and brought Abul Qasim to the throne through a conspiracy. But Hasan bin Sabbah declined to accept the leadership of Abul Qasim and supported Nazar as the rightful successor to the throne. It is because of this that Hasan bin Sabbah's party is also called Nazaria. Hasan bin Sabbah left Egypt and reached Khurasan via Asia Minor and Mosul.

The Governor ruling Taliqan and Qahistan had entrusted the Alamut Fort to an Alwi. Hasan bin Sabbah went to the Alwi who greeted him with respect and asked him to stay as his honored guest. Hasan enjoyed his stay in the Fort as a devout Muslim but kept his mind engaged in planning how to bring the Fort under his control. With the completion of his plan, he turned the Alwi out of the Fort and began to rule it. This event took place during the period of Malik Shah Seljuk. When his Minister Nizamul Mulk Tusi heard of this event, he sent an army to chastise Hasan bin Sabbah. By then Hasan bin Sabbah had gained strength and stabilized his position. Fighting between the two broke out and lingered on. In the meantime, Hasan bin Sabbah persuaded a section of the Batiniah sect to do away with Nizamul Mulk. He was killed and the army he was leading went back. This initial success worked as a great encouragement and Hasan bin Sabbah's expansionist urge began to increase. During these days a man, named Munawwar from the Sassanid dynasty was the Governor of Qahistan. His relations with the Seljuk rulers worsened and the situation took such a serious turn that Munawwar sought help from Hasan bin Sabbah who gave it without loss of time and he captured Qahistan. Hasan bin Sabbah's power and influence progressed rapidly. In the meantime, civil war broke out among Seljuk chiefs, and they had to seek help from Hasan bin Sabbah instead of making an offensive against him. As a result of this, the area of his power and influence kept expanding very rapidly. King Berkeyaruq had to seek help from the Batiniyah sect to take on his brother Muhammad. Such a development added only to their importance. However, King Berkeyaruq then ordered the massacre of the Batiniyahs.

Ahmad bin Attash had established his own rule after occupying Shahwar Fort but the Seljuks surrounded Ahmad bin Attash and his companions and many of them had to buy peace on the condition of leaving Isfahan and its outskirts and joining Hasan bin Sabbah in Alamut Fort. They were granted amnesty on these terms alone. Ahmad bin Attash was arrested and killed and his wife committed suicide. This was how the Batiniyah sect met its doom in Isfahan however, the power of Hasan bin Sabbah increased more and more. Hasan bin Sabbah was the founder of a strong rule also he was the founder of a new faith and sect. He came to be addressed as "Sayedna" by his followers. He passed thirty-five years of his life in the Alamut Fort and he did not come out of the Fort for a single day.

Death Of Hasan Bin Sabbah

He died on Rabia al-Akhir 28, 518 A.H. at the ripe old age of 90. He collected human material from wild and savage men of hilly areas and turned them into such a fortified band and they would do anything at the command of their leader. They were known as the party of "Fidais" (pledged devotees). Aided and abetted by these "Fidais" it became easy for him to get powerful kings, commanders and antagonists assassinated in their own houses and, in this way, he had became a terror to everyone.

Kiya Buzurg Ummid

After the demise of Hasan bin Sabbah, one of his disciples named Kiya Buzurg Ummid, succeeded him and occupied Alamut Fort. His dynasty reigned up to 655 A.H. Kiya Buzurg Ummid was succeeded by his son Hasan bin Muhammad who was succeeded by his son Muhammad, the second bin Hasan who was succeeded by Alauddin Muhammad bin Jalaluddin Muhammad who was finally succeeded by Khurshah bin Alauddin.

Ruknuddin Khurshah

He was the last king of the "Fidais" who was arrested by Hulagu Khan the grandson of Genghis Khan and part of the Khan dynasty and his country and empire were destroyed with the destruction of Baghdad. Although the Fidais ruled over Alamut Fort and its suburbs for about one hundred years, during this long period the entire territory witnessed no sign of progress or development. When Genghis Khan began to ravage Muslim countries, the Fidais also sprang into action with their expansionist designs. They were still fulfilling their plans when they were invaded by Alauddin Khwarizm Shah who struck a deadly blow to their power. He wrested from them all the forts and razed them to the ground allowing them all to take refuge in Alamut Fort. At last, Hulagu Khan put them all to death.

Those Assassinated By The Fidais

Among those killed by the atheist *Fidais* were Khawaja Nizamul Mulk Tusi, the Prime Minister of King Alp Arsalan and Malik Shah Seljuk, Fakhrul Mulk bin Khawaja Nizamul Mulk, Shams Tabrizi, Maulana Rum, Nizamul Mulk Ma'ud bin Ali, Minister of Khwarizm Shah, Sultan Shahabuddin Muhammad Ghouri, some Christian kings of Europe and others. Sultan Salahuddin Ayubi and Imam Fakhruddin Razi were also threatened with murder but they remained unharmed.

Chapter 16

Ganghisid Mongols, Turks and Tartar Mongols

Removal Of A Doubt

A student of history faces difficulty in making differences among the Turks, Mongols and Tartars, Turkmen, Kara Tartars etc. and their origins. He sometimes finds that the Seljuks, Alp Arsalan and Tughril Beg were Turks and Genghis Khan appears to him as a Mongol. At another place, he comes across the same Genghis Khan who is a Turk, and a third place his campaigns are being mentioned as the trial of the Tartars. Now he comes to the natural conclusion that the Mongol, Turk and Tartar are one and the same people. But, later on, he finds the Mongols and the Turks fighting with one another, which gives him to believe that the Mongols and the Turks do not have common origin. When he goes through Indian history, he finds to his wonder that some Generals and Commanders are called Turks and they have entered into relations with the Mongols and in the 10th century A.H., we find India ruled by the Mughals. It also comes to his notice that the Mongols are called as "Mirza and they necessarily carry `Beg' as their title. But the reader finds `Mirza' attached to the names as a title when he meets the Persian Kings in the pages of history. Uthmanid Turks have also adopted Bek, Bey or Beg as titles. European historians sometimes describe the Mongol empires as Turkish empires. Therefore, it appears proper to clarify the differences between the Turks and the Mongols so that the student of history faces no confusion while going through the books of history.

Application Of 'Turk'

Adam, the Second, Prophet Nuh (Noah) (ﷺ) had three sons named Ham, Sam and Yafith. The progeny of Yafith inhabited the eastern countries, China etc. From among them was a man named 'Turk' whose progeny spread all over China and Turkistan and were all known as 'Turk'. Some people consider Afrasiyab also as a Turk although he belonged to the Keyanid royal family of Persia and was the descendant of Faridun. Since he was the king of Turkistan, he is mistaken as belonging to Turks. The progeny of Turk bin Yafith flourished in China, Turkistan, and Khatan etc. In order to keep themselves organized and united they came under a chief and, gradually, every emerging tribe had its separate chieftains. However, all the chieftains were considered subordinate to the main chief. Every tribe belonging to the progeny of Turk bin Yafith came to be called 'Turk' and all the people inhabiting China, Khatan, Turkistan were known as Turks.

Turkan Ghez

Some of these Turk tribes crossed the river Oxus and committed robbery and banditry in the interiors of Persia, Khorasan (between the Amu Darya [Oxus] and Syr Darya-rivers in modern Uzbekistan and Kazakhstan). These tribes are known as Turkan Ghez. Historians have found proof of their reaching up to Europe, Africa and Morocco.

Seljuks

Among these same tribes was one tribe known as the Seljuk. Among the progeny of Turk bin Yafith this Turkistan tribe of Seljuk was, perhaps, the first to confess Islam and it gave birth to great and powerful kings like Tughril and Alp Arsalan whose names spread into every nook and corner of the world.

Mongols And Tartars

Before the Seljuks' embracing Islam and before their exodus to Khurasan (northeastern Iran, southern Turkmenistan, and northern Afghanistan), two new tribes emerged by the name of two full brothers and came to be known as Mongol and Tartar. About the time of the Seljuks converting to Islam and gaining fame, these two tribes were almost a nonentity. Gradually, the progeny of the Mongol and Tartar multiplied and both the tribes settled in different countries and separate territories under various chiefs.

It happened that among the Turks there was a person named Anjah Khan who had twin sons named Mongol and Tartar. They raised two separate peoples and they were called by these names, Mongol and Tartar. Mongol Khan's son was Qara Khan whose son was Arghun Khan who was the chief of his tribe. During his time, a man of his tribe invented a cart for carrying loads. Arghun Khan liked the carriage and entitled the inventor as 'Qangli.' Thus, a carriage or conveyance is called Qangli in Turkish. His progeny brought the Qangli tribe into being. Arghun Khan had a number of sons, and one of them was Tanghez Khan whose son was Mangli Khan and his son was named Eil Khan and his son was called Qeyan. Qeyat tribe emerged from the progeny of Qeyan Khan who was succeeded by his son, Temur Tash whose son was Mangli Khan and his son was Yeldoz Khan Junea Bahadur who had a daughter named Alan Quwa. She was married to her cousin Dububayan and gave birth to two sons Yalkadai and Yakjudai. Alan Quwa's husband Dububayan was the ruler of his tribe. But he died leaving his two sons of tender age behind. The Mongol tribe entrusted Alan Quwa to be their chief after the demise of their chieftain Dububayan, the husband of Alan Quwa.

One night Alan Quwa went to bed. She had not yet slept when she noticed a light coming through the window of her room. This light entered her mouth. She got up in embarrassment and informed her mother and girl friends of this event. A few days later, she showed signs of pregnancy. When the news spread, the people rose to condemn her. But the queen Alan Quwa assembled the elders and asked them to stay for a few days near her room to know the facts. They saw with their naked eyes that a light descended from the sky, entered the room of the retiring queen and then went back to the sky. Now they believed the statement of the queen and accepted her pregnancy as miraculous. On the completion of the pregnancy, Alan Quwa gave birth to triplet sons who were named Bugun Qaiqi, Yusfain Salji and Buzbakhar Khan. Thus, she became the mother of five sons, two from Dububayan and three without a father.[1] While Yalkadai and Yakujdai's progeny formed the Darlekin tribe, Bugun Qaiqi's progeny came to be known as Qaiqain tribe and those of Yusfain Salji's were called Saljeut; the progeny of Buz Bakberqan gained fame as Buzbakhar. Buzbakhar succeeded his mother Alan Quwa after her demise. He called himself the son of the son. This Buzbakhar produced Genghis Khan, Temur and many other famous Mongol tribes.

As mentioned above, there came a man named Anjah Khan from the progeny of Turk bin Yafith who had twin sons named Mongol Khan and Tartar Khan. The progeny of these two brothers came to be known as Mongol and Tartar. Their people chose two different areas to settle in. The Mongol tribe settled in China and Mongolia, while the Tartar tribe inhabited the area along the bank of the river Oxus and the region became known as Tartar or Turkistan. Since from the Keyanid royal family of Persia Faridun's son Tur ruled the territory in the past, it is also called Turan.

In the Keyani ruling dynasty of Persia, Afrasiyab attained great fame and found a prominent place in the *Shahnema* of Firdausi. The progeny of Afrasiyab lived in Turkistan or Turan and mixed with the Tartars. Since Turkistan was closer to Islamic territories, the tribe of Turks that first made progress into Islamic territory was the Tartars, which consisted of many sub-tribes. Among them was the tribe of the progeny of Afrasiyab. They were ambitious and respected and they

---

[1] This and same these Vevents and stories describe the old nations to magnifects their rulers and monorchs to link their relations with heavenly power, but these stories have no any base and ground.

were the beginning of a magnificent empire. The saying of Seljuk, the Great seems true when he said: "We are the progeny of Afrasiyab." A man named Seljuk in the suburbs of Bukhara was the first to confess Islam along with his tribe. The progeny of this Seljuk is called the Seljuk tribe. Seljuk had five sons. Among them, one was Israel and another one Michael (Mika'il). Sultan Mahmud, the Ghaznavid imprisoned Israel in the Fort of Kalinjar and Mahmud's son Sultan Mas'ud freed him then he rejoined his tribe. Mika'il's son was Sultan Tughril while another brother of Tughril named Chughri preg had a son who was Sultan Alp Arsalan Seljuk. If the Seljuk tribe is acknowledged to be the descendent of Afrasiyab, it was not totally Turkish in origin but also Persian Keyani. The Turks or Tartars living in Turkistan invaded Iran and Khurasan more than once. One among those tribes, the Seljuk's, laid the foundation of the Ottoman Empire, which came to be known as Turkish Ottoman.

The Word 'Mongol'

It is a fact that the Mongol Tribe comes from Mongol Khan's progeny and every individual of that tribe is called Mongol. The short form of Mongol is Moghal. Some people consider 'Mongol' as the plural of Moghal, which is totally wrong.

Fara Tartar

Mongol and Tartar would most frequently go to war because they had inhabited different territories and would compete for each other's land. The Keyani dynasty kept lending support to the Tartars until it ruled Turan and the Mongols remained subdued. During these battles, the Tartars captured Mongol women and children and from these women their offspring were called slave girl children and had no right to property. When such children became numerous and were married to their same class they all together made a separate people. Some historians believe, that such people were called Turkaman. It is because of the Tartar's dislike of the Mongols that they did not consider the children from Mongol women on par with their own, other than this tribal distinction The Mongol tribe and the Tartar tribe were actually the offspring of the same father.

Removal Of A Misunderstanding

Some people mistake the Uzbeks for the Tartars, although the Uzbeks are a tribe raised from the progeny of Genghis Khan. This misunderstanding took route because the Mongol kings kept fighting with the Uzbek rulers. The Uzbeks those days were the kings of Turkistan and so some historians mistook them for the Tartars. However, the Ottoman Empire came from the Tartars. Mongol tribes had a number of branches like Qachaq, Ighor, Khalj, Qachar, Afshar, Jala'ir, Arlat, Daghlat, Qantrat, Saldoz, Arghun, Qauchin, Tarkhani, Taghai, and Qaoshal.

It might have been clear by now that the word 'Turk' is a general term applied to all the tribes of the Mongols and the Tartars for both the Tartars and the Mongols are two branches of the Turkish tribe. Later on, the Tartars came to be called 'Turks' and the term 'Turk' was particularly applied to the Tartars. With the passage of time Turk and Mongol gained fame as two different peoples.

Being stronger than the Mongols, the Tartars came out of Turkistan and took Khurasan (northeastern Iran, southern Turkmenistan, and northern Afghanistan), Persia, Iraq, Syria, and Asia Minor by storm and spread over these territories leaving Turkistan behind. They had learned cultured manners and had become civilized by that time.

Genghis Khan

Features Of The Mongol

The features of the Mongols as described by the historians make them resemble the Turks to a great extent. They are known for their wide chest, flat face, small buttocks and wheatish complexion, quick action and sharp intellect. When they plan an endeavor, they never express their opinion and pounce upon their enemies catching them in a state of utter unawareness and do not allow them to retaliate. Their women fight along with men and never lag behind in the art of combat with their enemies. They eat flesh of all kinds and reject nothing. No spy can intrude their land for he is easily recognized by his features and movements. They make no concession, in killing anybody and kill women, children, the old and young alike. When attacking their enemies, they ravage the entire population. It seems that they are governed by a sense of greed and they rather enjoy devastating the entire human world.

Administration Of The Mongols

The territory ruled by the Mongols was divided into six provinces or parts, each governed by one person. All these governors were subordinates to one sovereign ruler who lived in Tamgach. One of these provinces or parts was ruled by Buzbakhar ibn Alan-quwa until the leadership came to the period of Tumna Khan ibn Bayasnaqar Khan. Tumna Khan had eleven sons out of which nine came from one mother and two were born as twins from another mother. He had named these two sons as Qabl Khan and Qachuli Bahadur.

Qachuli's Dream

One night Qachuli Bahadur had a dream that a star emerged from the collar of his brother, Qabl Khan and rose to the sky and began to give light to the earth. Shortly after that, the star disappeared then another star appeared in the same spot. That too went out of sight after a little while giving place to the third one. Following the disappearance of the third star the fourth one appeared so brightly and forcefully that the entire world was illuminated. When this big star too went out of sight, a few small stars became visible and with this sight Qachuli Bahadur's eyes opened. He was still musing over the interpretation of the dream when he again fell asleep. In a fresh dream, he saw that this time one star came out of his own collar, rose to sky and began to shine in the sky. It was followed by the second and the third and thus seven stars in all, appeared. Following the seventh one appeared a very big and bright star, which illuminated the whole world. The disappearance of this big star was followed by the appearance of a number of small stars. Following this Qachuli woke up and he related both these dreams to his father.

Interpretation Of Tumna Khan

Tumna Khan interpreted the dream by saying that a great king would emerge in the fourth generation from Qabl Khan and another great king in his (Qachuli Khan's) eighth generation and thus his dynasty would rule for long. Following this Tumna Khan counseled his both sons to keep united. He then wrote down a document and had his sons to sign it and then he handed it over to his treasurer to preserve it for the coming generations and he put his own signature on it before putting it under lock and key. The document stated that the empire and rulers would come from the progeny of Qabl Khan while the military leadership would remain with the progeny of Qachuli Bahadur. Accordingly, Qabl Khan came to the throne following the demise of Tumna Khan.

Birth Of Genghis Khan

Maisuka Bahadur, the descendent of Qabl Khan had a son born on Dhul Qadah 20, 549 A.H. The same year the Great Khan of Mongolia, King Tamuchin died. For this reason Maisuka Bahadur named his son Tamuchin and who later gained fame by the name Genghis Khan. When Maisuka Bahadur died in 562 A.H., Tamuchin was only 13 when he came to the throne of his small kingdom. The people looked down upon him because he was a child and they showed signs of revolt.

Dream Of Genghis Khan

Tamuchin dreamed that he had swords in his both hands and when he stretched his hands towards the east and the west, the tips of the swords touched both the horizons. When he narrated the dream to his mother, she was convinced that her son would shed blood and commit large-scale carnage. She also knew that, at the time of birth, Tamuchin's both fists were tightly closed. When the fists were opened, they had frozen blood in them. From this event, they also had inferred that the child would cause much bloodshed. The insurgence in Tamuchin's small kingdom reached a point that except for Amir Qaracha Bahadur from the progeny of Qachuli Bahadur, the entire progeny of Qachuli Bahadur also rose against Tamuchin. Tamuchin sought help from Aurang Khan, the ruler of the bordering state and practically took refuge with him. Aurang Khan welcomed him whole-heartedly and looked after him like his own son. Shortly after that, Genghis Khan sprang into action against his benefactor and hid in a protected mountain pass along with his comrades. In a fierce encounter Aurang Khan was fatally injured by an arrow shot by Amir Qaracha and another chief, Yang Khan, killed him while he was escaping. Peace between Tamuchin and Yang Khan was the most expected outcome because Yang Khan had helped him by killing Aurang Khan. However, following this victory, Genghis Khan attracted a number of tribes around him and they, finding him brave and determined, offered their allegiance to him. With a large band of organized fighters, Genghis Khan led an attack on Yang Khan who was killed during the encounter and his vast territory fell to Genghis Khan. As a result of these victories, Tamuchin rose as a center of power and leadership among all the Mongol tribes. He then emerged as rival to the ruler of Mongolia and the power of the Great Khan himself.

Change Of Name

Meanwhile, a man named Tankiri, who commanded respect from among the Mongols for his piety and devotion, came to Genghis Khan. He said to him, "I saw a red man in red garments mounted on red horse asking me to tell the son of Maisuka Bahadur to change his name from Tamuchin to Genghis Khan for God Almighty has decided to make you the emperor of many countries." Although Genghis Khan took him to be a liar, nevertheless, he began to be called Genghis Khan. In Turkish "Genghis" means emperor or is a synonym for emperor. A few days later, some dispute arose between Tankiri and a courtier of Genghis Khan. He caught Tankiri by his neck and knocked him so violently on the ground that he died on the spot.

Gradually, Genghis Khan brought all the tribes and Mongolia under his control and after the killing of the Great Khan in an encounter Genghis Khan was acknowledged as the Great Khan. Following this Genghis Khan turned to the Tartar tribes. The Tartar king found himself too weak to face Genghis Khan and bought peace by giving his daughter in marriage to Genghis Khan. In the wake of this peace treaty, Tartar chiefs rose against their king and they sought Genghis's help. After large-scale bloodshed, the Tartar king poisoned himself to death and Genghis's territory expanded again. Genghis Khan was very brave and shrewd among the Mongols. His performance bears testimony to his wisdom and intelligence.

Religion Of The Mongols

The Faith and religion of the Mongols lie in the darkness of history. However, they had the concept of one Powerful Creator, they believed in God Almighty. They worshipped much in the way as the non-Aryan inhabitants of India did. A Prophet must have been sent to that region but the Mongols had sent him into oblivion with the passage of time along with his message. They had lost sense of right and wrong, lawful and unlawful. They ate what they found and did anything they liked. Due to the climatic effect and tribal feuds, some historians have written that their religion was simply killing men. They also worshipped stars and natural phenomena. They were not Magi even though they worshipped fire. Genghis Khan rose as a reformer in a people so low in moral decay and immersed in abject ignorance. He first established a mighty empire in a comparatively short time and then he took time to bring about reforms in the moral and social conditions of the Mongols.

Sultan Muhammad Khwarizm Shah

During this time, Sultan Muhammad Khwarizm Shah had been in full control of Iran, Khurasan, Kabul, and Turkistan and was planning to annihilate Baghdad, and was undoubtedly considered the mightiest Muslim king on the Asian continent. When a dispute between the Abbasid Caliph Nasiruddin and Muhammad Khwarizm Shah took a serious turn, Khwarizm Shah decided to invade Baghdad and the Caliph sent Sheikh Shahabuddin Sahrwardy as his envoy to the court of Khwarizm Shah. He addressed the king and the courtiers and counseled them to hold back from plundering Baghdad. Khwarizm Shah said "Sheikh! You are a great admirer of the Abbasids, therefore you go back to Baghdad. I, myself, prefer the Alwis to the Abbasids and want to help the Alwis by devastating the Abbasid caliphate. I shall invade Baghdad by all means."

Curse Of Three Saints On Khawarizm

Sheikh Shahabuddin Sahrwardy's mission failed to bring any fruit and he cursed Khwarizm Shah saying: "O Allah! Set some tyrants over him". When Khwarizm Shah led his army, he found the way closed with heavy snowfall and he had to postpone his campaign until the next year. One day, in a state of inebriation, he ordered to put Sheikh Majduddin to death and he was martyred. When he returned to consciousness, he expressed deep regret and sent blood money to Sheikh Najmuddin. He remarked: "The ransom for the martyred Sheikh is the head of yours and mine and thousands of Muslims will be killed in retaliation". They say that Khwarizm Shah was overtaken by calamity because he invited curses from Sheikh Shahabuddin Suhrawardy, Sheikh Majduddin and Sheikh Najmuddin.

Peace Steps Of Genghis Khan Towards Khawarizm

When Genghis Khan established a mighty empire out of small states conquered by him, he thought it proper to establish peaceful friendly relations with his rival Sultan Khwarizm Shah for their borders were meeting each other. As a prelude to peace efforts, Genghis Khan sent a letter to Muhammad Khwarizm Shah through his emissaries, which contained, "I have conquered vast lands and I have under my banner such a large number of warring tricks that I have no desire to win any other country. Similarly, you are also in occupation of many countries and happen to be a great king. Thus it seems proper that we establish friendly relations between us and promise to live in peace and harmony so that each of us pay attention to human welfare and prosperity." He had further written in the letter, "I shall keep you dear like my own son." Having received the letter Khwarizm Shah evidently signed a peace document and showed the utmost courtesy to the emissaries but he disliked the last sentence which treated him as his son', which appeared somewhat degrading to him. According to the peace treaty, both the rulers agreed to free trading activities between the two empires and the traders enjoyed full freedom of crossing one another's borders. Genghis Khan, though an unbeliever, is praiseworthy for winning peace against the threat of a formidable power. The mention of trading facilities in each other's country is again a sign of Genghis Khan's wisdom and at that time he did not intend to plunder the Islamic countries.

In the wake of this peace agreement Caliph Nasiruddin Abbasi is reported to have shaved the head of a person and inscribed on the persons head a letter addressed to Genghis Khan. In this strange letter, he had advised Genghis Khan to attack Muhammad Khwarizm Shah without delay and consider him as his supporter. When the person's head grew a little hair the person was sent to Genghis Khan as an envoy. He met Genghis Khan and said, "I am the envoy of the Caliph and, I have a message inscribed on my head and you can read it by having my head shaved. Having read the letter Genghis Khan offered his apology that he had already struck a peace agreement with Khwarizm Shah and could not, therefore, fight with him. Following this letter from the Caliph, Genghis Khan addressed a letter to Khwarizm Shah assuring him of his love and friendship in great magnitude. It is one more proof of Genghis Khan's wisdom that he cared more for the enemy bordering him than a number of other countries far from his borders.

The Mistake Of Khawarizm Shah

Henceforward starts the misfortune of Khwarizm Shah. Genghis Khan handed over a letter to an emissary and dispatched him along with the four hundred and fifty Muslim traders who had come to Mongolia on a trade mission and were then on their return journey. The trade caravan was well placed and had access to the court. When the caravan reached Anzar, the official of Khwarizm Shah on duty arrested the merchants and put them in prison. The merchants tried their level best to assure him that they were only traders and had been to Mongolia on a trade mission. Moreover, they were also Muslims as well as the emissaries of the Mongol Empire. But all these arguments fell on the deaf ears of the official and he wrote to Khwarizm Shah that some spies from Mongolia had tried to cross the border in the guise of traders and emissaries and were duly caught; what should then be done about them? Khwarizm Shah ordered to kill them all and the official implemented the order and seized their merchandise. One escaped and related to Genghis Khan the calamity that befell the trade caravan.

Genghis Khan addressed another cautious letter to Khwarizm Shah condemning the unworthy act of the administrator of Anzar and asked for some deterrent punishment to the offender or to hand him over to him (Genghis). Having gone through the letter Khwarizm Shah put the emissary to death. As per some historians, Genghis Khan wrote a third letter saying: "Killing of an emissary is not proper for a king and their duty is to give protection to traders. Therefore do consider my points." But Khwarizm Shah killed the third emissary also.

In view of the situation, Genghis Khan began to build a huge army of the warring tribes of Mongolia and Turkistan and ceased to mention Khwarizm Shah as a king. He rather referred to him as a thief to him, for a king does not kill an emissary. Meanwhile, a frontier chief named Tug Tughan showed signs of revolt. In view of the situation, Genghis Khan sent his son Juchi Khan to chastise the insurgent chief. Tug Tughan moved to Mawaraunnahr (between the Amu [Oxus] and Syr rivers in modern Uzbekistan and Kazakhstan) where Khwarizm Shah was also staying in those days. Juchi Khan chased and arrested Tug Tughan. Khwarizm Shah having observed this, Juchi requested him not to attack his army for he had not been sent to fight with him (Khwarizm). He had rather come to catch the insurgent and he had already completed his mission and he was returning to his own territory. Khwarizm Shah paid no heed to his explanation and launched a massive attack on Juchi Khan. The day long fierce battle produced no result and in the night Juchi Khan left his camp in a blazing fire and gave an account of the entire event to Genghis Khan. Genghis Khan was infuriated and marched towards Persia and the other Islamic countries at the head of a massive army.

Genghis Khan Turns To Islamic Countries

Genghis Khan marched towards the Islamic countries in 615 A.H. and ordered his three sons Juchi Khan, Ogdai Khan and Chogatai Khan to besiege Anzar. He then sent Alag Nuyan and Mungkubuga with the armies of Khajand and Nabkat respectively and, he himself marched to Bukhara accompanied by his youngest son, Tolui Khan. Being informed of the Mongol invasion Khwarizm Shah dispatched a force of sixty thousand troops to the administrator of Anzar and thirty thousand cavaliers to Bukhara, he deployed two hundred and ten thousand men to keep Samarkand safe and sixty thousand fighters to fortify the Fort and tower and he himself left Samarkand for Khurasan (northeastern Iran, southern Turkmenistan, and northern Afghanistan).

Cowardice Of Khwarizm Shah

The biggest mistake or an act of timidity on the part of Khwarizm Shah was his personal evasion of Genghis Khan. His departure to Khurasan was certainly discouraging for his army. Even more disheartening and injurious was his remark at the time of his departure that if Mongols dropped their whips into this trench it would get totally filled. This remark filled the force of Samarkand with great terror. Khwarizm Shah first reached Balkh and dispatched his wives and children and treasures to Mazandan. It is here that he held consultations with his nobles and courtiers about adopting the ways and means to combat the Mongols. Among the seven sons of Khwarizm Shah, one named Jalaluddin, having seen his father extremely terrified said, "You may go to Iraq with pleasure but confer on me the command of the army and I shall attack the enemy and Allah willing, I shall pitch my tents across the Oxus River. Moreover, let me guard Mawaraunnahr (between the Amu [Oxus] and Syr rivers in modern Uzbekistan and Kazakhstan) and you take the responsibility of Iraq and Khurasan (northeastern Iran, southern Turkmenistan, and northern Afghanistan)". But Khwarizm Shah did not like the suggestion. He proceeded from Balkh to Herat. Meanwhile, the news of the seizure of Bukhara by the Mongols and the massacre of the whole population came to him as a great shock. He hurried to Nishapur and indulged in luxury.

In 617 A.H., a commander of Genghis Khan crossed the river Oxus at the head of thirty thousand troops. This news sent terror into the heart of Khwarizm Shah who dispatched his wives and children and treasure to Qarun Fort and he himself left for Asfarain. The Mongols felt utterly encouraged when they found Khwarizm Shah evading engagement and running away from one place to another for his safety. With this in mind, they embarked on chasing him and surrounded Qarun Fort where he had kept his wives and children and his possessions. He then ran away to Asterabad and then to Amal.

Death Of Khwarizm Shah

From Amal he fled to an Island and took refuge there. It was there that he got the soul shattering news that the Mongols had seized Qarun Fort his possessions, wives and children. He succumbed to the shock and was buried in the garments he was putting on. Next, the Mongols took the entire Khurasan (northeastern Iran, southern Turkmenistan, and northern Afghanistan) and Persia by storm and filled the territory with death and destruction. Only one of his sons named Jalaluddin, a brave, courageous and ambitious young man saved himself.

During this period, the Mongols conquered Bukhara and Samarkand and plunged the entire population into a river of blood. Genghis Khan himself crossed the river Oxus in Rabia al-Awwal 617 A.H. and massacred the population of Balkh and Herat. When the wives and children of Khwarizm Shah were produced before Genghis Khan, he took no pity and ordered them all to be put to death. This large-scale massacre also enveloped Nishapur, Mazandan, Amal, Rayy, Hamadan, Qum, Qazwin, Debal, Tabriz, Tiflis, and Maragheh where nobody, old or young, women or child, was spared. This scene of carnage and destruction filled the Muslim hearts with so much terror that an alone Mongol woman could ransack a house without any resistance. The people of Hamadan spared until then had mustered enough courage to assassinate a weak Mongol Governor bore the brunt of the Mongols' wrath in such a wild and violent way that no one has ever repeated such a brutal action ever since.

Jalaluddin Bin Khwarizm

Soon after the death of his father Jalaluddin bin Khwarizm came to Tabriz from an island in the Caspian Sea. He took some brave friends with him. Although the Mongols attempted to arrest him, he tore apart their ranks and escaped along with his friends. He reached

Ghazni and received the support of a band of persons there. The nearby Mongol troops attacked his party but he fought them back and this was perhaps, the first defeat conceded by the Mongols at the hands of Jalaluddin. With this news Genghis Khan rushed to Bamyan where his grandson the son of his son Chogatai Khan was killed by an arrow. Genghis Khan grew so furious that he ordered the death of everyone. Even the pregnant women were not spared and their babies were taken out by splitting their wombs and killed. Following the defeat of the Mongol troops, Jalaluddin fortified his position and took the field against Genghis Khan. Unfortunately, some Generals changed sides during the engagement and went over to the Mongols. Jalaluddin was left with only seven hundred fighters. He didn't lose his courage and dashed against the mighty force of Genghis Khan. Jalaluddin showed exemplary bravery and spirit and he pushed back the Mongols wherever he turned against them. He frustrated the attempts of the Mongols and a large Mongol army always had to come to their rescue. However, Jalaluddin could not win the battle owing to dearth of fighters on his side. But he succeeded in establishing his prestige in the heart of Genghis Khan. He did not yield even when only one hundred fighters were left to fight under his command. In such an hour of crisis, he took off his coat of mail and threw it away, took his crown in his hand and plunged his horse into the river Indus. His companions followed suit. Even though Genghis Khan wanted to give chase to that valiant fighter and his followers it was not easy for his troops to face the surging waves of the deep river. Genghis Khan and his troops stopped at the bank of the river Indus and began to shower their arrows at the handful of fighters braving the dashing waves of the river. Many of them lost their lives bravely and only seven of them were left to stand by valiant Jalaluddin across the river. He put off his garments and spread them over the bushes to dry them and stuck his lance into the ground and put his crown on its and lay down under it to take a rest. He also put off the saddle of his horse and placed it in front of himself to dry out.

Genghis Khan was watching all this from the other bank with a feeling of surprise. He called his sons and commanders and said: "I have never seen the like of such a brave and courageous person. His companions are also matchless in bravery and crossing such a vast and turbulent river is the work of brave men only. I am afraid, if this man remains alive, he will erase the name of the Mongols from the face of the earth. Let us work out a plan to do away with him as soon as possible". But, finding no way to fulfill his plan, Genghis Khan returned disappointed. This event took place in 620 A.H.

Following this Sultan Jalaluddin won some victories in the Sind province. His supporters and well wishers kept joining him here. A few days later, he crossed the river and reached Kirman an and then to Shiraz. In the meantime, he inflicted defeats on the Fidai known as Batini and razed their forts to the ground save the Al a Mut Fort. The Fidai or Batini people were happy with the news of the Muslim massacre and destruction at the hands of the Mongols. Since they were themselves, sworn enemies of the Muslims like the Mongols they were not at all afraid of the Mongols. They had expanded their territories in the wake of the Muslim disaster. The uprooting of the Qaramatians should be reckoned among the deeds of Sultan Jalaluddin. It was the time when the Mongol flood was raging in the north. Sultan Jalaluddin proceeded to Baghdad to seek Caliph Nasiruddin's help and support so that the Mongol campaigns against the Islamic countries could be warded off. Since Nasiruddin hated Jalaluddin's father he deployed his nobles to stop Jalaluddin and drive him out of the territory. Facing this situation, Jalaluddin took the field and fought back the nobles. He then turned to Tabriz instead of Baghdad and moved to Girijistan after occupying Tabriz. He was greeted by the nobles with honor and they expressed their satisfaction over his arrival.

Now Sultan Jalaluddin gained strength and stability once again and when he came face to face with the Mongols near Isfahan, he repulsed the attack and drove them back. Now the whole country of Girjistan and its suburban territories came under the occupation of Jalaluddin. The Mongols attacked Jalaluddin once again with large-scale preparations. In view of the massive Mongol attack, Jalaluddin sent his emissaries to Baghdad and other Islamic countries to seek help but none rose to his help because they did not want to invite any risk to their countries by lending help to such a valiant fighter like Jalaluddin. At last he alone rose to face the Mongol attack but on account of being misinformed by his spies that the Mongol troops were far away from him he was caught unaware by the Mongols in a midnight attack and lost the battle in spite of fighting gallantly. In a state of utter disappointment, he went away to an unknown place and remained untraceable for the rest of his life.

End Of Jalaluddin

Two kinds of narratives have gained currency concerning his end. According to one, he took refuge in a hill where someone assassinated him for his costly garments and horse. Another one says that he joined the company of Muslim Sufis and saints and passed the rest of his life in long journeys, piety and prayers.

Genghis Khan's Interest In Islam

Being relieved of the campaigns of Sultan Jalaluddin Khwarizm, Genghis Khan left his son, Chogatai Khan in Makran and came back to Mongolia in Dhul Hijjah 521 A.H. after an absence of seven years. In route to his native land and upon reaching Bukhara he ordered to produce before him the most learned Muslim scholar to learn from him the facts about Islam. Seven years of fighting and carnage had impressed upon him that although, the Muslims had become weak at the time, Islam was not an ordinary religion it had a magnificent system and high moral teachings. Qadi Ashraf and a learned Muslim scholar were produced before Genghis Khan. On inquiring about Islam, those two Muslim scholars first explained to him about faith in one God (Tawhid). Genghis Khan acknowledged the faith. Following this they put before him the creed of Prophethood which he readily accepted saying that God Almighty used to send His envoys for the guidance of mankind. He also accepted the prayer and fasting as obligatory. However, he held pilgrimage to Ka'bah as unnecessary. Qadi Ashraf declared Genghis Khan a Muslim but another scholar differed.

From Bukhara Genghis Khan came to Samarkand and showed much kindness to the Muslims there. During seven years of his absence from his homeland, he kept plundering and ravaging Muslims indiscriminately was now coming home but spiritually defeated and dominated by Islam. Genghis Khan's grandson Kublai Khan and Hulagu Khan were then ten and nine years old respectively. Both of them came out to welcome Genghis Khan home, hunting a rabbit and a deer on the way. Since it was the first hunting affair of the boys Genghis Khan celebrated the occasion with a feast and festivities.

Nomination Of A Successor

After everything being settled Genghis Khan assembled his sons, grandsons and commanders at a place where he said, "Since my last days are approaching and I have won a vast country for you all, I want you to choose someone as my successor." They all said in one voice, "We are perfectly obedient to you. We shall, therefore, obey anybody of your choice." Genghis Khan said, "If you leave the matter to me, I shall nominate Ogdai Khan as my successor. Now, it is your duty to obey him and carry out his orders." Following this he ordered to take out the document made out by Tumna Khan and signed by Qabl Khan and Qachuli Bahadur. He showed the document to everyone and had all of them sign it. He then declared that the deserts of Karakrum (in modern Turkmenistan) and Khazr (southeastern section of modern European Russia), Alani (Russia northeast of the Black Sea), Russia, and Bulgar (territory at the confluence of the Volga and Kama rivers) would be ruled by Juchi Khan. Mawaraunnahr (between the Amu [Oxus] and Syr rivers in modern Uzbekistan and Kazakhstan), Khwarizm (territories of present day Turkmenistan and Uzbekistan), Kashgar (city in extreme western China), Badakhshan (in present day Afghanistan), Balkh, Ghazni and the territory up to Indus River would go to Chogatai Khan. Moreover, Qarachar Chogatai Khan and Amir Qachar would keep the same relation as stood between Qarachar and himself. Chogatai Khan would be the king and Amir Qachar his Commander-in-chief. Both would remain faithful and loyal to one another. He then made out a fresh document bearing the new settlement and put his own seal and signature on it. Amir Qarachar was the great grand son of Qachuli Bahadur. A part of Mongolia and a part of the command of Ogdai Khan would remain attached to Tolui Khan. He then ordered that all the brothers would consider their elder brother Ogdai Khan as their monarch and never think of turning away from him.

Death Of Genghis Khan

Genghis Khan died in the Ramadan 624 A.H. at the age of 73 after a reign of 25 years. He was buried under a tree as per his will. In the first year, a thick forest grew around his grave until it became impassable and invisible and untraceable by the ensuing generations.

A Review Of The Genghis Khan's Reign

Genghis Khan emerged among the Mongols as a very wise and far-sighted man. It was due to him alone that the unknown Mongol race achieved renown all over the world. He had established firm and appreciable principles of governance. He grew well aware of the basic fact that a savage and ignorant people like the Mongols must not be allowed to go without engagements otherwise they would perish by killing each other. On one hand, he taught the Mongols the virtues of unity and solidarity but worked out such laws and principles that would not leave the Mongol army out of action on the other. He also compiled a set of laws for the purpose, which came to be known as the "Torah of Genghis". The Mongols revered this book of statutes of Genghis Khan like a divinely religious book. The Torah of Genghis contains laws and principles for hunting as well, it was incumbent on Mongol kings to go hunting along with their troops when there were no campaigns to launch.

Along with the carnage and plunder, it is worth noticing that Genghis Khan would avoid the use of haughty words. In a letter to a king, he would generally say; "Obey me, otherwise, God Almighty knows, what will happen." He would never claim to have a strong and formidable army to crush the enemy. Similarly, he would never hold his huge army responsible for the victory. He would always say that his victory was only due to the Grace of God and He was the One who made him king. Moreover, he would not allow anybody to write about him words of acclaim and lofty praise. He would do ordinary work like ordinary soldiers. He covered long distances on horseback and had his soldiers to do it as well. He would so often say, "We should be adopted to hard labor and diligence. Our excellence and leadership lie therein."

Genghis Khan himself was tall, strong and stout. During battle, he was in the first row and dispersed the enemy ranks wherever he charged at them. The secret of his outstanding victories also lay in the fact that his sons were also mighty warriors and had been endowed with soldierly qualities and temper. Furthermore, he had done away with tribal feuds and rivalries and forged unity and accord among the Mongols.

He married five wives and every wife belonged to a different tribe. In this way, he won the confidence and support of all those tribes. One of the laws of his book of statutes entitled the "Torah of Genghis" was that, in case of the conquest of a new city, a large-scale massacre was a must, for it created deep terror in the hearts of the defeated people, never allowing them to gather courage to rise against the victor. Genghis Khan practiced it in all of his victories. It is an undeniable fact that in those days, no ruler was above the danger of revolt and murder and such insurgencies and uprisings caused untold miseries and sufferings to the population at large. The revolts of the Persians, Shiites and Ubaidites never ceased to occur. When Genghis Khan was acquainted with these ways and practices throughout the conquered territories, he used this device to create awe and fear in his subjects and it paid him dividends.

The Mongols of that time had conquered the entire Asian continent and some parts of Europe except Iraq, Arabia and India. The Islamic states suffered most at the hands of the Mongols and their swords killed large numbers of Muslims. At times, it appeared that Islam would go out of existence but Allah Almighty saved His Religion and only the deviated Muslims were overtaken by the calamity. With the passage of time, the anti-Islamic force of the Mongols surrendered to the mighty moral and spiritual forces of Islam. The swords, which were used to wipe out all traces of Islam, were now being used to guard it. When Christianity made an attempt to turn the Mongols might and magnificence towards itself the Mongols found nothing in it to attract an ambitious and adventurous people. Mongols were, in truth, like a clean slate concerning religion and faith and had nothing against others. Allah Almighty had taken the Mongols out of the mountains to make a victorious entry into Asia and to become civilized and enlightened. This is a splendid sign of the truth of Islam that it has the power to cast its impact both on the victor and the vanquished.

Ogdai Khan

After the demise of Genghis Khan his elder son, Ogdai Khan succeeded him while his brothers took charge of their respective territories as allotted by Genghis Khan. Two years later, Ogdai Khan invited his brother to join him in a feast and other festivities. At the end of the celebrations, Ogdai Khan said addressing his brothers, "I now abdicate the throne and you all are at liberty to choose someone else as your Great Khan". But Chogatai Khan and the other brothers and commanders insisted on him to continue as emperor. They seated him on the throne and worshipped the sun according to their practice. Hatu Khan, the son of Juchi Khan and grandson, Guyuk Khan and Mungku Khan, the sons of Tolui Khan were commissioned to invade Russia, Cherkessia (southwestern Russia) and Belgrade. These princes conquered all those countries after fighting long campaigns over seven years. The commander Arghun was then entrusted the duty of rehabilitating the cities of Khurasan, which were once devastated by the Mongols.

Ogdai Khan, the son of Genghis Khan was very sober and gentle. He paid heed to welfare programs and developmental plans for his subjects at large. He was particularly very sympathetic to the Muslims. He held them in high esteem and paid them special attention. Taking a bath by diving into the water was a major crime according to the Mongol law. Ogdai Khan and Chogatai Khan were going together somewhere. They noticed a Muslim having bath in a river. Chogatai Khan issued an order to have him executed. Ogdai Khan immediately ordered to arrest the Muslim and have him executed in full view of the public. Ogdai Khan then met the Muslim in private and advised him to say that he had a purse full of gold coins which he wanted to hide under the water for fear of robbers and that was his sole purpose for entering the river. Ogdai Khan then had a purse dropped into the river at the spot where the Muslim was bathing. When the accused Muslim was brought for execution, he advanced the same argument as was instructed by Ogdai Khan. Following his statement, men were sent in search of the purse and it was found. In this way, the truth of the statement of the Muslim was established and Ogdai Khan set the Muslim free along with the purse and with a few others by way of reward for his truthfulness.

Once a certain person came to Ogdai Khan and said, "Last night I saw Genghis Khan in dream. He told me to convey to Ogdai Khan my utmost desire that the Muslims must be wiped off of the surface of the earth without any delay." Ogdai Khan said to him, "Do you know the language of the Mongols?" He said, "I know only Persian and can speak and understand this language alone." Thereupon Ogdai Khan said, "Genghis Khan knew the Mongol language and could neither speak nor understand Persian. How did you know what he said?" Saying this Ogdai Khan ordered that he be killed for he was a liar, and he was put to death on the spot.

It was a common opinion about Ogdai Khan that, even though he had not confessed Islam openly he had secretly embraced it by acknowledging its power and virtues. His capital was Karakorum where he had stored the gems and jewels and other possessions they had collected as a result of their pillaging and plundering all over the world. But the proverbial generosity of Ogdai Khan attracted men from far off places like Khurasan and Syria to Karakorum who would come back rich and prosperous. The atrocities and bloodshed from which the father had collected phenomenal wealth the son distributed it among the people with exemplary generosity, kindness and sympathy. In consequence of this the awe and terror of the inhuman treatment and wanton behavior of the Mongols turned into love for Ogdai Khan. Even though Genghis Khan laid the foundation of the Mongol Empire, it was, in truth, Ogdai Khan who lent stability and solidity to it.

Guyuk Khan

When the end of Ogdai Khan came his son, Guyuk Khan was far away from Karakorum. Thus, in accordance with the Mongol practice, they gave the throne to Turkina the widow of Ogdai Khan so that the empire could be spared any trouble. When Guyuk Khan

returned   to Karakorum, he spoke nothing about the throne
following the Mongol practice and the Torah of Genghis and passed
his days like a   common person. After sometime Turkina sent
invitations to the kings and rulers all over the world to attend a
great occasion. The Kings of Khurasan, Persia, Kipchak, Rome,
Baghdad, and Syria sent their ambassadors as their representatives.
The Caliph of Baghdad sent his Chief Qadi Fakhruddin and Amir
Arghun came from Khurasan, while Sultan Ruknuddin Seljuk came
from the Seljuk Sultanate of Rome (modern Turkey), Shahabuddin
and Shams from Ala-Mut and Qahistan and envoys from the
European kings. Two thousand camps were pitched for the Muslim
guests; this let us know the scale of the celebration and the number
of visitors and participants. Now the question of choosing a worthy
man for the throne was raised. All men present on the occasion
chose Guyuk Khan for the job. Mungku Khan, the son of Tolui Khan
caught hold of the hand of Guyuk Khan, made him sit on the throne
and put the crown on his head. Guyuk Khan's wife was a Christian
woman; therefore, Christian representatives received special attention
and honor. However, the representatives of the Batiniyah sect were
turned out with disgrace.

He showed hospitality to the Muslims too. But the Christians made an
all out attempt to make Guyuk Khan hate the Muslims. At last, they
succeeded in causing Guyuk Khan to write an edict enjoining all the
commanders to rise as one man to wipe out the Muslims from the face
of the earth. When he came out after putting his signature and seal on
the order, his hunting dogs charged at him and chewed his testicles.
Although Guyuk Khan remained alive, he was seriously injured and
from that day on the Christians were terrified and they could not
muster courage to oppose the Muslims.

Death Of Guyuk Khan

A short time later Guyuk Khan went to Samarkand and died there.
When Ogdai Khan was alive, his younger brother and the youngest
son of Genghis Khan, Tolui Khan lived with him and was the
commander of his army. Tolui Khan loved Ogdai Khan very much.
Once Ogdai Khan fell ill, Tolui Khan prayed to God to either heal him

or give him death instead of Ogdai. From that time, Ogdai Khan began to recover and Tolui Khan's health started deteriorating. At last, Ogdai Khan was completely cured and Tolui Khan passed away. Tolui Khan left his four sons behind namely, Mungku Khan, Kublai Khan, Arigh Boke and Hulagu Khan. Ogdai Khan loved them most. Guyuk Khan also showed his kindness to them all. After the demise of Guyuk Khan, Batu Khan, son of Juchi Khan, the king of Qabchag was considered strong and wise. The majority of them turned to Batu Khan for the choice of the Great Khan however, some of them opposed his right to choose but the choice of Batu Khan prevailed and Mungku Khan came to the throne with a broad consensus.

Mungku Khan

Mungku Khan entrusted the reign of Khitai (northern China) to his brother Kublai Khan and sent another brother Hulagu Khan towards Persia at the head of a huge army. Mungku Khan came to the throne in 648 A.H. and treated the Muslims kindly and favorably.

Death Of Mungku Khan

Mungku Khan died in 655 A.H. after reigning for 7 years. A year before his death Mungku Khan wrote to the Chinese king to obey him and invaded China upon his refusal.

Kublai Khan

Mungku Khan died in Chankad during the same journey and his brother Kublai Khan, who had accompanied Mungku Khan on the journey was enthroned in Chankad right away. On receipt of this news, Arigh Boke advanced his claim on the throne at Karakorum and declared himself the king of the Mongols. When Kublai Khan turned to him, Arigh Boke came out to meet him with his army. The two brothers faced each other at Kuluran and Arigh Boke was defeated after a fierce battle. But he escaped unhurt. Kublai Khan entered Karakorum and sat on the throne. Arigh Boke collected troops in Khitai (northern China) and rose again to fight against his brother but tasted defeated once again and fled to Kashgar (city in western China) and attacked Kublai Khan again. In short, fighting between the two brothers spread over a period of four years. At last, Arigh Boke was arrested and put in prison where he breathed his last.

After coming to throne in 655 A.H. Kublai Khan sent orders to Hulagu Khan that he was responsible for looking after the territory from across the Oxus river to Syria as the ruler. As a consequence of long battles between Arigh Boke and Kublai Khan, the central rule of the Mongols and awe of the Karakorum court was diminished to a great extent and the heads of a number of provinces threw off the burden of the central rule and declared their sovereignty. These events happened at a time when a number of princes of the Genghis Khan dynasty had embraced Islam and Islam was spreading among the Mongols.

Getting rid of Arigh Boke, Kublai Khan invaded China and won the whole of China after a protracted battle. He then laid the foundation of a new city named Ta Tu (later Pei-p'ing corrupted to Peking by westerners and now known as Beijing) and shifted his capital from Karakorum to this city and forced Siam, Burma, and Japan to pay tribute.

Kublai Khan appointed four ministers belonging to four different religions one among them being a Muslim named Amir Ahmad Banakti. All other Mongol rulers acknowledged the sovereignty of Kublai Khan. At this time, the Mongol rule spread from China to Europe. Muslim rule was then weak and unimpressive. The Christians, Magians and Jews, after getting access to the Mongol court, made all out efforts to instigate the ruler against the Muslims. Abaqa Khan, the son of Hulagu Khan once wrote to Kublai Khan from Khurasan: "The Jews and the Magians have informed me that the Qur'an, the Book of the Muslims enjoins upon them to kill the polytheists wherever they find them. What's your opinion about this injunction? In case, the Muslims are bound by their faith to kill us without discrimination their very existence is a menace to our own." Kublai called some Muslim religious scholars and sought their opinion saying "Does your Qur'an contain such an injunction?." "Yes there is such an order in the Qur'an." Thereupon Kublai Khan said, "Why don't you kill us?" They said, "It is because we don't have power to do so. We shall start killing you when we get such a power."

At this Kublai Khan said, "Since we have such a power at present, we should kill you." Saying this he had the Muslim scholars killed and issued orders to kill the Muslims wherever they were found. Having heard this Badruddin Baihagi and Hamiduddin Samarkandi reached the court of Kublai Khan and asked the reason behind his orders for the mass killing of the Muslims. Kublai Khan said to them, "What do you mean by "kill the idol worshippers." Both the scholars explained, "Allah Almighty had commanded His Prophet and his Companions to kill the idol-worshipers because they had thirst for Muslim blood. It was just a safety device. But this order doesn't apply to you for you hold God Almighty as one and write the name of God at the head of your orders and edicts." Hearing this Kublai Khan grew happy and abrogated his first order.

This event proves beyond doubt that Mongols had a very sensitive feeling regarding religion. But they kept coming close to Islam with mental development and cultural progress and all efforts to present a distorted view of Islam fell flat on the ground.

Death Of Kublai Khan

Kublai Khan died at 73 after reigning for 35 years and was succeeded by his grandson, Temur Khan who came to the throne in China. During his reign, the public administration suffered a setback and complete disorder. Temur the Great Khan died in 700 A.H. Although a number of rulers succeeded him one after another following the final departure of Temur Khan, it was more a formality than actual rule. The Mongol empire had, in fact, ceased to exist from the death of Temur Khan.

Hulagu Khan

When Mungku Khan took charge of the Mongol empire in Karakorum, he received the complaint that Batiniyah Ismaili's mischief had crossed all limits and they hated everyone holding a high position like kings, commanders, high officials and men in power. They passed sleepless nights owing to their acts of murder and terror. Along with this he also got the news that the Caliph of Baghdad, although considered a weak ruler, could prove formidable to the Mongols by virtue of his glory and magnificence, if he rose to face the challenge. Mungku Khan sent his brother Hulagu Khan at the head of a huge army of one hundred and twenty thousand men and instructed him not to launch an attack if the Caliph meant peace but to fight him to the finish in case he showed signs of belligerency. Moreover, he was asked to annihilate the Ismailites and their ruler by attacking the Ala-Mut Fort. Amir Ichol, son of Amir Qarachar was ordered to accompany the army as commander.

Hulagu Khan reached Khurasan and Iran in 651 A.H. The Rulers of Azerbaijan, Shirvan (part of modern day Azerbaijan) and Girjistan presented themselves before Hulagu Khan and offered their allegiance to him. Arghun Aga Obrat proceeded from Khurasan to meet Mungku Khan. Hulagu Khan arrived in Khurasan and, being acquainted with the prevailing situation, paid attention to the disturbances created by the atheist Ismailites and went on seizing their forts one by one. Ala Mut Fort fell in Dhul Qadah 656 A.H. Ismailite ruler, Shah Ruknuddin Khurshah was arrested and produced before Hulagu Khan, who sent him to Mungku Khan in Karakorum with the instruction that he should be done away with on the way. His order was implemented and Ruknuddin's wife, children and relatives were all put to death. However, Khawaja Nasiruddin Tusi who was one of the courtiers of Khurshah received a position as a courtier of Hulagu Khan by virtue of his flattery and cleverness. All the treasures and buried possessions of the Ismailites were plundered by the Mongols and their reign met its doom.

Shortly after that, Nasiruddin Tusi persuaded Hulagu Khan to invade Baghdad and the Minister of the Caliph of Baghdad, Algami conspired with Hulagu Khan through Nasiruddin, which resulted in the devastation of Baghdad. Hulagu returned from Baghdad to his capital Maragheh laden with gems and jewels and immense valuables and slave-girls and sent all this to Mungku Khan in Karakorum. Atabak S'ad bin Abu Bakr, the ruler of Persia, Badruddin Lulu, the ruler of Mosul, and Sultan Azizuddin Seljuk, the ruler of the Seljuk Sultanate of Rome (modern Turkey) appeared before Hulagu and offered their allegiance. In Ramadan 657 A.H. Hulagu sent some renowned Generals at the head of an army as vanguards towards Syria. He then moved ahead conquering Nasibain, Harran, and Halab massacring people and reached Damascus and won Damascus in the same way. He then put Syria under his governor Kasuqa and turned towards Khurasan. Shortly after that, the Egyptian army invaded Syria and fought back the Mongol troops. Hulagu was enraged and decided to restore Syria but the death of Mungku Khan stopped him. During the same time discord began between Hulagu and Berke Khan the son of Juchi Khan the ruler of the Kipchak Khanate (the Golden Horde).

It is said that a close relative of Berke Khan lived with Hulagu Khan. Berke who was killed by Hulaqu. Khan became infuriated and remarked, "Hulagu Khan killed the Caliph of Baghdad and massacred a large number of Muslims without any rhyme or reason. I shall avenge him for all his crimes." He then dispatched an army against him and Hulagu's army was defeated. However, the fight continued until at last, Hulagu Khan himself led his army against Berke Khan in 661 A.H. and won the battle. Shortly after that, Berke Khan launched a massive attack on Hulagu Khan and gave him a decisive defeat. This ignominious defeat left Hulagu Khan dejected and frustrated.

Hulagu Khan's Death

After losing the battle to Berke Khan, Hulagu Khan sent a General to Syria to bring tribes of the Kara Tartar to be dispatched against Berke Khan. The General went to Syria and winning the Kara Tatar tribes to his side, revolted against Hulagu Khan. When Hulagu received this shocking news in Maragheh, his capital, he suffered such a deep frustration that he died in 663 A.H. in a state of coma, at the age of 48 years and after reigning for 8 years. In Maragheh, he set up a planetarium with the help of Nasiruddin Tusi and other scientists. He gave the reign of Iraq and Khurasan (northeastern Iran, southern Turkmenistan, and northern Afghanistan) to his son Abagha Khan and Azerbaijan to his second son. Dayar-e-Bakr and Dayar-e-Rabi'a he gave to Saldoz, the ruler of Turan and appointed Khawaja Shamsuddin Muhammad Jawini as his Minister. Ata al-Mulk Alauddin, the son of Shamsuddin Jawini was made the ruler of Baghdad. Hulagu Khan was buried in a strange manner according to the Mongol practice. Instead of a normal grave, a grave room was made ready for burial. After putting the dead body in the grave room, a few young girls, wearing costly garments and ornaments, were brought to the grave room to serve the dead man and be his companion in solitude. Following this, the opening of the grave room was firmly closed leaving the beautiful young girls to die with the dead man. Sultan Balban ruled over India during the reign of Hulagu Khan. Although he used to keep himself acquainted with the events and affairs taking place under Balban he never attacked India. Although some Mongol Generals invaded India from time to time the credit goes to their leaders who repulsed their attacks every time. At a time when the entire world of Islam was overtaken by disturbances and disruptions, India was one country where the Islamic rule was strong and mighty and so this country remained safe from the Mongol's expansionist designs.

Abagha Khan

Shortly after the death of Hulagu Khan, the nobles and courtiers convened a meeting of the Mongol celebrities and chose Hulagu Khan's son Abagha Khan for the throne. However, Abagha Khan refused the throne in the absence of permission from the Mongol Emperor Kublai Khan. He yielded to the insistence of the Mongol court and came to the throne on Ramadan 2, 663 A.H. He lavished rewards on Mongol Generals and soldiers and made his brother Bashmut the ruler of Shirvan (part of modern day Azerbaijan), Mazandaran (historic region of northern Iran, bordering the Caspian Sea on the north) and Khurasan to his next brother, Teshen. Rome (modern day Turkey) was given to Tuhan Bahadur, the son of Sonjak. The territories near Rome (modern day Turkey) were given to Turan, the son of Jalair Darlakin. Arghun Aga was given the duties of Finance and Khawaja Shamsuddin was made Prime Minister and Arghun Khan was appointed the instructor of his son Mehrtaq Nawyan Birlas.

Abagha Khan resumed fighting against Berke Khan who died during these battles. The Generals and relatives of the Mongol rulers targeted Abagha Khan on all sides. Baraq Khan Chogatai captured Khurasan and Abagha Khan defeated him after a series of fights and, gradually, re-established his rule. Attempts to expand to the southwest failed and every time the Mongol army clashed with the Egyptian troops, it tasted defeat.

Abagha Khan's Death

Abagha Khan died in 680 A.H. He was a great devotee of Sheikh S'adi Shirazi and Jalaluddin Rumi and would often attend them. His son, Nakudar Aghlan, succeeded him.

Nakudar Aghlan

Nakudar Aghlan called Ahmad Khan had embraced Islam during the time of his father. He adopted the appellation of Ahmad Khan shortly after coming to throne and appointed Sheikh Kamaluddin Abdur Rahman al-Rafe'i as his Minster. Sultan Ahmed provided all facilities for the Muslims and conferred upon them high posts. He obliterated the blasphemous rites and practices of the Mongols and made an all out effort to propagate Islam. With the efforts of Ahmad Khan, other Mongols also came to the fold of Islam. With an eye to the harm caused to Mongol's glory and leadership at the hands of Ahmad Khan, as a Muslim ruler, his brother Arghun Khan started to plot a revolt against him.

Martyrdom Of Nakudar Aghlan

Arghun Khan, the son of Abagha Khan brought other courtiers and Generals around to his view and revolted against Ahmad Khan. Sultan Ahmad's army also joined hands with the conspirators, with the result Sultan Ahmad Khan was arrested and martyred after a reign of 3 years. This event took place in 683 A.H.

Arghun Khan

Arghun Khan came to throne and appointed S'adullah, a Jew as his Prime Minister and issued orders, at the instance of his Prime Minister to kill Muslim religious scholars in every city under his rule. In the wake of this order, thousands of Muslim scholars were put to death. Arghun was deeply devoted to a Hindu ascetic and received from him a herbal medicine to extend his age, but it resulted in producing one disease after another and he succumbed to disease in 690 A.H.

Gaykhatu Khan

Arghun Khan (son of Abagha Khan) was succeeded by his brother Gaykhatu Khan. The first use of currency notes in 693 A.H. is a notable event of his reign. The Mongols called it "Yut." It was a small piece of paper bearing Testimoney of Faith (There is no God but Allah and Muhammad is His Messenger) on its both sides and the name of the king and the value thereof were written below. This created a great outcry throughout the country and caused a bad effect on trade and commerce. The people looked upon the piece of paper with amazement and remarked: "How can we accept this piece of paper instead of gold coin." Thus, due to strong opposition from his subjects, Gaykhatu Khan discontinued its circulation.

Gaykhatu Khan's Martyrdom

Mongol commanders martyred this king too for his attachment to Islam.

Baydu Khan

Baydu Khan, the cousin of Gaykhatu Khan succeeded him. He was the grandson of Hulagu Khan. Arghun Aga Awirat, who ruled over Khurasan (northeastern Iran, southern Turkmenistan, and northern Afghanistan) for about 30 years on behalf of the Mongol kings, died in 696 A. H. Prior to his death his son Amir Nawruz Beg went to Prince Ghazan Khan, son of Arghun Khan, grandson of Abagha Khan, joined his court and persuaded him to accept Islam. Ghazan Khan was then the Governor of Khurasan. Since Ghazan Khan, considered himself the rightful heir to the throne it became the point of discord between Baydu Khan and Ghazan Khan. Led and persuaded by Nawruz Beg, Ghazan Khan called for Sadruddin Hamwi and Ghazan Khan embraced Islam at his hand; his Islamic name was Mahmud Khan. In the wake of his acceptance of Islam, many other Mongol Commanders became Muslim. Following this, the gulf of differences between Baydu Khan and Sultan Mahmud (Ghazan Khan) widened so much that it resulted in fighting and killing.

Assassination Of Baydu Khan

Sultan Mahmud Khan won the battle and had Baydu Khan assassinated and he came to the throne in 694 A.H.

Mahmud Khan Ghazan Khan

Sultan Mahmud Ghazan Khan was the son of Arghun Khan and the grandson of Abagha Khan. Having come to throne, Mahmud Khan appointed Nawruz Beg as his Minister and Commander and engraved *Kalimah-e-Taiyabah* on the coins and ordered to write "Allah, the Most High" at the head of the Seal and on all edicts. A short time later, he sent Nawruz Beg to Khurasan as the Governor. Two Mongol commanders, named Istimur and Arsalan agreed on a plan to do away with Sultan Mahmud Khan and Nawruz Beg and the same date was fixed for the event by each of them. However, their plan failed and one was killed by Sultan Mahmud Khan and another by Nawruz Beg. Following this some commanders and ministers conspired to turn the king against Nawruz Beg by inventing stories about Nawruz Beg's secret plans to revolt against him. As a result of constant conspiratorial campaigns, Sultan Mahmud brought about the death and destruction of Nawruz Beg and his family members. The Minister, Khawaja Sadruddin also met his doom at the hands of the same conspirators and Khawaja Rashid uddin took his place. The event took place in 699 A.H.

When the situation returned to normal, Sultan Mahmud Ghazan Khan wrote to his counterpart in Egypt that since his ancestors had conquered Syria and it remained occupied by his ancestors and the Egyptian army had usurped it, it was better to vacate the territory and offer allegiance to him. But the Egyptian reply was rather degrading. Moreover, the Egyptians came out and invaded some of the territories under the occupation of Sultan Mahmud Ghazan. The Egyptian troops even desecrated mosques and massacred the Muslims indiscriminately. Sultan Mahmud Khan invaded Syria at the head of 90 thousand troops in 699 A.H. The Egyptian king also came out to combat the Mongols. The battle broke out in Hims and the result was a defeat for the Egyptians. Mahmud Khan then occupied Syria and Damascus and appointed his viceroys to govern them. The Egyptian king invaded

Syria once again and the Mongol commanders in Syria fought valiantly but conceded defeat and Taitaq, the Mongol commander was arrested while fighting gallantly. Hearing this Mahmud Khan resolved to invade Syria once again. However, news came to him that Juchi's offspring ruling over Kipchak Khanate (the Golden Horde) had staked their claim to Persia and Khurasan. Sultan Mahmud Khan changed his mind and he never had the opportunity again to turn towards Syria.

Death Of Mahmud Ghazan Khan

Sultan Mahmud Ghazan died in 703 A.H. During the tenure of this king Islam flourished among the Mongols and the Muslims were largely benefited from his favor. On the eve of his death, he made a will that he would be succeeded by his brother Oljeitu, known as Muhammad Khudabanda.

Sultan Muhammad Khudabanda Oljeitu

He came to the throne in Dhul Hijjah, 703 A.H. and adopted "Muhammad Khudabanda" as his appellation. All the great commanders greeted him on the eve of his enthronement. Soon after becoming the king, he ordered to enforce Islamic codes all over the country and to obliterate all anti-Islamic practices. His rule gained quick popularity and he was acknowledged as a sovereign ruler from Russia, Khwarizm (territories of present day Turkmenistan and Uzbekistan), Belgrade, Seljuk Sultanate of Rome, Syria to Karakorum, Sind and Iraq.

His Death

The noble and pious king breathed his last on the night of Eid-ul-Fitr, 716 A.H. after reigning for 13 years. He had founded a new city named Sultania, made it his capital and was buried in the same city. His son Abu Sayeed Bahadur succeeded him.

Abu Sayeed Bahadur Khan

Abu Sayeed was 14 at the time of his enthronement. Although feuds erupted among the Mongol commanders, they controlled their differences knowing the consequences. Sultan Abu Sayeed appointed commander Chaupan as his Prime Minister and enhanced his power and position. Commander Hasan Jalair, the son of Commander Chaupan was married to a woman named Baghdad Khatun. Sultan Abu Sayeed fell in love with this woman and he wanted her to be divorced by commander Hasan. But commander Chaupan did not agree to this and their differences took such a turn that Commander Chaupan rose in revolt and occupied Khurasan. Herat was then ruled over by Chogatai dynasty and they had a strong hatred against the Hulagu dynasty. However, one of the Chogatai commanders named Turma Shirin Khan was brought around to Commander Chaupan's view and gave his active support. Sultan Abu Sayeed Bahadur Khan prepared for a fight, and after a series of encounters, Commander Chaupan was arrested and assassinated. His son, Commander Hasan Jalair divorced Baghdad Khatun and gave Sultan Abu Sayeed an opportunity to marry her.

Abu Sayeed's Death

Uzbek Khan, the king of Kipchak Khanate (the Golden Horde) invaded Persia with a huge army. Sultan Abu Sayeed also proceeded to take on the enemy. But he fell ill at Shirvan (part of modern day Azerbaijan) because of the unfavorable climate and succumbed to it on Rabia al-Awwal 13, 736 A.H. Since he was without children, anarchy and troubles of the worst nature overtook his kingdom.

Arpa Khan

Arpa Khan came to the throne with the common consent of the Mongol commanders. He proclaimed that he needed no comforts and luxuries in life and preferred a mace to a golden waistband, a felt cap to a jeweled crown. Since he was about to face Uzbek Khan's force, Arpa Khan was bent on making preparations courageously and wisely and he deployed troops to stop the invaders. Meanwhile, Uzbek Khan received shocking news of an emerging insurgency in the Kipchak Khanate (the Golden Horde). He left the capital to put down the revolt. Then Amir Ali rose up against Arpa Khan. Amir Ali succeeded in his attempt particularly because Arpa Khan had started killing the offspring of Hulagu Khan wherever he found them. Most of the commanders grew disheartened with these new developments. Two different camps developed one supporting Arpa Khan and one supporting Amir Ali.

Assassination Of Arpa Khan

The two forces faced one another in 736 A.H. It resulted in the arrest and assassination of Arpa Khan. After achieving success, Amir Ali seated Musa Khan, the son of Baydu Khan and the great-grandson of Hulagu Khan, on the throne.

Musa Khan

With the enthronement of Musa Khan, the power and influence of Amir Ali Aviran and other Avirat commanders took firm root and flourished. Amir Hasan, the Governor of Rome (modern day Turkey), invaded Musa Khan, fought against him and killed Amir Ali. Defeated and frustrated Musa Khan was succeeded by Sultan Muhammad Khan, the son of Qatlaq Khan the descendant of Hulagu Khan. His rule was also weak like that of Musa Khan. A few others succeeded each other from the Hulagu dynasty but only in name. By 744 A.H., Hulagu Khan's descendants ceased to rule and the countries conquered by Hulagu Khan came to be ruled by a number of other sovereign rulers.

Progency Of Juchi Khan

Juchi Khan was the eldest son of Genghis Khan. Soon after conquering Khwarizm (territories of present day Turkmenistan and Uzbekistan), Juchi Khan won Kipchak Khanate (the Golden Horde) and settled there. The other sons of Genghis Khan were not sympathetic to Juchi Khan. Like him, his country also fell far off from the center of Mongol authority. Most of Juchi Khan's descendants were called Uzbek. Juchi Khan expired during the lifetime of Genghis Khan, who then entrusted his vast territory to his son Batu Khan who was eldest among Juchi Khan's seven sons.

Batu Khan

When Batu Khan marched from Kipchak to invade Khazr and Russia,. Ogdai Khan, the son of Genghis Khan ordered his son Guyuk Khan, Tolui Khan, the son of Mungku Khan and a son of Chogatai Khan to accompany Batu Khan on his mission. Batu Khan first conquered the whole of Russia and attacked Moscow and won it before invading Poland and occupying it. Being informed of the advancing troops of Batu Khan, the European powers concentrated their army in a vast field to collectively combat their common enemy. Batu Khan had a large number of Muslims as well in his army. When Batu Khan came to know that the Christians had collected troops several times more than the Mongol army had, he ordered the Muslim section to assemble at a place to invoke victory. The Battle broke out thereafter and the Christians were ignominiously defeated, and Batu Khan conquered the whole of Hungary. Batu Khan founded a new city in Europe and named it Sarai (near modern day Volgograd). The rest of Batu Khan's life passed in conquering and administering European territories and he died in 654 A.H.

Berke Khan

His brother Berke Khan succeeded Batu Khan. Batu Khan was a Muslim in name like Genghis Khan but Berke Khan openly embraced Islam, with the result that the Muslims enjoyed peace and safety from the Mongols' excesses during his tenure. Hulagu Khan killed a relative of Berke Khan, he was terribly enraged at this action, and Berke Khan sent Buga Khan at the head of thirty thousand troops to invade Hulagu's country. Hulagu also sent a commander to face the enemy, but he was defeated. Hulagu Khan's army was defeated at first but Berke Khan's forces were later repulsed.

Thirty persons among the progeny of Juchi Khan came to the throne one after the other. Berke Khan was succeeded by his son Mungku Temur Khan who was later succeeded by Tugtai Khan. A fierce battle was fought between Tugtai Khan and Tugai Khan and Tugtai Khan was victorious and embarked on a peaceful administration. He then wrote to Ghazan Khan that Hulagu Khan and his descendants had annexed Azerbaijan within their country although, according to the allotment of Genghis Khan, Juchi Khan's offspring had a right to the territory. It is therefore proper for this territory to be handed over to him (Tugtai) otherwise; he had the power to capture it by force. Ghazan Khan replied in the negative and expressed his readiness to take on the invaders. But the situation was saved as Tugtai Khan changed his mind.

Tugtai Khan was succeeded by his son, Tughril Khan and his son, Uzbek Khan came to the throne after his demise. Uzbek Khan is renown as the founder of the Uzbek tribe, which was named after him. Uzbek Khan had a large number of descendants and all of them were known as Uzbek. The Uzbeks invaded Sultan Abu Sayeed Bahadur Khan, the king of Persia in 718 A.H.; they plundered some of the Persian area and returned. Uzbek Khan launched another attack on Persia in 735 A.H. Sultan Abu Sayeed came out to face the invading force but died on the way and Arpa Khan came to the throne. Uzbek Khan abandoned his campaign and returned and died after a long reign.

Jani Beg Khan Uzbek then came to the throne. The progeny of Juchi Khan, who as we have stated are known as Uzbek broke away from the central rule and set up their own separate kingdoms. Jani Beg Khan was succeeded by his son Bairwi Khan. A king named Shadi Khan ruled over Tabriz in 809 A.H. Urs Khan Uzbek was a contemporary of Temur Sahabe Qur'an (the companion of the Qur'an). Urs Khan's son was Temur Malik Khan Uzbek whose successor was Tugtamish Khan Uzbek who ruled over the Kipchak Khanate (the Golden Horde) who was defeated by Temur Sahabe Qur'an. Faulad Khan Uzbek conquered and ruled over Turkistan in 815 A.H. Sultan Sayeed Mirza Shahrukh married a girl of his family. Muhammad Khan Uzbek came to the throne after Faulad Khan. Burraq Khan Uzbek, from the progeny of Urs Khan, took help from Ulagh Beg Temuri and attacked Muhammad Khan Uzbek and occupied Turkistan. Ulagh Beg Khan Temuri and Burraq Khan then clashed with each other and Ulagh Beg was defeated. As a result of this defeat, Sultan Sayeed Mirza Shahrukh Khan attacked and punished Ulagh Khan. Following the invasion of Mirza Shahrukh Khan, Burraq Khan returned from Samarkand. However, Sultan Mahmud Khan and Buraq Khan were later assassinated and with this ended the Uzbek Empire.

In 855 A.H., Sultan Abul Khair Khan and Badaq Khan Uzbek captured Samarkand and established their rule. Abul Khair Khan's son was

Badaq Khan and Badaq Khan's son was Abul Fath Muhammad Khan, who was the contemporary of Zahiruddin Babar. This Sultan Abul Fath Muhammad Khan Uzbek is also known as Shebani Khan Uzbek who was killed fighting with Ismail Safwi. He was a gallant fighter and had dislodged Babar from Turkistan and Farghona (eastern Uzbekistan). Sultan Abul Fath Khan Uzbek was later seated on the throne by the Uzbeks.

Jani Beg has found mention above; his son was Iskander Khan whose son was Abdullah Khan, who defeated the Persians decisively. Abdullah Khan Uzbek was the contemporary of king Akbar of India. He was also in correspondence with Akbar. Abdullah Khan died in 1006 A.H. and was succeeded by his son Abdul Momin Khan but was, within a few days, killed at the hands of his uncle, Rustam Sultan. Following this event the Uzbek kingdom was torn into pieces. Abdullah Khan's sister's son Wali Muhammad Khan occupied Turkistan after Abdul Momin Khan, entrusted Mawaraunnahr (between the Amu [Oxus] and Syr rivers in modern Uzbekistan and Kazakhstan) to Imam Quli Khan and Badakhshan (in present day Afghanistan) to his sister's son Nazar Muhammad Khan. Within a short time, Wali Muhammad Khan was dislodged by Nazar Muhammad Khan. He took refuge with King Abbas of Persia. The Uzbeks had previously established a kingdom in Khwarizm (territories of present day Turkmenistan and Uzbekistan) but it was not strong or impressive.

Offspring Of Chogatai Khan

Genghis Khan had given Turkistan, Khurasan, Ghazni and the entire territory around river Indus to his son Chogatai Khan and made Commander Qarachar Birlas his commander-in-chief. After the death of Genghis Khan, Chogatai Khan always remained loyal and faithful to his younger brother Ogdai Khan. Chogatai Khan was very brave and wise. He died in 640 A.H. Following the death of Chogatai Khan Prime Minister Qarachar seated Qarabalaku Khan, the grandson of Chogatai Khan on the throne. Guyuk Khan, son of Ogdai Khan objected to this arrangement on the plea that how could the grandson be enthroned in the presence of Chogatai Khan's son Maisu Mungku

Khan. Thus, Maisu Mungku Khan was enthroned by dethroning Qarabalaku Khan. But, shortly after the demise of Maisu Mungku Khan, Qarabalaku Khan was brought to the throne once again. After his death, his wife Warghana Khatun was seated on the throne and Alghu Khan of Chogatai tribe succeeded her. But, he too died after reigning for one year. His son Mubarak Shah Chogatai then became the king of the Mongols.

Chogatai tribe joined hands with Tolui Khan's progeny in all their campaigns and adventures even though these two tribes were rivals in the past. The progeny of Tolui Khan, son of Genghis Khan had attained utmost greatness and grandeur due to Hulagu Khan's style of governance and Chogatai Khan's progeny had fallen behind in this field. Even though the Chogatai kept their control over Herat and its adjoining territories, they by time, conceded to the authority and supremacy of Hulagu Khan and his progeny and sometimes declared their own sovereignty. Among them Sultan Ghayasuddin Muhammad Buraq Khan, son of Maisun Tuwan Khan had attained much fame and came into serious conflict with Abagha Khan in Khurasan. His descendant Turma Shirin Khan came to the throne and invaded Qandahar. He also fought against Amir Hasan Saldoz in the suburbs of Ghazni in 716 A.H. and lost the battles. Turma Shirin Khan had also launched an attack on India. After Turma Shirin Khan his brother, Faulad Khan became the king of the Chogatai tribes and died in 735 A.H. He was succeeded by Aghlan, son of Dawa Khan.

During his tenure, Amir Temur Sahabe Qur'an came to the throne of Khurasan. A series of battles were fought between Temur Sahabe Qur'an and Khidr Khawaja Khan. At last, Khidr Khawaja was defeated and bought peace and safety from Temur by giving his daughter, Khanam Khan in marriage. Khidr Khawaja Khan was succeeded by his son Muhammad Khan and then his brother Jahan Aghlan son of Ibn Khidr Khawaja Khan came to throne. Jahan Aghlan was succeeded by Sher Muhammad Khan who came into conflict with Ulagh Temuri, King of Khurasan and Mawaraunnahr in which Sher Muhammad Khan was defeated. Among his descendants were Mahmud Khan and Ahmad Ulja Khan, sons of Yunus Khan. Zahiruddin Muhammad Babar sought help from these two brothers against Shebani Khan Uzbek and they gave it, but both the brothers were captured fighting on the battlefield. They were produced before Shebani Khan and he set them free. But both of them committed suicide out of shame shortly after being released and thus the Chogatai dynasty came to an end.

Although Mansur Khan, son of Sultan Ahmad Ulja Khan became the king of Mongolia it was only in name and the territory was actually ruled over by Shebani Khan.

The Mongol dynasty may be divided into two parts or classes Genghisid Mongols and Temuri Mongols. The Genghisid Mongols have already been mentioned above and will now be summarized. We will then discuss the Temuri Mongols.

A Glance At Genghisid Mongols

The greatest event of Islamic world was the devastation of Baghdad caused by Hulagu Khan. Prior to this, Hulagu's grandfather Genghis Khan had reddened Iran and Khurasan with Muslim blood. Their plunder and carnage had turned the Genghisid Mongols into a curse and scourge in the eyes of the Muslims. Dynastic rule had germinated so many ills and paved the way to the throne for such a large number of unworthy souls that the Islamic character was dreadfully eroded and Islamic glory was brought down. During this era of depravity, nothing was practically done to reform the situation and to put a check on the fall and decline of Islamic values.

By the end of the sixth century Hijri, Islamic rule particularly the Caliphate of Baghdad had become incorrigible. The Seljuks and other mighty empires could, in spite of having glory and magnificence, did not dare to do away with the Caliphate. The creed that none save the Abbasid dynasty could do any good for the Muslims had gained firm ground in Muslim minds. This wrong creed proved very harmful because dynastic rule had spread over a very long period and almost stopped the birth of able and worthy rulers. Fortitude, determination, enterprise and soldierly attributes of Muslims had disappeared. In such a precarious state of degeneration, Allah Almighty brought to the fore unknown and unnoticed, savage and ignorant Mongols to punish the unworthy and depraved Muslims and then to inject pure and fresh blood into the veins of Islam. The Genghisid Mongols, through their plunder, arson and large-scale bloodshed of the Muslims, established their own empire and demolished the so-called caliphate carried by evil and unworthy elements in the name of Islam. This caliphate was, in truth, a deep scar on the spotless face of Islam. Islam is a system of governance, which let the uncivilized and unequipped Muslims conquer the magnificent Empires of Caesar and Choroes. But the day they renounced the teachings of Islam they kept falling into the quagmire of disgrace and ignominy. The Mongols won victories over the Muslims not because they deserved it more; they did it because Allah Almighty wanted them to become a source of a rude awakening to the inert and forgetful Believers in Islam.

The Mongols, as a whole, were neither sympathetic nor antagonistic to Islam. Even when they developed in them a natural desire to be acquainted with the teachings of Islam, they accepted what they could comprehend and rejected outright what lay outside their power of comprehension. Now it can be safely said that the Muslims gained more from the Mongols morally and spiritually than they lost physically and materially. Islamic rule, instead of losing its existence, was rewarded substantially when the pure and truthful teachings of Islam subdued their minds and conquered their hearts. The conquerors were themselves conquered by the mighty sword of Islamic values. Countless Mongol swords once raised against Islam became devoted to the service of the Religion of Allah Almighty. Had the wild and wanton conquests, plunder and carnage not been committed by the dashing and haughty conquerors like Genghis Khan and Hulagu Khan the might and dominating spirit of Islam which conquered their hearts in a very short time could not have been comprehended. Moreover, their forthright feelings and straightforward behavior allowed Muslim scholars and preachers to propagate the moral and spiritual values and impart the truthful and trustworthy teachings of Islam all over the Mongol territories without any fear of being called to account or taken to task. Free from all kinds of religious bigotry they allowed their receptive minds to absorb the true spirit of Islam.

Very few historians have paid attention to the fact that Islam received an easy access to Mongolia, China, and Turkistan while the people of Syria, Egypt, Tripoli, Morocco, Iran, Khurasan, and Baluchistan put obstructions in the way of Islam and resisted its entry into their territories. They turned to Islam only after large-scale bloodshed and destruction.

Islam had stepped in eastern Turkistan and Tibet during the Caliphate of Uthman Bin Affan 🌸. Flourishing fast in China and Turkistan Islam had enveloped the entire population by the very first century Hijrah. However, conspiratorial activities of the Alwis and the destruction of the Umayyads had caused damage to the growing tree of Islam. Moreover, selfish designs and personal rivalries of the Governors blocked the preaching efforts and the army of Islam and thus lost attraction for the non-Muslims even though China and Turkistan had fertile lands for Islam. Seljuk tribes embraced Islam without fear or greed and did splendid service to Islam. Ghaznavid Turks had entered the Islamic countries as robbers and plunderers and confessed Islam of their own. Even today, Islam has a large number of followers in China and they have all embraced Islam not due to any military campaign; they are direct descendants of the ancient inhabitants of China. Genghis Khan and his comrades had victoriously stepped into Islamic territories but they showed their interest in being acquainted with the reality of Islam from the very outset. They accepted this Religion of Truth and served it with sincerity. The offspring of Genghis Khan also accepted and served Islam through difficulty and ease. It is a strange fact that in the countries to the extreme west, Morocco and Spain they marched victoriously with swords in their hands while in the countries of the extreme east, China and the Pacific islands traders and preachers conveyed Islam to the bulk of population. They preached the message of Islam both as a vanquished and a victor.

It is human nature that during the days of ignorance, the most suitable form of governance is autocracy. Democracy in a state of ignorance can bring only lawlessness, disorder and disruption. The Mongols also lived in the hills and mountains like Bedouins and the ignorant. They had a very high concept of a chief or a king. Their leaders wielded so much power that the tribes looked upon them in the same position. It may rather be safely said that king-worship was a characteristic feature of the eastern countries. Since the Mongols had seized the crowns and thrones of the eastern countries after some time, and the earlier concept of king-worship remained intact with them and it continued even after their becoming civilized and well mannered. Both Islam and human nature go against king-worship. But this king-worshipping proved beneficial to Islam as the acceptance of Islam by two or three Mongol kings led all of their subjects to the fold of Islam with the exception of Juchi Khan and his progeny who were late in embracing Islam because of their being at such a great distance from the world of Islam. The Uzbeks welcomed Islam with open arms and history bears no evidence that the Mongols ever rose against their rulers simply because of their coming into the domain of Islam. Even when they revolted against their Muslim kings, the sole reason was material and temporal gains. Since the Mongols accepted Islam as kings, they could not reconcile themselves with the nature and taste of Islam until several generations and remained like those converts still in the process of conversion to Islam and not as pure Muslims. It is because of this that the Mongols never showed an active interest in spreading Islam. Keeping the above-mentioned facts in view, one should not express surprise over some of the religious irregularities of King Akbar of India.

The Tartars were more acquainted with Islam than the Mongols. It is because of this the Mongols never took an active part or showed such a deep interest in Islam and its moral and spiritual tenets and values as the Tartars and the Seljuks did.

Chapter 17

Brief Supplement Of the Islamic History Of Persia

Even though a greater part of Persian history has found place in the history of Islam as a whole, those who have written an exclusive history of Persia have followed quite a different order in mentioning events and their order was defined to suit their purpose. Since Muslims have been more closely attached to Persian history it seems proper to narrate it briefly so that some of the events left out during placement by the majority of historian and their classification can find a proper reference.

Saffariah Dynasty

In the history of Persia, the Saffaria dynasty finds an important place as a sovereign rule. Since Abbasid caliphate had received active support from the Persians, it was not reluctant at all in providing the Persians opportunities to expand their power and influence against the Arabs. It came into their minds the thought of establishing their own royal empire. But the Persians could not attain success while the Abbasid dynasty retained their fighting quality, fortitude and determination. However, when Abbasid Caliphs took to a life of luxury and comfort and lost their spirit and courage, Yaqub bin Laith succeeded in setting up his own independent regime. He belonged to a family of brass vessel makers therefore he was called "saffar", which comes from the word brass in Arabic. He achieved this success simply because of his soldierly character. Yaqub was matchless in friendliness, generosity and simplicity. He easily made friends and served them wholeheartedly even at the cost of his own comfort. Due to these honorable traits, he was able to gather around him a very large circle of friends, supporters, followers and well wishers. As a king, he never ignored his childhood friends and gave them opportunity to attain high social and political positions. Even during his tenure as a ruler, he behaved like an ordinary soldier. He never showed any reluctance in sleeping on the ground and digging trenches. He abhorred the life of luxury and debauchery. He showed firmness and determination in whatever task he performed. These are the reasons why he reached the pinnacle of power and glory from a very humble position. He became so mighty and formidable that the Caliphate of Baghdad was never able to overpower him by any means.

Following the death of Yaqub, bin Laith, his brother Amr bin Laith came to the throne. He expanded his territory. Even though he is said to be superior to Yaqub in wisdom and sagacity, he lacked the soldierly character and simplicity of his brother. He was once defeated by Muwaffaq, the brother of Caliph Mu'tamid. But he lost no time in restoring his position and became a terror for the caliphate. At last, the caliph sent Ismail Samani, Governor of Mawaraunnahr to take on Amr bin Laith. Ismail Samani came out with twenty thousand horsemen against Amr bin Laith's seventy thousand strong cavalry, which had come across the river Oxus to give battle to his enemy. However, during the fierce fighting Amr bin Laith's horse carried him to the battle line of Ismail Samani's army where he was easily captured.

Ismail Samani sent him to Baghdad and thus the greatness and grandeur of the Saffaria almost met its doom.

The greatest difference between Yaqub bin Laith and Amr bin Laith lay in the fact that, while Yaqub could live on dry bread and face hardships with a smile on his lips Amr bin Laith lived a luxurious life with all the royal comforts and splendor at his command.

In the morning of the day Amr bin Laith was captured his cook had complained that three hundred camels were not enough to carry the load of his kitchen so he needed more beasts of burden. The same evening Amr bin Laith was captured, he complained about hunger to his cook who was also in prison with him. The cook found a pot there, which he put on with some water and a little half-ground cereal. Nothing else was available to eat. Amr bin Laith was impatiently waiting for the food and at last the cook removed the pot from the stove and left the spot for an urgent piece of work. Meanwhile, a dog came in, caught the edge of the pot in his mouth and made off with the pot. Amr bin Laith called out to his cook and said to him, "In the morning you had complained to me that three hundred camels were not enough to carry the load of the kitchen. Behold now! How a single dog is carrying my entire kitchen."

Since the demise of Amr bin Laith, his descendants ruled over the limited area of Sistan (eastern Iran and southwestern Afghanistan) but only in name. Yaqub bin Laith's maternal grandson named Khalaf took over as the ruler and ruled over Sistan until the time of Mahmud Ghaznavi. Khalaf's son rose against him but he was killed by Khalaf. The citizens of Sistan complained to Mahmud Ghaznavi against Khalaf to save them from the atrocities of Khalaf. King Mahmud Ghaznavi invaded Sistan. In the wake of the fall of his fort, Khalaf appeared before Mahmud Ghaznavi, kissed his stirrup and said after rubbing his beard with his feet, "Forgive me O' Sultan." Mahmud Ghaznavi liked the word "Sultan" from the lips of Khalaf and adopted it as his appellation. He gave Khalaf no punishment. He took him to Ghazni where he passed away after four years.

Samanid Dynasty

Asad bin Saman reckoned himself among the descendants of Behram Chaubin. He took his four sons to Caliph Mamun Rasheed Abbasi at Merv. Mamun had succeeded against his brother, Amin in coming to throne with much active support from the Persians. Therefore, Mamun had a favorable attitude towards Asad bin Saman and his progeny, which evoked no wonder. From that day, the Samanids made rapid progress and consolidated their position. Ismail, the grandson of Asad bin Saman attained the position of a king after subduing Amr bin Laith. The Samanids remained nominally attached to the Caliphate of Baghdad positioned against the Saffar dynasty.

Ismail Samanid ruled over Mawaraunnahr (between the Amu [Oxus] and Syr rivers in modern Uzbekistan and Kazakhstan) and Khurasan (northeastern Iran, southern Turkmenistan, and northern Afghanistan) for seven or eight years. Caliph Mu'atazid Abbasi of Baghdad had issued him credentials to rule over Khurasan. His son Abu Nazir Ahmad succeeded Ismail.

Ismail was noble and good-natured and relied exclusively on Allah Almighty. He was well aware of the principles both of conquests and administration. His subjects loved him.

But Ahmad bin Ismail displeased his courtiers and relatives. His six-year rule was fraught with conspiracies against him and at last, his slaves assassinated him.

His son Nasr bin Ahmad succeeded him at the tender age of 18. He took after his grandfather, Ismail. Shortly after accession, he expanded his territory and ruled for thirty years with all his energy. Nasr bin Ahmad died and was buried in Bukhara.

His son, Nuh bin Nasr acceded to the throne and died in 343 A.H. after ruling for thirteen years and was succeeded by his son Abdul Malik bin Nuh. He died falling from his horse while playing polo.

His brother, Mansur bin Nuh came to the throne as his successor. He married the daughter of Ruknuddaula Dailmi. His rule was acknowledged in the provinces of Iraq and Persia too. His Minister, Abu Ali bin Muhammad had the history book of Tabari translated into Persian. He had tenure of fifteen years.

His son, Abul Qasim Nuh II succeeded him. With his accession, the Samanid dynasty was overtaken by decline and calamity and his courtiers rose against him and invited Bughra Khan, the king of Mongolia to attack him. Bughra Khan defeated him and seized Bukhara. But Bughra Khan died following his conquest of Bukhara and his army returned to its country. Nuh II then occupied Bukhara and consolidated his rule. It was the time when Ghazni was ruled by Sebuktigin, the founder of the Ghaznavid Dynasty.

After getting rid of Bughra Khan, Nuh II wanted to chastise his unfaithful and insurgent nobles. But they escaped, took refuge with Fakhruddaula and with his support invaded Bukhara. Nuh II sought help from Sebuktigin once again who took on the insurgents near Herat and repulsed their attack after a fierce fight. Sebuktigin's son Mahmud Ghaznawi showed his swordsmanship and gallantry in this battle. Nuh II grew happy and conferred upon Mahmud Ghaznawi the title of Saifuddaulah. Nuh II ruled for 22 years but his reign was beset with feuds, battles and revolts. He continued fighting his enemies his whole life as a king and yet lost his provinces one by one.

Nuh II was succeeded by his son, Mansur II. His father's detractors and opponents kept him anxious and embarrassed all the time and, at last, forced him out of Bukhara. Later on, they acknowledged him as a king but took the administrative affairs under their own control and appointed a new ruler for Khurasan. But Mahmud Ghaznawi drove their new ruler out and captured Khurasan.

During this period, the commanders dethroned and blinded Mansur and seated his brother Abdul Malik II bin Nuh II on the throne. Then they led him to attack Mahmud Ghaznawi. But Mahmud Ghaznawi defeated Abdul Malik II and his troops and drove them towards Bukhara. Elaj Khan, the ruler of Kashgar (a city in the extreme western part of China) seized Khwarizm (territories of present day Turkmenistan and Uzbekistan) and attacked Bukhara, with the result Elaj Khan arrested Abdul Malik II and occupied Bukhara. Abdul Malik II's third brother Muntasir escaped from Bukhara in disguise and was killed after wandering with pirates for a short time and with this the Samanid dynasty came to an end.

Delmid Dynasty

The Delmid and the Samanid dynasties were contemporary but rival powers. The Samanids had occupied Mawaraunnahr (between the Amu [Oxus] and Syr rivers in modern Uzbekistan and Kazakhstan), Khurasan (northeastern Iran, southern Turkmenistan, and northern Afghanistan) while the Delmids ruled over Persia, Iraq, and Azerbaijan. All of Persia was ruled over by these two dynasties for a short period.

Although the Samanid Dynasty was replaced by the Ghaznavids, the Delmids's weak and wretched rule dragged on for some time.

Ghaznavid Dynasty

Abdul Malik bin Nuh had appointed Alaptagin as the Governor of Khurasan. When Mansur bin Nuh, the Samanid succeeded Abdul Malik in 350 A.H., Alaptagin came to Ghazni for he had expressed himself to be against the accession of Mansur. Ghazni was then a small settlement. Alaptagin consolidated his position there and established a sovereign state.

On the death of Alaptagin in 367 A.H., his son Ishaq Ghaznawi came to the throne, but, in a very short period, he proved himself unworthy and was either deposed by the military commanders or died a natural death. With his end, they acknowledged Sebuktigin, the commander-in-chief and son-in-law of Alaptagin as their king.

It is said that Sebuktigin was the slave of Alaptagin but it so happened only by circumstance. Some robbers once found him alone on the road and sold him in Bukhara. Sebuktigin's lineage meets with that of King Yazdgard. However, it is difficult to prove the authenticity of this claim. Some historians have held him as a Turk, while others have claimed that he was Turk from his father's side and Persian from his mother's. Nevertheless, he was a noble person by his birth and genealogy. In accordance with the Asian practice the nobles, commanders and men enjoying high positions did not feel any disgrace in calling themselves a slave of the king. May be, Sebuktigin would have called himself the slave of Alaptagin owing to being the commander-in-chief of his army. Sir John Malcom, *The History of Persia from the Early Period to the Present Time* (1815) holds the same view. Sebuktigin conquered scores of cities and ruled for about twenty years. He won the battle of Herat and defeated and arrested Raja Jaipal Singh of the Punjab and Sind who had invaded his country and released him only on promising tribute. But Jaipal Singh committed a breach of promise and launched another attack with a huge army of three hundred thousand. However, Sebuktigin gave him a smashing defeat with a few thousand troops and captured him again but set him free on the promise of being loyal to him. Nuh bin Mansur had offered him the title of Nasiruddin and his son Mahmud was entitled with Saifuddaulah. Sebuktigin expanded the Ghaznavid rule before his final departure in 387 A.H. His son, Ismail succeeded him in Balkh but was subdued and deposed by his brother after a fight.

Mahmud bin Sebuktigin came to the throne of Ghazni in 387 A.H. Caliph Qadir Billah Abbasi conferred upon him the title of Yaminuddaulah and Aminul Millat. After accession, Mahmud Ghaznawi began his campaigns very ably. The opponents instigated Abdul Malik against Mahmud but he was defeated at the hands of Mahmud and fled to Bukhara. Elej Khan or Elek Khan, the king of Kashgar (a city in the extreme west of China) captured Bukhara and arrested Abdul Malik. Mahmud Ghaznawi attacked Elej Khan, son of Bughra Khan and annexed Bukhara. He later defeated the Mongol Commander Tugha Khan, son of Altu Khan and expanded his territory up to the Caspian Sea, besides occupying Khwarizm (territories of present day Turkmenistan and Uzbekistan). While Sistan (eastern Iran and southwestern Afghanistan) and Khurasan (northeastern Iran, southern Turkmenistan, and northern Afghanistan) were already part of the Ghaznavid dynasty from the time of Sebuktigin, Mahmud defeated Majuddaulah Delmi and occupied Isfahan. He also launched a number of attacks on India. In short, Mahmud Ghaznawi extended his rule from Sutlej River (the largest of the five rivers that give the Punjab, meaning five rivers, its name) to the Caspian Sea and from Mawaraunnahr (between the Amu [Oxus] and Syr rivers in modern Uzbekistan and Kazakhstan) to Baluchistan and Iraq in a comparatively short period.

Mahmud Ghaznawi is reckoned among the mightiest and most renowned emperors of the Asian continent. During his tenure, the Persians made rapid progress. He was a true and pious Muslim and a great lover of learning. It was during his period that Firdausi composed *Shahnameh*, *The Book of Kings*. The Samanid court conferred upon him the title of "Amirul Umrai" "Prince of Prices." But, in 389 A.H., Mahmud declared himself a sovereign ruler and dropped the name of Abdul Malik Samani from the address.

Mahmud Ghaznawi was born on Muharram 9, 361 A.H. and died at the age of 60. He was the mightiest Muslim emperor of his time. He had divided his empire between his two sons during his lifetime; giving Khwarizm (territories of present day Turkmanistan and Uzbekistan), Iraq, Persia, and Isfahan to his elder son Mas'ud and Mawaraunnahr (between the Amu [Oxus] and Syr rivers in modern Uzbekistan and Kazakhstan), Khurasan (northeastern Iran, southern Turkmenistan, and northern Afghanistan), Ghazni, and Punjab to his younger son, Muhammad. However, shortly after the death of Mahmud both the brothers fell out with each other. Muhammad seated on the throne of Ghazni and Mas'ud came to the throne of Rayy (southeast of Tehran). First of all the two brothers came to clash over the question of the order of mentioning their names in the official addresses. Mas'ud, being the elder brother, wanted his name to be placed above that of Muhammad. However, Muhammad contended that his name should be mentioned above for he was seated on the throne of his father. All of the discussion was just a false pretence, they, in fact, wanted to subdue one another. At last, Mas'ud attacked Ghazni, captured it and blinded Muhammad after having him arrested.

Mas'ud then occupied Baluchistan (in modern day one Province of Pakistan) and Makran (on the Persian and Pakistan coastline). Family feuds resulted in a series of revolts and Sultan Mas'ud bin Mahmud could not maintain his territorial integrity. The Seljuk Turks started their acts of plunder in Khwarizm (territories of present day Turkmenistan and Uzbekistan). Provisional Governors in the Punjab and other parts of India also rose in revolt, with the result his empire began to disintegrate. But Sultan Mas'ud showed his courage and determination and came out to put down the rebellions. He gave a series of defeats to the Seljuks of Khwarizm and Khurasan. In the meantime, he invaded India as well and demolished the strong forts of Sarsuti (northwestern India, on the edge of the Great Indian, Thar, Desert) and Hansi (northwestern India in Haryana state). He then hurried back to Ghazni where he found a large number of Seljuks arrayed against his country.

Sultan Mas'ud had recruited a large number of Hindus in his army. He had under him a number of Hindu regiments and he had appointed some of the Hindus as commanders. Mas'ud loved to build Hindu regiments by giving them military training and teaching them manners. With this purpose in view, he sent some Hindu commanders to India to recruit their relatives and bring them to Ghazni. When Hindu soldiers came to Ghazni, Mas'ud paid them salaries more than what he would pay to the Persians and the Afghans. A Hindu named Tilak was given the title of Maharaja and was appointed as the commander-in-chief of his army. Since Maharaja Tilak was the son of a Hindu barber, his high position disheartened most of the Muslim commanders and nobles and they lodged complaints to Mas'ud against appeasing the Hindu fighters. Even the fall of Makran due only to the timidity of the Hindu regiment did not alter his mind or change his policy, although they had escaped from the battlefield pushing Sultan Mas'ud and the Afghan troops into an arena of death and destruction. Mas'ud saved his life with the sacrifice of his true and faithful companions and he brought with him a feeling of shame arising out of his ignominious defeat. He took a very strange decision to eliminate his sense of shame and frustration. He left his Minister and son, Maudud in Ghazni, loaded all his treasures and possessions on elephants, camels, bullock carts and men and proceeded towards India in the company of his Hindu commanders and their regiments with a plan to make Lahore the seat of his Government. Since Sultan Mas'ud had already disclosed his plan, his nobles and commanders tried their level best to persuade him to change his mind and they also tried to ensure that the defeat could be successfully avenged. However, he would not pay any heed to their pleas. He left Ghazni after removing the treasures and took away all the jewels, ornaments, gold, valuable utensils and costly garments. Before his departure, he wrote to his son Maudud who was then in Balkh and Badakhshan (in present day Afghanistan). "I hereby appoint you ruler of Ghazni and Khurasan. You keep obeying the orders I shall be issuing in your name. Moreover, you should make an all out effort to end the Seljuks' occupation of your land."

As soon as Sultan Mas'ud crossed the Indus River the Hindu regiments and their Hindu commanders betrayed him and fell upon the royal possessions and robbed all, of what Sebuktigin (founder of the Ghaznavid dynasty) and Mahmud Ghaznawi had collected over a span of 40 or 50 years. They left leaving Sultan Mas'ud at the mercy of a small band of his Muslim comrades.

In the wake of this soul-shattering event, this small body of the Muslims deposed him for his mental imbalances and brought his blinded brother Muhammad to the throne after releasing him from prison. With the enthronement of Muhammad, many of the evasive Hindu soldiers gathered round him for they no longer feared any punishment from Mas'ud.

When Mas'ud was produced before Muhammad he, instead of taking revenge for his blindness, he asked him what was his preference. Mas'ud told him that he should be allowed to stay in Kiri Fort and Muhammad conceded his request forthwith and sent him there along with his wife and children.

Ahmad, son of Muhammad, went to the Kiri Fort without permission and without his father's knowledge and avenged his father's blindness on his uncle, Mas'ud. Muhammad expressed his deep regret at this unpleasant event. In a letter to his nephew in Balkh Muhammad informed him that he had no hand in the assassination of his father, Mas'ud and that Ahmad had committed this heinous act of his own accord. Maudud marched at the head of an army to fight for his rights. Muhammad's troops made an attempt to stop him at the bank of the river Indus but Muhammad's army was defeated and Maudud captured Muhammad and his wife and children and killed them all. Following this Maudud went to Ghazni and sat on the throne in 435 A.H.

Maudud also fought a number of battles against the Seljuks like his father, Mas'ud however, he had to be content with his rule over Mawaraunnahr, Ghazni and India. The rest Khurasan, Khwarizm, and Iraq slipped out of his hands forever and the Seljuks began their rule over them.

Maudud bin Mas'ud died in 440 A.H. then his son Ali came to the throne. His son, Abdur Rashid, succeeded him but in a matter of days, he was killed by a commander named, Tughril who occupied the throne but was assassinated by the nobles, and Farkhzad, son of Mas'ud came to the throne in 444 A.H.

Farkhzad showed his courage and caliber. He built his army to force out the Seljuks from Khurasan and he succeeded in his initial campaigns. However, his fight against Alp Arsalan Seljuk proved disastrous to him and he could not win Khurasan.

Ibrahim bin Mas'ud, the brother of Farkhzad succeeded Farkhzad in 450 A.H. Sultan Ibrahim was virtuous, pious, brave and wise. He made peace with the Seljuks. Following this treaty, they began to consider themselves within their rights to rule over Khurasan (northeastern Iran, southern Turkmenistan, and northern Afghanistan). After winning peace on this front Sultan Ibrahim turned to India. In the wake of feuds and fights against the Seljuks, they could not maintain sufficient attention on India for very long. A number of commanders and Rajas (Kings) showed defiant attitudes and stopped giving tribute. Sultan Ibrahim launched a number of attacks on the insurgents in India and consolidated his rule. He died in 493 A.H. after reigning over a span of 42 or 43 years.

Mas'ud bin Ibrahim then came to the throne and died in 509 A.H. after a reign of 16 years. Mas'ud bin Ibrahim had also made Lahore his capital for a short period.

Mas'ud was succeeded by his son Arsalan and ruled for three years. Sultan Sanjar Seljuk conquered Ghazni and brought Behram bin Mas'ud bin Ibrahim, brother of Arsalan to the throne of Ghazni.

Behram reigned for 35 years. He also invaded India several times to punish the insurgents. He passed most of his time in Lahore. The book entitled *Kalila wa Dimna* and the *Khamsa Nizami* were written during his rule. During the last days of his rule, the Ghouries invaded Ghazni and ousted him from Ghazni. He escaped to India and died in Lahore in 347 A.H. The Punjab was left to be ruled by the Ghaznavids while Ghazni came under the rule of the Ghouries.

Following the death of Behram his son, Khusrau Shah came to the throne. He made a great effort to take Ghazni out of the clutches of the Ghouries but his attempts failed to materialize any positive results. He died in Lahore after reigning for 8 years.

His son, Malik bin Khusrau was seated on the throne in Lahore in 555 A. H. The Ghouries captured Malik bin Khusrau and occupied the Punjab. This ended the Ghaznavid dynasty.

Seljuk Dynasty

A Turk named Waqaq with Temur Taligh as his appellation was related to Paigu, the king of Turkistan. His son was Seljuk by name. He claimed his genealogy to be meeting with that of Afrasiyab in the thirty forth generation. He also had access to the court like his father. Seljuk became displeased with Paigu and shifted to Samarkand and Bukhara along with his sons. This occurred when Nuh II Samani was ruling over Bukhara. Persuaded by the Muslim Governor of Jund, Seljuk embraced Islam; the Jund was a tributary of Paigu, the king of Turkistan. A short time later, Paigu's collectors came to collect tribute. Thereupon Seljuk told them that the idea of the Unbelievers collecting tribute from the Muslims was intolerable to him. Seljuk's courage infused new spirit into the people and they with Seljuk attacked the collectors sent by Paigu and were successful. Seljuk shot in to fame and his act of valor was inspirational for everyone. The people of his tribe rushed to cluster round him. When Elej Khan attacked Nuh II, Seljuk sided with Nuh II and fought valiantly. Seljuk's son, Mika'il was killed in the battle. Mika'il's two sons were then raised by Seljuk. Seljuk had four more sons named, Israel, Yunus, Yanal and Musa. Showing exceptional valor during a battle was the best way to power among the Turk and Mongol tribes. Thus, Seljuk and his sons attained renown and power in a very short time and the Turks gathered around them. Elek Khan and Paigu joined hands to destroy the Seljuks. Meanwhile, Seljuk died. His grandson Chager Beg wanted to march on Armenia to wage a holy war against the Christians. However, the province of Tus (in the area of present day Meshed, Iran) was in between Bukhara and Armenia, which was a part of the Ghaznavid Empire. However, the Governor of Tus let him pass through the territory as a matter of cooperation with his holy campaign. Mahmud Ghaznawi was a sensible and far-sighted man. When he came to know of the Seljuk army's passing through his territory, he called for an explanation from the Governor of Tus for he anticipated a possible assault and plunder on his territory by them. On way back from Armenia, their strong force had grown stronger, and they started grazing their animals in the suburbs of Balkh and they halted there for this purpose. Being acquainted with the state of affairs, Mahmud Ghaznawi called the Seljuk chief to his court through his governor. With respect to age and sensibility Israel, the elder son of Seljuk was considered more suitable for the job. When he appeared before Mahmud Ghaznawi, he was greeted with esteem. After a preliminary chat, Mahmud Ghaznawi came to the point and said, "How many men can you provide if I am in need of troops?" Putting his arrow before Mahmud, Israel replied, "If you send this arrow to our tribes in the forest you will find one hundred thousand men standing before you." Thereupon Mahmud said, "In case I need some more men how many more could you give me?" Placing his bow before him Israel said, "If you send this bow to our tribes, two hundred thousand men will turn up to serve you." Now Mahmud Ghaznawi could easily determine the strength of the Seljuks. He then held Israel as a guarantee for peace and sent him to India where he remained a captive in the Kalinger Fort for 7 years. The Seljuk rule went to Tughril Beg and Chagher Beg, these two brothers ruled over the tribes with accord and amity.

Mahmud Ghaznawi gave a piece of land to the Seljuks in Mawaraunnahr (between the Amu [Oxus] and Syr rivers in modern Uzbekistan and Kazakhstan) to serve as a pasture. Moreover, he allowed them to cross the river Oxus and settle in Khurasan. Objecting to this decision Arsalan Jadeh, the Governor of Tus and Balkh questioned, "Why do you allow them to come across the river Oxus? They are a contentious people and they are bound to give trouble". Mahmud was aware of his own strength and besides, he has a plan to recruit them into his army to serve his purpose plus Israel's confinement was still a point in his favor, which he could exploit. When Mahmud passed away, Sultan Mas'ud set Israel free and he joined his nephews. With his arrival, the Seljuks rose to power. Sultan Mas'ud had not yet consolidated his position when Chagher Beg seized Merv and Herat and Tughril Beg occupied Nishapur. When Mas'ud Ghaznawi decided to punish them, they gave him so many anxious moments that, at last, he gave the entire territory of Khurasan to them.

Tughril Beg then shifted his capital to Rayy, while Chagher Beg stayed in Merv. The official addresses carried the names of both the brothers. Chagher Beg then annexed Khwarizm (territories of present day Turkmenistan and Uzbekistan) and made a successful attack on the

Romans (present day Turkey). They reached Baghdad and put an end to the Delmid rule. He was then appointed as the prime Minister of the Caliph of Baghdad and received a title and royal robes from the Caliphate. Tughril Beg's name was mentioned in the address delivered in Baghdad in 447 A. H. He died in 455 A.H. at the age of 70, while Chagher Beg had already passed away in 451 A.H.

Since Tughril Beg died without any children his nephew, Alp Arsalan bin Chagher Beg succeeded him. After reigning for nine years, he died in 465 A.H. He was a devout Muslim and the greatest Muslim king of his time. He once defeated a huge Christian force of three hundred thousand soldiers with a cavalry of 12 thousand and also captured the Caesar of Constantinople Romanus IV Diogenes.

Malik Shah Seljuk came to the throne after his father, Alp Arsalan. Qawurd, the brother of Alp Arsalan opposed his nephew but was captured and killed. Malik Shah then annexed Syria and Egypt. He had an empire even larger than Alp Arsalan's. He died in 484 A.H.

His son, Barkeyaraq succeed him and this was the beginning of the decline of the Seljuks. His brother, Muhammad bin Shah came to the throne in 496 A.H.

Sanjar bin Malik Shah was seated on the throne in 509 A.H. and was known as Sultanus'salatin (Sultan of Sultans). Sultan Behram Ghaznawi had agreed to pay tribute to him under compulsion. When Sultan Alauddin Ghouri Jahan Soz dislodged Behram and occupied Ghazni, Sultan Sanjar Seljuk appeared on the scene and captured Alauddin Ghouri. The Oguz Turks once arrested him in the suburbs of Balkh and he passed four years as a captive. During this period, they ravaged the entire territory of Khurasan. At last, Sultan Sanjar got free and occupied Khurasan. Following this, the former servant of his father Anustegin and Governor of Khwarizm rose against him and laid the foundation of a new dynasty known as Khwarizm Shahiya (territories of present day Turkmenistan and Uzbekistan). After the demise of Sultan Sanjar, his sister's son Mahmud Khan came to the throne in Nishapur in 550 A.H. During his time, the Gourids seized a part of Khurasan and the Khwarizm Shahs occupied the rest and wiped out all traces of the Seljuk dynasty.

Ten kings, the progeny of Qawurd, the brother of Alp Arsalan, are known as the Kermanid Seljuks. Kerman is bounded by Baluchistan and Sistan on the west, Yazd on the north, and Khorasan on the northeast. Their capital was Hamadan (west central Iran). Qawurd was killed in 465 A.H. opposing Malik Shah his nephew. His son, Shah Kerman succeeded him by the order of Malik Shah, son of Alp Arsalan. When he died after reigning for 12 years his brother, Turan Shah came to the throne and ruled for 13 years, and was succeeded by his son; Iran Shah and his end came after a reign of 42 years. His son, Mughithuddin then got the throne and held it for 14 years and made his final departure leaving behind his son, Mohiuddin Tughril Shah to occupy the throne and he ruled for 12 years. His son Behram Shah came to power after whom a number of persons namely, Arsalan Shah, Turan Shah, Muhammad Shah came to the throne one after the other ending the Kermanid Seljuk Dynasty.

Sultan Alp Arsalan Seljuk had sent Sulaiman Qatlamish bin Israel bin Seljuk to Asia Minor as Governor. He founded an independent state there. His progeny produce 14 kings who were called the Seljuks of Rome. The city of Konya was their capital. They ruled until the end of the seventh century Hegira and continuously fought against the Romans. They were followed by Ottoman Empire.

Khwarizm Shah Dynasty

A Turkish slave of Malik Shah Seljuk named Qutbuddin bin Anustegin had access to Sultan Sanjar. Sultan Sanjar Seljuk appointed Qutbuddin as the Governor of Khwarizm. Whenever Qutbuddin came to Sultan Sanjar, he would serve him as usual in his royal garments. He served as governor of Khwarizm for a long time and came to be known as Khwarizm, His descendants also adopted the same title.

Qutbuddin remained loyal to Sanjar Seljuk but following Sanjar's arrest by the Oguz Turks, he (Qutbuddin) proclaimed sovereignty and invaded Mawaraunnahr. He was succeeded by his son Atsaz Khwarizm Shah.

Atsaz died about 540 A.H. and was succeeded by his son Arsalan Shah in 557 A.H. He and his brother, Ala ad-Din Tekish remained at odds with each other all the time, which often led to armed conflict. At last, Ala ad-Din Tekish came out victorious and became the Khwarizm Shah. Ismail bin Hasan, author of *Dhakirah-e-Khwarizm* and the poet, Khakani belonged to his period. He had Tughril III Seljuk assassinated and expanded his own territories by capturing Khurasan (northeastern Iran, southern Turkmenistan, and northern Afghanistan) and Iraq.

After his death his son, Khwarizm Shah Muhammad bin Tekish came to the throne in 590 A.H. He ruled for 21 years and brought about a major territorial expansion. During this expansion, his relations with the Caliph of Baghdad deteriorated. After the demise of Shahabuddin Ghouri, Khwarizm Shah's territory extended up to Ghour and Ghazni. He defeated Atabak S'ad of Persia as well as Atabak Uzbek, the king of Azerbaijan. He then revolted against the Caliph of Baghdad and led an army against him intending to replace the Caliph by his spiritual guide, Sayed Ala al Mulk Tirmidhi. The caliph sent Sheikh Shahabuddin Sahrawardy to meet Muhammad Khwarizm Shah and have him reconsider such an action and to make peace. The mission bore no fruit and Muhammad Khwarizm Shah was determined to complete his plan. However, a natural calamity in the form of a heavy snowfall forced him back from attacking Iraq and he had not yet returned to his capital from this campaign when his country was stormed by Genghis Khan.

Sultan Muhammad bin Tekish Khwarizm Shah was a mighty king of his time. Even far off kings feared him. But, following the misfortune of snowfall, he suffered such a swift decline that he died in a state that he did not even have a burial shroud.

Sultan Muhammad ibn Tekish Khwarizm Shah had seven sons and three of them namely, Ruknuddin, Ghaythuddin and Jalaluddin were Governors of the different provinces however, they all had strained relations, with the result they could not join ranks to face Genghis Khan and they were all routed one by one.

Jalaluddin Khwarizm Shah was the most famous among them. He fought Genghis Khan valiantly at the bank of Indus but without any result. He went to India but returned after a short stay in the Sind. On his way, back he broke the back of the atheists of the Alamut Fort. He fought the Mongols on one hand and the Romans on the other. He won victories no doubt but the opposition was so powerful that he failed to regain his lost empire and died unknown and unnoticed. Historians mention his name with love and respect because of his bravery, which he had proved on several occasions. His end brought about the end of the Khwarizm Shah dynasty.

Ghourid Dynasty

Ghour (modern day Ghowr) is a vast region in the west central of Afghanistan. Mahmud Ghaznawi conquered it and made it a province of his empire. The Ghourid people confessed Islam in the beginning of the second century and none but the Afghans inhabited the entire region. Mahmud Ghaznawi appointed a noble man as the Governor of Ghour whose ancestors enjoyed this position for a long period. Circumstantially, the relations between Sultan Behram Ghaznawi and Qutbuddin, the Governor of Ghour became strained and resulted in an armed conflict in which Qutbuddin was killed. Qutbuddin Ghouri's brother, Saifuddin invaded Ghazni and turned out Behram Ghaznawi from Ghazni and won the throne. Behram Ghaznawi secured help from the surrounding countries an attached Ghazni and had Saifuddin mercilessly tortured to death.

Being informed of the event his third brother, Alauddin, in order to avenge the assassination of his two brothers, invaded Ghazni. Behram Ghaznawi made an attempt to lure away the enemy troops with gems and jewels and win peace by this way but the memory of the ignominious and torturous assassination of Saifuddin did not allow their burning anger to be appeased with wealth. Thus, the crafty device of Behram failed and Alauddin conquered Ghazni. Behram Ghazni fled to India, but Alauddin Ghouri, by way of revenge committed a large-scale slaughter of the people of Ghazni. He demolished the tombs of Ghaznavid kings and set the houses on fire and this carnage continued for a week. Because of his wild and wanton carnage, he came to be known as Alauddin "Jahan Soz" (the burner of the world). He also took with him a large number of captives, put them all to death and used their blood for kneading the clay to be used in the fortification of the city. This event took place in 547 A.H.

Alauddin Ghouri left for Ghour after appointing a viceroy for Ghazni and Ghazni became a province of Ghourid Empire.

Since Behram Ghaznawi had acknowledged the leadership of Sultan Sanjar Seljuk, he dispatched a letter to him from India informing him of the events. Sanjar Seljuk conquered both Ghour and Ghazni the next year and brought Behram back from India to rule over them. He arrested Alauddin and took him to his country.

What Alauddin did to devastate Ghazni was out of a sense of revenge and retaliation that overpowered his senses otherwise; he was a farsighted, able and sensible Sultan. Sanjar was so impressed with the behavior and abilities of Alauddin that he set him free and he came back and took over the reign of Ghour. Shortly thereafter, the Oguz Turks arrested Sanjar and this diminished the awe and power of the Seljuks. Sanjar passed four years in captivity. But it was a confinement similar to king Jehangir's of India by Mahabat Khan. The Oguz Turks would seat Sultan Sanjar on the throne in the day and treat him as a king but during the night, they would put him into confinement again. Shortly after the captivity of Sanjar, Alauddin ousted Behram Ghaznawi from Ghazni and he died a natural death after a number of days.

Alauddin Ghouri should be considered as the first sovereign King of the Ghourid dynasty. His son, Saifuddin II sat on the throne of Ghour and was assassinated by his own Commander during a battle with the Oguz Turks.

Alauddin Ghouri's nephews, Ghayas ud-Din and his brother named Shahab ud-Din Ghouri had practical experience in leading campaigns and administration, were co-rulers like the two brothers Tughril Beg Seljuk and Chugher Beg Seljuk. Both Ghayas ud-Din and Shahab ud-Din lived in accord and amity and both were considered as kings. Shahab ud-Din regarded his older brother, Ghayas ud-Din as his elder and made it his sacred duty to carry out his wishes and instructions.

After annexing most parts of Khurasan, the Ghourids turned to India because they considered themselves the true successors of the Ghaznavid dynasty and thought it to be within their rights to bring under their control the entire territory ruled by the Ghaznavids. The Punjab was then under the rule of the descendants of Behram

Ghaznawi. Shahab ud-Din wrested the Punjab from them and he arrested Khusrau Malik Ghaznawi in Lahore in 582 A.H. and sent him to his brother, Ghayas ud-Din Ghouri in Ghour and he himself occupied Lahore and began to rule over it.

Ghayas ud-Din Ghouri died in 599 A.H. and was succeeded by his younger brother Shahab ud-Din. He had invaded India during the reign of his elder brother, Ghayas ud-Din and arrested and killed Prithivi Raj. He appointed his slave Qutbuddin Aybak as ruler in India. During his tenure as king Shahab ud-Din went to India. On his return journey, the Fidais or the Kakhars killed him by mistake. Following the death of Shahab ud-Din Ghouri, the Ghourid dynasty came to an end. Qutbuddin Aybak consolidated his position and laid the foundation of the Slave Dynasty in India . The throne of Firozkoh (south of the Central Elburz mountains in Iran) was occupied by Shahab ud-Din's nephew, Mahmud Ghouri, son of Ghayas ud-Din Ghouri.

Mahmud Ghouri was also assassinated in 607 A.H. His son, Bahauddin who was later arrested by Khwarizm Shah, succeeded him. Ghour was then ruled over by a number of nominal kings related to Shahab ud-Din and thus came the hasty end of Ghourid Dynasty.

Atabeks Of Shiraz

Atabeks were the teachers to whom were entrusted the Seljuk princes for their education, training and learning of high morals. Gradually, these teachers or Atabeks rose to such heights that they were given the high post of ministers and rulers. In the wake of the Seljuk dynasty's decline, these Atabeks established their own sovereign rule in various countries and provinces. A number of Atabek dynasties remained in power in Syria, Iraq, and Persia and some of them attained eminence in the world of Islam.

During the reign of Sultan Sanjar Seljuk, Muzaffaruddin Sangar bin Maudud Salghari was the Governor of Persia. Following the death of Sultan Sanjar, he chose the title of "Atabek" and established his sovereign rule over Persia. He died in 556 A.H.

He was succeeded by his brother, Muzaffaruddin Atabek and ruled until 571 A.H. and his son came to the throne after his demise and ruled for 20 years.

Following his death, Atabek S'ad bin Zangi acceded and died in 622 A.H. after reigning for 28 years. Sheikh Muslehuddin Shirazi adopted "S'adi" as his pen name after Atabek S'ad.

After his death, his son Atabek bin S'ad Zangi acceded to the throne and it was during his tenure that Baghdad was annihilated by Hulagu Khan. He had accepted to give tribute to the Mongols and survived.

Following his demise, his grandson Atabek Muhammad sat on the throne. In short, this dynasty ruled over Shiraz and Persia until 663 A.H. but remained a tributary to the Mongols throughout. Afterwards, viceroys were sent by the Mongols to look after the administration of Shiraz. When the Mongols showed signs of decline and disturbances, Shiraz once again had an independent sovereign rule, which was then taken over by the Temur era.

Sistan Kings

Sistan (eastern Iran and southwestern Afghanistan) is also called "Nimroz." King Sanjar Seljuk had appointed a man named Abul Fazl Tajuddin as the Governor of this country. In the wake of the degeneration taking place in the Seljuk Dynasty, he claimed an independent rule. His son Shamsuddin succeeded him but his atrocities attracted the hate and anger of his people. At last, his subjects mobbed and assassinated him and brought a man named Tajuddin Herb bin Izzul Malik to the throne who belonged to the same dynasty. He was good-natured and able. During his reign, Khurasan was a part of Ghourid Dynasty. He ruled over a span of 6 years and following his demise, his son Yaminuddin Behram Shah acceded to the throne but was killed by atheists. His son Nusratuddin came to the throne after him. His brother Ruknuddin staked his claim to the throne, which led to armed conflict between the two. Nusratuddin was killed by Ruknuddin and Ruknuddin was killed by the Mongol invaders. Tajuddin Herb's son Shahabuddin Muhammad then was seated on the throne as the last member of the dynasty but he too was arrested and killed by the Mongols and with him, his dynasty desisted.

Muluk Dynasty In Karat And Herat

A man named Izzuddin Umar belonging to Seljuk Dynasty was the Minister of Ghayas ud-Din Ghouri. Ghayas ud-Din later sent him as the Governor of Herat where he built royal palaces and mosques. He came to be known as Izzuddin Karat. He was succeeded by his son, Ruknuddin in 643 A.H. They came to be considered as kings of Herat in the aftermath of the destruction of the Ghourid Dynasty. Shamsuddin Karat sat on the throne of Herat. He and his father both had offered their allegiance to the Mongols like the Atabekan of Shiraz. The Mongols caused no harm to their rule and left them to rule over Herat as their viceroys.

Ruknuddin, son of Shamsuddin Karat sat on the throne of Herat following the death of Shamsuddin Karat. Abagha Khan, the Mongol king had conferred upon him the title of Shamsuddin Kahin". His son, Fakhruddin came to the throne after the demise of his father. Fakhruddin was succeeded by his brother, Ghayathuddin and Ghayathuddin by his son Shamsuddin in 729 A. H. Shamsuddin was succeeded by his brother, Malik Hafiz and he by his brother, Muizzuddin Husain in 721 A.H. He died as a king of Herat in 771 A.H. His son, Ghayathuddin Babar Ali came to the throne after him. During his tenure, Temur arrived in Herat and he rose to obey Temur while Temur gave his daughter to him in marriage.

Atabeks Of Azerbaijan

Among King Mas'ud Seljuk's slaves was a man named Shamsud Din Eldeguz who was racially a Turk. He made a start as an ordinary servant but gradually, he rose to the position of a teacher and then began to show his power and influence in administrative affairs. At last, he was married to the widow of Tughril II and he became the Governor of Azerbaijan. He was then appointed the Prime Minister and Commander-in Chief of the Seljuk Dynasty and brought much of Persia under his control. When he died in Ramadan, his elder son, Muhammad Ata Beg became the Prime Minister and the teacher and guardian of Tughril III, who was then 7. Ata Beg enjoyed power for 13 years. When he died, his brother Qazl Arsalan was put in this high

post. He then assassinated Tughril III and captured the throne but he
died the day he was to be crowned. Following this event Ata Beg Abu
Bakr took over the reign and consolidated his position by confining
himself to Azerbaijan and began to rule peacefully. Suddenly, Abu
Bakr's brother Qatlagh Khan rose in revolt against him. Qatlagh was
defeated in the encounter. He escaped and took refuge with
Khwarizm Shah and persuaded him to attack Azerbaijan. However, a
commander of Khwarizm Shah assassinated Qatlagh. Ata Beg Abu
Bakr died after a few days and was succeeded by his brother Ata Beg
Muzaffar. He also occupied Iraq and ruled for fifteen years. Finally,
Jalaluddin Khwarizm Shah the last of his dynasty conquered
Azerbaijan. Thus, the end of the dynasties of the Khwarizm Shah and
Eldeguzid of Azerbaijan came at about the same time with the
onslaught of Genghis Khan.

Alamut Atheists' Dynasty

Hasan bin Sabbah founded his rule by capturing the forts of Alamut
and Qazwin at the time when the Seljuk Dynasty was going very
strong. Many things have been mentioned by historians about Hasan
bin Sabbah. His physical strength may be measured with the event
that when once his two sons disobeyed him, he grew angry at both of
them and with one slap to each of them they fell down dead.

He led a very simple life and wanted the same life for his wife and
children. Once, anticipating the Seljuks' siege of the fort and attack, he
felt the need of shifting his wife and children to another fort. He
instructed the officer in charge of the fort not to provide them food
and drink like a guest and leave her to earn it herself by spinning yarn.

Following the death of Hasan bin Sabbah, Kiyabuzurg sat on the
throne and fought with King Muhammad Seljuk until the death of
Muhammad Seljuk. Kiyabuzurg then seized several forts of the
Seljuks and plundered Gilan.

On the death of Kiyabuzurg, his son Muhammad took the throne.
During his period, the Fidais began to kill kings and the celebrities
here and there. When such events crossed all limits, the Persians
appeared before King Sanjar Seljuk and cried out for assistance and
the religious scholars also gave their fatwa (verdict) against the Fidais

and declared their killings as invalid. However, king Sanjar sent his emissary to Alamut to determine their greed and actions. An assembly was convened to make arguments and counter-arguments. The atheists defended their beliefs and actions with all the arguments at their command with the result that the matter remained undecided. King Sanjar practiced caution in ordering their massacre at large.

Three years later Muhammad bin Kiyabuzurg Umid died and was succeeded by Hasan bin Muhammad. He promoted atheism beyond all limits. When he died in 561 A.H., his son, Alauddin Muhammad came to the throne. During this period, Imam Fakhruddin Razi came from Azerbaijan to Rayy and began delivering sermons and wise counsel. He used to target the atheists' beliefs to keep people from joining the Fidais. In view of his campaign, they reached Rayy and threatened him with death. Following this, the Imam shifted to Ghour and joined Ghayathuddin Ghouri and his brother. Shahabuddin Ghouri had accompanied the latter during his journeys to India. He was appointed as Imam to lead the Muslim army in prayers. In the wake of Shahabud-Din's attachment with the Imam, the Fidais assassinated him in 602 A.H. Imam Fakhruddin Razi then went to Khwarizm Shah.

After Alauddin his son, Jalaluddin Hasan took the throne. He renounced the faith of his father and grandfather and informed the Muslim world of his conversion to the true faith. Following this he came to be known as Jalaluddin, the neo-Muslim (convert to Islam). Caliph Nasir Abbasi grew happy with him. Thus, when Jalaluddin Hasan's mother went to perform the Hajj, King Muhammad Khwarizm Shah's standard was kept behind that of Jalaluddin Hasan's mother. This was done simply to appreciate and encourage Jalaluddin Hasan. However, King Muhammad Khwarizm Shah took exception to this and this resulted in his campaign against the Caliph of Baghdad. Since Jalaluddin Hasan's son was only 9 at the time of accession disturbances and disruptions overtook the entire country. Nasiruddin Tusi belonged to this period. Muhammad passed away in 653 A.H. and was succeeded by his son, Ruknuddin Khurshah. Hulagu Khan attacked and arrested Ruknuddin and demolished his forts and with this came the end of the dynasty.

Chapter 18

Brief Supplement Of The Islamic History Of Egypt And Syria

Following the decline of the Seljuks, the Seljuk Dynasty itself broke into pieces and established several separate independent states. In the same way, Atabeks also set up their own states. Thus, there appeared a large number of small Muslim states in Persia, Khurasan, Iraq, Iran, Syria and Asia Minor. Konya was the capital of the Asia Minor rule, which came to be known as the Seljuks of Rome. This dynasty existed until the Ottoman Empire came into being. Similarly, an independent Atabek rule was established in Syria, which was known, as the Syrian Atabek Rule.

Syrian Atabek Rule

Atabek Imaduddin Zangi laid the foundation of his sovereign rule in Syria in 521 A.H. when he died in 544 A.H. he left behind three sons Nuruddin Zangi, Saifuddin Zangi and Qutbuddin Zangi. Each of them set up separate states in different cities of Syria and chose Nuruddin Zangi as their emperor. Like the Seljuks of Rome, the Atabeks of Syria were preoccupied with countering the Roman Christian attacks.

Sultan Nuruddin Zangi was very brave, devout and good-natured. Bait al-Maqdis was under the possession of the Christian since 490

A.H., and they had founded their rule there. This Christian rule in Bait al-Maqdis had the help and support of the whole European continent. In spite of all efforts, bravery and determination Sultan Nuruddin Zangi failed to take Bait al-Maqdis from the Christians during his lifetime.

It was for Sultan Salahuddin Ayyubi to fulfill this mission. The Abbasid Caliph of Baghdad had conferred upon Nuruddin the title of "Sultan" and credentials to rule over Syria. During this Sultan's rule, the Christians exerted pressure on Egypt. Thereupon, Azid, the Egyptian ruler and the last among the Ubaidi rulers sought Sultan Nuruddin's help. Responding to this request Nuruddin sent his commander Sherkoh along with his nephew Salahuddin to Egypt, within a short time the Ubaidi ruler passed away and Egypt came under the control of Salahuddin. Nuruddin Zangi died as well during this time period and his son Malik Saleh succeeded his father on the throne of Damascus in Syria. Shortly thereafter, Saifuddin bin Qutbuddin established his separate rule in Mosul and finally Syria too came under the possession of Sultan Salahuddin Ayyubi. Salahuddin Ayyubi practiced favor and concessions to the children and family members of Nuruddin and they enjoyed ruling in Syria until the invasion of Hulagu Khan. However, they were rulers in name while Salahuddin was the virtual ruler.

Ayyubid Dynasty Of Egypt And Syria

Najmuddin Ayyub was a Kurd by race and held the post of commander in the army of Imamuddin Zangi. Imamuddin Zangi was very kind to Salahuddin, the son of Najmuddin Ayyub and he had made some special arrangements for the education and training of Salahuddin. Following the death of Sultan Imamuddin Zangi, Nuruddin Zangi appointed Najmuddin Zangi as garrison commander of the Damascus Fort and his son Salahuddin as his helper. After the death of Najmuddin Ayyub, Nuruddin Zangi appointed his brother Sherkoh as the commander-in-chief and Salahuddin as the garrison commander of the Damascus Fort.

Following the death of Azid Ubaidi, Salahuddin Ayyub became the ruler of Egypt. When differences erupted regarding the accession after the death of Sultan Nuruddin Zangi, Salahuddin Ayyubi came from Egypt to Damascus and enthroned Malik Saleh, the son of Sultan

Nuruddin Zangi. From that day on Syrian rule came under the power and influence of Sultan Salahuddin Ayyubi. Yemen and Hijaz also conceded to his rule the same year.

This was a most crucial period for the world of Islam. The united force of Europe invaded Egypt but Salahuddin Ayyubi stood like a mountain in their way. The Alamut atheists were on the other hand playing havoc in the region by killing Muslim kings, ministers, nobles and commanders. They had threatened Sultan Salahuddin Ayyubi too with death but, by the grace of Allah, he escaped.

At last, all the commanders unanimously conceded Salahuddin as the ruler of Syria. And with this, he began to make all out efforts to take Bait al-Maqdis from the rule of the Christians. Following a heavy fight Salahuddin Ayyubi was able to capture the Christian King of Bait al-Maqdis on the battlefield and liberate the territory in 583 A.H. However, he set him free on the promise that he would never fight against the Muslims in future. Salahuddin then marched ahead and occupied Aakka and conquered Bait al-Maqdis in 588 A.H. From 490 A.H. to 588 A.H. a period of 98 years, Bait al-Maqdis had remained under Christian control. When the Christians had won it from the Muslims, they let flow a river of Muslim blood. However, when Salahuddin Ayyubi took over Bait al-Maqdis not a drop of Christian blood was spilled anywhere.

With the Muslim conquest of Bait al-Maqdis, the entire European continent was overtaken by a tumult of the worst nature and every Christian household raised a great clamor over the unexpected and ignominious defeat. In the wake of this historic defeat Phillip, the Emperor of France, Richard, the Lion-hearted Emperor of England, Frederick, the Emperor of Germany along with a large number of small kings, dukes and nobles built a huge army and led it to conquer the entire Asian continent and to wipe out all traces of Islam. They first targeted Syria. But Salahuddin Ayyubi with a comparatively small army fought against them several hundred battles within a span of four years and he did not allow them to touch the walls of Bait al-Maqdis. Defeated, disgraced and frustrated the Christians returned with their dreams smashed and souls shattered. Even at the height of these inimical relations, the kindhearted Salahuddin Ayyubi allowed them to visit Bait al-Maqdis as pilgrims.

During the previously mentioned battles, Salahuddin Ayyubi showed so much human feeling, generosity, kindness and dignity that, even today, European nations and the Christian world remember him with respect and consider his name synonymous with bravery and nobility. Sultan Salahuddin Ayyubi passed away in 589 A.H. and was reckoned among the Friends of Allah due only to his piety, devotion and fear of Allah Almighty.

Following the death of Salahuddin his son, Uthman came to the throne with Malik al-Aziz as his title. He ruled for 6 years with a good character and reputation. Following his death in 595 A.H., his son, Malik Mansur came to the throne but was deposed after a year and was succeeded by Malik Adil, brother of Sultan Salahuddin Ayyubi. He was virtuous and praiseworthy. He died in 615 A.H. He was succeeded by his son, Malik Kamil. He too was a king of lofty ideals and character. When he died in 635 A.H. his son, Malik Adil Abu Bakr came to the throne. Two years later, Egyptian nobles put him in confinement and seated his brother, Malik Saleh bin Malik on the throne of Egypt. He ruled for a decade but was martyred during a fight against the Christians. Following him Malik Mu'azzam Turan Shah Malik Saleh came to the throne in 647 A.H. but was assassinated after reigning for only a few months. After him Queen Shajratud'dur came to the throne in 648 A.H. and was deposed after a few months and Malik Ashraf was brought to the throne in 648 A.H. The slaves of the same dynasty in 652 A.H. deposed him and the Ayyubid dynasty came to an end.

During his reign, Sultan Salahuddin Ayyubi passed his days either in Syria, the city of Damascus or on the battlefield. However, his successors confined themselves to Egypt with the result that Syria slipped out of their hands and they had to be content with Egypt under their possession. The last rulers carved out a policy to purchase slaves from Kharjiah and Armenia to build a massive army to combat and punish any insurgent commander. Gradually, these slaves rose to such strength and power that they laid the foundation of Mamluk Dynasty.

Mamluk Dynasty Of Egypt (Category I)

When the Ayyubid dynasty suffered a decline and all administrative affairs came to be managed by the slaves, they chose one Malik Mu'iz

Azizuddin Aybak as their king. He married Shajratud'dur, the slave girl of Malik Saleh Ayyubi who ruled for a short period. He was assassinated in 655 A.H.

Following his death, they chose his son Mansur for the highest position. However, he abdicated the throne after 2 years. Malik Muzaffar replaced him as a king but only for a short span of eleven months. During his tenure, Hulagu Khan attacked Egypt but was defeated. Malik al-Zahir Ruknuddin captured the throne by assassinating Malik Muzaffar in 658 A. H. He ruled successfully for 17 years and was succeeded by Malik Sayed Nasiruddin in 676 A.H. but he was deposed after one year. Malik Adil Badruddin was then brought to the throne but he too was deposed after four months. Thus ended the first category of the Mamluk Dynasty of Egypt in 678 A.H. In total, they ruled for 26 years. However, some of their attributes are worth mentioning. Firstly, they introduced the voting system and elected their kings by majority vote. Secondly, they repulsed all attacks of the Mongols who had once devastated the entire civilized world.

Mamluk Dynasty Of Egypt (Category II)

It is also called the Qulauniyah Dynasty. After Malik Adil Badruddin, Abul Ma'ani Malik Mansur Qala'un was elected the king of Egypt and he was considered the first king of the second category of the Mamluks. He ruled for 11 years.

Egyptian territory expanded during his tenure. Following him Malik Ashraf Salahuddin Khalil came to the throne but abdicated it on his own after a few days however, the people forced him back to the throne and his reign spanned over 44 years and came to an end only after his death in 737 A.H. Malik Adil Katbagha Mansuri succeeded him but he did not rule for even a month. After him, Mansur Hosamuddin ascended the throne. He was assassinated two years after his ascension and Malik Muzaffar Ruknuddin was elected for one year. Following him Malik Mansur Abu Bakr was given the throne in 741 A.H. but he was sent into exile. Malik Ashraf replaced him but he was also exiled after eight months, and Malik Nasir Ahmad received the throne. Following his assassination in 745 A.H., Abul Fida Malik Saleh Ismail came to the throne. His reign lasted for not more than one year. Malik Kamil

Sh'abani ascended the throne in 746 A.H. but was deposed only after a few months. Malik Muzaffar Hajji was given the throne in 747 A.H. but was assassinated within a year. Nasir Hasan then acceded the throne in 748 A.H. He too was assassinated after reigning for 14 years. Malik Saleh then came to the throne in 762 A.H. and was deposed in 765 A.H. and was replaced by Malik Mansur bin Hajji and he too, was deposed after a tenure of two years and the throne came to Malik Ashraf Sh'abani who was assassinated after 11 years and was replaced by Malik Mansur Ali in 778 A.H. and died after 5 years. He was replaced by Saleh Hajji in 783 A.H. and abdicated the throne passing a duration of 8 or 9 years, and with this ended Qalaukiah Dynasty. This dynasty covered a period of 114 years. Category one and two showed no substantial difference in respect of style of governance.

Mamluk Dynasty of Egypt (Category III)

It is also known as the Cherkesy (Circassian) Dynasty. Malik Tahir Barquq replaced Malik Saleh Hajji who belonged to the Cherkesy (Circassian) tribe, from northwest Caucus. Since kings from the same tribe later ruled Egypt, Malik Tahir Barquq came to be known as the first king from the Ayyubid slaves. His reign covered a period of 9 years between 792 A.H. to 801 A.H. and he was replaced by Malik Nasir who ruled for 4 years. Even though Timur made Egypt a tributary for 5 years during his tenure by and large, the Mamluk Dynasty remained safe. Malik Nasir was instrumental in setting up Hanafi, Shafe'i, Maliki, and Hambali prayer carpets at the Ka'bah. At the outset, religious scholars opposed this new arrangement but it subsided in due course for this step created no disruption in the religion. He was followed by a number of kings like Malik Mansur, Abu Nasser Sheikh, Malik Muzaffar Ahmad, Malik al-Zahir Abul Fath and Malik Saleh Muhammad who ascended the throne in 822 A.H. and abdicated on his own after four months and was replaced by Malik Ashraf Abu Nasir. He was a devout Muslim and loved to hear Quranic recitations. He ruled until 841 A.H. and was replaced by Abul Mahasin Abdul Aziz, but was deposed only after 3 months. Following him Malik Abu Sayeed, known as Malik Al-Zahir came to the throne and died after reigning for 15 years. He was very good-natured and gracious. He was replaced by Malik Mansur Uthman who was deposed in 857 A.H., after ruling for a few months.

Following him Malik Ashraf Abu Nasser ruled until 885 A.H. and then Malik Muayyed came to the throne but was deposed within a few days. Malik Zahir Abu Sayeed Khushqadam who reigned from 865 A.H. to 892 A.H. and died a natural death then replaced him. Malik Zahir Abu Sayeed Malyas then took over as king but was sent into exile after a few months and was replaced by Malik Zahir Abu Sayeed Tamrigha who was put in prison within two months. Malik Ashraf Abu Nasir then came to the throne and ruled till 902 A.H. and was replaced by Malik Abu al-Sadat who was assassinated after ruling for two and half years. Malik Ashraf Qalduh came to the throne after him but was lost after 11 days and was never found. Malik Zahir Abu Sayeed Qalduh remained on the throne until 906 A.H. Malik Hanbalat replaced him but was exiled within a year. Malik Adil ascended the throne in 907 A.H. but was killed after four and half months. Malik Ashraf Abu Nasser Qalduh then came to the throne and reigned over the country for 15 years.

Sultan Salim I Uthmani invaded Egypt in 922 A.H. and brought about an end to the Cherkesy Dynasty by defeating Malik Ashraf Tuman, and annexed Egypt to his kingdom and along with this ended the nominal Abbasid Dynasty of Egypt.

This third category of Ayyubid slaves, which is known as Cherkesy Dynasty, covered a period of 130 years. Subsequent to the Ayyubid Dynasty, three categories of the Mamluks reigned over Egypt for a total period of 270 years. In the beginning of these Mamluks, Hulagu Khan had devastated the Abbasid Dynasty in Baghdad, but in a very short time, as mentioned above, the Abbasid dynasty was revived by these Mamluks and continued until their end in 922 A.H. Even though these Abbasid caliphs were treated only like spiritual guides or figureheads they after all, held a unique religious status and were very useful to the Mamluks for no Muslim ruler would dare commit aggression against them. Similarly, the Mamluks never posed a challenge to the Abbasid Caliphate and they passed their days in peace and safety.

It appears proper to give below a list showing clearly which Abbasid Caliph corresponded to which king. It also should be kept in mind that a new king had to seek credentials from the Abbasid Caliph and a new Caliph was installed with the approval of the Egyptian king. Nevertheless, there were examples where some caliphs enjoyed such a strong position and power that an Egyptian king would not dare oppose their installation. However, at times, relations between the caliph and the king suffered setbacks and fluctuations. The caliph enjoyed the support and sympathy of the Muslim masses while the Egyptian king lived by his power. However, King Salim Uthmani did away with such a conflicting situation and assimilated spiritual leadership and kingship into one and he manifested that.

Abbasid Caliphs of Egypt

No.	Name of the Caliph	Year of Accession
1	Mustansir Billah bin Zahir Bi-Amrillah bin Nasir Li-Dinillah	659 A.H.
2	Hakim Bi-Amrillah bin Mustarshid Billah	660 A.H.
3	Mustakfi Billah bin Hakim Bi-Amrillah	701 A.H.
4	Wathiq Billah	702 A.H.
5	Hakim Bi-Amrillah bin Mustakfi Billah	742 A.H.
6	Mutazid Billah	753 A.H.
7	Mutawakkil Alallah	762 A.H.
8	Mustasim Billah bin Muhammad Ibrahim	778 A.H.
9	Musta'in Billah	808 A.H.
10	Mu'tazid Billah	815 A.H.
11	Mustakfi Billah	845 A.H.
12	Qasim Bi-Amrillah bin Mutawakkil	858 A.H.
13	Musta'id Billah bin Mutawakkil	858 A.H.
14	Mutawakkil Ali bin Yaqub bin Mutawakkil	872 A.H.
15	Mustamsik Billah	903 A.H.

Sultan Salim Uthmani conquered Egypt and Caliph Mustamsik handed over to him the scepter and other relics, which were signs of the caliphate, and pledged his allegiance to him. Sultan Salim Uthmani took Mustamsik with him from Egypt to Constantinople where he died.

Chapter 19

Ottoman Dynasty

We have now covered the early part of 10th century Hijri however, in order to deal with the birth of the Ottoman Dynasty, we have to go back as far as to the seventh century.

The plundering Turk tribes, known as Oguz and Ghazan Turks, had injured and eroded the prestige of the Seljuk Dynasty by entering Iran and Khorasan. Histories ranging from the Chinese province of Hanchu to Morocco bear witness to the adventures of these Oguz Turks. By capturing Sanjar Seljuk, they had sent people into terror. With the rise of Genghis Khan, their power had diminished considerably. Their remaining ability to strike awe in their enemies suffered a complete setback after the bloodshed and destruction caused by the Genghezids. They had already divided themselves into a number of tribes and foreign invasions made them spread widely in all directions. A certain tribe drifted to Egypt and joined the Egyptian army, while several other of their tribes left Egypt and settled in Armenia and Azerbaijan. Since no mighty king rose among them, history is silent about much of their activity. By virtue of their being in Iran and Khorasan as conquerors, they had imbibed the qualities of mind and spirit and learned Islamic manners. However, even amidst power and conquest they had not given up the love of pastoral life. Therefore, most of these tribes settled in the green postures and forests of Khorasan, Iran and other such countries.

When the Mongols invaded Khorasan, the Oguz Turks of Khorasan shifted to Armenia and settled there. Their chief was Sulaiman Khan. He and his comrades were devout and true Muslims like the Seljuks. The courage, determination and his behavior with his people attracted many other Oguz Turks who were still unsettled and this added to his strength. It was the era of Genghezid invasions and plunder and every head of a family had to rely on his own strength and resources to withstand the onslaughts. In such a delicate situation, only their unity and solidarity could save them from utter destruction. Actually, Sulaiman Khan, by acting wisely and cautiously, not only added to his power and strength but also spared it for the future. The destruction of the Khwarizm Shah Dynasty provided him with an opportunity to make use of their men and materials for his own purpose.

Three years before his demise, Genghis Khan sent a huge army in 621 A.H. to invade the Konya based Seljuks. Konya was then ruled over by Alauddin Kaiqbad Seljuk. It has already been mentioned that the Seljuks rulers of this Empire continuously fought with the Romans (Christians). Now, with the passage of time, this Empire showed weaknesses and decline. When Sulaiman Khan came to know that Alauddin Kaiqbad was targeted by the Mongols, he felt very sad for the Sultan who was a Believer while the Mongols were Unbelievers. Moreover, the Konya kingdom was constantly engaged in holy war against the Christians while the Mongols had devastated the world of Islam.

Sulaiman Khan ordered his tribesmen to march ahead to join Alauddin and reinforce his army so that he could have an opportunity to be honored with martyrdom. Even though the actual number of Sulaiman's troops is not known, he sent his son Artughril at the head of 444 fighters as a vanguard. One of the strange things of history occurred on this occasion. These warriors in defense of faith were marching ahead from Armenia when, about the same time, a Mongol force appeared from another side to take on Alauddin Kaiqbad's troops. Now, as the battle between the Mongol and Seljuk forces broke out and the Mongols were about to gain the upper hand Sulaiman Khan's son Artughril appeared on the scene with Muslim soldiers. He witnessed two forces fighting against each other and one party about to be defeated when he joined the weak and dominated side without identifying it and gave such a fierce fight that the Mongols were uprooted and they took to their heals leaving behind nothing but dead bodies. Alauddin Kaiqbad Seljuk who was facing certain defeat expressed his utmost joy over this sudden and most unexpected victory. He hugged Artughtil out of love and thankfulness. Artughril on the other hand, expressed his happiness over extending timely help to his Muslim brethren fighting in the way of Allah Almighty. Artughril and Alauddin were still in an ecstasy of delight when Sulaiman Khan also reached the battlefield. Alauddin's joy knew no bounds and he not only thanked but also honored the father and the son with costly garments. He then bestowed on Artughril an estate near Angorah, present day Ankara, and appointed Sulaiman Khan as the Commander-in-chief of his army.

Alauddin's prudence is commendable when he gave Artughril the best piece of land under his possession. The Konya Empire was very vast. But, gradually, the northern and western parts of Asia Minor were occupied by the Romans and with their expansionist designs they were going ahead capturing one area after another. The Mongols had separated the southeastern areas on the other hand, and their thirst for more territory was going on unabated. Thus, the Konya Empire was being ground between two millstones. With the result, it was reduced to a small State and was counting its days to extinction. In such a situation, it was rather a wise step on the part of Alauddin to allot Artughril an estate bordering the Roman Empire and appointed Sulaiman Khan as Commander-in-Chief to stop the advances of the Mongols. Sulaiman Khan was campaigning against the Mongols and while sailing along the Euphrates with his troops and crossing the river fell into the river and succumbed to death. But Artughril kept going ahead with his mission of wresting Christian lands and expanding the borders of his own country. The King of Konya looked upon his constant successes with appreciation and satisfaction.

Alauddin Kaiqbad died in 634 A.H. and was succeeded by his son, Ghayathuddin Kaikhusro. In the wake of the constant Mongol invasions, Ghayathuddin Kaikhusro was reduced to the position of giving tribute to the Mongols. However, Artughril was safe for he was governing a territory that was out of danger. The Mongols also had no time to turn to Asia Minor. Hulagu Khan, the grandson of Genghis Khan put out the lamp of the Abbasid Caliphate of Baghdad in 656 A.H. A son was born to Artughril in 657 A.H. who was named, Osman Gazi (or Osman I which is Turkish for the original Arabic Uthman). This is the same Osman Gazi after who the later Turkish kings came to be known as Ottoman kings. Artughril died in 687 A.H. when Osman was 30. The King of Konya issued Osman Gazi credentials for ruling over the entire territory once ruled by his father. Being highly impressed with his all-round abilities, Ghayathuddin Kaikhusro appointed Osman Gazi as the Commander-in-Chief of his army and gave him his daughter in marriage. Now Osman Gazi settled in Konya and, in a very short time, he rose to become the Prime Minister and held the status of delivering Juma (Friday) addresses instead of Ghayathuddin Khusro.

Osman Khan

Ghayathuddin Khusro was killed during a Mongol disturbance. He had no son but a daughter, who was married to Osman Gazi. Thus, Osman Gazi was unanimously chosen as the king of Konya. Since then the Empire founded by the descendants of Israel bin Seljuk in 470 A.H. ended in 699 A.H. giving place to the Ottoman Empire which continued until the recent past. Israel bin Seljuk was the person whom Sultan Mahmud Ghaznawi had confined in the Kalinjar Fort in India.

At the time of Osman Gazi's accession, the Konya Empire was weak and powerless and it was unable to withstand the two-pronged onslaught of the Romans and the Mongols. But Osman Gazi injected new life into the dying Empire and the secrets of Osman Gazi's success lay in his generous and polite attitude towards everyone. Osman Gazi was a devout Muslim on one hand and was endowed with bravery of the highest order on the other. First, he wrested the city of Eskisehir (Dorylaeum of ancient times) from the Romans and set up his capital there. This choice proved auspicious. Right after his accession to the throne, Osman Gazi had to deal with the enmities and intrigues of his rivals, which he ultimately put down and silenced his detractors and opponents. Had Osman Gazi shown weakness at any stage his rivals would have rose in open revolt but his bravery, courage, determination and utter fearlessness stood him in good stead on every occasion. Thus, when the Christians built a strong army to invade Konya at the initial stage of his coming to power, Osman Gazi called his courtiers for consultations. On this occasion Osman Gazi's uncle the brother of Artughril, an old man, expressing his opinion, said, "We must avoid conflicts with the Christians and keep peace and friendship with them because in case of an engagement with the Mongols other Turkish commanders will invade our country in support of the Christians and we may not be able to face the joint attacks of our enemies." Osman Gazi grew furious at these discouraging words of his old uncle and he shot an arrow at him, which led to his death on the spot. This horrible scene choked off the dissenting voices, if any. Thus, Osman Gazi launched a massive attack on the Christians and conquered and brought Eskisehir under his control; and shifted his capital from Konya to Eskisehir. Following this victory, Osman Gazi marched ahead against the Christians winning one city after another and forced them out from Asia Minor as well. Witnessing the surging flood of Osman Gazi's victories with utmost anxiety the Caesar of Constantinople in route to induce the Mongols to invade Osman Gazi's country from the eastern side. His plan was to turn the tide towards the Mongols. The plan bore fruit. Instigated by Caesar, the Mongol invaders began to launch attacks on Osman Gazi's country. But the victorious army of Osman was in high spirits and boisterous form bubbling with zeal and determination. Osman Gazi dispatched a part of his army under his son, Orkhan, a fighter matchless for his gallantry, to combat the Mongols and he himself rose against the Christians with added force and determination. Orkhan repulsed every Mongol attack and forced them to give up their mission. After the successful campaigns against the Mongols, Orkhan hurried to his father and the joint command of father and son left no choice for the Christians but to vacate city after city and the marching Muslim fighters and the flood of Muslim victories reached the coast of the Black Sea conquering Asia Minor rather easily. Orkhan, on the other hand, pushed the Christians back and conquered Bursa, which was a magnificent city of Caesar of Rome situated near the western coast of Asia Minor. At the time of the conquest of Bursa Osman Gazi was on a sickbed in Eskisehir. When the good news on the conquest of Bursa came to him, Osman Gazi at once decided to go to Bursa. He asked his commanders to have him buried in Bursa even if he died on the way. However, Osman Gazi arrived in Bursa and died a few days after reaching there in 727 A.H.

Osman Gazi said addressing his son, "I don't feel sad over my fast approaching death for a worthy son like you is going to succeed me. Make it a point not to give up devotion to Allah Almighty, piety, mercy and justice. Your first and foremost duty should be to put into practice the codes of Shari'ah (the Islamic system of law)." At the end, he urged his son to make Bursa to serve as the center of his Empire. The choice of Bursa to be the capital also pointed to his wisdom and farsightedness. He knew fully well that a section in Konya was at enmity with his dynasty and they could at any time rise against his successor. He was also aware of the fact that the Mongols were against the Muslims not because of their faith and they were, bit by bit, coming into the fold of Islam. Thus in case of Konya being the capital unnecessary conflicts and campaigns would continue. Moreover, the Christian countries were a better field for the Muslim fighters. In addition, Bursa as a capital would serve as a deterrent to the Christians having expansionist designs. And, above all, Ottoman kings would find it easier to target Europe and conquer the Balkans. Osman was thinking on the right lines and his descendants followed suit.

Osman Gazi was brave and he was an outstanding horseman and a very handsome person. His power of judgment was unique and he could easily arrive at a decision in the most intricate matters and his opinions proved right. In beneficence and benevolence, he was matchless. His intelligence and presence of mind had no parallel.

The Seljuk kings of Konya used the crescent on their flags. Osman retained the Crescent on his flags and standards and it became his national symbol and it is an object of love for the Muslims even today.

Osman Gazi died at the age of 69 years and a few months reigning powerfully and magnificently for 27 years. His piety and abstinence may be gauged from the fact that he left nothing save his armor, sword and girdle as personal property. This is the same sword, which used to be fastened to the waist of every Ottoman king at the time of his accession to the throne. Let it be clear that when Osman Gazi left Konya he brought members of the old Seljuk dynasty to power as rulers or governors and kept in tact their rights and practices that were enjoyed by them in the past. In other words, Osman Gazi had set up Konya as a principality under his rule that existed for a long time. This act of Osman too lends support to the view that Osman Gazi was, undoubtedly a noble, generous and farsighted by all standards.

Chapter 20

Ottoman Empire

A brief note on Roman Empire

Osman Gazi was succeeded by his son Orkhan, the second in the Ottoman line. It seems expedient to describe what led to the emergence of the Roman Empire so that the conditions leading to successful campaigns and conquests of Orkhan can be comprehended.

Nearly six hundred years before the birth of Isa (Jesus), a virgin from Italy named Silviya gave birth to twin sons. One of them was named Romulas and the other was called Rimos. It is said that both were born of the seed of Mars. The virgin girl, Silviya was the priestess in the temple of the goddess Westa where she was conceived by the god Mars. Shortly after their birth, the boys Romulas and Rimos were put in a boat on the river and the waves pushed the two to a forest or to the foot of a mountain. A female wolf came and suckled them and began to take care of them. Accidentally a royal shepherd appeared, lifted both the babies and produced them before the king. The Queen brought them up under her care. After having grown up, they laid the foundation of a city, which came to be known as Rome or Roma. Their descendants founded such a terrible and magnificent Empire that it is counted among the greatest Empires that ever existed on the earth. Although the Empire founded by Romulas and Rimos disappeared, Rome is still the capital of Italy. At its highest point of power and development it was divided into two, giving birth to Eastern Rome and Western Rome. Eastern Rome had Constantinople as its capital while Rome itself was the center of Western Rome. Western Rome later came under constant attacks by savage people of northern Europe and Russia and lost much of its power and strength and, at last, it was also divided into two parts, Genoa and Venice. They had their separate governments, and with the passage of time, these two were also divided and subdivided into a number of independent states. However, Eastern Rome suffered fewer foreign attacks and a time came when Rome also came under the control of Constantinople. The Arabs and the Persians knew nothing about Western Rome. When the ruler of Constantinople confessed Christianity and propagated Christianity the Christian world held him in esteem and obeyed him. When almost all Europe came to the fold of Christianity, Caesar of Rome gained special prestige in Europe. When Christianity spread in Roman held territories, the Arabs and the Persians began to call every Christian a Roman. Since the Empire of Caesar of Constantinople was founded on the ruins of the Greek Empire and Caesar of Rome was in command of the territories once ruled by Alexander the Great of Greece, the Roman Empire also came to be called the Greek Empire. Since Asia Minor and Syria too were parts of the territory ruled by the Caesar of Constantinople, during the early days of Islam, Asia Minor was considered as a part of the Roman Empire. Even though Christian rule ended before long in some of these territories, its rule in Asia Minor remained for a long period. Thus, Asia Minor was popularly known and considered as Rome. When a section of the Seljuks set up their government in Asia Minor it came to be called the Seljuk State of Rome. When Osman Gazi I occupied most of Asia Minor, he also came to be known as the Sultan of Rome and Ottoman kings are referred to by this title even to this day.

When the Caesar of Constantinople accepted Christianity, this Christian state and the Magian state of Persia remained constantly at war with one another. These conflicts were still going on when the Islamic State in Arabia appeared on the scene and replaced them in the region. The Magian Empire broke into pieces and virtually ceased to exist shortly after the advent of Islam but the Christian Empire of Constantinople survived the onslaughts of Islam for a long time.

During the times of the rightly guided Caliphs, the Christian rule of the Caesar of Rome was routed in Syria, Palestine and Egypt. And the Umayyads and Abbasids were constantly at war with the Caesar of Rome. Asia Minor had been the cause of disagreements between the Muslims and the Christians for seven hundred years. Sometimes the Muslims pushed the Christians back as far the Danube pass (Iron Gate), and the Christians sent the Muslims back to Iran and Kurdistan. However, the reason behind the long stay of the Christian rule in Asia Minor was the feuds and civil wars among the various Muslim States.

But the Ottoman Turks did the needful and because of this, they became appreciated by the Muslims in general. The period we refer to here is one when the European forces had flooded the vast fields of Syria and Palestine repeatedly and every time they were driven back by the Muslim fighters. But, even though they lost battles, they enriched themselves with light and learning and something of the moral heights of the Muslims and used all these to educate and enlighten their own people. Thus, Europe embarked on a new way of life and showed signs of progress and development. The argument advanced by the European historians that the Roman Empire was then weak and negligent is quite misleading and a sheer travesty of facts. The Christians were then bubbling with rage against the Muslims and the Constantinople Court was playing a pivotal role in uniting the Christians for a decisive battle between the Cross and the Crescent. Constantinople was comparatively stronger and more powerful and knew the art of warfare better than most of the Christian powers. The Crusaders had brought all the warring powers together. Moreover, the Caesar of Constantinople used to establish friendship with powers antagonistic to the Muslims. Thus, Christian emissaries carried their mission of friendship up to China. They would offer even their daughters in marriage to attract their rivals to peace and friendship. Their heinous act of creating discord and dissension in the Muslim ranks and thus weakening them in not a new development of the present age but rather an old strategy. If the Muslims gave up feuds, civil wars and infightings no power on earth could stand in their way. Since Osman Gazi and his descendants were fully aware of this plain fact, they always spared themselves from armed conflict with the other Muslim states. They kept their resources preserved for combating the Christians.

Orkhan

Osman Gazi left behind two sons, Alauddin being the elder and Orkhan, the younger. Alauddin, although matchless in learning, insight, courage and determination, Osman Gazi was more impressed with the military acumen and fighting spirit of Orkhan, and so he appointed him as the successor to the throne. They were expected to fight for the throne. But Alauddin, who deserved the throne, preferred the will of his late father to his own rights and placed the crown on the head of his younger brother with pleasure and pledged his allegiance to him. He simply wanted a piece of land in a village to pass the rest of his life in perfect peace. But his younger brother wanted something else. He entreated his elder brother, with the active support of his courtiers, to accept the role of Prime Minister, which he did after some reluctance. Even though it was not highly respectable to become the Prime Minister of his younger brother, he made this sacrifice for the stability of their dynastic rule. He managed the affairs so adequately that his name might top the list of the persons who held that post.

Within one year of his accession, he expanded the borders of his country up to the Danube Pass and ended Christian occupation of Asia Minor. He, with the wise counsel of his elder brother, issued and enacted such orders and laws, which played a principal role in organizing and regulating the administrative affairs of the country. Until then, it was the common practice that military commanders were allotted small pieces of land free of levy, for this they had to provide the required number of soldiers when the country was at war. Thus, each feudal lord had to serve as a commander on the battlefield. A large number of Muslims lived in Asia Minor. However, northwestern Asia Minor had a Christian majority.

Janissaries

With the fall of the northwestern part of Asia Minor to the Ottoman Turks, a large number of Christian prisoners of war were brought to their capital and many more Christians settled in the Muslim territory as Dhimmi (non-Muslim citizens of an Islamic State).

Prime Minister Alauddin put into the mind of his younger brother that the big feudal fiefdoms possessed large armies and often posed a danger to the central rule. The feudal lords could use the influx of Christians against the central rulers. Thus it appeared wise that the young boys from the Christian prisoners and subjects be brought up and trained by the central power and an army be built out of them after teaching them Islam. This army was to be considered as the royal army and they were not expected to rise against the state. Moreover, they could prove their mettle as devout Muslims and in such a case, their relatives would not think of going against their own sons who made up the royal army. When the plan was put into practice and several thousand young Christian boys, when properly taught and trained, rose to such a respected position, the Christians themselves rushed for admission of their sons into these training centers. When the first batch of the young Christian trainees was posted as the bodyguards of the Sultan, he took them to a religions scholler for his blessings. The sage put his hand on the shoulder of a young trainee and invoked Allah's blessings for the new recruits, which was taken as a good omen. The teachings of Islam and exclusive military training made them very pious and devout Muslims on one hand and soldiers of the top rank on the other. These soldiers had nothing to do with their relatives and they were solely the virtuous servants of Islam and royal bodyguards. This wonderful army eliminated the danger of revolt against the central rule and the commanders and feudal lords could not even think of such an action. Prime Minister Alauddin opened new madrasas (schools) in different parts of the country and the Christians were given the same rights that the Muslims enjoyed. They were given full facilities to carry out their trade activities and allotted lands for their churches. This graceful behavior of the rulers caused large number of Christians to enter the fold of Islam. However, they were free to make their own choice regarding religion and accepted Islam on their own desores with full understanding of what they were doing.

This Janissary force was very modern. Alauddin brought about certain reforms in the army, gave it uniforms according to ranks, divided them into various regiments and made them follow military rules very strictly. One hundred, five hundred and one thousand soldiers were put under separate commands. The army was also divided into infantry and cavalry. A set of separate laws was enacted for the volunteers. Reforms were also made in the revenue department and separate civil and criminal courts in cities and towns were setup. Alauddin paid attention to the police and municipal departments. Tribes, which were fond of plunder and piracy, were given similar tasks to perform. They were organized as a separate force to be sent to enemy countries to terrorize them with their acts of plunder.

Prime Minister Alauddin paid special attention to construction works and built mosques, madrasas, hospitals and inns. He also constructed magnificent parks and palaces in big cities, bridges over the rivers, set up police posts along the roads and constructed roads to facilitate trade activities and military movements. He did everything he could do for the progress and development of Asia Minor and for the peace, integrity and solidarity of the country as a whole. For these reasons this territory remains the abode of the Turks and they are still going so strong within its bounds that no one could dare drive them out of this land.

The Caesar of Constantinople of the day had become disappointed with the loss of Asia Minor and the fall of many other occupied territories in Asia. In addition, he was apprehensive of the Turks landing on European coasts by crossing the sea. However, Orkhan preferred to consolidate the reforms and developmental works carried out by his elder brother Alauddin in Asia Minor than to expand their territory. He devoted twenty long and precarious years of his life to major reforms in all the departments of his administration. Had the following generations conformed they would have been ruling in Egypt, the Balkans, and Tripoli also.

Caesar's grandson rose in revolt against him. This civil war among the Christians proved somewhat advantageous to the Ottomans. The insurgents sought help from Prince Umar Beg the Turkish Governor of Iden. He crossed the sea with a fleet of 380 ships and an army of 28 thousand fighters and besieged the city of Demotika in Thrace, Greece. Afterwards, he took a detachment of two thousand cavalry soldiers and made progress into Serbia. Caesar held Umar Beg or

Umar Pasha back from helping the insurgents by giving him a substantial payment. Thereupon Umar Pasha returned to his province. However, Caesar's grandson went out of control, deposed Caesar and captured the throne. Following his death in 742 A.H. John Palaeologus ascended the throne of Constantinople. But, the late Caesar's grandson deposed Palaeologus and occupied the throne in 748 A.H. and ruled until 794 A.H. Two more Caesars replaced him until 857 A.H. after which the Turks occupied Constantinople. Soon after ascending the throne of Constantinople Caesar Cantacuzenus conceded Sultan Orkhan to be the ruler of Asia Minor and made all out efforts to establish good relations with the Sultan. Thus, Caesar sent word to Orkhan that he wanted to give his exquisitely beautiful daughter to him in marriage. Caesar knew that Orkhan was then 60 and his daughter was quite young. He was not unaware of the difference in religion. Orkhan accepted the offer and married Theodora, the daughter of Caesar. Thus, Caesar bought peace to strengthen his position militarily. But, eight years after this event, something strange took place. Venice and Genoa, the two strong naval powers clashed over coastal areas and ports. Since Genoa and the Caesar of Constantinople had serious territorial disputes both powers were hostile to each other therefore, Caesar wished success for Venice. Orkhan Gazi, on the other hand, hated Venice for its hostile activities on the southern coast of Asia Minor and Venice looked down upon Orkhan's Empire. Thus, Orkhan was felt compelled to lend his support to Genoa.

At last, Genoa and Venice the two entered into armed conflict near the Bosphorus Straits. Orkhan's son, Sulaiman Orkhan was the Governor of the nearby coastal province.

One night Sulaiman Orkhan took only forty men and landed on the European coast from a Genoese boat and conquered the fort at Gallipoli (Turkish: Gelibolu, historical: Callipolis) on the coast, which was a source of strength for Venice. Following this several thousand Turks joined their victorious prince at the fort. Genoa felt happy and encouraged at this new victory while the allies of Constantinople were greatly disappointed after this development. He was about to write to Orkhan to direct his son to vacate his occupation of the fort when Caesar himself faced a revolt by his other son-in-law. When Caesar found his capital under threat, he sought immediate help from Orkhan. Sultan Orkhan wrote to his son, Sulaiman to leave the fort in return for a substantial amount of money. Sulaiman was on the verge of acting upon the order of his father when a violent earthquake erupted and the city wall of Gallipoli fell to the ground creating greater terror and panic among the citizens. Assuming it a support from destiny the two commanders Azdi Beg and Ghazi Fazil, accompanying Sulaiman crossed the broken city-wall and captured Gallipoli. Immediately after the seizure Sulaiman, had the walls repaired and deployed a strong Turkish detachment there. Caesar lodged a complaint with Orkhan against the occupation of Gallipoli Fort. Orkhan wrote back that his son with sword did not conquer Gallipoli. The possession of the city took place by an accident of the city wall falling because of the earthquake. However, he would write to him to vacate the occupation. But, since Caesar was constantly in need of military help from Sultan Orkhan and was himself involved in family feuds, he did not put further pressure for the return of Gallipoli and Sulaiman continued the occupation. The occupation of Gallipoli was very necessary to Sulaiman because it kept safe the western coast of Asia Minor from being usurped by Venice. Two years after this event, Sulaiman suffered a fall from his horse and died in 759 A.H. while hunting a falcon.

Sulaiman was a very promising, brave and wise young leader. Orkhan felt terribly shocked at his tragic death. Had he lived he would have succeeded his father Orkhan. It was, in fact, a severe blow for a father like him who succumbed to his frustration in 761 A.H. at the age of 75 years, after reigning marvelously for 38 years.

Orkhan put his father's will and policy into practice with courage and caution and extended his borders up to the European coasts. Orkhan was wholly and solely interested in European campaigns. The reason he buried his son at the Danube pass instead of Bursa was that he didn't want the Turks to ever think of deserting the European coasts.

Murad I

In the wake of his elder son, Sulaiman's death Orkhan declared his younger son, Murad as the crown prince. Following the death of

Orkhan, Murad ascended the throne in 761 A.H. at the age of 40 years. He had a strong desire to expand his territory in Europe but revolt in the Turk Seljuk State of Karaman engaged his attention and he was preoccupied with the affairs of Asia Minor. However, he descended on the European shores, conquered Adrianople and renamed it Edirne and made it his capital and from 763 A.H. to the conquest of Constantinople by Sultan Muhammad II the capital remained at Edirne. In the wake of the conquest of Adrianople the people of Bulgaria and Serbia grew anxious. The Caesar of Constantinople sent his message to the Archbishop of Rome to deliver sermons on the Crusade and dispatch reinforcements from all over Europe. The Christian kings of Serbia and Bulgaria also became alert. Thus, the united Christian forces moved towards Andrianople in 765 A.H. Murad I sent his commander, Lala Shahin at the head of 20 thousand soldiers. The Muslim force took on several hundred thousand Christian troops two stages ahead of Adrianople. This handful of Muslim soldiers gave a smashing defeat to the huge Christian army. They fled the battlefield leaving behind a large number of dead and many captives. Lala Shahin moved forward and conquered large tracts of enemy territory.

When the Christians witnessed that Sultan Murad I had consolidated his position in Adrianople, they made another attempt in 778 A.H. to end the Muslim occupation of European land. Thus, the united forces from Serbia, Bulgaria, Hungary, Bosnia, Poland, Constantinople and the Pope of Rome marched ahead to wipe out Murad I and the Ottoman Empire. The Muslim army was traditionally less than one-fourth of the Christians' joint command but the result was the same and the huge Christian forces had to taste an ignominious defeat. The king of Serbia bought peace with an annual payment in silver the availability one thousand horsemen at the time of war for the service of Murad I, while the ruler of Bulgaria saved himself by offering his daughter in marriage and promising allegiance. Caesar of Constantinople presented three beautiful daughters one to be married to Murad I himself while the other two were to become wives of his two sons. Caesar now cast out of his mind the idea of driving Sultan Murad I out of Europe. Overtly he was now making all-out efforts to maintain good relations with the Sultan instead. While covertly, he was making secret efforts to get rid of the Sultan. With this purpose in view he bore the disgrace of visiting the Pope in Rome and seek his moral support and military help for the expulsion of the Muslim ruler. When his mission fell flat, he grew afraid of Murad I and to atone for this he sent his son Theoders to the Sultan to grace him by recruiting him for the Janissaries. Sultan Murad grew happy with this gesture.

During these days, Sultan Murad I had to leave for Asia Minor to put down certain revolts and uprisings and handed over the administration of his occupied European territories to his son, Sawji in Adrianople. In the absence of the Sultan, one of the sons of the Caesar of Constantinople named Andronecus came to Adrianople and instigated Sawji against his father Murad I after establishing intimate friendly relations with him. He first expressed his dissatisfaction over the attitude of his own father and then allured him into capturing power in the absence of his father who was then far away in Asia Minor. According to his plan, he first invited Sawji to move along with his army to make a joint attack on Constantinople and capture it and following the conquest of Constantinople, they would jointly capture power in Adrianople. Thus, the Christian prince entrapped Sawji with the lure of power. They jointly besieged Constantinople and declared their sovereignty. When Murad I came to know of this development he quickly managed the affairs of Asia Minor and rushed back to Adrianople. Both the princes hurriedly crossed a river and began preparations to take on Murad I. Having reached Adrianople Murad I wrote a strongly worded letter to Caesar Palaeologus to present himself before him and explain how such a silly and improper thing could have happened. Why did he create such a situation by sending his son to that of mine? Shocked and frightened he, claiming his innocence, gave word that he would side with him in all actions taken by him against the insurgent princes. On his part, he proposed that both the princes be arrested and killed. With this reply Sultan Murad I himself proceeded and encamped on his side of the river and crossed it alone and called out at the insurgent camp: "Those who come to me even now will be forgiven." Recognizing the king from his voice, almost all the soldiers came out of the camp and joined him. Thus, both the princes fled the camp along with a few Turks and Christians. But both of them were rounded up and produced before the Sultan.

He first called his son before him and had him blinded and killed. Caesar's son was sent to his father in chains with the message that he should punish him as he had himself punished his own son. Caesar found himself in a terrible dilemma, as he could neither kill his son by his own hand nor invite the wrath of Murad I. However, he preferred to please the Sultan and blinded his son by dropping acid in his eyes but left him alive. Murad I became happy with Caesar when he knew that his order was carried out and did not object to his son being alive. But in fact, Caesar's son had not lost his eyesight completely and he regained it after some time.

In 789 A.H. Karaman Turks revolted against Murad I in the western part of Asia Minor. In a fight near Konya Murad I's son, Bayazid made a quick charge at his enemy and routed them. Being happy at the bravery and courage of his son he conferred upon him the title of Yaldaram or Yil'diram (lightning). Since the Turk Chieftain was also the son-in-law of Murad I, his daughter saved her husband by entreating her father to pardon his fault.

Sultan Murad I then left on a visit to Asia Minor. The crusading spirit and fiery speeches of the bishops all over Europe had plunged all of Europe into a fiery fury against the Muslims and in the wake of the fall of Romiliya and some other territories, their blood boiled. Murad was sitting in Asia Minor unaware of these new developments throughout Europe that in Serbia, Bulgaria, Albania, Hungary, Glacia, Poland, Germany, Austria, Italy, and Bosnia they had united to annihilate the Ottoman dynasty. In 791 A.H., Murad I received the shocking news while in Bursa, that the twenty thousand troops kept at Romiliya had been exterminated by Christian forces. The entire occupied territory in Europe along with the capital, Adrianople lay under threat of European assault. With the receipt of this news, Murad I reached Adrianople and took charge of the affairs. In 792 A.H. Ali Pasha, the commander of Murad I subdued the King of Bulgaria and forced him to obey once again. The king of Serbia gathered the forces of the different Christian countries at the borders of Serbia and Bosnia and after setting up his camp there, he himself threw a challenge to fight. Murad I was also ready for a decisive battle. He assumed charge of his entire army and appeared on the battlefield of Kosovo. When the Christians found the Muslim troops one-fourth of their number, they felt doubly encouraged. Since they had occupied the field from before, they had regained their freshness and energy unlike the Muslim army, which had arrived at the spot after continuous fighting and enduring a hard journey and were completely exhausted. Moreover, the Christians were well acquainted with the environs and surroundings of the area for they had friends, relatives and co-religionists there. With the arrival of the Muslim army, both the parties went into long consultations in their respective camps during the night. Some of the Christian commanders were of the opinion that the Muslim troops should be sniped at and exterminated before the daybreak. However, other commanders, filled with the pride and conviction of their victory spoke against this, pleading that a night attack would provide the Muslims an opportunity to flee in the darkness of night, and they did not like to spare a single soul. The Muslims, on the other hand, seemed awe-struck with the size of the Christian army. During consultations in the royal assembly, some Muslim commanders proposed rows of camels of burden to be set against the enemy fighters to serve as living fortifications. Moreover, during the fight these camels would strike fear into enemy horses setting their battle lines in disorder. However, Bayazid Yaldaram, the elder son of the Sultan differed for the reason that such a deceptive device was tantamount to declaring their weakness and fear. He wanted to take on the enemy in the open field. Thus, amidst conflicting views and suggestions, Sultan Murad I could not arrive at a decision. Furthermore, he experienced with anxiety the arrival of a strong dusty wind that had begun to blow against the Muslim troops covering their eyes and faces with dirt. It was certainly very injurious to the Muslim's fighting temper and spirit. Finding no way out Sultan Murad I fell prostrate, invoking Allah's help and succor in this hour of distress. His prayer continued until morning. He was crying in distress with his head touching the ground, saying: "This is the fight between Islam and infidelity; look not at our sins but protect the honor of Your Messenger (ﷺ) and his Righteous Religion". These prayers attracted the Blessings of Allah and it began to rain heavily by the evening settling the dirt and dust and making the weather pleasant. The rain and wind stopped after a while and the battle lines were drawn. Murad I put the feudal forces to the right under Prince Bayazid Yaldaram and those from the Asian territories to the left under Prince Yaqub, while Murad I himself took over the command of his bodyguards putting them in the center. He then sent irregular horsemen and infantry as the vanguard. The center of the army on the Christian side was under the command of Lazers, the king of Serbia, the right wing was given to his nephew, the left to the king of Bosnia. Both the armies clashed and kept fighting firmly until noon. Sultan Murad I had an iron mace and was striking dead anyone who faced him. Now the Christian troops showed signs of yielding and were uprooted at last. The Muslim fighters expedited their assaults and rounded up the king of Serbia, the Commander-in-Chief of the Christian army. They fled the battlefield leaving behind hundreds of thousands of Christians dead and almost all the prominent commanders as captive. When the King of Serbia was produced before Murad I, he ordered to keep him safe in prison. But a Serbian commander's cunning changed the jubilation of victory into deep sorrow. While running with the defeated ones he, all of a sudden, turned his horse towards the chasing Muslims and requested them to catch him alive and bring him before their king for he hated Christians and liked to join the Muslim camp after disclosing some important secrets directly to the Sultan. Moreover, he had decided to embrace Islam at that time. Thus, the Muslims caught him alive and produced him to the Sultan along with others, narrating what led to his arrest. The Sultan grew happy and called him near. He moved ahead very respectfully and put his head on the feet of the Sultan. This respectful gesture convinced the Sultan and his courtiers of his utmost loyalty. Now, raising his head from the Sultan's feet he took out a dagger from under his garment and struck it into his chest. The Sultan sustained a deep injury and those in attendance tore the Serb to pieces. When the wounded Sultan felt sure of his death, he ordered the assassination of the captive King of Serbia, which was implemented at once. After a while, the Sultan succumbed to his injuries. Bayazid Yaldaram succeeded his father. The Battle of Kosovo proved beyond doubt that even the allied forces of all Europe were unable to drive the Muslims out of their lands. Along with this, the battle put an end to the Christian invasions and crusades, for they had grown anxious for their own safety. The thought of conquering Syria had now left their minds. The Christians were now convinced that their numerical superiority was no match for the spirit and enthusiasm of the Muslim fighters. This defeat of the Christians is reckoned among the most horrible defeats they had ever tasted. This splendid victory rooted the Muslim's feet firmly and permanently onto European soil. The Christians of Spain and France who were once planning to put an end to the Muslim rule in Granada were now in a state of constant terror and gave the Muslims ample concessions and facilities of their own.

Sultan Murad I died at the age of 23 after ruling for 32 years. He was buried in Bursa. Murad I was a wise, courageous, devout and dervish like man.

Sultan Bayazid Khan Yaldaram

In 793 A.H., the second year of his succession, Sultan Bayazid Yaldaram heard that efforts were on against the Muslim rule and that Serbia and Bosnia were on the verge of revolt. Bayazid hurried to Europe and annexed the territory from Bosnia to the Danube River and extended his kingdom from the Euphrates to the Danube in Walachia (a principality on the lower Danube River). Serbia and Bosnia had become tributaries of Sultan Bayazid. In Persia, on the other hand, the Mongol Genghezids had lost their unity and integrity and broken into a number of small states ruled over by various members of the Genghezid House and were at odds with each other. In view of Bayazid's power and grandeur, the Caesar of Constantinople wrote a letter to Bayazid that since he (Caesar) was then in possession nothing more than Macedonia and some small Islands and these should be left to him in lieu of his sincere support for him. Bayazid Yaldaram granted his entreaty and left him free to rule his territories. Now, after buying peace from Bayazid he devoted his time and resources to hatching a plot against him. He sent his emissaries to Iran, Khorasan, Persia, Syria, and Iraq. He also attempted to establish friendly relations with the Muslim kings of Asia. The Muslim rulers of

Armenia, Kurdistan and Azerbaijan were, on the other hand, knocking at the door of western Asia Minor. Bayazid could easily crush the Turkmen of Asia Minor but his sénse of Muslim brotherhood held him back. The Ottoman dynasty from the very beginning had made it their directive principle to avoid conflict with the Muslim rulers and devote all time and resources in waging holy wars on the Christians and transform them into a civilized and enlightened people under the influence of Islamic culture and civilization. Thus, Bayazid also followed this tactic of his ancestors and never showed any interest in conquering Muslim territories. But in the wake of invasions by the Turkmen into Bayazid's territories in Asia Minor he was forced to proceed to Asia Minor in 795 A.H. and brought peace to the troubled areas by defeating, capturing and killing his enemies. The same year Bayazid obtained the title of Sultan form Mustasim Billah, the Abbasid Caliph of Egypt. Thus, Bayazid became the first "Sultan" of the Ottoman Empire as kings before him were called "Amir."

Sultan Bayazid was a brave man with all the traits of a soldier. However, he absented himself from campaigns from 795 A.H. to 799 A.H. and kept confined to his old capital, Adrianople and other parts of Asia Minor. However, he came to know in 799 A.H. that the allied forces of Europe were making serious preparations under the command of king Sajmund of Hungary. France and England had also joined the European camp against the Ottoman Empire. Even though Caesar of Constantinople was totally behind their hostile activities, he could not dare stand openly against Bayazid. The Ottoman ruler dashed into Europe with lightning speed. He witnessed the European nations mad with rage against the Ottoman rule for the Pope of Rome had already issued his verdict that anyone joining the crusade would be absolved from all sins. A short time before that France and England were involved in war but the Pope and other influential Christians brought peace between them and turned the waves of war against the Muslims as a whole. A separate strong army from Burgundy was also sent to Hungary under the Duke of Burgundy to reinforce the army under the command of the king of Hungary. Besides a huge force from France was mobilized under three cousins of the king of France namely, James, Philip and Henry. Forces from Germany, Pomerania (northwestern part of Poland on the Baltic Sea), Austria, Italy and Jerusalem concentrated in Hungry. The Christian king of Walachia (a principality on the lower Danube River) who had already offered his allegiance to Sultan Bayazid Yaldaram also joined the bandwagon when the Christian forces passed through his territory. However, the king of Serbia could only lend his secret support. Nevertheless, it deserves notice that the present Christian forces were not only armed to the teeth, it consisted of the bravest and most seasoned soldiers of the Christian world. The commanders of this army were so confident of their victory that they said most arrogantly and in one voice: "Even if the sky falls today we shall lift it at the point of our swords". The Christian army marched to the Ottoman Empire through two routes via Walachia and Serbia. Reaching within the bounds of Ottoman Empire, Sajmund, the king of Hungary and Commander-in-Chief of the allied forces ordered the invasion and the Christian troops began to conquer one city after another and every conquered city was reduced to ashes. Nobody was spared including young and old, women and children. Bayazid was informed of these reverses after a number of Ottoman cities had been totally destroyed. He hurried from Asia Minor to Adrianople. It was likely that Sajmund should have reached Andrianople by the time Sultan Bayazid would arrive and the latter would therefore suffer setbacks. But loot and arson on the way delayed his movements and provided Bayazid with many opportunities to organize his army and resources and to move ahead to face the enemy.

The Christians were still unaware of the approaching Muslim troops. When the spies communicated to Duke of Burgundy that the Muslim army was not far away, he left his lunch with other French commanders and requested Sajmund for an opportunity to be allowed to be at the vanguard.

Sultan Bayazid Yaldaram kept his forty thousand strong force behind an embankment so that the Christians could not measure the actual strength of the Muslim fighters. Following this, he mobilized his irregular detachment ahead. The French cavalry moved forward from the opposite side, while Sajmund followed it at a slower pace. The French cavaliers crushed the irregular Muslim troops in the vanguard and ascended the embankment in a fit of zeal after gaining an initial success. The Muslim detachments took advantage of the situation and moved behind the French invaders on the embankment. Thus, the Christian troops in the vanguard were besieged and smashed by the Turkish soldiers and very few of them escaped death to tell the story of their complete rout. The Christian camp became terrified. Following this Bayazid launched a massive attack with such immeasurable zeal and fervor that it came to them as a great shock. Bayazid's army worked like an iron mace, which demolished the sand walls of the Christians wherever it hit. Even though Bavaria, Austria and Hungry fought with determination, the ferocious swords of the Muslim army did not allow them to live any longer. The battle, which was fought on a very large scale, came to its logical end in a very short time. Never before had such a huge Christian army been routed so ignominiously in spite of being so large in numbers and resources. Sajmund, the king of Hungary fled for his life. A number of princes, dukes and commanders were either killed or caught. The Duke of Burgundy was among the captives. Not less than one hundred and fifty thousand Christian soldiers lost their lives on the battlefield. Following the victory the Sultan came to inspect the battlefield and found it covered with dead bodies. Since he also found the bodies of Muslim soldiers as well, he while expressing regret over their sacrifice, showed his determination to avenge their blood. He then ordered the captives to be brought before him. The prisoners were divided into several parts. Ordinary soldiers were made slaves and distributed among the Muslim troops while others were put to death. The Christian commanders' both their arms were tied behind their backs and sent to some of the big cities to highlight the Muslim victory over the Christians. A section comprising of princes and dukes and sovereign rulers numbering twenty-five including the Duke of Burgundy was brought to the Sultan. The Sultan took them and came to Bursa, his Asian capital. He then called all of them and said, "You people unnecessarily took the trouble of invading our territories, and I am myself determined to invade Hungary, Austria, France, Germany and Italy. I have resolved to feed my horse at the altar of St. Peter. I shall, therefore, meet you in your countries and I shall be very happy if you come to the battlefield with greater preparations than you made for our last battle. Had I feared you in the least I would have released you on your promise that you will never rise against me. Instead I insist on you to go to your respective countries and plunge into making hasty preparations against me." Saying this Bayazid set all the princes and commanders free.

Shortly after this, he hurried to Europe at the head of a strong army. He turned to Greece first, conquered Athens in 800 A.H. and dispatched 30 thousand Greeks to be settled in Asia minor. He then sent his commanders to Austria and Hungry along with troops and they won most parts of those countries. Being aware of the intriguing activities of the Caesar of Constantinople Bayazid decided to conquer and put an end to that Christian rule, but Caesar saved the situation once again on the promise of building a mosque in Constantinople for the Muslims with a Muslim Qadi (judge) to look after their affairs and provide all possible facilities for the Muslim traders besides paying a huge amount annually in tribute. Bayazid accepted to these conditions and left Constantinople.

However, Bayazid's conquests of Greece and Athens sent terror into the heart of Caesar and he sent an envoy to Timur (Tamerlane) with a letter delineating: "My dynasty exists from the days of old and we have been ruling Constantinople since the days of the Last Prophet and the Rightly Guided Caliphs. We have signed peace treaties with the Umayyads and the Abbasids and none among them ever desired to conquer Constantinople. But at present, the Ottoman Empire has annexed our territories and has its evil eye on Constantinople. In the wake of the existing situation, I find no way but to seek your help. Bayazid is making victory after victory in Europe and his power is expanding rapidly and, I am sure, he will invade your territories once he is free from his European campaigns and you will then find him a formidable adversary. Besides, Bayazid had given Sultan Ahmad Jalair and Qara Yusuf Turkman a place of respect in his kingdom when they had revolted against you and they have kept instigating Bayazid to invade your country. It is tantamount to showing utter disrespect on you when your opponent is so important and you are unable to do anything in this connection. Now it is the clear demand of the situation that you make no delay in launching an attack on Asia Minor and save me from the disastrous activities of Bayazid. I am ready to lend my help and support to you in your action within my power and resources." Even though the letter carried Caesar's selfish feelings and Timur was not so gullible to be entrapped by these words the issue of giving shelter to rebels did not go out of his mind. Caesar's letter came to Timur at a time when he was staying at Haridawar on the bank of the river Ganges in India. Timur read the letter and sent back the envoy in a hurry without showing any reaction. Although he was planning to attack the eastern provinces of India, the content of the letter agitated his mind in a way that he lost interest in further advances and the consolidation of his conquests and hurried to Samarkand. In Samarkand, he made all-out preparations against the Ottoman Empire to establish exactly who was worthy of being called the conqueror of the world. Bayazid was on his mission to feed his horse at the famous church of St. Peter after conquering Hungary and Austria when he came to know that Caesar was working hard to join hands with Timur against him. Although he had no fear of Timur nor was he sure that Timur would fight with him in support of Caesar, he decided to teach a lesson to Caesar.

Timur, on the other hand, arrived at the western border of Asia Minor and created large-scale loot, arson and carnage in Azerbaijan and Armenia and brought a reign of terror all over the region. Now the frontiers of Bayazid's Empire were within his reach. In the wake of Timor's conquest of Azerbaijan Bayazid dispatched a detachment under the command of his son Tughril. But Timur practiced caution and instead of plunging into a direct fight based his strategy on slow movements towards the cherished goal. First, he dispatched circulars to all his occupied territories ordering his seasoned soldiers and selected forces to join his camp without loss of time. Moreover, he had a large number of men under the guise of beggars, mendicants, Sufis, sermonizers, traders and tourists to enter the frontiers of Ottoman Empire. Furthermore, he sent expert and experienced spies into the forces of Sultan Bayazid to contact the Mongol soldiers forming part of the Ottoman army and cavalry to instill in their mind that their real leader and ruler was none but Timur and, hence, to fight under the banner of Bayazid Yaldaram, the Turkish ruler was nothing short of treachery, dishonesty and dishonor. This secret invasion of Timur worked wonders, and a big section of the Ottoman soldiers lost interest in the victories of Bayazid. The spies also put into the minds of the Mongol soldiers that while they were victims of Bayazid's miserliness Timur was very generous in matters of his soldiers' salaries and general welfare and spoils of war.

Being satisfied with these preliminaries Timur thought it proper to first conquer Syria and Egypt so that Bayazid could get no help from those two countries. He then wrote a letter to Bayazid to hand over the rebel, Qara Yusuf Turkman, otherwise he would invade his country. Following this he attacked Syria in 803 A.H. After the conquest of Syria and Egypt, Timur marched to Baghdad and conquered it also. He was in Baghdad when he received the reply to his letter from Bayazid, who rejected his demand with utter contempt.

Timur anticipated such a reply and had set himself to make preparations much before his writing the letter to Bayazid. However, he left Baghdad in a hurry and reached Azerbaijan and devoted his time and energy to organizing supply, communication and intelligence departments anew. Bayazid, on the other hand, sent an army headed by Qara Yusuf Turkman to vacate the Mongol occupation of Syria and do away with Timor's Governors, and he himself marched to take on Timur.

Timur had invaded the frontier city of Sivas where Bayazid's son, Artughril was stationed as a garrison commander. Artughril and his troops shut themselves in the fort and fought a defensive battle. However, Timur besieged the fort and used his devices to break the fort. He dug under the very foundations of the fort from the outside. When pits were formed at different spots under the walls the wooden beams that were set in those pits were set on fire with the result the walls sank in. Thus, finding no way out the inmates of the fort surrendered and were rounded up. They were four thousands in all. As Timur had applied a new device to sink the fort into the ground, so likewise he used a horrible and novel way of giving punishment. Instead of sparing their lives he ordered that their arms be tied behind their backs and fastened their heads to their knees like a bundle and threw them all into the deep trenches dug for this purpose. He then bridged the trenches with wooden planks and poured earth on it. Thus, the captives were all buried alive.

When Bayazid Yaldaram heard of these inhuman atrocities meted out to his son and his four thousand soldiers he boiled with anger and lost his balance and this was exactly the reaction that Timur wanted to produce in Bayazid. It was a situation where Timur was practicing calm and composure while Bayazid had not only lost his temper but his mental balance also.

Bayazid had the information that Timur had with him 5 hundred thousand selected soldiers. Bayazid was in great haste to avenge the blood of his son and so he took with him as many soldiers as he could and marched to Sivas where his son was buried alive and where his enemy was lying with his troops. Being informed that Bayazid was on way to Sivas with lightening speed, Timur played a trick and left Sivas at a time when he was sure that Bayazid could not change his route and shifted to Ankara and besieged it. When Bayazid arrived in Sivas, the sight of his son's burial ground turned him mad with anger and when he came to know that Timur had shifted to Ankara, which lay in the heart of Asia Minor, he could not put up with the loss of a moment to have his revenge. Had he practiced caution he would have first sent word to the Syrian and Egyptian commanders to make advance towards Timur, and he himself could have made all out efforts to cut all the supply lines of Timur. Moreover, he would have allowed Timur to move towards the western cities even at the cost of their destruction for those cities were thickly inhabited by Turks, the staunch supporters of the Ottoman Empire and could then target Timur on all sides. Thus, Timur could easily be surrounded and caught. But Timur expected no such acute sense of wisdom from Bayazid and he proved perfectly correct. Bayazid, in his fit of burning anger, rushed to Ankara with such a rage and speed that, out of 4 hundred thousand troops he could only arrive with one hundred and twenty thousand at the break neck speed he was traveling at and due to their continuous movement they were completely exhausted. It was a blunder that Bayazid committed and he had to pay dearly for it.

At the time when Bayazid reached near Ankara with his extremely tired army, Timur was there with his troops physically fresh and ready to combat his enemy. Besides, Timur had encamped at a place strategically very important and advantageous and he had dug trenches at various spots.

Bayazid came and, in order to show disrespect to Timor's military strength, led his troops to a high hilly spot to hunt wild animals. Thus, the exhausted army, instead of taking sometime to rest and regain freshness they were overtaken by more exhaustion. In addition, the soldiers had to go without water with the result that about five thousand soldiers died of thirst and the rest became disillusioned at his whimsical behavior. On his return, Bayazid found that his camp had already been captured by the enemy who had also turned the coarse of the stream that was to provide water for the Turkish soldiers. Now the military acumen of Timur and his strategies had already won the battle. Bayazid was left with no choice but to lead his thirsty and extremely exhausted soldiers against an enemy much superior in number, strength, strategy, spirit and freshness.

The Battle of Ankara

On Dhul Hijjah 19, 804 A.H. (July 20, 1402 A.C.) battle lines were drawn between Bayazid and Timur and troops from both sides came out to measure swords and the battle came to its logical end by sunset. Bayazid had to combat against five to eight hundred thousand fresh troops of Timur with his one hundred and twenty thousand exhausted and disillusioned soldiers. Besides, as was expected, the Mongol section deserted Bayazid during the fight and the Christian commanders showed weakness and timidity and turned the whole event into a disaster for the Ottomans. However, the principal reason behind this smashing defeat was Bayazid's shortsightedness and indiscretion. His idiocies and wild zealotry could not bring him anything else. Timur, on the other hand, showed patience, far-sightedness, military acumen and strategy of the highest order at every step. However, the backbreaking defeat of Bayazid caused immense and immeasurable loss to the world of Islam and Europe, which could easily have become a Muslim land but because of the defeat of Bayazid slipped into Christian hands.

Amir Timur had his battle-line as follows:

Prince Mirza Shah Rukh was put as commanding officer of the right wing which had forces commanded by Khalil Sultan-Sulaiman Shah, Rustam Birlas Sonjak Bahadur, Musa, Tawi Bugha, Amir Yadgar etc. Mirza Sultan Husain was heading a strong force to reinforce the right wing.

The left wing was commanded by Nuruddin Jalair, Barmazag Birlas, Ali Fanjain, Mubash'shere, Sultan Sanjar Birlas, Umar ibn Taban etc. and Prince Miran Shah was appointed as their commanding officer. The detachment to reinforce the left wing was under the joint command of Abu Bakr Amir Jahan Birlas and Pir Ali Salduz.

The right side of the main body comprised commanders like Tash Timur, Aghlan Uzbek, Ahmad Jalal Yusuf, Baba Hajji Suji, Sikandar Hindu Bogha, Khawaja Ali Airwi, Daulatemur, Muhammad Faujain and Idris Qarchi etc. while Beg Wali, Elchikdai Hari Malik, Arghun Malik Sufi Khalil, Esan Timur, Sanjar, Husain and Umar Beg, sons of Nekroz, Jon Arbani, Beri Beg Faujain, and Zirak Birles were given charge of reinforcements.

The left side of center was given to Tawak'kal Qara'qara, Ali Mahmud, Shah Wali, Sunjak Tankari, Bezish Khawaja Muhammad Khalil, Luqman, Sultan Birlas, Mirak Pir Muhammad, Shankram, Sheikh Aslan Ilyas, Kapak Khani, Daulat Khawaja Birlas, Yufus Birlas, and Ali Qabchag while its reinforcement was handed over to Muhammad Sultan, Pir Muhammad, Iskander, Shah Malik, Ilyas Khawaja, and Shamsuddin.

The above divisions of army apart, Timur took charge of the forty strong squads to be kept reserved for reinforcing the side needing it. Besides, he had employed a large number of mountain-like war elephants, which were put ahead of the army rows, while Bayazid had none.

Sultan Bayazid handed over the left wing to Sulaiman Chalpi, the right wing to his Christian brother-in-law, the brother of his wife, while he himself headed the main body and kept behind his three sons, Musa, Isa and Mustafa.

With the beat of the war drums, brave soldiers from both sides fell upon each other. The fight between the two was going on when Prince Abu Bakr launched such a massive attack on the Turkish army that it fell into complete disorder. Immediately after that, Sultan Husain made another attack on Sulaiman while Muhammad Sultan launched the third assault. Noticing reverses in the left wing of the Turkish troops, Muhammad rushed to reinforce Sulaiman Chalpi. The Turkish army fought so firmly and gallantly that the Mongols, despite their superior number, had to retreat to a plateau. Bayazid, in a fit of anger, lost his head and the fact that he was the Commander-in-Chief of his army went out of his mind. Instead of keeping an eye on the entire battlefield, he kept himself engaged throughout with the task of driving back attacks of the main body of the Mongols and he achieved his purpose. Now, without looking towards the right and left wings of his army and taking care of their needs, he ascended the Plateau and occupied it by dislodging six major Mongol commanders.

Timur, on the other hand, had his eyes on every part of the battlefield and was watching every move without getting directly involved in the fight. Like a seasoned commander, he was pushing ahead and drawing back his troops according to the need of the hour. When he noticed Bayazid's victorious advance, he directed his fresh squads to charge at the right and left wings of his enemy with the result Bayazid was separated from a greater part of his army. At this juncture, the Mongol troops deserted Bayazid's army and joined the Mongol camp and caused great harm to the Turkish battle line. Now Timur had the opportunity he was waiting for. He ordered his army to make an all-out attack on the enemy with the result Bayazid's right wing leader was killed in action and his wife's brother, a Christian commander fled the battlefield in a wretched condition. Bayazid himself was surrounded on all sides. But, in such a crucial moment, Bayazid and his devoted soldiers showed their mettle with their swordsmanship in a manner that they alone could do. Bayazid alone was more than a match for the Mongols and pushed them back wherever he made his swift but deadly charge. At times, he tore apart Mongol lines and reached the spot from where Timur was directing his soldiers. Now the darkness of night enveloped the surroundings and Bayazid, the Turkish lion was captured alive falling from his tumbling horse, while his devoted fighters had already laid down their lives and with his capture were laid to rest all the hopes of the Muslim world to conquer Europe.

If nature is not transformed man has it in his nature to admire its nobility. In spite of being a beast, the lion is held in high esteem by everyone throughout the world. Man likes to be likened to a lion and even though the ox and horse are so useful, nobody likes to be compared with them. The fame of Rustam and the greatness and glory of Khalid bin Waleed and Salahuddin Ayyubi center around their acts of valor. The event of Rustam's assassination as mentioned in *Shahnama* fills us with grief. When a valiant fighter meets with failure, we feel offended and Sultan Bayazid Yardarm's capture on the battlefield of Ankara is a soul-shattering tragedy of human history.

Had Timur been defeated in the battlefield of Ankara it would have been the loss solely of Timur and his dynasty not of Islam as a whole. In such a case the territories under the occupation of Timur would have been given to another Muslim king and not to forces antagonistic to Islam but Bayazid's defeat was a total loss for Islam, for the Muslim's advance towards Europe came to halt all of a sudden, reviving a Europe that was breathing its last.

Had the result of the battle gone in favor of Bayazid it could be linked to the battle fought in the battlefield of Asia Minor in 463 A.H. when Sultan Alp Arsalan Seljuk gave a severe beating to two to three hundred thousand Christian troops with his twelve thousand fighters or the third battle of Panipat where eighty thousand Muslim soldiers routed five or six hundred thousand Hindu troops. History bears witness to the glaring fact that whenever a small army clashed with a huge one the Muslim force was always much less in number but in the battle between Bayazid and Timur, both sides had Muslim fighters to combat one another.

Prior to this unfortunate clash one Muslim emperor named Bayazid Yaldararm had gone up to France and was knocking at the door of England while Timur, another mighty Muslim ruler had stormed the eastern world up to China and Japan and the marching steps of the Mongols had not been exhausted. There was none to stop Bayazid in Europe and Timur was more than a match for everyone in the east. Thus, almost the entire world would have watched the flags of Islam flying over it. But history had something very shocking in store for the world of Islam. The battleground of Ankara drew both forces of Islam to clash and it was the ground where the hopes of European conquest were laid to rest forever.

Bayazid's son, Musa was also captured with his father while Princes Muhammad and Isa fled the battlefield for life. Timur put Bayazid in an iron cage and kept him so through out his journeys. To keep in such a disgraceful confinement a mighty king like Bayazid and to put his defeat and dishonor on display did not befit a brave fighter and great king like Timur. His treatment was much below the standard of a valiant soldier and noble soul. Brave and noble minded persons show great respect to their worst enemies particularly when they are at their mercy. When Alp Arsalan Sejuk arrested the Caesar of Constantinople on the battleground of Maladhkurd, he released him with due honors and restored the occupied country to him. When the Raja of Punjab was arrested and produced before Alexander of Greece, he was not only released with honor and given back his rule but was allotted even more. Bayazid himself had arrested twenty-five princes on the battlefield of Nicopolis but set them free asking them to make more preparations for another round.

Unfortunately, the treatment meted out to a matchless fighter like Bayazid is a scar on the face of Timur. Although Timur had kept Bayazid, the Ottoman lion, in a manner a lion is kept in a cage it is not an acceptable sort of poetic simile. The point is that the good sense of Timur could not make a difference between man and animal.

The insult and indignity that Bayazid had to bear in the wake of his setback in Ankara was so heavy that he did not remain alive for more than eight months. The only act of grace on the part of Timur was that he handed over the dead body of Bayazid to his son, Musa and released him to take it to be buried in Bursa.

Timor's military activities remained centered on plundering Muslim territories and he never found in him a desire to wage war against the non-Muslims and propagate Islam in their territories. However, Timur also did not live long after the tragic death of Bayazid. He arrived in Samarkand and marched ahead to conquer China, his only campaign against a non-Muslim country, but Allah Almighty did not allow him to accomplish it, and he died on the way.

Bayazid's Sons at War

Following the defeat at Ankara there was, apparently, no hope of the survival of the Ottoman Empire, for Timur had distributed among the

Seljuks the small states of Asia Minor ruled by them prior to the conquest of Bayazid Yaldaram. In some parts, Timur had carved out new States.

When leaving for Asia Minor to fight with Timur, Bayazid had left his son, Sulaiman in Adrianople as his deputy. The Turkish disaster in the battle of Ankara encouraged the Christians to restore their lost territory, with the result all the occupied parts save Adrianople and its suburbs slipped out of the Ottoman Empire. The Caesar of Constantinople too, who was restlessly awaiting the outcome of the battle, found in himself a burning desire to expand his territory. Although apparently at peace, the Christian powers were still under the psychological fear arising out of their defeats and disasters in the past and hence they could not muster courage enough to force the Ottomans from Adrianople. Except for small pieces of European land and Asia Minor, the Ottoman Empire had lost everything. And, to add fuel to the fire, Bayazids' sons rose against each other in internecine fighting for the throne.

Bayazid Yaldaram had seven or eight sons and five or six had survived the Battle of Ankara. Sulaiman was substituting for his father in Adrianople; Musa was in prison along with his father; Isa who fled Ankara to Bursa had become its ruler; Muhammad, the youngest and the most worthy son of Bayazid was still ruling over a city in Asia Minor; and Qasim who was totally devoid of courage and determination lived with either Muhammad or Isa. Thus in the wake of Bayazid's captivity, Muhammad and Isa had their separate rules in the remaining Ottoman territories, while Sulaiman was in possession of the European territory under Ottoman rule.

Isa and Muhammad clashed with one another to establish their claim over all the parts of Asia Minor under Ottoman administration. After a fierce fight, Muhammad defeated Isa and the latter fled Asia Minor and joined his brother, Sulaiman in Adrianople. He then pressed Sulaiman to win his lost territory for him. Sulaiman captured Bursa and Ankara. What a misfortune that Bayazid's sons were at war with one another at a time when he was suffering captivity at the hands of Timur. Amid their burning desire to capture power, they must have forgotten their father passing his days in disgrace.

During the days Sulaiman was fighting with Muhammad in Asia Minor Bayazid Yaldaram breathed his last in a state of utter distress and Musa was carrying the dead body of his father home. Unfortunately, a Seljuk squad of Qarmania arrested Musa on the way. On hearing this, Muhammad wrote the Seljuk ruler to act gracefully to release his brother, Musa so that he, along with Musa, could fight with Sulaiman. The Seljuk ruler granted his submission without loss of time in order to gain benefit from the infighting of the Ottoman camp. Musa joined his brother, Muhammad immediately after the burial of his father. Since Musa had accompanied his father, Bayazid during his days in captivity, Ottoman nobles and soldiers held him in great veneration and Muhammad felt more encouraged and powerful and the battlefields of Asia Minor began to spit fire and blood. Muhammad and Musa on one side and Sulaiman and Isa on the other, each was thirsty of one another's blood. At last, Isa lost his life but Sulaiman fought firmly and did not allow his brothers to win the battle. Finding no way out Musa asked his brother Muhammad to give him a detachment to conquer the Ottoman occupied territories in Europe so that Sulaiman should turn to his European possessions giving up his campaigns in Asia Minor. Muhammad liked this suggestion and Musa reached Adrianople with his troops. As expected, Sulaiman rushed to the spot with the result a fierce battle broke out between Musa and Sulaiman. Sulaiman being the elder son and claiming for himself all the territories under Ottoman rule would not do any favors for his military commanders to keep them happy and spirited. Since Musa and Muhammad were making all out efforts to wrest power from Sulaiman but considered their claim weaker owing to their being younger, they showed more respect to the feelings of their commanders and kept them emotionally attached to their cause, with the result they preferred Musa to Sulaiman and brought about the defeat of Sulaiman. Defeated and dejected, Sulaiman was going to the Caesar of Constantinople when he was captured and assassinated on the way in 813 A.H. Now only two brothers were left to rule and thus the European part of the Ottoman rule went to Musa and Muhammad occupied the Asian Territory.

Musa then decided to punish the Caesar of Constantinople for his support of Sulaiman but he first turned to Stephen, the ruler of Serbia for he had favored Sulaiman openly. He invaded Serbia and gave it a smashing defeat with the result the Christians were overtaken by great terror. This victory won by Musa removed from the Christian mind any thought about the weakness of the Ottomans. Following this Musa besieged Constantinople.

Caesar was very shrewd and alert. During this period, Musa was engaged in Serbia, he established very cordial relations with Muhammad who was then ruling over some parts of Asia Minor and annexing the small States carved out by Timur. Even though Musa and Muhammad were in agreement to rule over European and Asian territories respectively, Caesar's clever moves turned Muhammad against Musa. In the wake of his country being under siege, Caesar requested Muhammad to come to his help. Muhammad having the least regard for brotherly relations reached there with his army to raise the siege. Thus, the European and Asian Turks stood face to face and both were ready to do combat when Mohammed was informed that one of his commanders had revolted against him. Thus, he rushed back to Asia Minor to put down the uprising. This revolt had taken place at the instance of Musa who wanted him to go back without extending his help to the Christian ruler. In his absence, Musa narrowed down his siege and Caesar found himself in great trouble. Muhammad put down the revolt and returned to Constantinople and wrote to Stephen, the King of Serbia to take up arms against Musa and assured him of his support. The king of Serbia rose against him and Musa raised the siege of Constantinople and rushed to Serbia. Muhammad chased him. Musa was killed in comb at with Muhammad and serbian king. Muhammad sat on the throne of Adrianople. He was now the only ruler of the entire Ottoman conquered territories. Now all civil wars ended for there was none to challenge him. However, Muhammad made it a point to establish his allegiance to his commanders, forces and subjects and, in order to do away with the least possibility of insurgence against him, he blinded his brother Qasim, who lived in Bursa and his nephew, the son of Sulaiman. These events took place in 816 A.H. It is, without doubt, one of the wonders of history how a dynasty, torn by eleven years of civil wars and family strife not only survived but also rose so powerfully.

Sultan Muhammad I

Sultan Muhammad, son of Bayazid Yaldaram ascended the throne in Adrianople in 816 A.H. He began to run the administration with wisdom and sagacity. He had already established cordial relations with the Caesar of Constantinople and the Christian King of Serbia. Hence, both of them conveyed their facilitations on Muhammad's coronation and sent him precious gifts. Muhammad, also in token of friendship and harmony, granted a number of concessions to the king of Serbia and gave away to the Caesar of Constantinople some such territories in the absence of which he felt perturbed. The democratic State of Venice, a mighty naval power and at enmity with the Turks, extended its hands of friendship in the wake of the Ottoman King's fame as a peace-loving ruler. Sultan Muhammad warmly welcomed this move. States like Walachia, Albania, and Bosnia had declared their sovereignty in the wake of the Ottoman setback in Ankara. But now all these Christian States were anxious for their safety and hence each of them sent its felicitation to the new Ottoman ruler through their emissaries. He greeted each of them warmly and told them while saying goodbye, "All of you should tell your masters that I offer peace to one and all and accept their peace offer as well. Allah Almighty loves peace and hates disturbances". With the expression of this friendly gesture, peace returned to Europe. In truth, the Ottoman Rule, which had very recently recovered from a long spell of illness, needed rest and a controlled diet and the wisdom and patience of Sultan Muhammad provided it in ample measure. Every step taken by him was directed towards consolidation of power and integrity.

But uprisings in Asia Minor were going on unchecked. At last, Muhammad marched to punish the insurgents. First of all, he put down the revolt in Smyrna (Izmir) and then silenced his enemies in Fermania. He then established peaceful relations with those states formed after the demise of Timur and which bordered the eastern part of the Ottoman territory. Thus, peace prevailed in the entire region of Asia Minor. On the return journey the Sultan's war fleet clashed with that of Venice and the Ottoman fleet had to sustain damage but a fresh agreement of peace was duly signed and normalcy returned.

Sultan Muhammad believed in internal strength and consolidation of power instead of expansion of territories. After winning peace, he paid his attention to the public welfare. He set up madrasas (schools) and extended honor to religious scholars. He brought peace and safety to the routes and thoroughfares and set trading activities in motion. Thus, his actions and activities brought him admiration both of friends and foes.

But, despite all this, his rule was also overtaken by strife of the worst nature. The man responsible for these disturbances was Qadi Badruddin.

It is said that a new-Muslim Jew turned apostate launched a movement that the Sultan be deposed and democracy adopted. The movement got the support of Qadi Badruddin. They jointly put an uneducated man named, Mustafa as their religious leader and launched their thoughts all over Asia and Europe. Thus, the movement gathered momentum and caused anxiety to Muhammad. It gained popularity among the Muslim masses particularly because they disliked their ruler's friendship and amity with the Christian powers. However, they didn't have the slightest idea that for the stability of Ottoman dynasty, a policy of peaceful relations with the Christian powers was the need of the hour, with the result, they were easily carried away by the ideas of revolt from the elements antagonistic to Ottoman rule. However, Muhammad stood against the poisonous campaign and put an end to it in a short time and all the three protagonists of democracy had to pay the price with their lives. Shortly after that, Muhammad had to face another trouble.

Mustafa, a son of Bayazid was killed in the battle of Ankara. But his body remained traceless. Even the search party sent by Timur returned without success. Thus, the killing of Mustafa became doubtful. Now, during the tenure of Sultan Muhammad in 824 A.H. a man staked his claim in Asia Minor to the Ottoman throne asserting that he was Mustafa, the son of Bayazid Yaldaram. Since he happened to resemble Mustafa, many Turks recognized his claim. The Ottoman Governors of Smyrna and Walachia joined the bandwagon for they were not happy with Muhammad. Aided and abetted by them the said Mustafa came to Gallipoli and captured a territory near Thasli. Muhammad rushed to the troubled spot and Mustafa fled to

Constantinople after being thoroughly beaten. Muhammad wrote to the king of Constantinople to send back Mustafa, the rebel. But Caesar refused to do so but promised to keep him safe in custody provided he keep sending him an amount to be spent on his maintenance. Since Muhammad was worried about insurgence here and there and didn't want to add to his trouble by coming into conflict with Christian powers, he accepted the demand and without showing any dissatisfaction, he moved ahead with his plans to establish better relations with Caesar and worked out a personal visit to Constantinople. Caesar also greeted him warmly and honorably. They together renewed the old agreement of peace and friendship. Following this, Muhammad left for Gallipoli where he passed away in 825 A.H.

A Review of Muhammad's Reign

Muhammad was 27 at the time of the Battle of Ankara. After the battle, he became the sovereign ruler of Amisiah, a town in Asia Minor and came into clashes with his brothers. In the wake of fighting with his brothers for eleven long years, he overpowered all others and ascended to the Ottoman throne. His 8-years tenure was beset with strife and disruptions. His soft policy and wise steps saved a dying Empire. Because of this some historians have called him the Noah of the Ottoman Dynasty.

Sultan Muhammad I was the first Ottoman king who fixed an annual grant for the maintenance of the House of Allah, the Ka'bah and for the poor and the needy Makkans. This sacred service of his attracted from the Abbasid Caliph, Mu'tazid Billah the enviable title of the custodian of the Sanctuaries of Makkah and Madinah. This title rose to such a height with the passage of time that the Ottoman rulers came to be called the Caliphs of the Muslims.

Sultan Muhammad died when he was 47. His son, Murad II, who was then 18, was proving his worth as the commander of the Ottoman Army in Asia Minor. The Ottoman ministers concealed the death of the Sultan Muhammad for 40 days and during this period, they sent couriers to Murad II to post him with the loss and bring him back to the capital for his coronation as the king of Ottoman Dynasty.

Following this, the body of the deceased was carried from Gallipoli to Bursa and was laid to rest.

Murad II

Sultan Murad II was born in 806 A.H. and ascended the throne in Adrianople. Shortly after ascension, the young Sultan was beset with difficulties and dangers. On hearing about the death of Sultan Muhammad, the Caesar of Constantinople called Mustafa from his confinement and had him to write a bond declaring that in case he became the ruler of the Ottoman territories he would hand over such and such strongholds to him (Caesar) and would ever act as a well-wisher of the Constantinople administration.

In the wake of the agreement, Caesar gave Mustafa a war fleet and they landed on the eastern part of the Ottoman Empire to occupy that area. Since his claim of being the son of Bayazid had not been decided as yet a large number of Ottoman soldiers joined him and added to his strength, with the result he went on winning city after city. The major part of the army sent to fight Mustafa joined his camp and the rest fled back after a thorough beating. Following this reverse Sultan Murad sent his commander, Bayazid Pasha at the head of an army to punish the rebels. But Bayazid Pasha was killed on the battlefield and his army was routed. This victory encouraged Mustafa beyond all limits. He was also very sure of help from Caesar as well as the Christian kings of the West against Murad and after his conquest of Asia Minor, he would be able to dislodge him from power. With this purpose in view, he began to storm Asia Minor. Murad II himself led his army to Asia Minor without delay and beat Mustafa. At this time, the Turkish soldiers had distanced themselves from the false claim of Mustafa and joined Murad. In view of the lurking danger around him, he fled Asia Minor and occupied Thasil in Gallipoli. Murad came chasing him to Gallipoli and routed his military strength. Mustafa fled to Adrianople to capture it but he was caught and hanged to death.

Shortly after Sultan Murad II turned to Genoa and signed a peace agreement with it because of its rivalry with Constantinople. Following this he started massive preparations against Constantinople. On hearing this news, Caesar grew anxious. He had, until now, escaped all such troubles by various crafty devices. But, finding no other means to save his country this time, he sent his emissary to Murad to seek forgiveness for his fault of lending his help to Mustafa. However, Sultan Murad returned the envoy with contempt.

Following this Murad reached Constantinople in 826 A.H. (June, 1422 A.C.) at the head of a 20 thousand-man army and laid his siege around Constantinople. Even though the occupation of Constantinople was not an easy job his expert use of explosive mines, catapults and moving towers brought him very near to success. Caesar too was clever to accept his defeat very easily. He had his own secret plans to cause armed insurgence in Asia Minor. Thus, Murad had to raise his siege of Constantinople and rush to Asia Minor when he was near to victory, like his grandfather who had raised his siege of Constantinople to hurry to Asia Minor to take on Timur.

Muhammad was survived by four sons two young and two of tender age. The eldest among them, Murad II was 18 and the next one, Mustafa was 15 at the time of Muhammad's death. After ascension, Murad II sent his youngest brothers to Bursa for upbringing and education and his brother Mustafa, younger than him by three years, to Asia Minor, as a governor or commander.

When Murad II got rid of his so called uncle, Mustafa, the Caesar of Constantinople started his efforts to bring the next Mustafa round to his view and kept convincing him through his emissaries and spies that he supported his right to the throne and he would lend all help in case he staked his claim. He then began to persuade the Seljuk commanders stationed in Konya and other cities as the feudal lords of the Ottoman Empire and most of them were related to the ruling family, to rise against Murad II and in favor of Mustafa, the brother of Murad and his efforts brought fruits.

At last, Mustafa took up arms against the Ottoman Empire with the active support of the Seljuk commanders. Thus, when Murad II was about to conquer Constantinople, Mustafa very hastily occupied a number of cities of Asia Minor and besieged Bursa. In view of the prevailing situation, the Ottoman troops in Asia Minor joined the camp of Mustafa. When Murad witnessed that Asia Minor was gradually slipping out of his hands, he grew anxious and rushed to the troubled spot to put a check on the advancement of his enemy. With the arrival of Murad II, the major part of Mustafa's army changed sides and returned to Murad's camp. Thus, Mustafa was beaten and killed and peace staged a comeback in Asia Minor. Following this victory, Murad was stationed in Asia Minor for about a year to punish all the insurgent elements and bring about complete peace and safety in the region. When Sultan Murad II came to Europe, the Caesar of Constantinople bought peace from him at the cost of paying 30 thousand Ducats annually.

Being free from these campaigns Murad II devoted himself whole heartedly to the welfare of his subjects and the development of his country and kept from any campaigns against Christian or non-Christian powers. However, he kept them following their agreements.

The King of Serbia, loyal and tributary to the Ottoman Empire, died in 831 A.H. and was succeeded by George Bernick. The new king was not so sober and farsighted, hence, the Caesar of Constantinople had an opportunity to hatch secret plots against the Ottoman rule with the help of the Serbian and Hungarian administrations.

After the fall of Venice to Murad II, Caesar felt aggrieved as it was on friendly terms with him. Thus, he multiplied his hostile activities. Murad II, on the other hand, plunged himself into the task of consolidating his position in Europe and in developmental works. Albania and Bosnia too joined the intriguing activities of the Christians like the Serbians and the Hungarians.

The Christians of Transylvania, a province towards the north of Serbia and Romania, took up arms in 842 A.H. but the Sultan put down the rebellion with such a heavy hand that 70 thousand Christians were killed on the battlefield and his name became a terror for them.

During those days a man named John Honey Deys or John Hani Das, the illegitimate son of King Sajmund of Hungary came back to Hungry after gaining rich experience in some of the battles fought in Western Europe. His mother was Elizabeth Marsi, a beautiful but loose woman. She secured for him the post of a Commander and he rose against the Turks. He succeeded in forcing out the Turks from Transylvania. The Turkish General Mazid Beg, who was the Governor and the administrator was killed along with his son and 30 thousand Turkish troops also died. Now, after a long exchange of letters the Sultan agreed to a peace agreement, as a result of which he recognized the freedom of Serbia and George Bernick as its king. He also handed over Walachia to Hungary and repatriated Muhammad Chalpi in return for sixty thousand Ducats. The peace document was written both in Turkish and Hungarian. Both the kings then put their seal on it and vowed to obey it like a religious scripture. The agreement was concluded for a period of ten years.

Now, in the wake of a ten-year peace treaty, and frustration caused by the tragic death of his son Alauddin, Sultan Murad II decided to abdicate the throne. Thus, he called his second son, Muhammad II to Adrianople and performed his coronation ceremony. Since he was a boy of tender age a council of experienced and brave ministers and commanders was constituted to advised him on crucial matters. Sultan Murad II then left for Asia Minor joined the assembly of the saints and divines and adopted a life of seclusion.

But the very thought of Sultan Murad II's abdication of the throne and the ascension of a boy of tender age excited the Christians' greed and they launched a secret plan to break the peace agreement and exterminate the Turkish race from European soil. Although the king of Hungary was reluctant to become a party to the peace breakers for he had not only signed the truce but also vowed to abide by it. However, the Bishop and his deputy Cardinal Julian prevailed by issuing a verdict that breach of agreement with the Muslims carried no sin and it was rather an act of reward. Hani Das was also not in favor of breaking the agreement of peace so soon for such an act brought disgrace to the Christian community but he was lured away from his position with the offer of Bulgaria. Thus, the Christians agreed on breaking the peace agreement within a month of its conclusion.

The Hungarian army launched an attack on the Turkish border security force. Hani Das besieged and conquered Warna. They killed all the Turkish soldiers found on the way and they made a new record in committing crimes against the Muslims.

Members of the Ottoman court, at last, went to Asia Minor and posting Sultan Murad II with the breach of agreement by the Christians and the latest development, requested him to come out of seclusion and lead his army to punish the defaulting Christians and save the Ottoman Empire. Therefore, Murad II rushed to Adrianople and then left for Warna where the Christian army was encamped. Hani Das's informers let him know that Sultan Murad II had given up his life of seclusion and had arrived nearby at the head of forty thousand troops to fight the Christians.

With this news, Hani Das and the king of Hungary held emergency consultations and decided to face the Ottoman assault. Following this, they drew their battle lines and placed the Walachian army on the left and the Hungarian troops on the right side. In addition, a huge army was put under the command of Cardinal Julian. The King of Hungary was in charge of the main body along with his commanders and brave cavaliers. The Polish army was behind all under the command of a bishop. Hani Das was the Commander-in-Chief of the entire army.

Sultan Murad II also set his troops right and raised his standard with a copy of the peace treaty atop. The battle was fought on the battleground of Warna. Hani Das made such a powerful attack from the right side that the Turkish troops were uprooted, the Walachian army too pushed back the Ottoman force. Sultan Murad II was watching the repulses from behind and was almost sure of a setback. In the meantime, the King of Hungary made a forceful charge at the Ottoman troops and reached where Murad II was standing in a state of anxiety and threw a challenge with utmost arrogance. The Sultan, without loss of a moment, shot an arrow and his horse fell down wounded. Khawaja Khairi, and old commander of the Janissaries, pounced on the King and cut his head off. He then placed the head on the point of his spear and lifted it high. The very sight of the head sent terror into the hearts of the Christian troops. However, Hani Das made a few desperate attempts to get back the head of the Hungarian King but the Ottoman army encouraged by the new developments, repelled one and all and, at last, they were beaten and driven back. Cardinal Julian, the worst enemy of the Muslims, the deputy of the Pope and the Commander-in-Chief of the Christian crusaders, was also killed. The Bishop and all other Christian commanders lost their lives. Hani Das was the only commander who escaped death.

In the wake of this marvelous victory, Serbia was annexed and Bosnia too became an integral part of the Ottoman Empire. The heinous act of the breach of trust on the part of the Christians boomeranged and a large number of Christian embraced Islam. Sultan Murad II expanded his territories deeply into Europe and consolidated and regularized the administration and went back again to a life of piety and seclusion by handing over the throne to his son, Muhammad II.

Shortly after the ascension of Muhammad II, for a second time, the Janissaries launched a demand for a substantial increase in salaries and stipends. When their undue demand was turned down, they took up arms and took to plundering. Thus, the Ottoman Empire was once again pushed into deep waters.

In view of the precarious situation prevailing throughout, the notables appeared before the Sultan once again and requested him to intervene. Murad II had to come out from his seclusion for the second time. He came to Adrianople in 849 A.H. On reaching the capital, he was warmly greeted by his army and subjects. On coming to the throne, Murad II sent his son, Muhammad II to Asia Minor to gain more experience regarding statecraft and warfare. After assuming charge of the administration this time he gave severe punishments to the opponents and the insurgents, with the result perfect peace returned to the country. The Sultan thought it improper to quit the throne for the third time nor did he want to give the Christians any opportunity to rise against the Ottoman rule. However, he never put anyone to trouble without any rhyme and reason. Even though the Caesar of Constantinople was the sworn enemy of the Ottomans and it was very necessary to uproot him, Murad II made it a point to ignore his mischief.

In 852 A.H., Hani Das made a bid to launch a fresh campaign against the Ottomans and he succeed in collecting Christian soldiers in about the same number as they had done in the past, but Sultan Murad II gave him a smashing defeat and annexed a number of Christian territories.

Following this, the Sultan had to spend much time in putting down disturbances in Albania, but he had not put an end to them when he was overtaken by death in 855 A.H.

Although the Turks conquered Albania since a long time ago, it had been left to the same ruling dynasty as a feudatory. In order to establish close contacts with Sultan Murad II the king of Albania sent his four young sons to the Sultan to be kept as hostage and to be brought up in the Janissaries. However, accidentally, three of them fell ill in the training center of Adrianople and passed away. The king of Albania smelled a rat in their sudden demise. He, therefore, wrote to the Sultan that he thought some of his enemies must have poisoned his sons to death. Sultan Murad II too felt unhappy over the incident. Now he made some special arrangement for the eldest son, Chastrait, and kept him in his palace. He was educated and trained like a Muslim prince. When he was eighteen, he was given command of a military squad and he came to be known as Sikander Beg and Lord Sikander. His father, John Chastrait died in Albania in 836 A.H. Sultan Murad did not think it right to send George Chastrait to Albania to succeed his father. The Ottoman Sultan loved him like his son and he was, in truth, in a better position with the Sultan than he could be as a ruler of Albania. Sultan Murad believed in his loyalty and he never thought of any challenge on his part at any stage.

But, in the wake of a reverse incurred by the Turkish army at the hands of Hani Das, Sikander Beg resolved to capture Albania by force. Suddenly one day he stormed into the camp of the superintendent of the office and made him write a letter addressed to the Junior Commissioned Officer of Albania forcibly to hand over the administration to Sikander Beg who was going as the viceroy of Sultan Murad II. He also had the letter sealed and then assassinated the superintendent and hurried straight to Albania. The Junior Commissioned officer handed over the administration of Albania to him immediately. Shortly after occupying the throne of Albania in this manner, he proclaimed that he had decided to return to Christianity and, in future, he would direct all his efforts to keep his country free from Turkish control. With this declaration, the Christians' jubilation knew no bounds but, at the same time, a large-scale massacre of the Turks became the order of the day, with the result, not a single Turk was spared in the length and breadth of Albania.

Since Sikander Beg was brought up, trained and educated in the Turkish environment he lived and behaved like a prince. He had grown very rich in courage and ambition and lost all respect for the Turks. Thus, partly because of his courage and determination and largely because of Albania being a hilly country with very difficult rocky pathways, it was not easy for foreign troops to make entry across its borders easily. Sultan Murad's pre-occupations with the affairs of his country held him back from making a full-fledged attack on Albania and a few small-scale campaigns failed to produce any result.

Since Sultan Murad II had brought Sikander Beg up like his son and did not like his ruin or death. He entertained the hope of his return to righteousness. When Sultan Muhammad II came to the throne after the death of his father, he also made peace with Sikander Beg as he looked upon him like a brother. Despite these concessions, Sikander Beg rose against the Ottomans and Sultan Muhammad II was forced to take action and the result was the fall of Albania. Sikander Beg shifted to Venice where he died in 872 A.H. and Albania became a province of the Ottoman Empire.

Sultan Murad II passed away in 855 A.H. and was buried in Bursa. He ruled over his country for 30 years and passed an eventful life. He played a significant role in consolidating the Ottoman Empire. He was, by all standards, noble, pious and devoted to the dictates of Islam.

Sultan Muhammad II, the Conqueror of Constantinople

At the time of Sultan Murad II's death his son, Muhammad II was in Asia Minor. He was then 21. Before this, Muhammad II had twice ascended the throne during the lifetime of his father when he was only 15 and again when he was 16. Murad II had a son from the daughter of the king of Serbia who was then only 8-months old. At the time when the coronation ceremony of Muhammad II was on, someone, without the knowledge of Sultan Muhammad II took the child to the bathroom and put him to death. Such a heinous crime was, perhaps, committed in the interest of Muhammad II because some parties were apprehensive of this child capturing the Ottoman Empire after growing up with the help of the Christian powers. But Muhammad II expressed his strong displeasure over this dastardly act and found the murderer and killed him avenging the blood of his half brother.

Since, during the lifetime of his father, he had ascended the throne twice at short intervals, they expected him to function as a weak ruler devoid of courage and determination. But he proved them wrong. He was not then a boy of 15 or 16 but a young man of 21 or 22. And these six years had not been passed in playing but in developing his skills as a ruler, administrator, fighter and warrior. His company of religious scholars and spiritual divines had enhanced his will power and qualities of mind and spirit.

European historians accuse him of murdering his half brother but these accusations were simply because of his being the Conqueror of Constantinople. However, it is a matter of common knowledge that a commander of the Janissaries killed the child. Moreover, they all agree that Muhammad II killed the accused in retaliation. It is simple logic that during the coronation ceremony Muhammad II must have anticipated no trouble from that small child of only eight months. Had he been apprehensive of the child he could have implemented his plan, if there was any in days to come using some clever device. Furthermore, the commander of Janissaries had not accompanied Muhammad II from Asia Minor to Adrianople, he was in Adrianople much before the arrival of the Sultan. If the Sultan had such a plan, he would have carried it out through any of the commanders accompanying him from Asia Minor who were his confidants. It was against all precautionary measures to give such an order at such a crucial moment. Besides, the accused did not divulge his secret even at the point of death. Mohammad's relation with his stepmother, the princess of Serbia was so pleasant that she had joined the coronation ceremony on her own. Furthermore, the future life of Muhammad II had no similar instances of such a stupid and cowardly act, which did not fit the profile of such a pious and courageous soul.

It is an undeniable fact that the Janissaries had endeared itself enough to the Ottomans and they so often committed undesirable acts on their own like those of a spoiled child. Sultan Muhammad II's period was not free from such instances. The accused commander of the Janissaries had done so in order to keep Sultan Muhammad II in his control by obliging him in this way. The Caesar of Constantinople was under the same delusion and it not only cost him Constantinople but his life as well.

In 852 A.H. three years before the death of Caesar John Palaeologus, Caesar Constantine XII came to the throne of Constantinople. He too was very clever and alert like his predecessor. Following the death of Sultan Murad II and the ascension of Sultan Muhammad II, he forged the opponents and detractors of the Ottomans in Asia Minor into a strong insurgent force and encouraged them to take up arms against the new Ottoman ruler, with the result Sultan Muhammad II had to go to Asia Minor to put the matter right and bring peace and order to the Ottoman territory. But, in the meantime, Caesar Constantine sent word to him that Orkhan, a prince of the Ottoman dynasty was in his custody and he should increase the amount sent from the royal treasury to be spent on the internee, otherwise he would be set free to wrest the country from him.

Since Caesar was aware of the weak disposition of Sultan Muhammad II, he attempted to extort money from him by threats. Had Sultan Muhammad II been as weak as Caesar thought him to be he must have yielded to the threat. But Sultan Muhammad II had courage and will-power more than Alexander of Greece and Napoleon of France. He, therefore, arrived at the conclusion that peace could not be maintained unless the Christian kingdom of Constantinople was eliminated. He thus sent away the Christian envoy without making any reply.

On his return from Asia Minor, Sultan Muhammad II, entered into a three-year peace treaty with Hani Das, the king of Hungary. With the conclusion of this agreement, his northern borders became safe. The next step taken was that he punished the commanders of the Janissaries and cut them down to size. After a short interval, Caesar Constantine sent his emissaries to Adrianople with the same demand and threatened to set Orkhan free. Reacting sharply to this stupid demand the Sultan ceased the maintenance allowance and turned out the emissaries. Following this Muhammad II set himself to preparing to invade Constantinople. Now Caesar's eyes opened and he acknowledged his mistake. The man thought to be a fox turned out to be a lion. But Caesar Constantine too was a distinguished fighter and he started making preparations for the ensuing battle without loss of time. The enlightenment and far-sightedness of Constantine is commendable in that he brought about unity between the two major factions of the Christians. In those days the entire Christian world was divided in two parts one following the Pope of Rome the leader of the Roman Church and the other one, which followed the Greek Church and considered the Archbishop of Constantinople as its religious guide and Caesar of Constantinople had the pride of enjoying his patronage.

Caesar Constantine wrote to the Pope of Rome to bury the differences and rise united against the Muslims. He assured the Roman Pope of his acceptance of the Roman creeds and that the Church of Constantinople was to be led by the Roman Church.

This proclamation of Caesar of Constantinople stirred the entire Christian world and they rose united to crusade against the Muslims as they had done to conquer Bait al-Maqdis and Syria. Christians in large numbers rushed to join the military camp. Nicholas V, the Pope himself launched a strong campaign for the crusade, which produced deep, and favorable results. Huge armies from Spain and Castile joined the Christian Crusaders in Constantinople. The Pope collected a strong army, which was sent by warships under his deputy cardinal. The Army and Navy from Venice and Genoa also set off towards Constantinople. Constantine also began to fortify the city of Constantinople as a defensive measure. The city had a population of one hundred thousand. They were asked to contribute money and to make use of all their resources in safeguarding themselves.

Sultan Muhammad II ordered Arban, a blacksmith who was a new Muslim to make long-range heavy cannons. Arban was a citizen of Hungary and had joined the services of Constantine before coming to the fold of Islam. A number of such cannons were made and a few of them could fire heavy shells. Although, a few years prior, Sultan Murad II had already used cannons in battle they had not come to be considered an effective weapon yet. As for demolishing the walls of forts, those cannons made no major improvement over the catapults and it was difficult to move them swiftly from one place to another. Moreover, it could only fire seven to eight shells from morning to evening and so these cannons were not expected to be of much use during the siege of Constantinople.

First of all, Sultan Muhammad II paid heed to keep peace within his territories. Being free from this duty, he dispatched 50 thousand horsemen and twenty thousand infantry of brave and spirited soldiers to lay the siege around Constantinople.

Both sides had begun their all-out open preparations since 856 A.H. (1452 C.E.). Caesar Constantine had hoarded within the bounds of Constantinople large quantities of food grain. Furthermore, warships from European countries were carrying not only troops and war equipment but also supplies of food grain in large quantities. Besides, architects, engineers and seasoned military commanders had arrived in Constantinople to protect and fortify the city. They had tied strong iron chain on both sides of the sea and at the mouth of the port so that no warship could enter therein. However, they could loosen the chain to lower it to admit their own ships into the port. In this way, they had stopped the entry of the enemy warships. The walls of the city were very strong and fortified within a circumference of 14 miles and were virtually invincible. However, the walls were somewhat lower towards the port for they expected no attack from that side. Deep trenches were being dug around the City and outside of those walls were towers having cannons and squads of archers to provide safeguards to the trenches and fortifications. In short, all possible devices were put into service to fortify the defensive position of Constantinople.

Sultan Bayazid Yaldaram had built a fort at the narrowest place on the Asian coast of the Bosphorus Straits. When Sultan Muhammad II decided on conquering Constantinople, he built a fort in front of the first one. It was, in fact, the foremost preparation for war against Constantinople. The fort was ready in a very short time and cannons were fitted atop as was done with the former one. By this strategy, the door to Bosphorus Strait was sealed and separated from the Marmara Sea, which stopped the entry of Caesar's fleet into the Black sea. But these arrangements did no harm to Constantine since he was receiving help from the European countries through the Danube Pass. Sultan Muhammad II had three hundred small boats in all and none of them was equal in size to even the smallest ship in the Constantinian fleet consisting of fourteen ships.

Conquest of Constantinople

On Rabia al-Awwal 26, 857 A.H. (April 6, 1453 C.E.) Sultan Muhammad II appeared on the scene in front of the walls of Constantinople, while the Ottoman fleet was concentrated in the Marmara Sea and laid his siege to the Golden Horn, the port of Constantinople. The Sultan set up suitable squads at chosen spots. He then ordered his diggers to dig mines and carry parapets near to the city walls and archers were deployed to target anyone raising his head from the walls of the city. Sultan Muhammad II demonstrated his wonderful skill in keeping the siege not only in tact but narrowing its circle and reaching the walls of the city rather speedily. Cannons and catapults were set up at strategic spots and shells and stones were hurled at the walls.

The besieged were also not careless as regards their defense. John Ghatyas, the Commander from Genoa and Duke Notarus, the Greek commander put up the defenses with great skill and expertise and the Cardinal, the deputy of Pope Nicholas V, also showed his mettle as a brave and seasoned commander and fighter. Caesar Constantine assumed the overall charge of the allied forces. He remained in the saddle from morning to evening and even during the night and he seldom left it. He would inspect every part and wing of his army and cavalry personally, he encouraged his troops to fight gallantly and looked into the performance of various commanders. Shortly after the siege began, the citizens and Christian troops were filled with a new spirit and zeal. Bishops and clergies were moving about their side of the battlefield sermonizing and singing praises of the crusade and for laying down lives on the battlefield.

Sultan Muhammad II had pitched his camp in front of St. Romans, the gate of the city and the besiegers were targeting this avenue increasingly.

At first, the besieged began to target the besiegers coming out of their ramparts and the trenches. When this resulted in heavy loss of life at the hands of the Ottoman troops, Constantine issued orders that nobody should attempt to go out of the fortified city. However, the besieged began to reply to the besiegers in the same coin. At last, cracks appeared in the city-walls, but the besieged carried out repairs immediately. Sultan Muhammad II then took his troops near the trenches and made pathways by bridging these trenches and reached the city-walls. They could not gain control over the walls because the Christians started throwing blazing kerosene oil at the Muslim troops, with the result they had to retreat. Now the Sultan applied another device to achieve his purpose. He erected wooden towers as high as the city-walls with wheels to move them at will. A long ladder was fastened with each tower and all ladders were put on the walls, building bridges between the towers and the city-wall and Muslim soldiers started attempting to scale the walls. But the beleaguered made determined efforts to undo these attempts by hurling at them blazing shells of pitch and setting the wooden structures on fire. This new device also failed to produce any result.

On April 15, and the ninth day since the siege started, news came that four ships from Genoa loaded with shells, gunpowder and food grain reached the Golden Horn, the port of Constantinople tearing apart the blockade of the Turkish fleet. With this sensational news, Sultan Muhammad II rode to the seacoast and noticed that a fleet of five warships was advancing through the Marmara Sea. He ordered his navy commander to stop the approaching enemy warships. The Ottoman warships launched a heavy attack on the enemy fleet and broke the long row of the fleet so that they began to cluster together one by one and were surrounded by the Turkish ships. However, they failed to breach the high and heavy enemy ships and were not able to overpower them for their own ships were low and much smaller. After a short trial of strength, the giant enemy ships entered the Golden Horn, following which the Christians pulled up the iron chains stopping the chase of the Turkish ships.

Sultan Muhammad II witnessed the failure of his navy with his naked eyes and grew very sad. He called his navy commander, beat him thoroughly and ordered him to stay cautions and alert thereafter. In fact, the navy commander was not at fault for he could not board the giant enemy ships with his smaller ones. Nevertheless, the punishment meted out by the Sultan worked wonders and after that no enemy ship was able to pass by that route.

Sultan Muhammad II then showed the utmost steadfastness in the implementation of the siege but he had to sustain losses and reverses repeatedly which added much to the courage and determination of the Christians. There was no dearth of defensive material and food grain. Moreover, they were sure that the Hungarian king Hani Das would break the peace agreement and come to their aid and with his arrival the siege would be raised. In view of these setbacks and reverses, anybody else would have raised the siege putting off the task to some later occasion. But the Sultan's strong determination and invincible courage stood him in good stead and every failure enhanced his commitment and will.

When leaving for the campaign against Constantinople, Sultan Muhammad II had brought with him a party of religious scholars, Muslim divines and pious men. In the company of those slaves of Allah, he had taken lessons in determination and grit. During the lifetime of his father, he had spent six years continuously in Asia Minor in the divine company of Muslim saints and religious scholars and his qualities of mind and spirit had grown rich beyond all limits. Even during the present siege, he was satisfied with the consultations of these divines.

When the siege dragged on, he thought of a plan, which had never before come to his mind. On one side of the city lay the sea, the Golden Horn and was supposed to be safe from any siege. Up to now all siege activities were limited to land. The entire use of force was directed at St. Romans and all efforts were pointed to pull down the city-wall from this side. Thus, the city-dwellers were also putting up all their defensive measures on this front. Sultan Muhammad thought that a fresh assault from the seaside would divide their defensive power, with the result the city wall could be more easily broken. But in the presence of the chain across the mouth of the Golden Horn, there was no way the Turkish navy could enter the area. To the east of the Golden Horn was a ten-mile wide strip of land across which lay the Bosphorus straits and the Turkish ships could move freely therein. Sultan Muhammad II spread wooden planks from the Bosphorus to the Golden Horn on the moonlit night of 14 Jumad al-Awwal. He then had eighty ships pushed across the strip of land. Thousands of troops kept pushing the ships ahead. The men within the city-walls could not understand what caused the shouts and noises and what was the reason for the martial songs and drum beating. At last, the Ottoman ships were brought into the Golden Horn before dawn. All of Constantine's ships were kept towards the mouth of the port to block the entry of Turkish ships. With the morning sun, the citizens of Constantinople noticed to their utmost amazement the bridge of Turkish ships right below the city-walls. The Ottoman army and navy were then engaged in setting up cannons at suitable spots to shell the weak portions of the city-wall. A look at this scene sent terror into the hearts of the Christian fighters and citizens. The Christian ships made an attempt to move in and launch an attack on the Ottoman ships but heavy cannons on both sides of the port stopped them and a few of them sank as a result of the heavy shelling. It was the first occasion that Ottoman artillery worked wonders. The sudden attack from the seaside caught them unaware and they had to divide their resources.

The same day, May 24, Constantine sent his emissaries to the Sultan with a peace offer requesting him to grant him mercy and leave him as the ruler of Constantinople in return for as much tribute as he thought proper. Sultan Muhammad II, who was then at the helm of affairs, wrote him back that, in case of submission, he could be allotted the southern part of Greece instead of Constantinople. Sultan Muhammad II was too far-sighted to know that the existence of a Christian Constantinople in the middle of the Ottoman Empire would always remain a source of danger. Moreover, he had in mind that Constantinople could serve as the most suitable capital for the Ottomans. Moreover, the offer of a piece of land in southern Greece was the height of generosity in view of the losses sustained and the sacrifices made by the Ottomans during the long siege of Constantinople. Caesar Constantine was destined to be the last ruler of Constantinople, the old and magnificent kingdom of eastern Rome. However, Constantine did not like to avail himself of this opportunity and sought to oppose the Ottoman ruler more vehemently.

Thus, on Jumad al-Awwal 19, 857 A.H. (May 28, 1453 C.E.) Sultan Muhammad II proclaimed throughout his army that an all around attack would be launched the next day at dawn and the troops would be left free to plunder the entire Constantinople but without doing any harm to government buildings and the old, the women and children and the subjects seeking peace.

The news of a general attack the next morning filled the Muslim troops with utmost joy and they passed the night in shouting slogans out of zeal. Caesar Constantine, on the other hand, called a meeting of his commanders, nobles and notables in his palace to inform them about the ensuing Ottoman attack the next morning he induced them to fight gallantly and to the last drop of their blood. Caesar then went to St. Aya Sofia Church to pray for his victory. From there, he went straight to his palace, which was overtaken, by despair and harassment. After taking rest for a while he mounted his horse and came to St. Romans, which was, then under heavy attack.

Sultan Muhammad II, on the other hand, following the predawn prayer, requested the assembly of religious scholars and pious people to pray to Allah Almighty for the victory of Islam.

The Sultan then took ten thousand selected horsemen under his command and set off for the campaign ahead. His spiritual guide then asked the people to erect a separate booth for him and entered it alone to pray to Allah for an Ottoman victory. He put a gatekeeper to stop the entry of anyone. The Ottoman forces launched a multi-faceted attack and their cannons and catapults made cracks and holes in the city-walls. However, all their attempts to enter the city met with failure as the besieged troops and even the Christian women and children put up stiff resistance. Heads were rolling on both sides but neither side was losing courage. By noon, the battle turned hot. At this crucial moment, the Sultan sent one of his ministers or courtiers to his spiritual guide to pray and seek special Divine help. The situation was quite discouraging for the Muslim troops and they seemed to be losing hope of victory. Sultan Muhammad II also was growing anxious that if, despite an all-out attack, the city remained unconquered it would be almost impossible to win it later for the invading Muslim troops had devoted all the courage and power at their command to defeat the enemy. At such an anxious moment, the emissary of the Sultan arrived at the booth of the spiritual guide. The doorkeeper made an attempt to stop him from intruding but the emissary made his entry by force and he found the saint prostrate praying for a Muslim victory. On the entrance of the emissary the saint raised his head and said, "The city of Constantinople has already been conquered!" The emissary of the Sultan was greatly surprised. He hurried back and found to his amazement the Ottoman flag flying atop the ramparts of the city.

It so happened that at the very crucial moment when Sultan Muhammad II had sent his emissary to his spiritual guide to request him to make some special prayer for victory, the emissary had just left with the request when unexpectedly the city wall in front of the Sultan caved in all of a sudden and with the debris of the wall the trench filled up to pave the way leading to the city. About the same time, the Ottoman navy captured a tower and hoisted the royal flag atop. Noticing the flag flying and the frontal city-wall demolished the Turkish troops under the direct command of the Sultan launched a massive attack. Even though the Christians faced the Muslims firmly they could not overcome them in the hand-to-hand fighting that ensued. Besides this, the Muslim troops, on all sides, made a heavy charge at the Christian soldiers and there was nothing but a heap of dead Christian bodies. Sultan Muhammad II mounted on his horse and went straight to the church of St. Aya Sofia and called *adhan* therein without delay. He then offered prayer along with his comrades and thanked Allah Almighty Who had given them such a magnificent victory. Following this he sent the people in search of Constantine. Near St. Romans where the city wall had fallen, the Christians had given a good account of themselves and were killed in large numbers. Constantine's body was also lying among them. His body had only two wounds. They cut off his head and brought it to the Sultan. Thus was completed the conquest of Constantinople. The Sultan then turned to palace of Caesar but found there nothing but a state of wilderness.

The conquest of Constantinople had taken place on Jumad al-Awwal 20, 857 A.H. (May 29, 1453 C.E.). Some people view the conquest to be the result of the prayer of the divine saint. It is, therefore, generally said that Constantinople was conquered with a prayer. From that day, Sultan Muhammad II came to be known as "Sultan, the Conqueror."

During this campaign, more than 40 thousand Christians fell dead and about 60 thousand were taken as prisoners. Only a small number thereof were able to escape by land and sea. They settled in Italy and various other places. One of the grandsons of Caesar embraced Islam shortly after that and settled in Constantinople. However, the dynasty went out of existence.

Sultan, the Conqueror gave full protection to the Christian population and their wealth and properties remained safe. Christian shrines and churches except the church of Aya Sofia were left to their control. Sultan Muhammad II called the Archbishop of Constantinople and gave him good news of being left as the spiritual head of the Greek Church and his religious power would not be interfered with. Sultan, the Conqueror accepted the patronage of the Greek Church on his own. Thus, the Archbishop and other priests and clergy had powers that they had never enjoyed even under Christian rule. The Christian population had full religious freedom. Various churches received from him large pieces of property. He bought prisoners of war from his own soldiers and set them free and had them to settle in a particular locality of the city. When he saw that most of the houses had lost their dwellers and much of the charm of the city had become an event of the past he, in order to restore the lost glamour and splendor of Constantinople, brought five thousand families from Asia Minor and had them settled in Constantinople, with the result the city not only regained its past grandeur but more than what it had in the past.

History of the City of Constantinople

The conquest of Constantinople is considered as one of the marvelous events in world history. European historians have ended the Middle Ages with the conquest of Constantinople. It is from here that the Age of Enlightenment begins. On this occasion, it appears befitting to give a short history of Constantinople. The place where Constantinople city is now situated was first founded in the 8 century prior to Isa (Jesus) (عليه السلام) by a nomadic tribe who named it Byzantium. It witnessed quite a number of events and incidents and became with the passage of time a central city and the capital of a small State. The father of Alexander of Greece attempted to occupy the city. In the darkness of night, he led his force to Byzantium. At the time when his troops had reached the city-walls, a bright light appeared from the North and the citizens noticed the invading army and rose to defend it. The invaders retreated in view of the readiness of the citizens and the city was saved. The local population thought it to be the work of the Goddess Diana and built a temple there in her name and chose the moon as their symbol.

A short time later, Alexander conquered the city and thus avenged the failure of his father. Following the demise of Alexander, Byzantium suffered many setbacks and reverses. When Caesar Constantine conquered the city, he was pleased with its location and laid the foundation of a new city by adding some adjoining areas to it and decided to make it his capital. Although he named it the Modern or New Rome, it gradually came to be called Constantinople after the name of Constantine.

Constantine I populated Constantinople in 327 C.E. Before this time Constantine and his ancestors were idolaters but Constantine had converted to Christianity. Three years after its being populated he presented this city to Holy Maryam (Mary) and celebrated this offering on a very large scale. Thus, since 330 C.E., Constantinople became exclusively a Christian city and when the Roman Empire was divided into two parts, Constantinople became the permanent capital of the Eastern part. Caesar Justinian I, who ruled over it from 527 C.E. to 565 C.E., added to its glamour and beauty. This city suffered invasions at different times but it remained safe from destruction. The Muslims invaded it during the early period of Umayyad dynasty and Abu Ayyub Ansari ؓ was martyred in that campaign and was buried below the city wall. Although the Christians decided several times to destroy the grave of Abu Ayyub Ansari, they could not do so for fear of Muslims' displeasure. Sultan Muhammad II, the conqueror built a mosque adjoining the grave, which came to be known as Jami Ayyub.

During the Abbasid caliphate, preparations were made more than once to conquer Constantinople but it could not be done due to one reason or another. In 600 A.H., when the Crusades were on an army from Venice conquered and annexed it to Latin rule which, followed the Roman Pope as its religious guide. This rule spanned over 60 years. In 660 A.H. the Greeks, Eastern Romans, conquered it and laid the foundation of their Eastern Rule and they became free from the dictates of the Roman Pope.

Two centuries later, Sultan Muhammad II, the Conqueror put an end to the Christian rule and shifted his capital from Adrianople to Constantinople. It had come to the Muslim fold after eleven hundred years of Christian rule. After serving as the capital for four hundred and seventy-five years it ceased to be so when at the end of the Ottoman caliphate, Ankara became the capital of the Turkish democracy. However, it is still considered as a magnificent Muslim city.

The Remaining Deeds of Sultan the Conqueror

Following the conquest of Constantinople Sultan Muhammad II devoted his time and attention to developmental work and the welfare of the people of Constantinople. However, the southern part of Greece could not escape his attention and he decided on its annexation. It was particularly because a Christian Greece could serve as the hotbed of the hostile activities for Italy and other European states. Hence, he conquered and annexed the small Greek States. The same Southern Greece had a small State founded by the descendants of Caesar Constantine after escaping from Constantinople but following the conquest of their States, they all were converted to Islam.

Finding time from the conquest of the small States, Sultan Muhammad II turned to Venice but they bought peace by accepting the superiority of the Ottoman rule. In 601 A.H. a man from the royal family of Constantinople was expelled from the country during the disturbances arising among the Crusaders. He had set up a separate small State at Trabzon along the southern coast of the Black Sea, and it remained unnoticed, with the result, it remained intact for two hundred and fifty years. Whenever a Muslim ruler turned to it, it bowed its head in obedience and saved itself but it would stop paying tribute whenever it found the Muslim rulers engaged in feuds or civil wars. Following the conquest of Constantinople, Sultan Muhammad II thought it necessary to do away with this Christian State in Asia Minor for it was, nevertheless, sympathetic to Caesar Constantine.

The Christian ruler of Trabzon was the father-in-law of Hasan Tawil, the Turkman king of Iran. Hasan Tawil had occupied the whole of

Iran and Armenia. He was considered a strong king. Hence, Iran could anytime pose a danger to the Ottoman rule in Asia Minor. The Christian rule of Trabzon was, therefore, at liberty to create difficulties for the Ottoman rule. Sultan Muhammad II was fully aware of the intriguing activities of the Christian Caesar. Thus, he decided to eliminate this potential danger. He attacked Trabzon in 860 A.H. and annexed it. In spite of being a sovereign State, Trabzon was considered to be a part of the Iranian state and this event angered the ruler of Iran but he took no immediate action whatsoever.

Being free from the campaigns of Greece and Asia Minor, Sultan, the Conqueror came back to Constantinople in 860 A.H. and he, very soon, resumed his campaigns against Serbia and Bosnia. Although these two countries had become feudatories of the Ottoman rule, they were showing signs of opposition. Thus the Sultan, in order to put an end to the disturbing situation, conquered both Serbia and Bosnia and annexed both of them and sent his governors there.

Since the period of truce with Hungary had already ended and the Hungarian ruler had started his preparations against the Ottoman rule and had sought help from the Christian powers, Sultan Muhammad II thought it proper to initiate his campaign against him. Thus in 861 A.H. (July 1456 C.E.) Ottoman forces marched to Hungary. In the wake of the fall of Constantinople, the Christian powers and all the Christian states were raging with anger against the Ottomans. They also had in mind that if Belgrade, the capital of Hungary, were to fall, all of Western Europe would be within Turkish reach. Hence, forces from all over the European continent concentrated to save Belgrade. Sultan, the Conqueror led his troops up to Belgrade conquering the cities and towns on the way and besieged it. Hani Das too was a shrewd commander. He began to defend the capital with all the expertise at his command. And after much killings and bloodshed the Ottoman army, at last, made progress into a part of the city. This was the low-lying area of the city. But the Christians, instead of losing heart, ascended to the upper part and above the Turkish troops. The Muslim squads that had enter the city fought firmly the whole day but returned to their camp when evening set in. The Christians re-occupied the area left by the Muslim soldiers and refortified it even more strongly. This event took place on July 21. Although the Muslims scaled the city-walls more than once and plundered the city the strong defensive measures of the Christians did not allow them to conquer it. At last, Sultan Muhammad II launched a decisive attack and beheaded a number of Christian commanders and even wounded Hani Das, the king of Hungary and was near to victory when a Christian soldier struck him on his thigh and injured him so badly that he was carried away on a stretcher. The present state of the Sultan was discouraging for the Muslim troops to such an extent that their advance not only stopped they began to retreat with the result the Christian attack intensified. Even though the Christian commander, Hani Das was wounded, his casualty was unknown to most of his troops. Moreover, leadership of the Christian forces was shouldered by a number of commanders in addition to Hani Das, while Sultan Muhammad II was the only one commanding his troops. The retreat of the Muslim troops was such a boost for the Christians that the Ottomans could not find peace even at their camp and they had to take their wounded ruler to Constantinople. In short, a Muslim victory changed into defeat and Belgrade could not be conquered. The Muslim reversal was celebrated all over Europe. But there was something else in store. Twenty-one days later Hani Das succumbed to his injuries at about the same time Sultan Muhammad II, the Conqueror took a convalescent bath, marking his recovery.

It has already been mentioned that Sikander Beg was occupying Albania and his upbringing in the Ottoman palace had attracted concessions from Murad II to the extent that he never challenged his position as the ruler of Albania. But, in the aftermath of the recent Ottoman reverse in Belgrade Sikander Beg also, along with others, felt encouraged and began to show signs of insurgence. Although, at the initial stage, Muhammad II ignored his rebellious activities, when his opposition took a serious turn, Sultan the Conqueror invaded Albania. Since Sikander Beg was a shrewd ruler and loved by his subjects besides ruling a land with a difficult terrain, victory was not very easy for the Ottoman king.

However, after a long-drawn out battle, Sikander Beg sought peace in 866 A.H. and promised to remain loyal in future. Sultan Muhammad II acceded his request and granted him peace by withdrawing from Albania. But Sikander committed a breach of faith again and had, therefore, to suffer another attack that was so massive that he could not sustain it and escaped to Venice where he was warmly greeted.

Albania came to the fold of the Ottoman Empire. But Sultan, the Conqueror was no longer a terror for the Christian world following his setback in Belgrade. Thus, Venice, which had bought peace from the Sultan in the immediate past, started raising its head once again. The Ottoman ruler lost no time in crushing its revolt and conquered long coastal areas and annexed a number of cities. The defeat was so terrible that they sought a truce on ignominious terms surrendering the city of Shkodra to Sultan, the Conqueror who spread his borders up to the Adriatic Sea.

Sultan, the Conqueror appointed his commander, Ahmad Qaiduq as his Prime Minister in 878 A.H. and engaged himself in conquering Greek islands. During this period, Shah Hasan Awzun or Hasan Tawil continued increasing his strength. He had captured and assassinated Sultan Abu Sayeed Mirza Timuri in 873 A.H. Now he had a plan to challenge the power of Sultan Muhammad II in Asia Minor and avenge his setback in Trabzon. He was behind a number of uprisings in Asia Minor and each time the Turkish troops put them down. But Sultan Muhammad II had no desire to fight with the Muslim state of Iran. He had uppermost in his mind the desire of his forefather, Bayazid Yaldaram to conquer the city of Rome. With this purpose in mind, he expanded his borders towards Italy. In the aftermath of his setback in Belgrade, he occupied the entire territory up to the borders of the Hungarian capital and consolidated his position up to this point. Setting aside the conquest of Belgrade for a later period, he first conquered the Greek islands and Venice. At that time, Asia Minor and Iran were not on his mind. However, an opportunity surfaced all of a sudden.

In 879 A.H. Sultan Muhammad II, sent his Prime Minister towards the Black Sea to Conquer Crimea, which was, for a long time, under the rule of the Khans of the Genghezid race. However, in the recent past, Genoa had annexed Yaffa (modern day Feodosiya), a port on the Black Sea on the southern coast of the Crimea. The Khan of Crimea wrote to the Sultan for help to vacate the aggression and take him under his care. Sultan Muhammad II acceded to the request and sent Ahmad Qaiduq at the head of a huge war fleet manned by 40 thousand troops and conquered Yaffa after a siege of four days and held 40 thousand Genoese. Ahmad Qaiduq captured huge spoils of war and warships too. The Khan of Crimea offered his allegiance to the Sultan, which spanned over three hundred years. Yaffa was supposed to be another Constantinople and its conquest was even more necessary to keep Ottoman supremacy in the Eastern States and the Black Sea. Annexation of the Crimea and Yaffa by the Ottoman Empire made the Iranian ruler hot with anger. Hasan Tawil began to oppose the Sultan openly.

In 880 A.H., Sultan the conqueror sent his son, Bayazid as Commander to Asia Minor to look after the affairs there while he kept himself involved in European campaigns. He had already conquered Albania and Herzegovina and he started winning islands in the Mediterranean Sea one by one. In 882 A.H. Umar Pasha, a commander of Sultan Muhammad II reached the capital of Venice with his victorious army. However, the parliament of Venice finding Turkish troops below the city-walls, sought peace very humbly with the promise that, when needed, they would provide a fleet of one hundred ships. Thus, Umar Pasha concluded the treaty and returned from Venice.

A group of the Crusaders from Rhodes set up a sovereign state in 711 A.H. These people had been in occupation of this island along with the nearby islands and used to commit piracy on the ports of Syria and Asia Minor. Even the rulers of Venice and Genoa never challenged them. They actually appreciated their acts of robbery simply because the Muslims were the sole victims of their assaults. When the Ottoman Empire spread up to the borders of Rhodes the existence of such criminal elements became a source of constant trouble to the Muslim state. Sultan Muhammad II sent a naval expedition in 885 A.H. but it met with failure. Following this, the Sultan sent another expedition under a seasoned commander who surrounded the capital and conquered the entire island. But the moment the Ottoman soldiers were about to enter the city for plunder the commander ordered them not to touch anything. This order sent waves of disappointment and discomfort and the soldiers held themselves back from completing the conquest. This state of affairs led to a dispute between the commander and the troops and they had to return without conquering the island.

About the time the expedition was sent to Rhodes Sultan, the Conqueror sent another expedition towards southern Italy under his Prime Minister, Ahmad Qaiduq to start conquests in Italy. Thus, Ahmad Qaiduq descended on the coast of Italy and besieged the city of Otranto, which was called the gate to victory, the conquest of this city meant the conquest of Italy and Rome. At last, Ahmad Qaiduq conquered the city in 885 A.H. (August 11, 1480 C.E.) and killed or captured twenty thousand of the besieged forces. Now the conquest of Rome was not a difficult task. All of Italy was overtaken by such a great terror that the Pope of Rome was ready to flee the city.

Being informed of the setbacks in the conquests of Otranto and Rhodes Sultan, the Conqueror plunged into the task of collecting troops and making preparations for another round. Apparently, there was no impediment whatsoever in fulfilling Bayazid Yaldaram's wish to feed his horse in the Roman Church. Sultan, the Conqueror installed his military Flag on the coast of the Bosphorus Strait signaling the immediate arrival of the Sultan with a huge army under his command.

There were then three expeditions drawing his attention. One, he wanted to punish Hasan Tawil, the King of Iran who had started giving trouble to Prince Bayazid; second, to conqueror Rhodes and third, to enter Rome victoriously. In spite of massive preparations, Sultan Muhammad II kept his next target a secret. It was the practice of the Sultan that he would never disclose his next target when he would himself lead the expedition even to his commanders and Prime Minister. A certain commander once asked about his next campaign, Sultan Muhammad II had said in reply that if he knew that a single hair of his beard had come to know of his plan he would pull out the hair at once and put it into fire. However, troops from all parts of his Empire were concentrating in Constantinople. It was such a large-scale preparation that 886 A.H. set in. It was presumed that he would first punish the king of Iran and then conquer Rhodes before his expedition to Italy where his Prime Minister was awaiting his arrival rather desperately, and the Pope of Rome was ready to leave with the Sultan's entry into Italy.

But Allah Almighty had decided otherwise. With the departure from Constantinople Sultan Muhammad II developed gout and it took such a serious turn that the succumbed to it in Rabia al-Awwal, 886 A.H. (May 3, 1481 C.E.). This ended the massive campaign that he planned. The expedition returned with the dead body and buried it in Constantinople. His end came at the age of 52 or 53 after ruling for about 31 years. His death proved disastrous not only to the Ottoman dynasty but for the entire world of Islam.

The year Sultan Muhammad II, the Conqueror succeed his father in Adrianople, Sultan Bahlol Lodhi had ascended the throne in India and ruled for a few years afterwards. The same year, Safar 5, 886 A.H. Khawaja Jahan Mahmud Gawan, the Prime Minister of Sultan Muhammad Shah Bahmani was assassinated in Dakan (Southern part of India). And exactly eleven years after the death of Sultan the Conqueror, Rabia al-Awwal 1897 A.H. the Muslim rule in Spain ended. Had the Sultan lived for a few years and Italy was annexed by the Ottoman Empire the Christians would have no opportunity to do away with the Muslim rule in Granada.

A Review of Muhammad II's Rule

Sultan Muhammad II's rule was packed with campaigns and adventures. During his tenure, he conquered twelve states and more then two hundred cities and forts. The total number of Muslim soldiers martyred during his reign came to 8 hundred thousand although the number of his regular troops never exceeded one hundred and twenty five thousand. The Janissaries who were the Body Guards of the Sultan numbered around twelve thousand.

He promulgated such laws that did away with all the evils and disorders of military and administrative spheres and made those that benefited the Ottoman Empire most. A Sultan who spent his tenure in campaigns and expeditions could not be a first-rate lawmaker. But Muhammad II was first rate lawmaker. Moreover, his court had a team of religious scholars along with a cluster of ministers and commanders.

He set up madrasas in every city, town and village under his rule and their entire expenses were borne by the government. The syllabus for the Madrasas was also prepared by none other than the Sultan. All the Madrasas held regular examinations and awarded degrees to the successful examinees. These degrees were supposed to be the true measurement of abilities and everybody received service positions according to his academic qualifications. The courses of study contained almost all the subjects necessary for the betterment of this world and the next one. Sultan Muhammad himself was a great scholar. He was well versed in Quranic and Hadith literature, history, biography, mathematics and physics. He, therefore, chalked out the best of courses. He could speak Arabic, Persian, Turkish, Latin, and Greek fluently and eloquently. The laws promulgated in the length and breadth of his country were based on stated principles: first of all the Glorious Qur'an should be followed in letter and spirit and then the authentic Sunnah and Hadith followed by the four *fiqahs* and only after all these three stages royal orders should be acted upon. In case, any order issued by the king was against the injunction of the Qur'an and the Hadith the religious scholars were at liberty to prove it against Shari' at so that the Sultan would then withdraw it.

He had divided the territories under his rule into provinces and districts. It is quite amazing how such a warrior and conqueror could find time to devote to academic activities. He was so conscious of his prestige and position that he would never talk pleasantly and informally even with his Prime Minister. He would sit in his court or assembly only by necessity. He loved to pass his leisure in loneliness. Nothing absurd and devoid of wisdom ever came from him. He was devoted to religious scholars and valued them highly on one hand but his hate for the "ignorant scholars" and so-called pseudo-religious people was very strong. He was very particular in offering prayer and observing fast and preferred his prayers in congregation. His love for the Qur'an was the deepest. He showed kindness and tolerance to the Christians and men confessing other religious beliefs.

He was fully aware of the fact that so-called religious scholars practiced so much orthodoxy and adopted hard lines on trifles in a manner that Islam became something "horrible." Therefore, he was very much in favor of taking advantage of permission when the Islamic laws allowed it.

Sultan Muhammad II had his eyes on all the departments of his administration. He was very steadfast in punishing the culprits and rewarding the able and efficient ones. Although he loved solitude and did everything to maintain his prestige he appeared very close to his ordinary soldiers in the battlefield and helped them with everything at his command, with the result his soldiers were ready to sacrifice their lives for him. They held him like their affectionate father.

Sultan, the Conqueror was a man of medium height with a wheat colored complexion. He most often looked sad, but appeared very ferocious when in anger. He meted out cruel punishments to those committing any kind of corruption in public life with the result there was no trace of theft and robbery within the boundaries of his country. A complete absence of uprisings and revolts, misconduct and corrupt practices is the glaring proof of his administrative acumen and bold action.

Chapter 21

Civil Wars after Sultan the Conqueror

The Story of Prince Jamshed

Sultan the Conqueror left two sons, Bayazid and Jamshed. Bayazid was the Governor of Asia Minor while Jamshed was appointed as the Governor of the Crimea. At the time of the Sultan's death, Bayazid and Jamshed were 35 and 22 respectively. Bayazid was somewhat idle and mild while Jamshed was remarkably active, steadfast and enterprising. Neither of them were present in Constantinople at the time of the Sultan's death. Sultan, the Conqueror had appointed Muhammad Shah as Prime Minister before sending the Prime Minister Ahmad Qaiduq to the campaign against Italy as Commander. Prime Minister Muhammad Shah had a desire to enthrone Jamshed after the demise of the Sultan. He tried to keep the Sultan's death a secret and sent word to Jamshed to hurry to Constantinople however, the news was soon known. The Janissaries took up arms and put Prime Minister Muhammad Shah to death and replaced him with Ishaq Pasha. Bayazid was then informed of the death of the Sultan with the advice to come rushing to Constantinople. In the meantime, the Janissaries took Constantinople by storm. They began to extort money from traders and wealthy persons and captured the administration of Commander Ahmad Qaiduq who had completed his preparations to make advancements after conquering and fortifying Otranto. Ahmad Qaiduq grew uncomfortable and frustrated with the sad news of the Sultan's demise. He immediately rushed to Constantinople after deputizing a commander to look after the affairs in Otranto.

Bayazid, on the other hand, hurried to Constantinople at the head of four thousand troops and ascended the throne. The Janissaries, after demonstrating their power and strength, pressed the new ruler to make a substantial increment in their salary and holdings otherwise, he would be assassinated. Bayazid surrendered before the demand of the hostile soldiers. By accepting this demand, he set the tradition of conferring rewards to the soldiers on the eve of ascension and thus used a big portion of the public wealth. Moreover, this weakness of the new ruler provided ample proof of his being far from a strong ruler and very different from his father who was a man of courage and determination.

However, his being the elder brother of Jamshed, a man like Ishaq Pasha, as his Prime Minister and his having the total support of the Janissaries none could muster courage to challenge his position. A short time later Ahmad Qaiduq reached Constantinople from Italy. Since his rival, Prime Minister Muhammad Shah, was an opponent of Bayazid and supporter of Jamshed, Ahmad Qaiduq took the oath of allegiance with Sultan Bayazid II.

Jamshed got the news of the death of his father a little late and by that time, Bayazid II had ascended the throne in Constantinople. Jamshed began to occupy cities in Asia Minor and wrote to his brother after capturing Bursa that Sultan, the Conqueror had not appointed him (Bayazid) his crown prince, therefore he had no right to become the ruler of the entire country. It was better that the occupied territories in Asia should remain under his (Jamshed's) rule while the European territories be ruled over by him. Bayazid rejected this offer and replied that two swords cannot be put in one sheath. Sultan, the Conqueror's sister lived in Constantinople and she tried to make her nephew

Sultan Bayazid II understand that fighting between two brothers was not desirable and it was advisable that the territories of Asia Minor be given to Jamshed. However, Bayazid paid no heed to these words of wisdom. He said that the most he could do for Jamshed was that he could give him permission to live in Bait al-Maqdis with his family members and he would get an allowance from the income of state and in short, no avenue for accord was explored.

Jamshed was aware of the fact that if he did not win the throne Bayazid would not leave him alive. He was by the force of these circumstances compelled to fight for his safety. Sultan Bayazid took advantage of his commander, Ahmad Qaiduq's experience and decided to fight against his brother, Jamshed. The two forces fought in 886 A.H. (June 2, 1481 C.E.). At the moment that the battle became heated, a few commanders broke away from Jamshed along with the soldiers under their command and went over to the side of Bayazid, which brought about the defeat of Jamshed.

On one side the two brothers were at war and, on the other side the Pope of Rome who was about to leave Rome changed his mind owing to the news of Sultan the Conqueror's demise and sent word to the Christian powers of Europe to take advantage of the present situation and save Italy and drive the Turks out of Otranto. This desperate call drew Christians from Spain, France and Austria and the Christian forces laid a siege around Otranto. The Muslim troops of Otranto could not get any help from Constantinople. However, the Turkish force fought gallantly. Being disappointed at the absence of any help from Constantinople they sent word to the Christians that, although, in full command of the situation they no longer wanted to shed human blood. If they wanted to take back the city in peace the Turkish force could allow them to do so on condition that they were allowed to leave with honor and safety and go back to Constantinople. The Christian authorities accepted the peace offer without loss of time and sent them a signed peace treaty granting peace and safety to each Turkish soldier. When, according to treaty, the Ottoman troops began to leave the Christians committed a breach of trust and started killing Muslim soldiers. They surrounded the Ottomans on all sides and killed almost all of them. The lanes and streets of Otranto became red with Muslim blood.

This was a great shock and setback suffered by the Ottomans shortly after the ascension of Bayazid II and their foothold in Italy was lost. The door to the conquest of Italy that was opened by the Turks was closed once again, and the cloud of despair hovering over the Roman Church was removed at once. With this development, the expected help for Spain was also held back. Ahmad Qaiduq was not even able to avenge the blood of the Turkish soldiers killed by the Christians.

In the aftermath of his defeat, Jamshed found it inconvenient to stay in Asia Minor and he had little faith in his own commanders therefore, he preferred Egypt as his shelter. Egypt was at that time ruled over by the Mamluks and Abu Sayeed Qaid Bey of the Cherkesy dynasty was the ruler. Since the Abbasid caliph also had its seat in Egypt, the world of Islam looked upon it with reverence.

Jamshed, after his setback, left for Egypt along with his mother and wife. He was still within the confines of the Ottoman territories when a Turkish commander raided the caravan and looted whatever goods and chattels Jamshed had with him. He then crossed the borders of the Ottoman Empire hurriedly. The Turkish commander appeared before Bayazid in Constantinople to please the ruler by presenting to him his plunder. But Bayazid had him killed for plundering a defeated and afflicted caravan. When the Egyptian ruler heard of Jamshed's arrival, he welcomed him with honor, kept him as his guest and showed him grace and sympathy. Jamshed enjoined his stay with Abu Sayeed Bey for four months. He then left to perform Hajj. He came back to Egypt after performing Hajj to the House of Allah. In the meantime, exchanges of letters between Bayazid and Abu Sayeed had begun but the Egyptian ruler would not be persuaded to go against Jamshed instead he showed more respect and sympathy.

On his return from Makkah and Madinah, Jamshed plunged into making preparations and the Egyptian ruler extended all military and monetary help to him. Leaving his mother and wife behind in Egypt, Jamshed marched ahead to fight against Bayazid. Passing through Palestine and Syria he arrived at the southwestern part of Asia Minor. With this news, Bayazid moved ahead along with his seasoned commander Ahmad Qaiduq. Jamshed was defeated again after a fierce fight. This battle broke out in 887 A.H. (1482 C.E.) The second defeat was also led by his treacherous Turkish commander who first called him from Egypt to fight against Bayazid but changed sides when the battle took a serious turn, with the result that the rest of the troops lost their spirit and suffered a disaster.

Jamshed felt so frustrated and ashamed that he did not want to go back to Egypt and show his face to his mother, wife and the Egyptian ruler. Thus, he decided to leave for the Christian territories in Europe for rest and recuperation. Although he had opportunity in ample measure in Egypt, he chose Rhodes for the purpose and addressed the ruling group of Rhodes to allow him to stay for a short period. They responded that they considered him as the ruler of the Ottoman Empire and were ready to greet him to add to their own grace and honor. They also assured him all help for carrying out his campaign. With this encouraging but intriguing reply, he could not hold himself back and hurried to Rhodes along with 30 men who were with him. He found a large number of people on the coast to receive and greet him. From there, he was escorted to the capital with pomp and show. Dobson, the President of the Parliament gave him a standing ovation and made him stay as an honored guest. But very soon, Jamshed came to know that he was, in fact, held as a captive. Dobson then made Jamshed sign a bond declaring that, in case, he became the ruler of the Ottoman Empire he would give all kinds of concessions to the officials of Rhodes. Afterwards, he wrote to Bayazid that Jamshed was under arrest. Now if he wanted to keep peace they should be favored with freedom to make ingress and egress in all Ottoman ports and carry out normal trading activities. Furthermore, they should be granted exemption from all kinds of duties besides an annual grant of forty-five thousand Ottoman ducats to keep Jamshed confined otherwise they would set him free to stake his claim to the Ottoman throne. Bayazid accepted all the demands immediately and sent them more than forty-five thousand ducats annually. Dobson, on the other hand, wrote to Jamshed's afflicted and exiled mother to send them one hundred and fifty thousand annually as the price for not handing over Jamshed to Bayazid and keeping him in peace and safety, otherwise they would be compelled to settle the matter with Bayazid who was offering much more than what they were demanding from her. Jamshed's mother managed somehow to meet the cruel demand of the Christians and sent word that she would keep doing so annually without interruption.

Thus, the ruling party of Rhodes made Jamshed a permanent source of income. In view of the possibility of an invasion by Bayazid to take possession of Jamshed and depriving them of their newly acquired asset, they shifted Jamshed to a city in France, and continued shifting him from one city to another. They also kept Jamshed's companions separate from him until he was alone. When he was in a certain French city, Philipina Helena, the daughter of the administrator of the city fell in love with him, with the result he was put in a house build especially for him. Jamshed became a ward of the King of France as he had become a valuable property, which everybody wanted to keep. The King of France, the Roman Pope and other influential Christians of France wrote letters to Dobson to give Jamshed to them. However, Dobson was unwilling to do so. He neither agreed nor disagreed openly. Instead, he kept buying time under one pretext or another. Prince Jamshed remained in France until 895 A.H. During this period the ruling party of Rhodes continued receiving money from Bayazid II. Being apprehensive of losing Jamshed to the King of France, they wrote him to send Jamshed back. In addition, they wrote to the mother of Jamshed in Egypt to send them one hundred and fifty thousand ducats as a traveling allowance for Jamshed so that he could be brought back from France and then to be sent back to Egypt. That helpless lady met their demand immediately.

Although unwilling, the French King, Charles VIII allowed Jamshed's departure to Italy on condition that the Pope deposit with him as security the amount of ten thousand ducats which would be forfeited in case Jamshed was taken out of Italy without the permission of the French court. The Pope, on the other hand, wrote to the rulers of Rhodes that the benefit they were getting out of Jamshed if held back because of Jamshed's departure to Italy the Pope would cover their loss.

In short, Prince Jamshed entered the Roman city and was warmly greeted and was made to stay in the royal palace of the Pope. The French envoy accompanied the Prince.

When the French envoy and Jamshed went to meet the Pope the bishops and the commanders asked Jamshed to bow before the Pope as the French envoy and others were doing. But the son of Sultan, the Conqueror refused flatly to do so and moved forward rather carelessly and with an air of a conqueror, seated himself beside the Pope and began to converse with him in a royal fashion. During the exchange, he expressed his desire to say something in private. The Pope acceded to his request. During the private talk, Jamshed complained to the Pope about the breach of trust and disrespectful behavior of the Christian commanders. He also told his story of his long suffering and separation from his mother and wife in such pathetic words that his eyes were filled with tears. The Pope too heard it with tearful eyes. However, he told Jamshed that his departure to Egypt would prove fruitless and he would not be able to restore his father's throne. The Pope also told him to go to Hungary as the Hungarian king had invited him. But, last of all, the Pope told him rather emphatically to abandon Islam and convert to Christianity and this was for him the easiest course to get back the Ottoman throne for, in that case he would be entitled to the support of the entire Christian world. The Pope had spoken this much when Jamshed stopped him and said: "I am not ready to desert Islam in return for sovereignty over the entire world." Having heard this the Pope changed his way of speech and sent him out after giving him a common gesture only. Thus, he began to pass his days in confinement as he had been doing in France.

Having come to know of Jamshed's arrival in Rome the king of Egypt sent his envoy to welcome him and the Egyptian ruler anticipated that he (Jamshed) would be sent to Egypt. Sultan Bayazid II also sent his emissary to Italy with presents and offerings to Pope to settle the matter for it was a well known fact that the Pope had the power to send Jamshed anywhere he willed, and he was not bound by the desire of the people of Rhodes.

The envoy of the Egyptian king searched for Jamshed in Rome and when he got access to him, he greeted and welcomed him in a manner he did with the king of Constantinople. The envoy related to Jamshed the story about the amount of money Dobson had demanded from his mother in the name of travel expenses. Hearing this Jamshed approached the Pope along with the envoy and reported this case of extortion. The Pope put an end to the dispute by ordering the emissary of Dobson to pay Jamshed an amount although it was very little.

The Egyptian envoy returned empty-handed. Bayazid's emissary then contacted the Pope and struck a deal for the amount Bayazid would pay to Dobson. Being satisfied with the settlement, he too returned. Following this, the Pope made suitable arrangements for Jamshed and he began to pass his days as a captive.

Three years later, the Pope passed away and was replaced by another one. The new Pope was even more mischievous than the previous one. Shortly after assuming the office, he sent his emissary to Bayazid with the message that, in addition to the annual amount of forty thousand ducats, if three hundred thousand ducats as a lump sum were sent he would get him rid of Jamshed forever. George, the emissary of the Pope expressed himself so wisely and nicely in the royal court of Constantinople, that Bayazid suggested his name for the post of the deputy of the Pope. The emissary was staying in Constantinople when Charles VIII of France invaded Italy in 901 A.H. The reason behind this attack was to take Jamshed out of the possession of the new Pope. In the aftermath of this assault, Pope Iskander fled Rome and took shelter in the fort of St. Angelo and took Jamshed with him because Jamshed was a valuable part of the royal treasury. Eleven days after this an assembly was convened to work out terms and conditions for peace between the Pope and the King of France. The first condition that Charles advanced was that Jamshed should be put in his custody. At last, the Pope, Charles and Jamshed sat together in a separate room where the Pope said addressing Jamshed, "Well Prince! With whom do you want to live the king of France or myself?" Jamshed replied, "I am no longer a Prince but a captive, so you can keep me anywhere." Finally, Charles, the king of France took Jamshed to Naples and put him under the care of a commander with a team of military guards. Now all hopes of the Pope to extort money in the name of Jamshed were lost. Since the envoy of Sultan Bayazid had finalized a deal with the people to do away with Jamshed in return for 3 hundred thousand ducats, the Pope, having greed for money, wrote to Bayazid that he would bring his life to an end even in Naples and would be entitled to the amount as already settled. Following this, the Pope chose a Greek barber to carry out his plan. The barber had already converted to Islam and was named Mustafa. He, thereafter, turned apostate, came to Italy and had access to the Pope by means of his profession. The Pope sent him to Naples with a small packet to have Jamshed take it. It was the type of poison that would first cause the victim to fall sick and then die after a protracted illness; the poison also had no antidote.

Mustafa reached Naples and after some time got access to Prince Jamshed. Even the guards thought it unnecessary to prevent such an important person from meeting Jamshed. One day, he found an opportunity to have Jamshed take the poison, after which the Prince caught an incurable disease. In the meantime, he was given a letter from his mother but he was reduced to such a state of weakness that he could not even go through it. In such a terrible plight Jamshed invoked, "O Allah'. If these Unbelievers seek to inflict harm on Muslims through me, it is better You give me death today and save the Muslims from their mischief". Mustafa had not only given him poison but also shaved his head with a razor dipped in poison. The day he invoked Allah for his death his soul left his body. This happened in 901 A.H. Jamshed succumbed to his long suffering in prison. His dead body was sent to Sultan Bayazid as was demanded by him and was buried in Bursa. Bayazid paid the fixed amount to the Pope who kept Mustafa with him and later gave him a high post.

The detailed account of the sufferings of Jamshed and the treatment meted out to him show beyond doubt the ignoble and treacherous nature of the Christians and their greed for wealth and power and their breach of trust and promise. The highest and greatest among them went down so low that they, on one hand, minted money at the expense of Jamshed and stopped the Muslim invasion of their soil on the other.

Sultan Bayazid II

Bayazid II came to the throne in 886 A.H. and ruled over the Ottoman Empire until 918 A.H. He had a term of 32 years. Shortly after his accession, he had to face his brother Jamshed twice and both time he was victorious. However, his successes produced no fruit. He could not invade Italy and Rhodes because Jamshed had been under their control. His relation with the Mamluk Dynasty of Egypt became strained. Since Jamshed had taken refuge in Egypt and his mother and wife remained there until the end they started raiding the south-western parts of Asia Minor and occupied some border areas by beating Bayazid's forces in 890 A.H. Following a series of setbacks Bayazid made peace with the Mamluks at the cost of the cities and forts conquered by them.

Sultan Bayazid had a very bold and seasoned commander in the person of Ahmad Qaiduq. Bayazid could utilize his experience and talent for some great achievements. Ahmad Qaiduq was very popular with his forces and exhorted Bayazid to correct his ways. He was bold and outspoken and cared the least for royal majesty and kingly awe. However, Bayazid did not tolerate him for long.

In 895 A.H., he decided to contain the expanding power and influence of the Janissaries and was about to issue orders in this connection. Disagreeing with this decision, Ahmad Qaiduq warned Bayazid while in the court against such an injurious step and the prevailing tumult it would cause and the utility of the Janissaries in curbing the current state of chaos and confusion. He very emphatically said that a frustrated army could not be of much use against the insurgents and the very integrity of the country would be at stake. Although Bayazid kept silent in the court, he grew displeased at Ahmad Qaiduq's interference. Following this he decided to do away with Ahmad Qaiduq, who was later arrested. Being informed of the state of affairs, the forces under the command of Ahmad Qaiduq rose against Bayazid and besieged the royal palace. They threatened to kill Bayazid in retaliation in case their commander was killed. Thus, the Ottoman ruler changed his mind and handed over Ahmad Qaiduq to his 'devoted' forces and apparently showed respect to him. However, sometime later, Bayazid sent all the entire 'devoted' force to fight in some far off campaigns and put Ahmad Qaiduq to death. The assassination of the commander proved harmful to the Ottoman Empire.

In 896 A.H., the Ottoman and Russian Empires got in touch with each other. To start with, the Czar of Moscow sent his envoy to Sultan Bayazid in Constantinople with presents but the envoy was given no special treatment and he returned after a couple of days. The naval power of the Ottoman Empire made much progress during his reign. The Sultan was very particular about his naval power because of Jamshed's invasion with the support of Rhodes, Italy and France. Thus, on one side, he made peace with the Christian powers but he kept adding to his military strength and especially to his naval power on the other.

At a time when Jamshed was being shuffled from one place to another by the Christians, the Muslims of Spain, the King of Granada, sought naval reinforcements from Sultan Bayazid. Even though he could have extended significant help, he held himself back because of fear of the Christian support for Jamshed against him. He, however, sent to Spain a very small and ordinary fleet consisting of only a few warships under the command of Kamal, his naval commander. The fleet reached the Spanish coast and inflicted only a minor loss to the Christians and did not play a major role. But with the end of Jamshed, he attempted to occupy the islands and coastal areas lying between Greece and Italy and ruled over by Venice. In this way, he started a clash with the naval force of Venice. At last, the Turkish fleet decisively defeated the Venetian navy in 905 A.H. In 906 A.H. the Ottoman war fleet had to face the allied naval forces of Venice, the Roman Pope, Spain and France as a preemptive precaution against the quickly developing naval forces of the Ottomans. They had unanimously decided to do away with the Ottoman navy. However, the Ottoman naval commander, Kamal did a wonderful job by defeating the Christian war fleet. A large number of enemy warships were either sunk or captured and the rest escaped the deadly Turkish assault. Following this naval victory Kamal's fame spread everywhere and the Ottoman navy became the terror of the Mediterranean Sea. Only a few years before the Turkish naval victory, Muslim rule in Spain had gone out of existence in 897 A.H. Although Poland and Hungary also came to a clash with Bayazid II, their feeble attempts are not worth mentioning. However, in the aftermath of these encounters, the Polish made peace with the Sultan and the result was the Turkish occupation of some cities of Poland. Since Bayazid II was mentally inclined to peace Ottoman rule did not go beyond a certain limit in regard to grandeur and territorial expansion. During Sultan Muhammad II's period, the Christians had been so awe-struck that they were satisfied with a peace treaty with him and did not dare rise against him. We cannot, however, decry Sultan Bayazid II because during his rule, the Ottoman naval power made much progress and a number of islands and coastal areas came under Muslim control. However, he did not perform on a level worthy of his ancestors. He is generally known as a man of peace and virtue with a tinge of idleness and stupidity.

The year Sultan Bayazid II came to the throne Sheikh Abdur Rahman Jami dedicated his book entitled *Silsilatuz 'Zahb* to him. The Sheikh had also passed away on Muharram 10, 898 A.H. during Bayazid's tenure and was laid to rest in Herat. Columbus discovered America the same year, although, Spanish Muslims discovered it long before, notwithstanding Columbus is known for this accomplishment. During Bayazid's period the Portuguese king, Manuel sent Vasco de Gama with three ships under his command to discover India. He reached the port of Cannanore on the Malabar Coast and on Ramadan 20, 903 A.H. he lowered his anchor in Calcutta. During the same period, 906 A.H., Ismail Safwi, the founder of Safwi dynasty acceded to the throne of Iran. Sikander Lodhi was the contemporary of Sultan Bayazid II in India, but he died in 915 A.H., three years before the demise of the Ottoman king. On Shaban 29, 916 A.H. the Turkman king of the Shebani Dynasty was killed facing Ismail Safwi, the king of Iran, and one month later, Sultan Mahmud Beker the king of Gujarat died in Ahmedabad. The thirty-two year reign of Bayazid II was not so eventful, events occurring in other countries contemporary to his period have been mentioned here for the sake of giving the reader a historical perspective.

One more event of Sultan Bayazid II's period is also worth mentioning for it brings to focus the cold hearted and unmanly character of the Christians of that time. As already mentioned, Sultan Bayazid II had come into armed conflict with Hungary. During one such encounter, Ghazi Mustafa, a commander of Bayazid, and Ghazi's full brother were caught by the Hungarian troops. The Hungarian commander meted out such a ghastly treatment to them that the brother of Ghazi Mustafa was put on a spit and roasted over a fire like roasted meat while he was still alive. The height of the cruelty was that Ghazi Mustafa was forced to turn the spit to cook him. Following this gruesome punishment the king broke all of Ghazi Mustafa's teeth and freed him after torturing him and taking a ransom for his release. A few years later, when the same Hungarian commander was caught and produced before Ghazi Mustafa, he was simply killed without any torture or ill treatment. This single event proves beyond doubt the brute nature of the Christians in contrast to the righteous and civilized behavior of the Turks and their religious sensitivity and practice.

Towards the end of Sultan Bayazid II's reign, some internal troubles and disorders appeared. The issue of his successor was one such development. Bayazid II had eight sons. Five of them died young while the three remaining sons were named Ahmad, Qarqud and Salim. Among them Qarqud was the eldest and Salim was the youngest. The Sultan was fondest of the middle one and wanted to proclaim him as his successor. Ahmad, Qarqud and their sons were Governors in Asia Minor while Trabzon was ruled over by Salim. Salim was more valiant, adventurous and good-natured and because of these qualities, his commanders and soldiers preferred him to the others. After coming to power in Iran Ismail Safwi had spread the Shiites all over Asia Minor to teach the Ottomans Shi'a faith and make them supporters and sympathizers of the Iranian king. These efforts bore fruit and those ambitious among them rose to indulge in piracy and plunder within the confines of Asia Minor. Qarqud and Ahmad, ruling over the greater part of Asia Minor, sent their force to put down the insurgence and a number of encounters took place. However, owing to the negligence of the Ottoman Sultan and the idleness and wrong actions of the princes, bands of insurgents gathered under the leadership of a man named Shah Quli and they developed into a strong force. Shah Quli was a staunch supporter and well wisher of the King of Iran, Ismail Safwi. He left no stone unturned in pushing the Ottoman Empire into trouble. When the news of disturbances in Asia Minor reached Constantinople, Sultan Bayazid was under compulsion to send an army commanded by his Prime Minister to face the situation. During a fierce fight at Srimashk, both Shah Quli and the Ottoman Prime Minister were killed. The event took place in 917 A.H. These disturbances and disorders occurred in the territories under Qarqud and Ahmad's rule.

Trabzon, the territory ruled over by Salim was not given any chance to rise against the Ottoman power, which was undeniable proof of Salim's steadfastness and farsightedness. He had built a huge army to keep peace and order in his territory. When he found himself at the helm of affairs, he led his force against Serkeshia and won victories. Hearing this Bayazid II wrote to him from Constantinople not to expand his territories by invading foreign lands. Salim wrote back requesting his father to install him in a European province so that he could wage *jihad* on the Christians, because sitting idle and keeping silent was against his nature and he could not remain away from the battlefield. These events occurred at a time when Bayazid II was about to declare Ahmed his successor. When the 'devoted' forces and other commanders had an opportunity with Bayazid II, they expressed their resentment. Some of them spoke in favor of Qarqud for he was the elder son, while others favored Salim for his bravery and farsightedness. When Ahmad and Qarqud came to know of this conflict, they grew anxious about losing the throne. Because of this, all the three brothers started making efforts of their own to grab power by increasing their military strength and indulging in opposing one another. As per the wishes of the courtiers and Salim himself, he (Salim) was nominated for a European province called Samundra. In a situation when efforts were on to overtake one another, Salim also strengthened his position by occupying Adrianople in Europe. With the conquest of Adrianople, Bayazid himself rushed to punish Salim and the latter had to concede defeat easily for a large section of his army deserted him and went over to Bayazid's side. He fled the battlefield, took a ship and reached the Crimea to join his father-in-law and plunged into collecting fighters from among the Turks and the Tartars.

Ahmad, in Asia Minor, completed his preparations to conquer Constantinople and dethrone Bayazid. When Sultan Bayazid returned to Constantinople after driving away his son, Salim from Adrianople, he heard of the ensuing attack of Ahmad. In view of this situation, Sultan Bayazid became embarrassed and his courtiers started doubting his abilities as a ruler. Now, following the advice of his courtiers or on his own, Bayazid sent word to Salim to come to Constantinople along with his army and join the royal forces to put a check on the impending onslaught of Ahmad. This message filled Salim with joy and he took with him three or four thousand soldiers and arrived in Adrianople passing through difficult routes and passes and along the coast of Black Sea and from there he went to Constantinople. Hearing of Salim's arrival in this manner Bayazid sent him orders to go back to the province of Samundra, which he had been nominated for, as his help was no longer needed. But the courtiers and military commanders, on the other hand, sent word not to return but to come straight to Constantinople for he would never have such an opportunity again. Thus, Salim reached Constantinople and was accorded a warm welcome by the courtiers and military commanders. Salim then reached the gate of the royal palace and sent his message to Bayazid II to grant him an audience in the court. Thus, Bayazid convened an open court. The courtiers, religious scholars and jurists, advocates of the people and commanders expressed themselves with one accord that since the Sultan had grown old and weak it was desirable that he should abdicate his throne in favor of his son, Salim. Bayazid heard them patiently and declared Salim his successor without loss of time and quit the throne. Salim moved ahead and kissed the shoulder of the Sultan. Following this, the Sultan gave him some wise counsel and then got in the palanquin and moved on. Salim too walked along catching the foot of the palanquin. Bayazid II left Constantinople to settle in the city of Demotika and pass the rest of his life in peace and prayer. Salim escorted his departing father on foot up to the gate of the city. He then came back and ascended the throne. Bayazid passed away on the way before reaching Demotika city. He left behind three sons and nine grandsons among the grandsons was also Sulaiman, the only son of Salim. Bayazid II abdicated the throne on April 25, 1512 C.E. (910 A.H.) and died on April 29, 1512 C.E. Sultan Salim son of Bayazid II, ascended the throne in Constantinople.

The Ottoman Sultan Salim

When Sultan Salim came to the throne of Constantinople with the common consent and desire of the people and the military both of his brothers ruling in Asia Minor, could not muster courage to challenge his position. They apparently, showed their allegiance to Sultan Salim, but secretly, they engaged themselves in preparing against the central government. Salim was also not so gullible as to believe in the so-called sincerity of his brothers. But he initiated no military campaign against them. Now it came to such pass that Ahmad concentrated his forces in Amasya and filled his treasury with a large amount of money collected through heavy taxation. His son Alauddin, on the other hand, declared his sovereignty at the insistence of his father. Having heard of these insurgent activities Sultan Salim thought it necessary to personally march to Asia Minor to put down the uprisings. Thus, he himself led his army into Asia Minor. Moreover, he sent some warships along the seacoast. He caught and killed both Alauddin and his brother and occupied Bursa. He also found his nephews among the opponents and killed them as well. Having heard this Ahmad came out at the head of an army but fled the battlefield after being beaten. Following his defeat, he sent his two sons to Ismail Safwi, the king of Iran to live in safety, and he himself kept striving for success. In view of the sad plight of Ahmad and his son his elder brother, Qarqud ruling in the northeastern parts of Asia Minor became alert. The next step of Sultan Salim was his sudden attack on the territory of Qarqud with ten thousand cavalry soldiers. Qarqud was arrested after a slight resistance and was put to death for his claim to the Ottoman throne. However, the assassination of his brother left him sad for sometime during which he refused to take meals.

The assassination of the Ottoman princes in this manner must have naturally touched the emotions of the people and so Ahmad was able to build a huge army and challenge Salim to fight with him. Salim's army suffered several initial reverses also. However, Salim was a man of courage and determination and did not lose heart and concede defeat. He continued his recruiting drive on one hand and consolidated and regularized his military machine on the other. The result was the defeat and arrest of Ahmad and finally his assassination. This last battle with Ahmad resulting in his final setback took place on April 24, 1513 (919 A.H.).

By habits, manners and his direct course of action Sultan Salim was, beyond doubt, more valiant than his father, and a man of courage and determination like his grandfather. He was a constant source of terror to the Christian countries. However, when they witnessed that the Sultan was paying more attention to the Muslims and his internal problems, they advanced cautiously towards implementing peace agreements and keeping their western borders free from all conflicts. Shortly after dealing with his brothers, Sultan Salim got involved with Iran and Asia Minor. Had he not shown his firmness and determination against the Iranian ruler the Ottoman Empire would have disintegrated. Ismail Safwi considered himself among the descendants of Imam J'afar Sadiq and because of this, the Iranian people were emotionally attached to him. Shia-Sunni conflicts had not yet disappeared from Syria and Asia Minor. These countries had a climate favorable to the growth of the Shia faith. Moreover, these territories had a large Shia population. Ismail Safwi's maternal grandmother was a Christian lady and the daughter of the Christian king of Trabzon and wife of Hasan Tawil. Hence, Ismail Safwi had a desire to possess Trabzon, although it was a province of the Ottoman rule for a long time. Since Ismail Safwi had rose to power through Shia bigotry he knew very well how the Shia sect had played a significant role in instigating the Mongols to ravage Baghdad. Thus, the hate and enmity of an ambitious and mighty king like Ismail Safwi towards the Ottoman rule was not a matter of surprise. From the day he came to power he never failed to create trouble for Bayazid II in Asia Minor and winning the favor and support of the people there by propagating the Shia faith. Bayazid's government failed to put a check on those hostile activities. Moreover, his two sons ruling at that time in Asia Minor took no serious notice of these impending dangers. However, Salim, the ruler of Trabzon was fully conscious of Ismail Safwi's intriguing activities and he never allowed his secret plans to bear fruit. Ismail Safwi had already captured a few border areas during the reign of Bayazid II, and when his Ottoman Governors failed to restore those territories Bayazid paid no heed to the problem.

When Sultan Salim became involved in dealing with his brothers and nephews, Ismail Safwi was watching the developments not only with a sense of satisfaction but, he lent his active support to the insurgents through his agents in Asia Minor. That is why Ahmad was able to give Salim some initial defeats. Now Sultan Salim came to know of the nefarious design of Ismail Safwi to set Murad, the son of prince Ahmad and nephew of Salim, against him (Salim) in Asia Minor and then put him on the throne of Constantinople. He was able to do so for Murad was in those days under the care of the Iranian king. He also noticed that the cities, towns and villages of Asia Minor were stormed by Shia-Sunni conflicts, which were created by none other than Ismail Safwi himself.

After doing away with his brothers, he first of all, set up a large-scale secret service in Asia Minor and ordered his agents to prepare a comprehensive list of those who had converted to being Shiites by the teachings of Ismail Safwi and were ready to lay down their lives for their leader. When the list was completed, Salim was shocked to know that Asia Minor had seventy thousand such men who were ready to fight against the Ottoman king as soon as Ismail Safwi would launch his attack on the Ottoman territory. He, however, recovered himself and rose very cautiously to face this seemingly adverse situation. First of all, he sent troops equal in number to the traitors and rebels, and handing over the list of the disloyal persons to the commanding officers of each area, to tell every soldier under his direct command to kill one rebel at the appointed date and time. They were also enjoined not to disclose the plan beforehand. Thus, in response of the order given forth fifty thousand traitors were killed in the length and breadth of Asia Minor in a manner that the Ottoman soldiers sustained not even a scratch. Such large-scale killing of the Shi'a sect was extremely horrible. The rest lost heart and renounced their new faith. The undoing of the conspiracy of Ismail Safwi was, in fact, a marvelous victory for Sultan Salim. Although Ismail Safwi fretted much at this unfortunate happening, he kept silent. But shortly after that, he came out with the open declaration that he was about to launch an attack on the Ottomans to restore his ancestral throne by arresting and deposing Salim, the Ottoman. Having heard this Sultan Salim called a meeting of his courtiers and military commanders and informed them of his plan to invade Iran.

This declaration was made at a time when the episodes of Iranian power had gripped the mind of everyone and Turkish troops had already tasted defeat at their hands. Moreover, Shebani Khan, the king of Turkistan had already been killed by Ismail Safwi. Thus, to the audience of courtiers and military commanders any thought of attacking Iran was an act fraught with danger. They all, therefore, kept silent three times at the call of the Sultan. However, the doorkeeper, named Abdullah broke the silence. He moved ahead, knelt down before Sultan Salim and submitted that he and his companions were ready to fight under the royal banner and die for victory. Sultan Salim grew very happy and promoted him to the post of district collector. Other commanders also followed suit.

Ismail Safwi

Ismail's lineage is as follows: Ismail bin Haider bin Junaid bin Ibrahim bin Khawaja Ali bin Sadruddin bin Sheikh Safiuddin bin Jibril. Sheikh Safiuddin was the first man in the family to achieve a prominent name and was famous. He lived in Ardabil and served the people as a spiritual guide. It is after his name that the family came to be known as "Safwi." Following the demise of Sheikh Safiuddin his son, Sadruddin took up the patched garment of his father and replaced him as a spiritual guide. Sultan Bayazid Yaldaram and Timur were his contemporaries. Along with the defeat and arrest of Sultan Bayazid in 804 A.H. a large number of Turkish soldiers were also held by Timur.

When, following this victory, Timur reached Ardabil he attended the shrine of Sheikh Safiuddin. During the audience Timur said, "Can I be of any service to you?" Sheikh Sadruddin said, "Release all the prisoners held from the battle of Ankara." Timur carried it out immediately. After their release, all the Turkish prisoners became the Sheikh's disciples and began to live in attendance of the Sheikh. With the passage of time, the number of these "released" captives' progeny increased.

After the demise of Timur, his empire broke into pieces and was divided among his children. Soon after the death of Timur, the Turkmen of Kara Koyunlu tribe set up their rule in the territory lying between the Black Sea and Azerbaijan. Similarly, Kurdistan, the northern part of Iraq, had gone to Ak Koyunlu, another tribe of the Turkmen, which ruled over the territory as a feudatory with the authority of Timur during the his lifetime. Qara Yusuf, the chief of the Kara Koyunlu was at enmity with Timur and passed his days wandering in Egypt during the reign of Timur. Having heard of the death of Timur, he came back and occupied Azerbaijan rather easily. Ardabil was the center of Azerbaijan while Diyar Bakr was the capital of Kurdistan.

During the time of Sheikh Junaid, the great grandson of Sheikh Sadruddin, the number of the disciples increased so much that Shah, son of Qara Yusuf was embarrassed and asked Sheikh Junaid to leave Ardabil. In response to the order, Sheikh Junaid, along with his disciples, left for Diyar Bakr. Hasan Tawil of the Ak Koyunlu was then the ruler of Diyar Bakr (Kurdistan). When he heard of the arrival of Sheikh Junaid in this way, he grew very happy and accorded him a warm welcome.

Soon after his arrival, Hasan Tawil married his sister to Sheikh Junaid. Both Ak Koyunlu and Kara Koyunlu tribes of the Turkmen were old rivals. Since Sheikh Junaid had now entered into relations with a royal family and come out of the life of seclusion, leadership had now become part of his duties. He changed his disciples into soldiers easily as they were none but the progeny of Turkish fighters. Building an army out of those soldiers, he launched an attack on Ardabil. Since the ruler of Ardabil had driven the Sheikh out of Ardabil, this invasion was taken as a retaliatory action. Even his disciples and supporters thought so. Since the Sheikh was an inexperienced commander he suffered a setback and escaped from the battlefield and invaded the ruler of Shirvan, a friend and ally of Jahan Shah, the ruler of Ardabil. But the Sheikh suffered another defeat and fled for his life in this state of confusion an assassin's arrow hit him and he succumbed to it.

Following the death of Sheikh Junaid his son Haider succeeded him as the spiritual guide. Haider was a prince from the side of his mother and a dervish from his father's side. He had, therefore, in him both the temporal and the mystical and he drew more disciples than his father had. After the death of Sheikh Junaid, Amir Hasan Tawil made temporary peace with Jahan Shah and annexed Khorasan after killing Abu Sayeed Timuri. Afterwards, Amir Hasan wrested Azerbaijan from Jahan Shah and became the ruler of Iran. After that Hasan Tawil, the King of Iran married his daughter to his maternal nephew Sheikh Haider. Thus, Sheikh Haider became not only the son of the king of Iran but also his son-in-law. Hasan Tawil had married the daughter of the Christian king of Trabzon. His Christian wife gave birth to a girl who was named Parsa or Shah Begum. This very girl was given to Sheikh Haider in marriage and three sons named Ali, Ibrahim and Ismail were born to her. Sheikh Haider remained silent during the lifetime of Hasan Tawil. But, following the death of Hasan Tawil and the accession of his son Yaqub, Sheikh Haider built an army out of his disciples and invited others too to join his army to attack the ruler of Shirvan, southeastern Caucasus (part of modern Azerbaijan), to avenge the blood of his father. He held himself back from any such action during the lifetime of Hasan Tawil because he had made peace with Jahan Shah following the assassination of Sheikh Junaid and had also entered into a peace treaty with the king of Shirvan who had also abetted Hasan Tawil in assassinating Abu Sayeed Mirza Timuri. Thus, the peace treaty remained intact during the lifetime of Hasan Tawil, and Sheikh Haider had to delay his action against the ruler of Shirvan. Shirvan was under the rule of an Iranian dynasty for several hundred years and they claimed to be the descendants of Bahram Chubin. When Farkh Yasar of Shirvan heard of Sheikh Haider's expedition to avenge the blood of his father he also became ready to fight. These two forces came face to face in 893 A.H. and Sheikh Haider was killed like his father and was buried in Ardabil.

After the demise of Sheikh Haider his elder son, Ali was brought to the seat of his father as a spiritual guide. Disciples in large numbers also flocked around him. When Amir Yaqub, who had succeeded Hasan Tawil, anticipated Ali's attack on Shirvan like his father and grandfather he wanted the peace treaty conducted during the time of Hasan Tawil to continue. To avoid any trouble in the future he interned Ali and his brothers in the fort of Astakhar where they passed more than four years of their lives. When Amir Yaqub died and was succeeded by his son Ahmad Beg, Ali, along with his brothers, escaped from captivity, he reached Ardabil and set himself to the task of procuring disciples. Ahmad Beg sent down an army to punish Ali who came out to face the attacking army but was defeated and killed like his father and grandfather.

During the encounter Ali's younger brothers, Ibrahim and Ismail fled from Ardabil to Gilan in disguise. Ibrahim passed away shortly after arriving in Gilan. Ismail alone, who was still young, remained alive. Ahmad Beg did not, in view of his tender age, oppose him. Ismail's old family disciples gathered around him.

By 906 A.H., when Ismail was still 14, his disciples, who used to be under arms at all times, organized themselves in a well-disciplined strong army at a very short notice. Ismail took these troops with him and launched such a massive attack on Farkh Yasar, the ruler of Shirvan that he was not only defeated but also killed. Ahmad Beg was shocked to hear of this setback and left to punish the offenders. In an action taken in a hurry, he marched with a small army under his direct command and clashed with Ismail. The logical result of too much haste and the lack of preparation was his defeat which took a heavy toll of life including his own. Following this, another ruler belonging to the Ak Koyunlu tribe took on Ismail near Hamdan but was beaten. As a result of these continuous victories, countries like Iraq, Iran, and Azerbaijan came to the fold of Ismail.

Only four years before, a man who was passing a wretched life in Gilan had now turned to be a mighty ruler. The progeny of the Turkish soldiers never lacked in loyalty and took the descendant of their benefactor, Sadruddin of Ardabil to the throne.

How amazing it is that those who led Ismail bin Haider Safwi to power could not keep peace with the Ottoman Empire ruled over by people of the same race. Since Ismail Safwi had won victories from the very beginning, his reputation as a conqueror benefited him greatly and he became a terror to his opponents. Had Ismail Safwi not spread his net of conspiracy throughout the territories of Sultan Salim and kept peace with him, the Ottomans could have turned to Europe. Because of this, Salim had to renew his peace agreements with the Christian powers and they had a long respite of eight to ten years to increase and strengthen their military power.

The Battle of Chaldiran

Having heard of the war preparations of Ismail Safwi, Sultan Salim mobilized his armed forces in Yeni city in Rabia al-Awwal 920 A.H. (April 20, 1514C.E) and entered into Asia Minor. After a week, on April 27, Sultan Salim's intelligence officers caught a spy of Shah Ismail Safwi and produced him before Sultan Salim. But instead of punishing him, he gave him a letter addressed to Ismail Safwi. In addition, he sent an emissary to Iran. Sultan Salim wrote to him the following after praising Allah Almighty.

"I, Salim bin Sultan Bayazid bin Sultan Muhammad bin Sultan Murad, the ruler of the Ottoman Empire, the chief of the brave and the destroyer of idolaters and the enemies of true religion, tell Ismail, the ruler of Iran, that the Word of Allah Almighty is above all changes. But it contains countless secrets beyond the comprehension of man. Allah Almighty sent man to the Earth as His Khalifa (vice rergent) for man alone embodies both spiritual and physical forces at one time, and man is the only animal who can understand the Attributes of Allah and worships Him for His High Qualities. Man cannot acquire true knowledge from any religion but Islam and none can gain success except by following the Last Prophet (ﷺ). O Amir

Ismail, you can never attain success and prosperity for you have defiled the pure and sacred principles of Islam by going against the dictates of the *Shari'at* and gave up the way to salvation. You demolished the places of prayer and captured power in the East by foul and unlawful means. You have attained your present position by tricks and fraud. You have opened the doors to cruelties and mercilessness on the Muslims. You are not only a liar, merciless and an apostate but also unjust, a fabricator in religion and one showing disrespect to the Qur'an. You have created differences and dissension in Islam by wrong interpretations. Your have sowed the seeds of mischief and disturbance throughout and raised the banner of faithlessness. You have committed terrible excesses overpowered by your baser self, and you have permitted one and all use of abusive language against Abu Bakr, Umar and Uthman. Since you have committed infidelity in word and deed, our religious scholars have issued a verdict of capital punishment on you. They have also given a verdict that every Muslim should make it his duty to do away with the evils and impurities lying within you and your followers. Now, in order to implement the decisions of the religious scholars which are totally based on the dictates of the Qur'an and for strengthening Islam, the Religion of Allah and saving people from your atrocities, I have decided to put on armor by putting off royal garments and took up my flag for the battlefield, the flag that has never seen defeat, and attack you with a sword which goes mad when it is unsheathed along with soldiers whose swords inflict deep injuries on the enemy. We have already crossed the Straits and I am sure, by the Grace of Allah, I will very soon put an end to your cruelties and disruptive activities and take out of your mind the smell of arrogance which has driven you towards evil acts. But, since I follow the dictates of *Shari'at*, I think it necessary to put the Qur'an before you and invite you to follow the true religion. The best course to shun the evil is to take stock of the record of deeds, repent for the evils done and ward off all evil acts in the future. Moreover, give back to the possession of our junior commissioned officers those territories, which you have unlawfully taken away. Do carry out these orders if you hold your safety dear and do it immediately. But if you fail to give up the wrong acts of your ancestors you will see your fields covered with our camps and watch us showing our wonderful acts of bravery. The entire world will then see the verdict of Allah Almighty, the greatest of all judges."

As pointed out in the letter, Ismail had demolished all the tombs and mosques belonging to the *Sunni* sect and put them to untold miseries. The ancestors of Ismail were not Shi'a by faith. They all belonged to the Sunni sect and practiced Sunni faith. After the time of Sheikh Junaid when the family was engaged in warfare, they began to induce people to love of *Ahl-e-bait* (members of the Prophet's family) for they were sure of their easy success in bringing recruits in this way. But, gradually, they stuck to the Shia creed for political reasons. Ismail Safwi indulged in excessive exaggeration and began to propagate the Shiite faith all over the country. Since the Iranians were inclined to this faith, he achieved remarkable success in his attempt. But those Muslims who showed firmness in faith suffered terrible atrocities. He propagated his beliefs across the borders of the Ottoman Empire. Sultan Bayazid did not arrange to put a check on it but Sultan Salim paid immediate attention to this scourge.

Along with the letter, Sultan Salim had sent his emissary to demand the return of Prince Murad in case he (Ismail) was reconciled to the Sultan's way of thinking. Having gone through the letter he handed over the emissary to Murad who, at the instance of Ismail Safwi, cut the emissary into pieces. This step of Ismail was not only brutal but against the royal norms. Ismail sent the following reply to Sultan Salim:

"I couldn't understand the reason behind your burning anger. I think you have written the letter under the effect of opium. If you are set to fight, I am also ready to face you and leave the result to Allah. You will measure the merit only during the fight."

Along with the letter Ismail Safwi sent a small box of opium as a gift to Sultan Salim, meaning thereby that the Sultan's letter was from one addicted to opium and the letter was written under the effect thereof.

Having seen the box of opium and having gone through the letter
Salim fell in wrath and retaliated by killing Ismail's emissary. He then
organized his forces and marched to Tabriz, the capital of Ismail
Safwi. When he took stock of his troops in Sivas, they were comprised
of eighty thousand cavalrymen and forty thousand infantry. He
divided his forty thousand infantrymen into many parts and deployed
a company at every stage from Sivas to Kayseri with the instruction
that each company should move one stage ahead as the troops under
the command of the Sultan moved a stage ahead of Kayseri. The
arrangement was made to facilitate the movement of supplies. But as
Sultan Salim stepped into Iranian territory he witnessed that, by the
order of Ismail Safwi, the Iranians had destroyed all populated areas
and cultivation and burnt down all the vegetation, trees and grass and
had set a large army to ravage its own territory leaving nothing for the
Ottoman troops. The Iranian population was ordered to vacate the
area with what they could carry and set what was left on fire
otherwise the army would turn them out and reduce their goods and
chattels to ashes. In such a situation Sultan Salim faced difficulties
although he had already made adequate arrangements for supplies
from Constantinople and the European provinces to the port of
Trabzon by ship and from there on donkeys and camels up to the
military camps. Ismail Safwi kept moving back without putting up
any resistance and ravaging his own country. He had in mind that
Salim would not be able to lead such a huge army so far and would
have to retreat exhausted and discouraged and Ismail Safwi was not
very wrong. At one stage of the long march the tired army refused to
go-ahead and the commanders advised the Sultan against further
movement. The Sultan disliked the suggestion and kept moving ahead
instead of going back. Now the Ottoman force entered Azerbaijan via
Diyar Bakr (Kurdistan). At this stage, the commanders jointly sent
Hamdan Pasha the childhood friend and classmate of the Sultan to go
and persuade him to return. He called on the Sultan and entreated
him not to displease his troops and go back. Having heard this Sultan
Salim turned mad with anger and cut off his head. No one could even
make a murmur against the Sultan. However, at one stage of this long
and arduous journey the 'devout' forces, most courageous and valiant

of all, raised a unanimous voice against going ahead. In view of the behavior of the entire army, the next morning Sultan Salim came on horseback and stood among the 'devout' army and addressed the soldiers as a whole:

"I have not come here to go back unsuccessful. Those who are valiant and cannot bear the blame of timidity because of their inherent nobility and fear not the wounds of arrows and swords will certainly go with me. But those who prefer life to honor and want to go back home deterring the troubles ahead are permitted on my part to leave the company of our brave and mighty men. In case none of you accompany me and leave me alone I shall not go back without fighting."

Having said this Sultan Salim ordered the 'impotent' to leave and the brave and those having a sense of shame to march ahead without delay. The stirring words of the Sultan electrified the entire army and it set out without a single soldier staying behind. It was the blessing of his manly courage that at the next stage the Christian ruler of Caucasia sent a huge amount of supplies to the Ottoman troops. This generosity was given to win the heart and favor of the Sultan. Now Tabriz, the capital of Ismail was not far away. Sultan Salim then reached the valley of Chaldiran, and as he ascended a moun towards the west of the valley, he witnessed the Iranian force in the field facing him and he grew happy. In each letter addressed to Ismail Safwi until then Ismail had put him to shame by evading a fight with the Ottoman force. Had Ismail Safwi left his capital too, Sultan Salim would have stopped his march and not gone beyond Tabriz. But Ismail could not bear the Ottoman advances any more. Chaldiran lay a little more than twenty miles away from Tabriz and Ismail Safwi had chosen this place to give battle to Salim. Ismail Safwi's army was almost equal in size to that of Salim's but with a difference. While the Ottoman force was extremely exhausted, Ismail had a fresh army, armed to the teeth. Ismail Safwi's retreat was, in fact, a part of his war strategy and he was very sure of defeating an army that was overtaken by fatigue. In such a situation, it was reasonable for Sultan Salim to delay the clash for a day or two and allow his troops to take a rest and regain lost freshness and energy. But, since Sultan Salim was impatient to fight with Ismail Safwi, he could not hold back when he came face to face with the enemy. As the spies of Ismail Safwi had informed him, the Ottoman force was to appear from the front he had drawn his battle line accordingly and was determined not to give any respite to the exhausted Ottoman army. He had also come to know of the artillery with Sultan Salim besides the number of troops he had. As a war strategy, he divided his eighty thousand cavalry into two parts, each consisting of forty thousands and kept one part under his direct command while another part he entrusted to his Commander, Abu Ali. He then issued instructions that in case of an Ottoman attack, the front line soldiers should face the assault and the two cavalry corps should come around from the right and the left side to reach behind and fall upon the enemy troops. When Sultan Salim noticed the firmness of the Iranian force, he placed his troops drawn from Asia Minor under his Commander Sanan Pasha and those from Europe to Hussein Pasha and put Sanan Pasha on the right wing and Hussein Pasha on the left. He took his 'devout' soldiers with him and kept to the center. He then mobilized the feudatories and volunteers as the vanguard; the artillery was set up at a suitable spot. Since Ismail Safwi knew about the artillery of Sultan Salim, he had utilized the services of eighty thousand cavalrymen to neutralize its effect. This was, in fact, a commendable and wise strategy on the part of Ismail. Thus, as both the armies came closer and the confrontation started Ismail Safwi went around the Ottoman force and targeted its right wing with his forty thousand cavalrymen and Abu Ali did the same from the left side. As the battle broke out, calls of *takbir (Allahu-Akbar)* rose from the Ottoman side while the Iranian troops cried "Shah, Shah." Thus, while the war cry of the Ottoman force meant, "Allah is Great", the Iranian army was chanting the name of its king and both the forces could be identified by their distinctive chants. However, Ismail Safwi, evading the artillery fire, launched a fierce attack on the Husain Pasha's right wing from behind and took a heavy toll on the European corps. Ismail's Commander Abu Ali also attempted to give the same performance on the left side but did not achieve much success. A part of his cavalry came within the range of the Ottoman artillery and they lost their existence along with their commander, Abu Ali Sanan Pasha put Commander Ali's troops to rout rather easily. But Hussein Pasha was still struggling to beat the Iranians who were proving their worth as formidable fighters. Sultan Salim was watching the battlefield with the utmost caution. When he found Sanan Pasha in a dominant position and needed no help, he hurried to the rescue of Hussein Pasha with the selected squads under his direct command and launched such a massive attack that the Iranians were uprooted and Ismail Safwi himself fled the field.

Ismail Safwi was caught in his attempt to escape to safety but his comrade Mirza Sultan posed as Ismail and as the Ottoman soldiers turned their attention to Mirza Sultan, Ismail Safwi escaped. The entire battlefield was cleared of Iranian troops. When Salim captured the military camp, he found that the Iranian ruler had fled in such a state of fright and confusion that he left behind not only his treasure but also his beloved wife. Sultan Salim kept the women and children in custody and killed all the prisoners of war. The deserted look of the battlefield showed that fourteen Ottoman commanders and an equal number of their Iranian counterparts were lying dead. Sultan Salim was much aggrieved at the loss and buried them with honor. Following this Sultan Salim proceeded to Tabriz and entered the city only thirteen days after the battle of Chaldiran on August 22, 1514 C.E. (Rajab 20, 920 A.H.). Ismail Safwi had taken refuge in Tabriz but fled to Khorasan on hearing of Sultan Salim's march into the city. After a halt of eight days in Tabriz, the Sultan proceeded to Karabakh. During his stay in Tabriz, Mirza Badiuzzaman, a prince claiming to be the descendant of Timur called on the Sultan and was greeted warmly and honorably. Salim had in mind a march to Azerbaijan and to pass the spring there before leading his campaigns against the eastern countries but his force once again refused to go ahead and pressed Sultan Salim to go back home. The return of the Sultan was similar to that of Alexander who was forced by his army to return from the banks of the river Satluj. Even though Sultan Salim left from Karabakh, he did not go straight back to Constantinople. He halted at the city of Amasya in Asia Minor and after passing the spring there invaded Armenia, Georgia and the Caucasus territories and annexed them to the Ottoman rule. He had already occupied Azerbaijan. He was now planning to conquer Kurdistan and Iraq, which until then was under the rule of Ismail Safwi. In the meantime, news came from

Constantinople that the Ottoman force there was about to revolt and had shown disrespect to the Viceroy of the capital. This new development compelled him to return to the trouble spot, but he appointed seasoned commanders to complete his unfinished tasks who, in a short time, conquered Kurdistan, Iraq and up to the coastal areas of the Persian Gulf. Thus, half of Ismail Safwi's country became the part of the Ottoman rule. All future attempts of the Iranian ruler to restore his lost territories ended in defeat.

One of the gains of Sultan Salim in Tabriz was that he contracted about one thousand builders, architects and artisans and sent them to Constantinople offering them higher daily wages plus endowments. The builders and architects of Tabriz were at that time famous all over the world. Thus, he fulfilled the needs of Constantinople. On being defeated thoroughly, Ismail Safwi made a few attempts to make peace with Sultan Salim and divert his attention elsewhere but because of his strong dislike for the Iranian ruler he spurned his peace offers and refused to build any friendly relations with Ismail. Had Salim not been involved in the affairs of Syria and Egypt he would have invaded Iran once again to wrest from Ismail Safwi the remaining parts of his country. As a result of these conquests, the Ottoman Empire expanded deep into the eastern regions and a number of fertile provinces came under its control. Most importantly, the Ottoman rule was no longer under threat from its eastern borders. Ismail Safwi wrote to Sultan Salim to send back his wife who was still in the custody of the Ottoman ruler. Since he considered Ismail an apostate and faithless he refused to send his wife to him and married her to one of his soldiers, Ja'far Chalpi. When Ismail Safwi came to know that his wife was enjoying her married life with a Turkish soldier, he was downcast by this terrible shock and he lived and died in the same state.

Conquest of Egypt and Syria

It has already been mentioned that Malik al-Saleh of the Ayyubi dynasty had organized a force in Egypt based on the Mamluks, which may be called a slave army. Very soon, these slaves captured the Egyptian throne. About the same time, the Slave dynasty was in power in India too. While in India, only two kings from the Slave dynasty were actually slaves and the latter kings only belonged to that dynasty, in Egypt however, only a slave could succeed to the throne on the death of the slave ruler. Those slave kings were called Mamluks. They ruled over Egypt until the time of Sultan Salim and the Abbasid caliphs lived in Egypt only to provide a safeguard and to provide credibility to those Egyptian kings. The Mamluk rule of Egypt was also very respectable and mighty. The Mamluks extended two marvelous services to Islam. One, they saved Islam from the Christian assaults and did away with the crusades forever; two, they put a check on the surge of Mongol invasions and beat the forces of Genghis and Hulagu Khan. It is quite strange that the victorious Mongols were thrashed by the slaves (Mamluks) of Egypt were beaten again by the slave kings of India. Thus, the Mongols who took the most respectable and highest dynasties by storm were routed by the Muslim slave kingdoms.

The Mamluk dynasty of Egypt, which ruled in Egypt, Syria and the Hijaz from the end of the Ayyubi dynasty, had never been inimical to the Ottoman dynasty. However, when Prince Jamshed took refuge in Egypt after being defeated by his elder brother Sultan Bayazid II relations with Cairo and Constantinople turned bitter to the extent of causing a clash between the two and the Ottoman rule had suffered setbacks at the hands of the Mamluks. They were anxiously watching the victorious marches of Sultan Salim and especially the defeat of Ismail Safwi. They were anticipating Salim's campaigns against Egypt to restore the cities and forts occupied by the Mamluks during the rule of Bayazid II. Ismail Safwi, after being defeated by Sultan Salim, sent his emissary to the Mamluk ruler to establish friendly relations with Egypt. Qalzu Ghazi, the ruler of Egypt held the Iranian emissary in esteem and accepted the offer. The emissary also warned the Egyptian ruler against the impending danger of Salim's invasion. These new developments drew his attention to the demand of the situation and he himself came to the city of Aleppo (Arabic: Halb) and stationed himself there. Immediately after this, he mobilized an adequate number of troops along the Syrian borders. This was only done for precautionary measures. Sultan Salim had, perhaps, no intention of attacking the Mamluk rule for the Mamluks were devout Muslims and they had a common faith. However, the unfortunate Mamluks suffered a setback because of the secret planning of the Iranian ruler, which positioned Mamluk and Ottoman forces in apparently hostile postures.

On his return from Iran, Sultan Salim sat down in Constantinople to organize and regularize the internal administration in Constantinople. He no longer had any target other than the European borders and Christian states. His ancestors had been campaigning against the European powers from the beginning of their dynasty. In 922 A.H. Sultan Salim received a message from Sanan Pasha, Governor of the eastern part of Asia Minor, that he was unable to lead his expedition into the Euphrates valley because of the presence of a Mamluk force on the Syrian border for, according to him, they could possibly attack the eastern parts of Asia Minor in his absence. Sultan Salim called an emergency meeting of the commanders, scholars and ministers in Constantinople and sought their advice on how to deal with the Mamluks. After a long discussion his superintendent of the vernacular office Muhammad Pasha made a fervid speech and said that the Ottoman Empire must demonstrate its might, and the Mamluk rulers do not deserve to serve the Sacred Sanctuaries of Makkah and Madinah and keep the Hijaz under their control. Hence, the Sultan must achieve this honor and this would be considered as a great service to Islam. Thus to fight against the Mamluks was valid and lawful. Sultan Salim liked the suggestion and appointed him as his Prime Minister.

Sultan Salim was determined to fight the Mamluks, first he sent his emissary to Qalzu Ghazi, the ruler of Egypt demanding from him obedience and tribute and threatened to invade in case of failure of implementation. When Sultan's emissary called on Qalzu in Aleppo, Qalzu was angered and imprisoned him. On receiving the news, Sultan Salim proceeded from Constantinople at the head of a force. When the Ottoman force drew near the Mamluk ruler got embarrassed and sought peace from the Ottoman ruler and released his emissary at once. But Sultan Salim paid no heed to the request and kept moving ahead. Thus the rival forces came face-to-face at Marj Wabiq, where lies the grave of Prophet Daud (عليه السلام) (the Prophet David). On August 24, 1516 C.E. (922 A.H.), two years after the battle of Chaldiran. Although the Mamluks were not deficient in bravery and courage, they were then overtaken by internal strife and rivalries and could not withstand the onslaught of Salim's huge force. The Mamluk ruler, who was an old man, fought gallantly and died in action. With this news, the Mamluks troops lost ground and Sultan Salim seized Aleppo (Halb).

But this initial defeat failed to frustrate the Mamluks for they considered the Ottomans unequal to them in valor. However, they returned to Cairo to elect a new Sultan. The Mamluks had twenty-four commanders who had the right to unanimously elect a new ruler and they all had to be present in the capital on such an occasion. Syria was now open to Sultan Salim in the absence of the major Mamluk commanders. Salim seized the opportunity and took full advantage thereof and brought Damascus and Bait al-Maqdis (Jerusalem) under his control. The Mamluks did not put up a strong resistance on their part.

The Mamluks elected Tuman Bey as their new ruler. Immediately after accession, Tuman sent a big force to the borders of Egypt and Syria to put a check on the advance of Sultan Salim and he set about building a huge army. In the meantime, Sultan Salim, fortunately, found a big treasure in Damascus, which belonged to the Egyptian rulers. This treasure played a role in the future conquests of Sultan Salim. With this huge amount he won the hearts of religious scholars, orators, religious groups and judges and donated lavishly to building mosques, madrasas, bridges and the carrying out of welfare projects besides, providing camels of burden and other necessary materials to be used in attacking Egypt. The Egyptian force moved up to Gaza, the bordering strip of Egypt. Sultan Salim led his troops passing through populated and flourishing areas of Syria. While entering the deserts, he loaded enough water on camel back and gave away rewards to his soldiers to enhance their courage and determination. He than handed over the artillery to Pasha by appointing him as the Commander of a huge army and sent him ahead as the vanguard. He himself took the remaining troops and marched forward with great caution. This ten-day long journey passed safely. Sanan Pasha fought with an Egyptian column at Gaza under the Mamluk commander Ghazali. Even though the Mamluk soldiers fought very valiantly, the Ottoman artillery routed them thoroughly. They lost the battle because their bravery was no match for the artillery of the Ottomans. This victory added much to the courage and determination of the Ottoman force and they shook off the fear of the Mamluks.

Clash between the Mamluks and the Ottomans in Egypt

On being thoroughly beaten in Gaza Ghazali came back to Cairo and gave the shocking news of their disaster caused by the Ottoman artillery. But the irrepressible Tuman Bey instead of losing courage he grew more determined. He mobilized his troops along the road leading to Syria and waited for the arrival of the Ottoman force. Sultan Tuman Bey was a noble man and a brave fighter. At times, the forces of destiny go against able and noble souls and so it happened with Tuman Bey. His election as the head of the country was opposed by a section of the commanders but they could not raise their voice openly at that time and kept smoldering with anger. Had Tuman Bey found time he could have pacified his opponents but his military engagement immediately after accession allowed him no opportunity for this noble work.

Two among those opposing commanders were Ghazali and Khairi. They started making secret plans to bring about the defeat of Tuman Bey in his efforts to save Egypt. They entered into secret correspondence with Sultan Salim and acquainted him with all the war preparations and military strategies of the Egyptian ruler.

In order to render Sultan Salim's artillery inoperative Tuman Bey worked out a plan that the Egyptian cavalry should attack and capture the artillery before it was set into action and then hand-to-hand fight with swords and lances would be started. But those two traitors informed Sultan Salim of this strategy with the result the new plan of the Egyptian ruler was unfulfilled. Thus, Sultan Salim was fortunate enough to get supporters from among the Mamluks themselves.

Both the forces drew their battle lines at Ridwaniah on January 22, 1517 C.E. (922 A.H.). Since Salim was already alert, he gave Tuman Bey no chance to implement his plans and the Mamluk force had to fight in front of the artillery. As the battle broke out, the two treacherous commanders joined the military camp of the Ottomans. However, the Mamluk troops fought with exemplary valor. At one stage, Tuman Bey took a squad of his cavalry armed to the teeth and launched a fierce attack on the main Ottoman force. Two brave Mamluk commanders who had vowed to either catch Sultan Salim alive or kill him on the spot supported Sultan Tuman Bey.

This attack of a small band of Mamluks was like an earth tremor, which shook the entire Ottoman army. Nothing could stop them from making inroads into the enemy's heart. Rending the enemy lines and killing them in large number, they reached the spot from where Salim was watching and directing his troops. But, taking Sanan Pasha as Salim, Tuman Bey targeted him so accurately with his spear that he fell down dead on the spot. Similarly, the Mamluk commanders, Alan and Qarat, killed two Ottoman Commanders mistaking them for Sultan Salim. None of them were able to recognize Salim. However, Tuman Bey and his Commanders killed Salim's Commanders under his nose and escaped unhurt. Since Salim was safe, the fighting continued without a break.

Sultan Salim was left bewildered at the bravery shown by the Mamluk fighters. If it was not for his guns and artillery, he was sure he would not have had an edge on the Mamluks just because his force was large. However, Sultan Salim, without losing his composure made the best use of his artillery and kept killing enemy troops before their access to the first row of his army. It is a unique example in the history that the Mamluks died fighting just to show their valor. Twenty five thousand Mamluk soldiers fell in the battle but did not surrender, with the result only a few remained alive. And they tenaciously led Tuman Bey to safety in Azubia. It is a fact that all the Mamluks that died perished in the artillery attacks while the Ottoman soldiers were killed by sword or spear. The Mamluks had not a single gun to fire at their enemy because they considered the use of guns while fighting below their standard of valor. Since Tuman Bey was led to Azubia, Cairo was lying undefended and so seven days after the clash Sultan Salim occupied the Egyptian capital. In the meantime, the scattered Mamluk soldiers gathered around Tuman Bey in Azubia and a small force came into being.

On hearing, that Sultan Salim had occupied Cairo Tuman Bey took his troops and launched an attack on the Egyptian capital. Salim was then in his military camp outside the city. Tuman Bey made a sudden advance into Cairo and began to kill the occupying Turkish troops in a manner that none of them were able to save their lives. Tuman Bey restored the city and fortified every lane and by-lane every house in the city. When Sultan Salim attempted to enter the city, he experienced many impediments and hurdles everywhere and at the same time, it would have been a shameful sign of weakness for Sultan Salim leave Cairo unconquered. Even three days after continuous clashes, the Turkish army could not make any headway. Finding no way out he called the Mamluk commander Khairi, who had joined his camp during the battle of Ridwaniah, and asked him to suggest the way to success. Khairi told him to announce that those among the Mamluks laying down arms would be given peace and safety. With this declaration, fighting came to a halt and a number of Mamluk soldiers appeared before the Ottoman Sultan on their own while others were forced by the citizens to join the Turkish camp. Thus, eight hundred Mamluks very easily became captives of Sultan Salim. They all were killed on the advice of Khairi followed by an all-out massacre in the city.

Losing all hope of resistance Tuman Bey left Cairo and went to the desert tribes. The Ottoman force acted brutally and massacred fifty thousand Mamluks. During this action Qarat Bey, the right hand of Tuman Bey, went underground in Cairo. Shortly after finishing his task, Sultan Salim ordered his soldiers to go in search of Tuman Bey and Qarat Bey. On being informed that Tuman Bey had escaped the territory while Qarat Bey had gone into hiding in Cairo, he announced that, since the Mamluks had already lost their power, it would be an act of wisdom on his apart to join him on the promise of safety of his life. Qarat Bey, being sure of his arrest in the immediate future accepted the offer and came to Sultan Salim.

Salim looked upon Qarat Bey and remarked: "On the day of the battle of Ridwaniah you appeared very brave on your horse but, at present, your are keeping silent. Qarat Bey told him that I am as brave as ever but the Ottomans are coward enough to make use of guns to establish their bravery. During the rule of Sultan Qalzu Ghazi a European came with a gun and told him that it would be wise to distribute guns among the Mamluk soldiers. But the Sultan and his courtiers said in one voice that even the holding of a gun was an act of utter disgrace for them. The European then remarked before the open court that you would one day lose the rule of Egypt to the guns and you have won victory only at gunpoint. I believe that guns cannot become the basis of victory or defeat; swords and arrows can play a more effective role in warfare. We have been affected only because Allah Almighty has decided so. But your rule will also come to an end one day. Dynasties also have their limited age on this earth like men. Never think that you have achieved victory because you are more valiant". Thereupon Sultan Salim said, "Why have you been produced before me as a captive if you are so brave?" Qarat Bey replied, "By Allah, I don't consider myself as a captive. I have come here of my own and by trusting you. I am, therefore, quite free." The exchange of words between Salim and Qarat Bey had reached this point when Qarat Bey noticed Khairi Bey who was then among the supporters of the Ottoman ruler. He turned to Khairi Bey and condemned him in the strongest possible words. He then said addressing Sultan Salim, "He (Khairi) deserves to have his head cut off and thus punishing him for his guilt otherwise he will carry you to Hell also". On hearing this Sultan Salim fell in wrath and said, "I had decided to entrust some important military position to you. But you have violated the dignity of the royal court and behaved impertinently. You are perhaps, unaware that anyone who behaves rudely in the royal court deserves disgrace and punishment." Qarat Bey replied fearlessly "May Allah not bring me the day that I am employed by you and become one of your supporters."

Hearing this Sultan Salim grew furious and called his executioners. At this Qarat Bey said, "What's the use of cutting off my head when thousands of brave men are after your head, and Tuman Bey is also alive and working hard to take revenge on you"? However, when the executioners came and got ready to behead him he turned to Khairi Bey and said, "Come and carry my head and put it in the lap of your wife." These words were coming out of his lips when his head was cut off.

Tuman Bey had already started collecting Arab tribes to fight along side of him. When he succeeded in organizing a reasonable force he began to make attacks on the Ottoman troops. Salim kept sending corps after corps to face the Mamluks' attacks but they all were torn apart. Tuman Bey's force consisted of two parts because some scattered Mamluk fighters had joined him and he had organized some Arab tribes into a force. Both the Arabs and the Mamluks had developed hate against their rulers and hence they jointly rallied to Tuman Bey but the growing rivalry between the two parts of his force was causing concern to him.

Sultan Salim, after suffering a series of setbacks, sent word to Tuman Bey that on condition of his obedience and submission, he would recognize him as the king of Egypt, stop occupying their land and leave all the Egyptian territories for him. Since Sultan Salim had killed their Commander Qarat Bey and committed carnage in Egypt they tore the emissary into pieces. When Sultan Salim came to know of it, he killed three thousand Mamluk captives in retaliation, and sent a strong army along with artillery to take on Tuman Bey. The two forces clashed near the pyramids of Egypt. During the battle, the Arab and Mamluk soldiers fought with one another and started killing each other. The Ottoman artillery was, on the other hand, killing them both. Thus, the force under Tuman Bey was wiped out quickly. Frustrated and dejected, Tuman Bey escaped to an Arab chieftain who owed much to him but that ungrateful person caught him and sent him to Sultan Salim.

When the Ottoman ruler came to know that Tuman Bey was caught, he said in a fit of joy: "Egypt is conquered." When Tuman Bey drew near, Salim welcomed him like a king and held him in high esteem and kept him as an honorable guest. Sultan Salim's treatment of Tuman Bey filled Khairi and Ghazali with anxiety for these two traitors were sworn enemies of the Egyptian ruler. Sultan Salim now had the opportunity to implement his scheme of installing Tuman Bey as the king of Egypt by way of obligation and leave for Constantinople. They, however, spread their net very cautiously and began to give Sultan Salim information from various sources that tremendous efforts were being made to free Tuman Bey and put him on the Egyptian throne and after being free, Tuman Bey would pose a grave danger to the Ottoman Empire. Sultan Salim, who was suffering from these troubles since he arrived in Egypt ordered Tuman Bey killed without loss of time. Thus came the end of Tuman Bey, the last Mamluk king on April 17, 1517 C.E. (922 A.H.).

Following the assassination of Tuman Bey the Ottoman ruler was under no threat from the former Egyptian rulers. However, he knew very well that keeping Egypt under Ottoman possession was not an easy task. The Mamluks were ruling in Egypt for several hundred years and were the inhabitants of Egypt. They had increased their population by purchasing slaves from the Caucasus. Gradually, they rose as a very strong and formidable ruling class in Egypt but the Arabs too were in such a large number that Egypt was considered an Arab country. Moreover, the Arab population of Egypt commanded much respect and influence religiously as well as politically because of their close relations with Syria and the Hijaz. The Copts and the Jews, the indigenous population of Egypt also wielded influence because of their services rendered as officials in the Accounts and Agricultural Departments. The people inhabiting the west-southern frontier provinces and territories had the capabilities of invading Egypt and occupying it at anytime. In the case that Sultan Salim appointed somebody as the Governor of Egypt, he wanted to be careful that he was not likely to rise in revolt with the support of Syria, the Hijaz and the people of the western territories. Also, if such a person were to be put in power that lacked courage and determination, he would not be able to put down any future revolt. Had Sultan Salim gone back immediately after the conquest of Egypt, the conquered country would have risen in revolt creating trouble for the Sultan. Salim, therefore, made a long stay in Egypt and studied the situation minutely. He had a plan to march to Tripoli and bring the entire of North Africa up to Morocco under his control but his troops refused to go ahead, with the result he had to go back to Constantinople.

After the conquest of Egypt it was very easy for Sultan Salim to annihilate the Mamluks from the country but he, very wisely, kept their number and strength intact and appointed Mamluk Commander Khairi as the Governor of Egypt with the permission that they could hold their 24-member council or parliament as usual. They had the power and ability to elect a new ruler after the death or deposition of the one in power. Although the number of the members of parliament was to remain unchanged, the consent of the Ottoman king was declared as necessary. Along with this, the post of the Chief Justice was limited to the Arab commanders and this was certainly a wise decision. Collection of money and other financial responsibilities were entrusted to the Copts and the Jews. After setting up a three-tier system in administration Sultan Salim deployed five thousand cavalry and five hundred infantrymen from his own force under his renowned Commander, Khairuddin with the instructions that he should keep Cairo city and the central forts under his direct control and must not, in any case go out of the fixed limits. Thus, all the possible dangers were eliminated.

Following the conquest of Egypt Sultan Salim offered his Friday prayers in the Grand Mosque of Egypt. A very costly carpet was spread for the Sultan. When he came to the mosque, he disliked this preferential treatment and asked for the carpet to be removed and performed his prayers like the commanders. During the prayer, he was so overwhelmed with tender feelings that he began to weep bitterly. Following the conquest of Egypt Sultan Salim sent a team of first-rate architects and artisans to Constantinople as he had done in Tabriz. One can gauge from this his strong desire to enhance the beauty and grandeur of his capital. It is strange that despite his long stay in Egypt he took no interest in the Egyptian pyramids and never visited them. However, his interest in the mosques and madrasas of Egypt was very high. He added to the grace and dignity of the religious scholars and increased their daily allowance. Sultan Salim had decided while in Egypt that the conquest of Arabia was even more necessary. The sacred cities of Makkah and Madinah were under the control of Arab chiefs and no military action was needed to occupy these cities. What was necessary was the conquest of the hearts of the citizens. With this in mind, he lavished favors on the Arab chiefs and Sultan Salim was undisputedly recognized as the king of the Hijaz following the end of the Mamluk rule. The Arab chiefs could have opposed Sultan Salim as the ruler but, because of his favors and kindnesses, they themselves sent greetings to the Ottoman ruler and gave him the title of the Servant of the Sanctuaries of Makkah and Madinah. The Abbasid Caliphs lived in Egypt with so much stately splendor and brotherhood as did the Roman Pope or Akbar Shah II and Bahadur Shah in Delhi. Even though they had neither any sovereignty nor a country nor any force but the rulers of Islamic countries would try to get from them some title to add to their power and position and they were treated as religious leaders.

Sultan Salim felt the power and influence of the Abbasid Caliphs. Thus, he made the last Caliph agree to abdicate the Caliphate and hand over the standard, the sword and the shield to the Ottoman ruler and recognize him (Salim) as the Caliph of the Muslims. He then pledged his allegiance to Sultan Salim. Now a real Caliph took over the charge of the Caliphate instead of a nominal one. The Caliph is the highest authority for the Muslims and Sultan Salim was, undoubtedly, the mightiest Muslim king of those days. In 923 A.H. Sultan Salim set out from Egypt along with one thousand camels loaded with gold and silver. He also took the last Abbasid Caliph with him. He had covered a distance of a few miles from Cairo when he told his Prime Minister, Yunus, who was marching and talking along with him on his own horse, that very soon they would step into Syrian territory. The Prime Minister said in reply that they were going back after spoiling half of their troops and handing over the charge of Egypt to the very people they had taken it from. Yunus also said to him that he could not understand what benefit they had gained by invading Egypt. Hearing this Sultan Salim ordered the cavalryman accompanying him to cut off his (Yunus's) head and the order was implemented at once. Sultan Salim was very hard on his ministers and courtiers but was equally soft on religious scholars. Yunus was, in fact, against the conquest of Egypt right from the beginning and he had opposed the original decision to invade and he had only repeated his position. However, this much can be said without any fear of contradiction that the conquest of Egypt had enhanced the glory of the Ottoman Dynasty. Sultan Salim took about two years in conquering Egypt and making his return journey. During this period, he had brought Syria, Arabia and Egypt to the fold of the Ottoman rule and the greatest benefit of all, was that he had invaded Egypt only as Sultan Salim but he was the Caliph of the Muslims and the leader of the Muslim world on his return.

Sultan Salim stayed in Damascus for several years. Some accounts support the view that from Damascus he went to perform Hajj while others contradict it. However, Sultan Salim established relations with the Arab chiefs and took the oath of allegiance from them. From Damascus, he came to Aleppo (Halb) and made a long stay there. In order to make the administration work efficiently he divided Syria into small parts under separate governors, thus, putting an end to the threat of revolts. From there, he reached Constantinople in 924 A.H.

On his return to Constantinople, Sultan Salim received the tribute of Cyprus from Venice, which it paid to the Mamluks of Egypt in the past. The Venetians not only paid the tribute but promised to keep on paying in the future also.

The Christian ruler of Spain sent his envoy to Sultan Salim requesting him to give protection to the Christians going to Syria and Palestine as pilgrims. Immediately granting the petition the Ottoman ruler gave word that Christian pilgrims would suffer no harm within the confines of his rule. The peace treaty with the king of Hungry was also coming to its end. Thus, the Hungarian ruler also requested for an extension and Sultan Salim granted it immediately. The Ottoman Sultan's conquests in Asia and Africa did not go unnoticed as far as the Europeans were concerned. Sultan Salim extended his territories considerably and was conferred with the title of the Caliph of the Muslims. European powers were shuddering at the very thought of an Ottoman invasion. Thus following the return of Sultan Salim from Egypt the European powers began to send peace proposals along with their offers of allegiance. Although Sultan Salim was temperamentally very harsh, he was very far-sighted too and had his eye on the consequences of every step taken. He was not so gullible as to be carried away by flattering remarks. He was also well aware of mischief and activities of intrigue. He had established a large and mighty empire by conquering Egypt, Syria, the Hijaz, Iraq and western Iran. Thus, his empire had extended over the three continents of Asia, Africa and Europe. His next target was the conquest of Europe as a whole and he was not at all negligent in this regard. He knew very well that his ancestors had been making all-out efforts to conquer the continent. Historians are unanimous that Sultan Salim was a devoutly religious person and was full of a religious sense of honor. However, it seems strange that Sultan Salim had always been engaged in fighting with the Muslim states and he conquered Muslim countries throughout his reign. It was because his experience and observation had taught him that the religious sense among the Muslims had considerably weakened and evils of all kinds had made progress against their Islamic character. The open clash between Timur and Bayazid was the clear evidence of this malaise. Sultan Muhammad II had brought peace to some extent by putting an end to the Christian rule in Constantinople but periodic revolts in Asia Minor remained a source of constant worry for the Ottoman kings. Ismail Safwi's mischief and secret planning had occupied Sultan Salim's attention right from the day of his accession. Hence, he managed to ward off threats from the eastern side by punishing the Shiite's of Iran and annexing its provinces. The large-scale massacre of the Shi'a sect in Asia Minor had minimized the possibilities of any plot against his territories. Since the Islamic rulers of Egypt had made use of force against the Ottomans in connection with Prince Jamshed, the Egyptian threat was not considered at all small. Sultan Salim thought it proper to bring Egypt under control before dealing with the Christian countries otherwise the Christians could instigate the Egyptians against the Ottomans. Now the European conquest was his next obvious step but Sultan Salim was prudent enough to avoid any hasty measures against the Europeans following his return from Egypt. He gave preference to the task of putting internal affairs of his country on right lines and finding time for strengthening his military machine. In the meantime the Christian kings, one after another, began their efforts to make peace with him and he readily accepted their peace proposals but without stopping his war preparations. Shortly after his return from Egypt, he started building ships and set up several shipyards. One hundred and fifty warships, each weighing about seven hundred tons, were ready in record time. One hundred small ships were built in addition. There was a total ban on taking the ships out to sea for sailing. Once he saw a warship sailing along the coast of Constantinople and grew so furious that he was about to order the killing of the Admiral. However, some commanders and ministers saved the Admiral by convincing the king that the ship was on a test run shortly after being built.

Besides shipyards, Sultan Salim set up a number of arms factories for manufacturing guns, artillery and gunpowder. Along with this, a large-scale recruiting drive was on. Moreover, a strong force armed with modern weapons was ready to come into action on very short notice. Sultan Salim's ministers were, in view of these large-scale preparations of the land force and navy, awaiting a big event but they were still unaware of what was going to happen. Although he consulted his minister and advisors on various issues, he kept crucial matters a secret. He never took any step in haste but once he resolved to do something, he would not budge from his decision. He was a man of courage and determination and anybody asking him to change his opinion would lose his life. Thus after a long campaign against the Muslim rulers and conquering a number of Muslim countries he was certainly making military preparations against the European powers. Since he wanted to leave nothing to chance, he was reorganizing his forces leaving no loophole anywhere.

Sultan Salim was desperately engaged in his military preparations when he passed away on Shawwal 6, 926 A.H. (September 22, 1520 C.E.) and left the task of conquering Europe to his son Sultan Sulaiman Azam.

Sultan Salim marched from Constantinople on Shawwal 1, 926 A.H. to Adrianople. He was encamped on the way to Adrianople when he developed a boil on his thigh. His physicians advised him against riding but he would not pay heed until the boil took a serious turn and he succumbed to it.

A Review of the Reign of Sultan Salim

Sultan Salim ruled for eight years, eight months and eight days, but he achieved such marvelous success as a conqueror that many mighty kings with longer reigns did not approach. The greatest trait of his character was that even at the height of rage and fury he held religious scholars in esteem. He put ministers and commanders to death for slight mistakes and hence they feared him greatly. But religious scholars and guides were free from his wrath. Once he grew angry with the officials of the Finance Department and issued death sentences for them. When Qadi Jamali of Constantinople heard of it he called on the Sultan and asked him to withdraw his order for they were not liable for capital punishment. Sultan Salim told the Qadi that he should not meddle in administrative affairs. The Qadi said to him: "You keep your eye on the welfare of your country, but I want your welfare in the next world. Whatever the expediency behind your order is, it will bring you destruction in the life Hereafter. Allah Almighty bestows his favor and reward on one who shows pity and chastises the cruel. Thus, the wise counseling of the Qadi caused Salim to change his mind and he ordered all of them set free.

Similarly, Sultan Salim once ordered that the export of silk to Iran be stopped. As a follow-up action, he ordered the arrest all such traders in Constantinople and those carrying silk to Iran. They were four hundred in all and their properties were to be confiscated and their heads were to be cut off by the order of the Sultan. At the time, Sultan Salim was about to leave for Adrianople and Qadi Jamali was accompanying him. He interceded with the Sultan for those condemned to death. The Sultan replied, "It is rather justified to kill one-third for the welfare of two-thirds of the citizens and what could be more of a major corruption than going against the orders of the king". The Qadi replied, "They can not be held responsible for the court order had not reached them." Had the Prime Minister talked to the Sultan so boldly he would have lost his life. But even at the height of anger, he could ask the Qadi not to meddle in the state affairs. Qadi Jalali grew furious and left without seeking permission and without showing due regard to the Sultan. Sultan Salim kept staring at him silently in a state of amazement. A few minutes later, he bowed his head, thought for sometime and ordered the release of the condemned traders along with the confiscated goods. Following this Sultan Salim sent a message to Qadi Jalali appointing him the Chief Qadi of the entire Ottoman Empire. Although Qadi Jalali declined the offer, Sultan Salim kept showing favor to him.

Sultan Salim's reign was noted by the world for its religious significance. During his period, the Ottomans replaced the Islamic Caliphate of the Abbasids, and Caliphs with power and authority were now at the helm instead of nominal ones. Martin Luther began reforms in Christianity at the same time, which was a result of the coming of the Muslims into Europe. Kabir Das started his own religious order in India during the same period. Kabir had died at Magher near Gorakhpur in 924 A.H. He was contemporary of Sultan Sikander Lodhi. During the Reign of Sultan Salim, in 922 A.H the pocket watch was invented.

Sultan Salim had in mind that following his conquest of the Christian countries he would bring all the Christians to the fold of Islam and wipe out all foreign elements from his territories. Thus, he expressed his opinion to convert churches into mosques. Having heard this some Christians appeared before the Sultan and submitted that his forefathers had given them full religious freedom and promised protection to their churches and non-interference with their religious affairs. Religious scholars of Sultan Salim's courts supported the statement of the Christians and Qadi Jamali also interceded for them. Thus, the Sultan held back from such an action. Christian historians appear to be very unhappy with Sultan Salim and held his religious interests to be his demerit but this is sheer prejudice on their part. Their dislike of him is a glaring proof of his divine nature and virtues and the countries conquered by Sultan Salim remained under Turkish control. Sultan Salim did not rule for long and died at the age of 52 had he lived a little longer he would have conquered Europe as a whole. He was also the first Caliph in the Ottoman Dynasty.

THE END

[Personal Notes]

[Personal Notes]

[Personal Notes]

[Personal Notes]

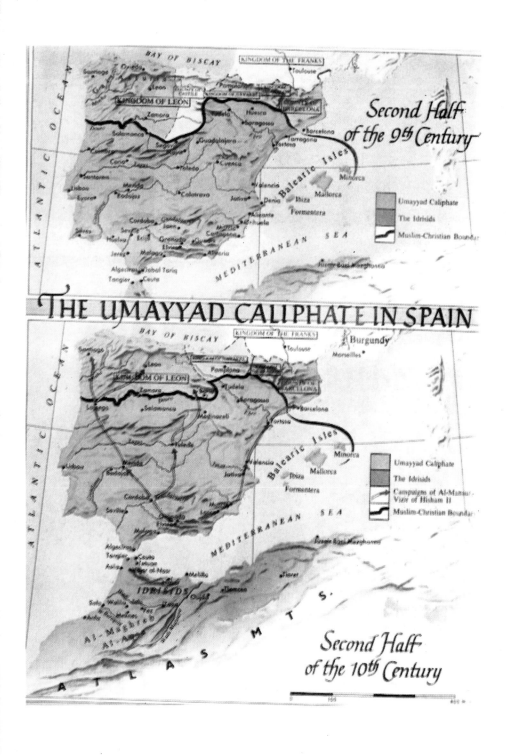

THE UMAYYAD CALIPHATE IN SPAIN

Map 1 (top): Second Half of the 9th Century

KINGDOM OF THE FRANKS
Toulouse
BAY OF BISCAY
ATLANTIC OCEAN

Santiago · Oviedo · Leon
Zamora
KINGDOM OF LEON
KINGDOM OF NAVARRE
Pamplona
Huesca
BARCELONA
Zaragoza
Barcelona
Tarragona
Tortosa

Salamanca
Segovia
Guadalajara
Ebro
Coria
Toledo
Cuenca
Santaren
Merida
Calatrava
Jativa
Valencia
Denia · Ibiza · Mallorca
Badajoz
Formentera · Minorca
Balearic Isles

Cordoba
Murcia · Cartagena
Huelva · Sevilla
Granada · Elvira · Almeria
Jerez · Malaga

Algeciras · Jabal Tariq
Tangier · Ceuta

MEDITERRANEAN SEA

Legend:
Umayyad Caliphate
The Idrisids
Muslim-Christian Boundary

Map 2 (bottom): Second Half of the 10th Century

KINGDOM OF THE FRANKS
Toulouse
Burgundy
Marseilles
BAY OF BISCAY
ATLANTIC OCEAN

Santiago · Leon
KINGDOM OF LEON
Pamplona
Zamora
Tudela
BARCELONA
Zaragoza
Barcelona
Salamanca
Tortosa

Lisbon
Toledo
Balearic Isles
Minorca
Valencia
Jativa
Ibiza · Mallorca
Formentera

Cordoba
Sevilla
Elvira

Algeciras
Tangier · Ceuta
Asila
Melilla
Tierer

IDRISIDS

Fez

AL-MAGHREB
AL-AQSA

ATLAS MTS.

MEDITERRANEAN SEA

Legend:
Umayyad Caliphate
The Idrisids
Campaigns of Al-Mansur, Vizir of Hisham II
Muslim-Christian Boundary

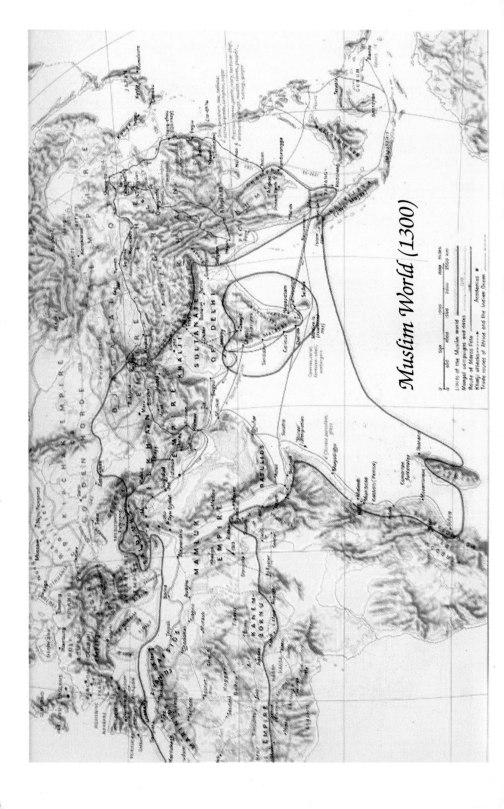

Muslim World (1300)

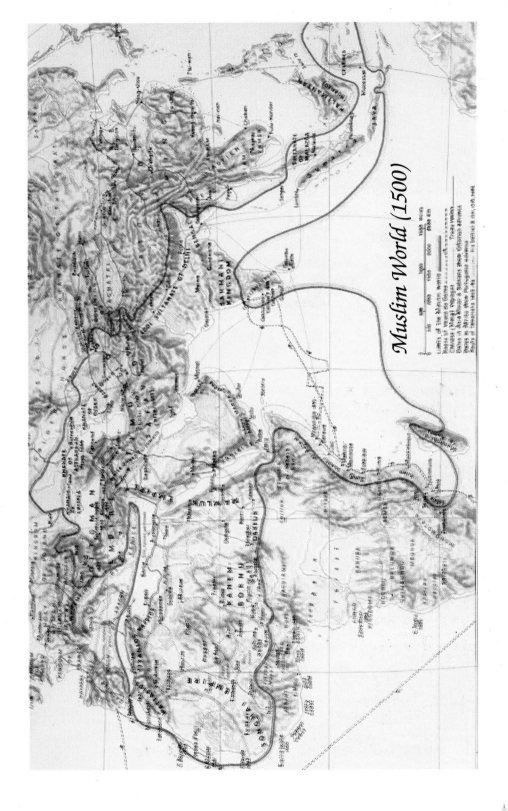

Muslim World (1500)

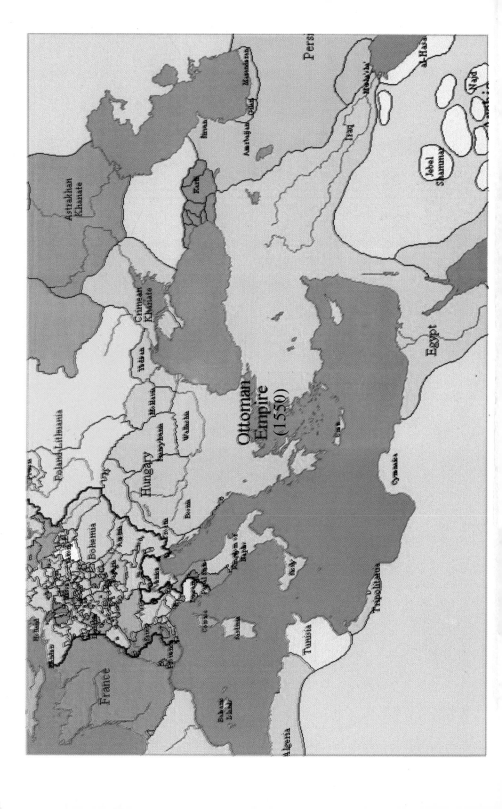